A Source Book
prepared by the
Personality growth and Learning Course Team

Personality growth
and
Learning

Published by Longman
for The Open University Press

LONGMAN GROUP LIMITED
London
Associated companies, branches and representatives
throughout the world

This collection © The Open University 1971

First published 1971
Second impression 1972
Third impression 1973

ISBN 0 582 48054 X Cased
ISBN 0 582 48055 8 Paper

Printed in Great Britain by
Western Printing Services Ltd
Bristol

PERSONALITY GROWTH AND LEARNING

A Source Book

Contents

Acknowledgements

This source book was put together for the Course Team by its academic members, whose names appear in the Introductions to the sections for which each was responsible. Overall editorial supervision was carried out by Asher Cashdan and Joan Whitehead.

We are grateful to the following for permission to reproduce copyright material:

Aldine-Atherton Inc. and Professor Robert D. Hess for 'Maternal Influences upon Early Learning: The Cognitive Environments of Urban Pre-school Children', by Robert D. Hess and Virginia C. Shipman, reprinted from Robert D. Hess and Roberta Meyer Bear (eds.), *Early Education* (Chicago; Aldine Publishing Company, 1968), copyright © 1968 by Robert D. Hess and Roberta Meyer Bear; American Psychological Association and Dr Donald O. Hebb for 'Drives and the Conceptual Nervous System' by Donald O. Hebb, abridged from *The Psychological Review*, 1955, 62, pp. 244-7, 250-4; American Psychological Association and J. P. Guilford for 'Creativity' by J. P. Guilford from *The American Psychologist*, 1950, 5, pp. 444-54; American Psychological Association and H. A. Witkin for 'Psychological Differentiation', abridged from *Journal of Abnormal Psychology*, 1965, 70, pp. 317-36; Beacon House Inc. and J. L. Moreno for 'Organisation and Conduct' from *Who Shall Survive?* by J. L. Moreno; The British Psychological Society for 'The School Psychological Service' from A Report by *The British Psychological Society*, 1962; Duke University Press for 'The Person, the Product and the Response: Conceptual Problems in the Assessment of Creativity' by Philip W. Jackson and Samuel Messick from *The Journal of Personality*, 1965, 33, pp. 309-29; Educational Technology Magazine for 'Using Intrinsic Motivation to Teach Young Children' by J. McV. Hunt from *Educational Technology*, Feb. 1971, Vol. 11, No. 2, pp. 78-80; International Universities Press Inc. and Jerome Kagan for 'Development Studies in Reflection and Analysis', abridged from *Perceptual Development in Children* by A. H. Kidd, J. E. Rivoire (eds.), pp. 487-505, 517-22; The Controller of Her Majesty's Stationery Office for 'Cigarette Smoking in School Children' by Dr Leila M. Watson from *Health Bulletin*, 1966, 24; Colin Lacy for 'Some

Sociological Concomitants of Academic Streaming in the Grammar School' from the *British Journal of Sociology*, 1966, 14, pp. 245–62; The Merrill-Palmer Institute and Forest Harrison for 'Relationship between Home Background, School Success and Adolescent Attitudes' by Forest Harrison from *Merrill-Palmer Quarterly of Behaviour and Development*, 1968, 14; Methuen, Publishers for 'The Development of Scales to Measure Junior School Children's Attitudes' by Joan C. Barker Lunn from the *British Journal of Educational Psychology*, Vol. 39, 1969, 'Teaching Approach and the Development of Divergent Thinking Abilities in Primary Schools' by F. A. Haddon and H. Lytton from the *British Journal of Educational Psychology*, 1968, Vol. 38, 'Divergent Thinking Abilities in Secondary Schools' by H. Lytton and A. C. Cotton, from the *British Journal of Educational Psychology*, Vol. 39, 1969; 'Questionnaire Measures of Maladjustment' by J. Tizard from the *British Journal of Educational Psychology*, Vol. 38, 1968, 'Personality in Primary School Children' by H. J. Eysenck and D. Cookson from the *British Journal of Educational Psychology*, Vol. 39, 1969, 'Aggressive and Withdrawing Children in the Normal School' by E. A. Lunzer, from the *British Journal of Educational Psychology*, Vol. 30, 1960, 'Factors Associated with Maladjustment in Educationally Subnormal Children' by M. Chazan from the *British Journal of Educational Psychology*, Vol. 35, 1965, 'A Comparative Study of Children's Behaviour at Home and School' by S. Mitchell and M. Shepherd from the *British Journal of Educational Psychology*, Vol. 36, 1966, and 'The Self-Picture as a Factor in the Classroom' by J. W. Staines from the *British Journal of Educational Psychology*, Vol. 28, 1958; National Foundation for Educational Research for 'British Behavioural Counselling' by R. H. Woody from *Educational Research*, Vol. 10, No. 3, and 'Social Class and Achievement Motivation' by D. F. Swift from *Educational Research*, Vol. 8, No. 1; Remedial Education for 'Maladjustment and Reading Difficulties—Recent Research and Experiment' by M. Chazan from *Remedial Education*, 1969; Schenkman Publishing Company Inc. for 'Reading Research Articles' by T. R. Sarbin and W. C. Coe from *The Student Psychologist's Handbook*; Schenkman Publishing Company Inc. for 'Sources of Information' by T. R. Sarbin and W. C. Coe, © 1969 Schenkman Publishing Company; The Society for Research in Child Development, Inc. for 'Experience and the Development of Motivation: Some Re-interpretations' by J. McV. Hunt from *Child Development*, 1960, 31; Spastics International Medical Publications for 'Promoting Optimum Learning in Children' by S. W. Bijou in 'Planning for Better Learning' edited by P. Wolff and R. MacKeith from *Clinics in Developmental Medicine* 33; Sweet and Maxwell Limited and Association of Programmed Learning for 'The Influence of Personality and Task Conditions on Learning and Transfer' by G. O. M. Leith and E. A. Trown from *Programmed Learning*, 1970, 7.

GENERAL
INTRODUCTION

The growth of children's personality has always been a major area of study in educational psychology. Several different threads can be unravelled from the work that has so far been carried out. On the one hand are the studies which are concerned to determine the structure of personality and to chart the way in which different personality structures emerge as children grow older. On the other hand are those studies which are more concerned with the determinants of personality characteristics and which seek to establish these determinants in the experiences of childhood. Some clinical studies in this latter group seek to emphasise the earliest experiences which the child gains in the context of his family relationships in infancy, whereas other studies are concerned to explain personality growth in terms of later experiences, not only in the family but also in the context of the school and of society.

Children's learning has been another of the major areas of interest in educational psychology. Again several different lines of work can be distinguished. As with personality growth it is possible to isolate a descriptive approach, concerned to establish the structure of abilities and attainments, and an explanatory approach, concerned to understand learning in terms of response to environmental circumstances. It is an over-simplification to separate these two approaches completely, but there is no doubt that these two threads can be observed in an examination of recent published work in educational psychology.

More recently it has become increasingly clear that these two normally distinct areas of study, personality growth and learning, are in fact closely linked. There is a sense in which the existence of the link has been known for a long time. The early followers of the 'structure of abilities' school, relating children's learning at school to such concepts as general intelligence, were very ready to report that the abilities which their investigations led them to establish could never account for more than a proportion of the success which children showed in the school situation. As a result of these early enquiries, it was suggested that the explanation of children's learning could be improved if we were to add an 'X factor' to the abilities which were used to explain learning. This X factor was considered to represent qualities such as interest, attitude, motivation etc.—in fact, personality qualities.

The way in which personality qualities such as those mentioned above have determined learning has not been studied to any marked extent until recently. There are various reasons for this—for example, the measurement of personality qualities has only recently become a fairly well-established science; reasonably reliable scales for measuring children's personality characteristics were not developed until scales for assessing attainments had been in common use in educational practice for many decades.

Another reason for the limited study of the effect of personality on learning is the dynamic nature of the interaction; not only does personality affect learning, but the consequent learning will itself affect personality. Success in school alters those very personality variables which may themselves have given rise to the success. This is therefore a more difficult model for educational psychologists to study than the simple ability-attainment model, which held that school progress could be determined by a number of relatively fixed abilities.

This source book brings together a collection of articles which form a basis for thinking about the relationship between personality and learning. The material is gathered together under the heading 'Personality growth and learning' since we are concerned with the relationship as it exists in children. There are two main reasons for the existence of this collection. First, it serves as a source book for students following the Open University course of the same name. Reference is made to the articles at appropriate points in the course. Second, it makes available to any other interested students the collection of readings chosen by the Course Team.

The choice of material has been guided by a number of principles. The concept of personality has been viewed in terms of emotions, attitudes, interests, etc. and not in terms of intellect. Although, as the course material explains, some psychologists tend to place qualities of intellect under the general heading of personality, this wider point of view has not been adopted in the course nor has it been reflected in the choice of articles for this Reader.

Second, learning has been interpreted where possible as learning in the school setting. Aspects of learning such as the learning of relationships with parents, or the learning of early play activities, have been avoided, important though they may be.

Third, articles which are very technical have been avoided as much as possible. However, it is not easy to follow the argument of a few articles without a little knowledge of educational statistics. Students following the Open University course will have some help over this in their correspondence material. Others will find it useful to consult an introductory statistics book. A list of the recommended reading for students following the Open University course is given on p. 406; the list includes an elementary statistics text.

The purpose of the Open University course is to illuminate the way in which classroom learning situations can be managed through studying the relationship which exists between personality growth and learning. This reader brings together a collection of articles which provide source material for this purpose.

This introduction is followed by excerpts which are intended to help students read and evaluate the material in the rest of the Reader. The first of the excerpts comments in a simple way on the sources of the information which underlie most of the articles, and also discusses ways in which designed experiments have been used to treat this information. The second of the two excerpts discusses ways in which research articles can be read and evaluated. These two extracts should be tackled before going on to read any of the articles which follow.

Section One moves straight into one of the interesting areas in which personality and learning are closely related—that is, the study of learning styles and strategies. These are ways in which individuals vary in their methods of learning (not their abilities). Then come two pieces which illustrates the way in which one learning style (convergence-divergence) can be affected by the characteristics of the school. The latter half of this section takes creativity as an illustration of a theme in educational psychology which demonstrates the interplay between personality growth and learning.

The next section consists of a single article which discusses the ways in which personality dimensions, established by the factor analytic method discussed in the Guilford article in the first section, are related to school performance. This is an important article, but not an easy one. It needs some acquaintance with statistical concepts; and their interpretation is discussed in the section's introduction.

The third section continues to examine the influence which personality has on learning. The main foci in Section Three are aspects of personality such as the self-concept, but the three articles, especially the

Lacey contribution, make us aware of sociological factors which affect personality and learning in the school situation.

Section Four stays firmly at the personality end of the relationship and considers two aspects of personality—motivation and attitude—and the relationship which these have to learning. The first two articles are fairly technical and cover theoretical issues. The articles concerned with attitudes include one which reports attempts to alter children's cigarette-smoking. This is not an aspect of learning which is of immediate relevance to the teacher in the classroom, but the article illustrates a careful enquiry into the effect of different methods of health education on changing children's attitudes in an important area.

One of the more interesting avenues of study is the way in which an examination of unusual conditions often sheds considerable light on the way in which normal development proceeds. So the next section, Section Five, examines the relationships between personality and learning in two groups of handicapped children, specifically the slow learners and the maladjusted. In this section there is a group of articles which examines some of the patterns of behaviour which maladjusted children show, and also deals with the relationships between maladjustment and scholastic performance, as in the first Chazan article. This section begins by considering children with personality problems and looks at the way in which these problems affect their school learning; later it moves to study children with learning problems. The Hess and Shipman article probes further, by looking at early experiences and how they may lay the foundations for school learning. In short, this section follows in miniature the theme of the whole Reader, by swinging from one end of the personality-learning relationship to the other.

The last section examines the ways in which the classroom teacher can intervene in the personality-learning relationship. It begins by looking at the process of behaviour modification in the classroom, using behaviour in the Bijou article to encompass both personality and learning behaviour. Then it moves on to look at the way in which the teacher can draw on outside services in order to help him with his intervention. The two services which are chosen for particular study are the counselling service and the school psychological service, both of which have a contribution to make to the personality-learning relationships which children show in the school situation.

P. WILLIAMS

I

T. R. Sarbin and W. C. Coe   Sources of information*

The ultimate worth of a scholarly work depends on the information used in its composition. Two major tasks are involved in obtaining information: locating it, and evaluating it. To locate information, one must know not only *where* to look but also *how* to look for it. In evaluating information, qualitative and quantitative aspects must be taken into account.

The quality of information is determined by considering the methods used in obtaining it. The way in which information is obtained indicates the degree of scientific rigour involved, and consequently, its usefulness to the particular project. The least rigorous sources of information are useful for speculation and for developing ideas, methods of moderate rigour serve to refine ideas and may provide some support for hypotheses, while rigorous experimental procedures provide the most definitive answers.

The quantitative characteristics of information are related to the degree of sophistication of measurement. Generally speaking, the more sophisticated the measurement, the more reliable the information. As quantification becomes more refined, one is better able to qualify his statements; statements may be made about different effects in relation to different degrees of a variable. For instance, information on responsiveness to hypnosis appears in different quantitative levels. One report will state a gross differentiation, '*most* people can be hypnotised', while another report will indicate the percentage of persons who reach different levels of depth as measured by a standard

* Reprinted from *The Student Psychologist's Handbook: A Guide to Sources*, Cambridge, Mass., Schenkman Publishing Co., 1968.

hypnotic scale. Although the two sources provide information on the same topic, it is clear that the information from the latter report is more refined than that of the first. Increasing quantification also increases the possibility that a study can be repeated by other investigations. And the repetition of experiments (when the outcomes are congruent) adds confidence to the validity and reliability of the information.

Observation is the basic source of scientific information. Scientists, indeed most people, base their ideas about the world on what they and others have observed. Many observations are made directly; that is, we record what we perceive through our senses. For instance, an observer may record the different behaviours exhibited by two children playing hop-scotch. Other observations are made indirectly with the help of measuring instruments. Body temperature is observed with the aid of a thermometer, although it may also be observed less precisely by placing a hand on the subject's forehead. In psychology, it is common to measure personality characteristics indirectly through questionnaires and other testing devices constructed for this purpose. The psychologist may make inferences about personality characteristics from the subject's response to questions of the type: 'do you ever have nightmares?' 'do you enjoy playing games?', 'do you like to watch television?'

Obeservations may be placed in two major categories—personal observations, and the observations of others. The remainder of the chapter will be devoted to examining these two sources of information; our emphasis will be, first, how does one obtain the information? and second, how does one evaluate the information?

PERSONAL OBSERVATIONS

Several procedures are available for gathering information through personal observation. Although each differs in its qualitative and quantitative features, each may still be useful in planning and preparing a research project. We shall discuss the following kinds of personal observations: casual observation, focused observation, and controlled observation.

I. Casual observation

The source of information when we make casual observations follows from our everyday experiences. What we see and hear as we enact our various life roles provide the data of casual observation. We learn about people and events from participation in social life, and from gossip, old wives' tales, popular sayings and folk tales that have been passed along in our culture without formal codification. Such everyday occurrences as seeing a movie, a street fight, or a political event provide the new data of experience. Some observations are impressive and compelling but others are ignored because the source appears invalid. At any rate, information gleaned from casual observation is often the beginning of scientific hypotheses about people and their behaviour. For instance, we may know students who are 'achievers' in their college work and wonder what accounts for their excellence. It is often heard that they are talented, or intelligent, yet we may also observe that they seem different in other ways: even casual observation suggests that they spend a good deal of time at their studies; they appear to have well-organised study and work habits; some seem to hold a general attitude that achieving in school and in life is important. Some of these students appear to do well in almost anything they encounter. Others, however, may seem unable to achieve a social sense, the 'book-worms', those who spend a good deal of the time by themselves and are in-frequently seen in the popular 'hangouts'. All these casual observations are a source of ideas for hypotheses about the factors associated with high achievement.

II. Focused observation

1. *Case study method* (naturalistic observation). Early in the develop-ment of a science ideas are often formulated by studying one individual, or by observing organisms in their natural environments. Casual observations may be supplemented by these methods. Retrospective accounts of a subject's activities and behaviours may be collected from people who have known him well, or information may be obtained directly from a subject by asking him (interview). Assuming we were interested in 'high achieving' students, we could ask room-mates about the subjects' study habits and the way in which the subjects approach their school work. The self-reports of 'high achievers' could also furnish information about their study habits, past successes, attitudes towards achievement, etc. After studying several successful students in this systematic way (peer reports, personal interviews) we may discover consistencies in their behaviour that lead to more refined hypotheses about high achievement.

Subjects whose lives are more easily controlled than college students (school children, prisoners, military personnel, hospital patients) are accessible to *time-interval* study. In such a study, subjects are selected for observation during specific time-intervals, for instance, each hour they are observed for a five-minute period, and their behaviour is recorded under predetermined categories such as social-approach responses, aggressive responses, or other responses that are believed to be important in posing a problem and in finding solutions. A quantitative estimate of behaviour occurrences may be obtained from time-interval observation. For example, during a five-minute time interval sampling of pre-school children, boys showed three times as many overtly-aggressive responses as girls.

The information obtained from case studies and naturalistic observations has limitations similar to information obtained from casual observation. However, the focus is sharpened on the variables believed to be important. The size of the sample is still limited, however, and caution is required in generalising from a few individuals to many. Also, the numerous factors that may affect the characteristics one wishes to understand are not systematically controlled; some idea of their differential importance may be gained, but only enough for statement of a refined hypothesis. Quantification is slightly increased over casual observation; therefore, a gain in precision is expected, i.e., the *number* of hours in study, the *intensity* of attitude towards achievement, etc. The primary usefulness of case studies is in refining hypotheses before they are submitted to more rigorous test.

2. Correlational analysis. The purpose of a correlational analysis is to determine the relationship between two variables. We want to find out what happens to one when another changes. Do they increase together? Does one increase as the other decreases, or does it make any difference?

In introducing the term *variable*, we mean that whatever it is we observe is measurable, and that it can be conceptualised as a dimension, e.g., height, weight, typing speed (words per minute), etc. Thus, to carry out a correlational analysis, it is necessary to provide measurements for the variables under study. For example, let us assume that casual observation leads us to believe that 'smart' people are 'high achievers' in college. To investigate the relationship between the degree of 'smartness', and the degree of 'college achievement', we must *define* each variable. It is important to stress that the definitions of variables in scientific work must not be mere verbal expressions. Definitions must be stated in terms of the 'operations' or the actions of the scientist with reference to the events under scrutiny. Thus the operational definition for 'weight' is the movement of a pointer on a standard balance in units of pounds and ounces. We may decide upon a standard IQ measure as the operational definition for 'smartness', and perhaps grade-point average as the operational definition of achievement. Thus, two measurements (scores) apply to our subjects. To complete the analysis it is necessary to obtain scores for our subjects on both variables.

School records are a source of academic achievement scores (grade point), and administering an IQ test can provide a measure of intelligence. The remainder of the analysis entails statistical computations between the two sets of scores; the statistical results indicate the degree of relationship between achievement and intelligence as operationally defined.

Two statistics are commonly used to indicate relationship in psychological studies: the rank-order coefficient, rho (ρ), and the Pearson product-moment coefficient (r). Rho indicates how closely matched the two sets of scores are when both are ranked from high to low for all subjects. For example, if we had measures of achievement and intelligence on thirty students, we would rank our sample from highest to lowest on both of the variables. If our hypothesis was that higher intelligence indicates higher achievement, we would expect those students who rank high on the intelligence test also to rank high in school achievement. If this turned out to be the case, we would find a *positive* relationship between the two variables; that is, as one increases, the other increases, or, as one decreases, the other also decreases— they go in the same direction. However, if those who scored high on the intelligence measure scored low on the achievement measure, we would find a *negative* relationship; as one variable increases, the other decreases, and vice-versa. If there is *no relationship* between the two variables, the rank order coefficient would equal zero (or be very small); that is, when one variable changes it makes little or no difference in the direction of change in the other.

The Pearson product-moment coefficient is similar in theory to the rank order coefficient although the scores are not arranged into ranks; the pairs of raw scores are used by themselves and a different computational method is applied. The same explanation applies to the direction of correlation (positive, negative, or none.)

The range of both coefficients is from plus one (1·00) to minus one (−1·00); plus 1·00 is a perfect, positive correlation where the highest member in IQ would also be the highest in achievement, second in IQ would be second in achievement, and so on. A minus 1·00 coefficient indicates just the opposite; number one in IQ would be last in achievement, number two in IQ would be next-to-last in achievement, and so on. Varying degrees of relationship lie in between these extremes. Statistical tables are available to help determine the degree to which chance factors may have accounted for the magnitude of the obtained coefficient.[1]

Information from correlational analysis has limitations. The quality is

[1] For more detailed information on computing correlation coefficients and determining their probability of occurrence, the student should consult an introductory text in psychological or educational statistics.

improved over the previous methods because the sample size is usually larger; thus, generalisations to a larger population are more appropriate. However, other variables that may influence the results have not been systematically controlled, and their effect cannot be determined. Correlational analysis *never* shows that one variable *caused* the change in the other. A third variable may cause the change in both variables. For example, if we correlated the number of umbrellas on the street with the number of puddles in the street, we are likely to find a high, positive correlation; however, it would be absurd to say that one caused the other; clearly, a third variable, the amount of rain, was antecedent to both observations. On the surface, it might appear that cause-and-effect is demonstrated through correlational analysis; however, it is quite hazardous to make the assumption that change in one variable causes the change in the other.

Although there are limitations to correlational analysis, it is still a potent investigative tool and may serve as a source of further hypothesis formulation. Because of the difficulties in submitting many human behaviours to rigorous control, a correlational analysis is sometimes the only feasible procedure.

III. Controlled observation

Ideally, the more we are able to control variables, that is, keep them from interfering with our observations, the more likely we are to discover the conditions responsible for the changes we observe. The basic premise of controlled observation is: if all factors are held constant, except those we wish to observe, then any change observed is a result of the change in those factors, consequently, they must have caused the observed changes. The logic behind this premise is basically sound; however, in practice it is often extremely difficult to apply. The main problem lies in controlling (keeping constant) all of the variables that are not of immediate interest but which might affect the outcome of the experiment. Investigating human problems presents even added difficulty because ethical restrictions limit experimental control over a number of variables related to human behaviour, i.e., how the subjects are raised, their diet, their freedom of movement, etc., and all may affect the results of an experiment. For this reason, much controlled experimentation is carried out in a laboratory setting with animal subjects; however, psychologists more and more are developing suitable techniques of laboratory experimentation with humans. Controlled observations may be carried out in natural settings although the difficulties in controlling variables are multiplied because of the freedom of the subjects, and the inability to control the environment.

To minimise the problem of controlling extraneous variables, several procedures are available. One is the method of *random selection*. Experiments are made on a *sample* of subjects, i.e., a sample of a population to which the experimenter wishes to generalise his results. If one is interested in the achievement of college students, the population may be defined as *all* college students; however, experimentation is done with only a few in hopes that the results will apply to all. If we select a sample of students *at random*, we maximise the chances that factors unknown to us, but which may influence the experimental results, will balance themselves. That is, from a sample selected randomly, the chances are good that no one characteristic will be favoured. For instance, in selecting students to investigate learning ability we would expect that a truly random sample would provide us with a range of intelligence, and random placement of subjects into two groups that receive different experimental treatments should cancel out the biasing effects of intelligence level. Each group should contain essentially the same overall level of intelligence. However, the validity of the assumptions behind random selection depends on having the entire population available for selection, an assumption that is rarely met in practice. Any restrictions on population availability weakens the chances that a truly random sample will be obtained.

Another method of overcoming difficulties in control is to establish *matched samples*. If an investigator knows some of the important variables affecting the events he wishes to study, he may equalise these variables in the groups by matching the subjects on them. For instance, if we are interested in the effect of monetary reward on the 'need for achievement' it is possible that the variables of intelligence and age are important; therefore we construct our groups so they are equal on measures of intelligence and on age. By actively equalising the effects of such extraneous variables, we reduce the chance that they will have an effect on the experimental outcome.

Scientists further rely heavily on repeated *confirmation* to increase the certainty of their observations. If the same experimental findings are repeated (replicated) in a different setting, with different subjects, the likelihood is increased that the results followed from the manipulating of the antecedent variables. When findings in different settings are inconsistent, the experimental design must be examined for important variables that are not being controlled.

A *control group* forms an important part of a controlled experiment. The function of a control group is to provide an observation that cannot be attributed to the variable being manipulated. In examining the effect of a new teaching method on learning, for instance, it is necessary to observe two similar groups of children—one group being taught by the new method, and the other group, the control group, being taught in the usual way. At the termination of the experiment, the amount of learning shown by the group receiving the new method (the experimental group) is compared to the learning of the control group. Such a comparison furnishes assurance that the new method resulted in an increase over and above the increase that would normally occur over the same time interval.

To understand the controlled experiment further it will be helpful to look at an example. Suppose we are interested in designing an experiment to investigate high achievement, and we suspect that 'incentive' plays an important part in learning. Our hypothesis might be: if incentive is increased, then learning is increased. Thus, we are interested in observing the change in learning as we vary the amount (degree) of incentive. Since intelligence is likely to influence learning, we administer an IQ test to all subjects before the experiment and compose our experimental group and control group so both contain subjects of similar intelligence level. The experimental group is told that their performance on the task (learning a passage of material) will count towards their course grade. The control group is asked to learn the task, but not told that it will count towards their grade. After the subjects have studied the material we administer a test to observe how much they have retained. We then compare the amount of learning of the experimental group to the amount of learning of the control group. If the amount of learning of the experimental group is greater, our hypothesis is supported.

The variables in an experiment are referred to by specific names. In the example above, the *independent variable* is the degree of incentive. It is the variable we manipulate; we cause it to change in order to observe its effect on learning. In this study it is defined by the difference in instructions to the two groups, and we examined only two *levels*, i.e., *no* added incentive (control group), and *some* added incentive (experimental group). The degree of learning is the *dependent variable*. We wish to observe changes in this variable when experimental manipulations are applied. Changes in this variable are 'dependent' on changes of the independent variable. In the above case it is defined as the score on a test. Our other variable, intelligence level, is called a *controlled variable*. We equated it between the two groups in order to eliminate its effect on the dependent variable; its definition is the score on an IQ test.

The foregoing experiment was an example of the simplest controlled experiment, the *two groups design*. As with correlational analysis, specific statistical procedures are applied to the data in order to evaluate the possibility that the difference between the two groups could have occurred by chance. We test the difference between the mean scores (averages) of the two groups on the dependent variable to determine if they are actually different, or if their difference is such that it could be attributed to a chance occurrence. The computation of two statistics is generally used for the above purpose, the 'z' statistic, and the 't' statistic. If the sample size is large, greater than 30, the z-test is applicable; with smaller samples, we must use the t-test. Most elementary statistics books contain computational procedures for these statistics.

Controlled experiments may become more complex than the two groups design. A common procedure is to include more experimental groups so that multiple levels of the independent variable are examined. For instance, the above experiment could be expanded by including a third group that is told their achievement scores will apply to their grade and also that anyone obtaining a score over 80 per cent will be rewarded with $5.00. Thus, three levels of the incentive variable is investigated: (1) the control group receiving no extra incentive, (2) one group receiving a specific incentive, and (3) a third group receiving two forms of incentive. As a result, more is learned about the effects of incentive learning, and more precise statements about the findings can be formulated. If, for example, the three groups showed increased learning with increasing levels of incentive, the initial experimental hypothesis would be supported even further, i.e., increased incentive increases learning. However, assume that the two experimental groups did not differ in learning, although both were higher than the control group. In this case, the results would be qualified by saying that added incentive increases learning to a limited extent, but a point is reached where further incentive does not add to learning. A design such as this where one variable is examined on several levels, is called a *simple analysis of variance*.

Controlled experiments become more complex as more independent variables are introduced. To continue with the example, it is possible to examine the effect of incentive *and* 'achievement motivation' on learning. Achievement motivation can be measured by tests designed for that purpose. The subjects can be divided into groups of 'high achievers' and 'low achievers' based on their achievement motivation scores. Consequently, our design contains six groups of subjects matched on IQ, and varied on two independent variables, (a) achievement motivation, and (b) incentive. A group of subjects scoring high on achievement motive tests and a group having low scores would be exposed to each of the levels of incentive. The results would show the effects of achievement motive and incentive on learning, plus the 'interactional effects' between the two variables. For instance, an inter-actional finding might indicate that subjects who have high achievement motivation perform high in learning regardless of incentive level, while subjects with low achievement motivation show increasing performance as incentive increases. One would have evidence to conclude that incentive is useful for students who have not developed a personal need to achieve.

Most of the limitations of the controlled experiment have been discussed in relationship to the difficulty in obtaining control. In general, experiments that are performed in laboratory settings maintain better control than studies in natural environments. While the techniques of randomisation and matched sampling help to reduce control problems in subject-variables, the natural environment presents more difficulties because of the numerous variables related to the setting. The more frequently experimental studies are confirmed, the greater the degree of certainty that the results are valid.

OTHERS' OBSERVATIONS

The observations of other investigators fall into the same categories that were discussed under personal observations. The way that others make their observations will reflect the same limitation, and uses, as they would if the student had made the same observations. One of the primary tasks in using others' observations is to evaluate the way in which they were made in order to determine their usefulness.

Literature is the primary source for locating others' results. The major handbooks, manuals and periodicals relating to psychology will direct the student to many of the major sources of information.

2

T. R. *Sarbin and* Reading research articles
W. C. *Coe*

In writing his term papers, the student psychologist will benefit from using both original sources and secondary sources. In general, original source material is to be found in the periodical literature, i.e., journals, reviews, bulletins and research monographs. Textbooks, handbooks, and encyclopedias give secondary source material in bringing together the content of the periodical literature and research monographs.

Research reports may appear forbidding to the beginning student. Technical language is frequently used, charts and graphs may be confusing, the concise form of reporting seems cold, and mathematical equations may be intimidating.

The purpose of this chapter is to make research papers less forbidding. This brief statement is intended to facilitate the reading of research articles so the student can become more involved in the elementary steps of the scientific enterprise. By clarifying the form of the usual article and by suggesting certain aids, these hints will give the beginning student some direction, some hope, and some skill.

Research articles generally follow a more or less standard pattern. In the first few paragraphs, *the introduction*, the author usually poses the problem to be investigated. His introductory statements should outline the problem in a general way. Frequently, he places it in a historical context by reviewing the propositions of previous investigations, or citing and quoting results and theoretical statements that are pertinent to his problem. Having given the reader a general perspective, the author becomes more specific and presents the particular aspects of the

* Reprinted from *The Student Psychologist's Handbook: A Guide to Sources*, Cambridge, Mass., Schenkman Publishing Co., 1968.

problem in which he is interested. At this point, the central feature of the investigation is expressed. It may be in the form of a narrative statement that certain observations will be related; it may be stated as a formal hypothesis; or it may be expressed as an informal guess or hunch.

The second section of a research article is concerned with procedures and is usually labelled *method*. The author describes in elaborate detail his apparatus, techniques or tests, characteristics of the experimental setting, his selection and description of subjects, his instructions to the subjects, and the experimental design. Detail is necessary in the methods section so that other investigators may confirm the findings (or question them) by repeating the experiment without altering the conditions.

The authors and editors of psychological research reports have evolved a set of conventional symbols to designate certain standard features. The more commonly used symbols and their referents are:

N=the sample, the number of subjects (N=10 should be read 'the number of subjects was ten')
S=subject
E=experimenter
O=observer

The next section is labelled *results* or *findings*. Here the data are presented, sometimes in expository form, sometimes in the form of tables and graphs, and sometimes by both methods. Because experiments usually use a large number of subjects, the general practice is to provide descriptive statistics of the data. When inferences are to be drawn from samples to populations, various statistical tests are included in order to evaluate the significance of the findings. In reading for acquaintance or for comprehension, the beginning student need not have a thorough grasp of descriptive or inferential statistics.

A *discussion* may follow the presentation of the findings. The author tries to link his observations with the original hypothesis, or guesses, and may speculate about implications for theory or applications to practice. The results of the study are compared with the findings of other investigators; where contradictions occur, the author will try to explain them. At the end of the article, the author customarily writes a condensed version of his research, a *summary*.

A research article may be read with any one of three aims: (1) acquaintance, (2) comprehension, or (3) critical evaluation. After preliminary selection based on the title or abstract, the student should approach each article with acquaintance as his first objective, comprehension as his second, and, if he has sufficient background and interest, critical evaluation as his third objective.

If the aim of the reading is *acquaintance* with a research paper, the student should first read the introductory paragraphs to determine the nature of the problem being investigated. Then the method and discussion should be scanned briefly. Finally, the summary statements should be carefully scrutinised. (In many journals, a summary statement appears in the form of an abstract at the beginning of the article.) By following this procedure, the student will achieve at least a cursory acquaintance with the contents of the article and perhaps acquire a 'feel' for what it is all about. The beginning student should be cautioned against becoming over-involved in the fine details of research presentation, lest he lose sight of the general conclusions and their implications.

With acquaintance as a basis, the student can now concentrate on acquiring a more profound *comprehension* of the work. In order to do this, he must scrutinise rather than scan the article. That is to say, he will ask a number of questions in the course of his reading. Some of the typical questions students have found useful in scrutinising research articles are outlined in the following paragraphs.

The *introduction* will generally provide information to answer the following questions: What is the author trying to do? Is he trying to discover new relations among events? Is his work aimed at testing a hypothesis (a hunch) by systematic observation? Is he trying to confirm findings reported at an earlier time? Is he interested in determining the generality of a principle? Is he questioning a popular conception that has not been subjected to systematic examination through controlled experiments or careful observations? Is he interested in determining the fruitfulness of a method?

The *methods* section will generally provide answers to questions of this sort: How does the author convert his hunches or his beliefs into testable hypotheses? What operations does the experimenter employ to answer the questions to settle his doubts? How does the author specify the variables? For example, how does he justify his selection of an ink blot test as a measure of sexual interest? How does he select his subjects —are they randomly selected or selected according to some announced criteria? What kinds of manipulations or examinations of the subjects does he introduce? How are the control samples selected? Are the control samples adequate?

The *results* section will provide answers to these typical questions: What are the raw data from which the results are refined? Are they ratings, scale scores, speech samples, self-reports, physiological measurements, test scores, census data, and so on? Have the data been processed to give summary statistics, such as averages? Or are the original protocols provided, such as electronic tracings, verbal responses to questions, etc.?

The *discussion* section will usually provide answers to questions of this type: Are the results in line with predictions from the author's initial hypotheses? How does the author relate his findings to conclusions reached by other investigators? How does he explain differences between his data and the predictions generated by his hypotheses? How does he integrate his findings with other current attempts to answer the same or similar questions?

Having achieved *comprehension*, the student is in a position to evaluate critically the research report by asking a few additional questions. Such questions cannot be asked by the beginning student; they are based in part on familiarity with research design, statistical methods, and the logic of experimentation. However, students at any level of sophistication may use common sense as the basis for criticism.

The student will ask the following questions to help him achieve a *critical evaluation*: Are the investigator's research hypotheses clearly linked to the questions raised? Are the specifications of the variables reasonable? Is he justified in specifying, for example, that a score on a personality test is equivalent to 'ego-control'? Is he concerned with representativeness both in selecting his subjects and in specifying the behaviours to be observed? In what ways are his controls adequate, and in what ways inadequate? Are the statistical tests appropriate to the data? May conclusions other than those of the author be derived from the same data? In what way are the findings significant, i.e., do they contribute in any important way to our understanding of conduct? Can the efficiency of prediction and control of behaviour be increased as a result of the application of the findings?

It is not unusual for the undergraduate student to hesitate before critically evaluating a research article. This hesitancy is understandable; for years he has practiced accepting the written word as the final authority. The reluctance to criticise may be eliminated if the student will bear in mind that a research article, simply because it is in print, is not the last word, nor is it perfect. In keeping with one of the purposes of this book—to help the student solve the problems that arise in connection with his creative efforts—the student should recognise that any research study provides only tentative and imperfect answers to questions. It is not improper for the student to be sceptical, to doubt, and to raise questions. By asking penetrating questions, new hypotheses emerge and new research is undertaken. This is as it should be: new research is the hallmark of science.

To summarise: The student should first attain cursory knowledge of an article by scanning the introduction, reading the summary and conclusions, and superficially examining the rest. Reading for comprehension and for critical evaluation may follow. Some suggestive questions have been listed above as an aid to the student who seeks comprehensive understanding of research articles.

SECTION I

Learning styles and creativity

The first four articles in this section deal with cognitive styles, while the fifth and sixth deal with creativity. There is a very close relationship between all these articles, as the first of the two articles on creativity treats the relationship of the cognitive styles of convergence and divergence to creativity itself.

The Witkin article (3) forms a good introduction to the concept of cognitive style, though focusing heavily on the author's researches into the articulated-global (or field dependent–independent) dimension, which is discussed in detail. The Kagan article (4) covers two dimensions, reflectivity and analysis. The analytic style clearly relates to Witkin's work but reflectivity seems to be a quite independent style variable. Neither article has been edited, but the second half of the original Witkin article has been omitted and the middle section of the Kagan article, which presents a two-year longitudinal study, has also been left out.

Both these articles are examples of efficient methodology in psychology. They are not just theoretical contributions but embody the results of empirical research, and may well lead to further fruitful *researches. Although they both differ in many ways from traditional interpretations, Witkin's research can be accommodated to much other theory and research in the personality field, while Kagan's reflection-impulsivity dimension offers a promising new avenue of approach.*

The third and fourth articles, really an article (5) and a research note (6), deal specifically with two cognitive styles, rather controversial ones—convergence and divergence—and their relationship to school structures. Although it is useful to employ the terms, particularly when discussing whether or not the British educational system caters more for the converger than for the diverger, it must always be remembered that there is no such animal as a converger or a diverger. The terms refer to two polarities on a kline, with certain personality characteristics associated with them, reflecting tendencies to learn in different ways. The article by Haddon and Lytton and the research note by Lytton and Cotton show the practical implications this can have for the teacher, by analysing the effect of formal and informal schools on this type of cognitive style. In the article, where the research was carried out in primary schools, the results indicated that the formal schools catered for the converger at the expense of the diverger, whereas the informal schools provided a climate where the converger and diverger alike could flourish. Of considerable interest is the fact that the research carried out in secondary schools and recorded in the research note did not show similar results.

The fifth article, by Jackson and Messick (7), attempts a conceptual analysis of the term creativity, and tries to relate various aspects of this concept to such things as the differing personality characteristics of the learner. The compartments into which this article divides the various components are too comfortable, but it does attempt a useful analysis of the ways in which creativity can be used, other than by using an operational definition.

The last article in this section deals with the structure of creativity and the approach of factor analysis. The virtues of Guilford's article lie not in the introduction of any new empirical evidence but in the clarity with which the subject is treated and the way in which it is related to personality characteristics. Guilford stresses the advantages of an approach where the hypotheses are testable. He gives a concise overview of theories of creativity, and in many ways this article marked a renewal of interest in the subject of creativity.

V. J. LEE

3

H. A. Witkin   Psychological
                  differentiation*

Recent research has demonstrated that people show characteristic, self-consistent ways of functioning in their perceptual and intellectual activities. These cognitive styles, as they have come to be called, appear to be manifestations, in the cognitive sphere, of still broader dimensions of personal functioning which cut across diverse psychological areas. The fact that these broader dimensions may be 'picked up' in the person's cognitive activities, in the form of cognitive styles, has an important methodological advantage. Cognitive styles may be evaluated by controlled laboratory procedures, thereby providing an experimental, objective approach to personality study and assessment.

It is of interest, too, that the dimensions of personal functioning that have been identified through the cognitive-style work represent different ways of cutting the personality 'pie' from those traditionally used. New ways of looking at personality organisation are thus being suggested. Even if the personality dimensions that are now being explored as outgrowths of the cognitive-style work, prove, in time, to be congruent with our more traditional dimensions, the outcome will be to deepen and enrich our understanding of these traditional dimensions.

The approach to cognitive activity followed in the research on cognitive styles has been a functional one. A primary concern has been with the adaptive function of cognitive processes in the psychological economy of the individual. This has led to a search for connexions and consistencies across psychological areas. An outcome of this research enterprise has been to demonstrate further that the conventional

* Reprinted from *Journal of Abnormal Psychology*, **70**, 1965, 317–36.

categories often used in describing man's psychological life are not as separate as once believed. A by-product of the cognitive-style research has thus been its contribution to a more integrated, holistic view of personality.

In these and other ways the recent extensive research on cognitive style has significant implications for personality theory, for the methodology of personality research, and for some of the practical problems encountered by the clinician in his work on diagnosis and therapy. Some of these implications may be demonstrated by considering, as illustrative, the particular cognitive style with which we have been concerned in our laboratory (Witkin *et al.*, 1954, 1962).

INDICATORS OF EXTENT OF DIFFERENTIATION

Articulated v. global dimension of cognitive functioning

We first identified this cognitive style, and the dimension of personal functioning of which it is a part, in perception, where we called it 'field dependence–independence'. In a field-dependent mode of perceiving, perception is strongly dominated by the over-all organisation of the field, and parts of the field are experienced as 'fused'. In a field-independent mode of perceiving, parts of the field are experienced as discrete from organised background. There is now considerable evidence that a tendency towards one or the other ways of perceiving is a consistent, pervasive characteristic of an individual's perception.

From our studies of the field dependence–independence dimension there has emerged a variety of perceptual tests for evaluating individual differences along this dimension. In all of these tests the issue is whether or not the person is able to keep an object separate from organised field in perception. In one test, the 'object' is the person's own body; in another, it is a stick; in still another, it is a simple geometric design. A brief account of these tests will make clearer the nature of the perceptual dimension they assess.

One test, the Body-Adjustment Test, is concerned with perception of the position of the body in space. The test evaluates the person's ability to perceive his body apart from the surrounding visual field, through reference to sensations of body position. The apparatus for this test consists of a small room, which can be tilted left or right, within which is a chair, which can also be tilted left or right. The subject's task is to make his body straight while the room around him is tilted. Some persons in carrying out this task, move their bodies into alignment with the tilted room, and in that position report that they are straight, though objectively tilted as much as thirty-five degrees, or even more. In this kind of performance, which we call 'field-dependent', perception of body position is dictated by the relation between the body and surrounding world. There seems to be a fusion between body and field in experience. At the other extreme of the performance range, we find subjects who, regardless of the position of the surrounding room, are able to bring their bodies close to the true upright. Persons who perform in this fashion—we call it a 'field-independent' performance—seem to have an immediate sense of the separateness of their bodies from the surrounding world.

Another of our tests of field-dependence again involves perception of the upright, but the object of perception is a neutral external object, a stick, instead of the body. The apparatus for this test consists of a luminous rod and frame, the only objects visible to the subject in the completely darkened room. With the frame tilted, the subject is required to adjust the rod to the upright. Some subjects perceive the rod as straight only when it is fully aligned with the tilted frame around it. For these field-dependent persons perception of rod position is dictated by the context provided by the axes of the surrounding frame. They cannot keep rod separate from frame; in this sense their perception is global. Other subjects, at the opposite extreme, are able to adjust the rod more or less to the true upright, independently of frame position. These field-independent persons are able to perceive a part of the field as discrete from the field; in this sense, their perception is analytical.

Still another test of field-dependence, the Embedded-Figures Test, requires the subject to locate a simple figure in a complex design which is so organised as to conceal the simple figure. For some persons the simple figure almost 'pops out' of the complex design. Their perception is field-independent. Others are not able to find the simple figure within the five minutes allowed. Their perception is field-dependent.

People tend to perform in a consistent fashion in these three tests. The individual who cannot separate the simple figure from the complex embedding design also cannot keep his body apart from the surrounding tilted room or the rod apart from the surrounding frame. Going beyond the particular tests I have described, this same individual is unable to keep item apart from context in a wide variety of other perceptual situations (including such classical ones as the constancies, illusions, reversible perspective) and in situations involving other sense modalities, as touch (Axelrod and Cohen, 1961). Such consistency is indicative of a stylist tendency in perception.

The particular stylistic tendencies we have been considering are not limited to a person's perception; they manifest themselves, in congruent form, in his intellectual activities as well. Thus, persons whose perception is field-dependent do less well at solving problems which require isolating essential elements from the context in which they are presented and using them in different contexts, as, for example, the tasks employed by Duncker in his studies of functional fixity.

It is because these stylistic tendencies extend across both perception, where we are dealing with an immediately present stimulus configuration, and intellectual functioning, where we are dealing with symbolic representations, that we refer to them as *cognitive* styles. The particular cognitive style we have been considering may be described as follows: at one extreme there is a consistent tendency for experience to be global and diffuse—the organisation of the field as a whole dictates the manner in which its parts are experienced. At the other extreme there is a tendency for experience to be delineated and structured—parts of a field are experienced as discrete and the field as a whole organised. To these opposite poles of the cognitive style we may apply the labels 'global' and 'articulated'. As with the dimension of perceptual field-dependence, there is no implication here that the world is peopled by two kinds of human beings. Scores for any large group on tests of this cognitive style show a continuous distribution.

I may add that a more global or more articulated quality is a stable characteristic of an individual's cognitive functioning over time. There are also consistent sex differences in the articulation-global cognitive dimension. Boys and men show greater articulation than girls and women. Small but consistent sex differences in tests of field dependence have been found with groups in the United States, in a number of western European countries (see e.g., Andrieux, 1955; Bennett, 1956; Chateau, 1959; Franks, 1956; Wit, 1955), and in Hong Kong,[1] Israel[2] and Sierra Leone, Africa (Dawson, 1963) as well.

Evidence that the global-articulated style of cognitive functioning is part of a still broader dimension of personal functioning has come from studies of the relation of this cognitive style to nature of the body concept, of the self and of controls and defences.

Articulation of body concept

Let me consider first our studies of the body concept—that is to say, the systematic impression an individual has of his body, cognitive and affective, conscious and unconscious. Our concern has been with the cognitive, rather than the libidinal aspects of the body concept, and

[1] Personal communication from Robert Goodnow.
[2] Personal communication from Martin Rothman and Joel H. Kaplan.

with the articulated-global dimension in particular. In turning to the body concept, we are in effect shifting the spotlight from experience which has its primary source 'out there', our main concern to this point, to experience which has its primary source 'within'. There is now considerable evidence that children and adults who show an articulated cognitive style in their performance in perceptual and intellectual tasks of the kind we have been considering are also likely to have an articulated body concept—that it to say, they experience their bodies as having definite limits or boundaries and the parts within as discrete yet interrelated and formed into a definite structure.

Performance in the Body-Adjustment Test itself permits some inference about articulation of the body concept. Take, for example, the person who, in order to perceive his body as upright, aligns it with the tilted room, and in that position reports no experience of tilt. Such a fusion of body and field in experience, or inability to keep body and field separate, suggests a lack of clear body boundaries.

In another, more familiar approach to study of the body concept, we have used the figure-drawing technique. To evaluate extent of articulation of drawings of human figures, made in response to the request to draw a person and then to draw a person of the opposite sex, a five-point sophistication-of-body-concept scale was devised. This scale does not follow the usual projective uses of the figure-drawing technique but rather considers directly characteristics of the figures drawn. Three areas of the drawings are considered in making ratings: form level, identity or role and sex differentiation and level of detailing. In a number of studies, scores for the figure-drawing test have been shown to relate significantly to measures of cognitive style. In the drawings of field-dependent children, we find very little detail and unrealistic representation of proportioning and of body parts. Sexual characteristics are shown minimally or not at all, so that in some pairs of drawings it is difficult to tell which is male and which is female. In most cases, there is no attempt at role representation. On the other hand, in the drawings of children whose perceptual performance is at the field-independent extreme we find the body drawn in realistic proportion. Parts of the body are presented in some detail and fairly realistically. There is clear representation of sex and sex differences. Aside from indication of sex through body characteristics, the sex of the figure is also indicated by such externals as clothing. We also find attempts at role representation, suggesting a sense of the uses to which the body may be put. These differences among children in the way in which they represent the body on paper are significantly related to how they perform in the cognitive tests in the laboratory.

It may appear from the description of the kinds of drawings they make that field-dependent children, who tend to make relatively unarticulated drawings, are just not as bright as field-independent children, who tend to make highly articulated drawings. Significant correlations are in fact found between figure-drawing articulation scores and total IQ. Several studies have shown, however, that this relation is carried mainly by particular subtests of standard intelligence tests which, like the cognitive tests we use, have the task requirement of separating item from context. These subtests are block design, picture completion and object assembly which in past factor analytic studies of the Wechsler were shown to load what we would designate an 'analytical factor' (Cohen, 1957, 1959). There are only low, non-significant relations between figure-drawing articulation scores and scores for the Wechsler vocabulary, information and comprehension subtests which have been shown to define a 'verbal-comprehension factor'. I should mention that scores for tests of field-dependence, similarly, relate very highly to scores for the triumvirate of block design, picture completion and object assembly; and they do not relate to scores for the triumvirate of vocabulary, information, and comprehension (Goodenough and Karp, 1961; Karp, 1963).

The sophistication-of-body-concept scale is easily learned and applied, even by persons without experience in the figure-drawing technique. Checks on interjudge agreement in a number of studies have shown good reliability. And, as we have just seen, scores based on the scale relate well to scores of tests of the articulated-global cognitive dimension. These characteristics of the scale, together with the ease of obtaining figure drawings from subjects, make the scale a useful assessment technique.

Let me interpolate that other studies, using more experimental means to evaluate articulation, have confirmed the relation between articulation of body concept and cognitive style (Epstein, 1957; Silverman et al., 1961).

Sense of separate identity

To continue, persons with a more articulated or more global mode of cognitive functioning also differ in an important aspect of the self, namely, sense of separate identity. Persons with an articulated cognitive style give evidence of a developed sense of separate identity—that is to say, they have an awareness of needs, feelings, attributes which they recognise as their own and which they identify as distinct from those of others. Sense of separate identity implies experience of the self as segregated. It also implies experience of the self as structured; internal frames of reference have been formed and are available as guides for definition of the self. The less developed sense of separate identity of persons with a global cognitive style manifests itself in reliance on external sources for definition of their attitudes, judgements, sentiments and of their views of themselves.

The nature of this relation may be made clearer by considering a few studies from among the many that have been done in this area.

Konstadt and Forman (1965) observed that children with a global cognitive style, when taking a test under stress and so concerned about their performance, looked up at the *face* of the adult examiner about twice as often as children with an articulated cognitive style. Similarly, Crutchfield, Woodworth and Albrecht (1958) found that persons with a global cognitive style were relatively better at recognising and recalling faces of people they had been with earlier. Messick and Damarin (1964) observed that field-dependent subjects showed greater incidental learning than field-independent subjects when the incidental material consisted of human faces; the relation is in the opposite direction with non-human incidental material (Witkin *et al.*, 1962). These studies suggest that persons with a global style are particularly attentive to faces, the major source of cues as to what others are feeling and thinking. The reliance of persons with a global cognitive style on external sources for self-definition was demonstrated in quite a different way by Linton (1955). She found that in an autokinetic situation, such persons more often changed their judgement about movement of the point of light in conformance with the suggestion of a planted confederate. The results of these and numerous other studies may be summarised by saying that the person for whom the frame around the rod, or the room around his body, strongly influence the manner in which rod and body are experienced, is, similarly, strongly influenced by the immediate social context in his experience of himself.

I would like to mention here a recently completed study by Winestine (1964) on the 'twinning reaction' of boy twins because of the particularly direct way in which sense of separate identity was evaluated. The twinning reaction, assessed by interview, was rated as strong for a given twin if in his specific attitudes, feelings and actions he showed that he experienced himself as an integral part of the twinship rather than as individuated. Twins rated high on the twinning reaction were strikingly more field-dependent and their representation of the body in their figure drawings much more global. In fact, so specific a characteristic as whether the twins dressed alike or differently proved to be significantly discriminating with regard to both perceptual field-dependence and nature of body concept in figure drawings. It would be of interest to study the parents of twins in relation to strength of the twinning reaction. We might expect that mothers of twins who show a weak twinning reaction and who are field-independent to perceive their twins as separate individuals, rather than as a unit; to have a distinct relation with each child; and to foster the separation of the twins. These expectations are based on an earlier finding that mothers of more field-independent children, in their interactions with them, give their children greater opportunity for separation (Witkin *et al.*, 1962).

Differences between field-dependent and field-independent persons, as a function of difference in sense of separate identity, have even been observed in characteristics of their dreams. In an experimental study of dreaming, using rapid eye movements and Stage-1 EEG sleep as indicators of the dream state, Lewis *et al.* (1966) observed that field-dependent subjects more often dreamed overtly about the laboratory situation. Moreover, in a recent analysis of the data from that study we found a difference between field-dependent and field-independent subjects in the kinds of incorporation they made. Field-dependent subjects more often had dreams concerned with their relation to the experimenter. Apparently these subjects get 'caught up' more with another person in the laboratory situation, as we have found they do in general, and these feelings are carried over into the dream.

Specialisation of defences

Finally, let me comment on the relation between cognitive style and nature of defences. Studies have shown that persons who experience in articulated fashion tend to use specialised defences, as isolation. In contrast, persons with a global cognitive style tend to use such defences as massive repression and primitive denial. These latter defences involve an indiscriminate, total blotting out of memory for past experiences and of perception of stimuli. Compared to such mechanisms as isolation, they represent relatively non-specific ways of functioning.

The contrasting kinds of defences used by persons with a more global or more articulated cognitive style may be conceived in terms similar to those we used earlier in characterising their cognitive functioning. In the last analysis, defences help determine the content of a person's experience—what enters into consciousness and what is put aside. They do this, in part, through regulating the interrelation between affect, on the one hand, and ideation and perception, on the other. It seems true of persons with a global cognitive style that feelings strongly influence thought and perception, in other words, that feelings are not kept sufficiently discrete from thoughts and percepts. This is congruent with what we saw happen within their perception, where again they are unable to 'keep things separate'—as body separate from field, rod separate from frame or simply figure separate from organised ground. Persons with an articulated cognitive style, in their use of isolation, maintain the discreteness of feelings and ideas, although the feeling component may be 'split off'.

This view of communality in mode of functioning in the areas of cognition and of defences may be made more evident by considering a few representative studies.

Bertini (1961) carried out a study of the relation between cognitive style and defences, following this view. He considered that the 'capacity' to separate and isolate an idea from its emotional content, involved in the mechanism of isolation, parallels the capacity in field-independent perception to 'separate several elements from the phenomenal field in isolating them from a context'. To assess the use of isolation as a defence, Bertini relied on the Rorschach, basing his analysis on the work of Schafer (1954). The expectation that the tendency to use isolation would go with field-independent perception was confirmed.

A recent study by Minard[3] on perceptual defence effectively complements Bertini's study. Words matched in structure and previously found in a free-association test to be neutral or charged for the particular subject, were presented tachistoscopically. Persons who were field-dependent showed a considerable perceptual-defence effect; their speed of perception of words was markedly affected by whether or not the word carried an emotional connotation for them. Percept and feeling were, in other words, not kept separate. Field-independent persons showed no difference in speed of perception of neutral and charged words, suggesting discreteness of percept and feeling. In their use of denial and repression as characteristic defences, persons with a global cognitive style are in effect showing a particularly extreme influence of feeling on percepts and memories. In these instances the total experience, including both its cognitive and affective components, is 'split off'.

A particularly striking example of this kind of complete blotting out of experience by field-dependent persons is found in their tendency to forget their dreams, presumably because of their use of repression as a characteristic defence. A connexion between field-dependence and dream recall has been found by Eagle[4] in one study of ten-year-olds

[3] Personal communication from James Minard.
[4] Personal communication from Carol Eagle.

and in another study of seventeen-year-olds. It has been observed by Linton[5] and Schonbar (1964) with groups of college students. More recently it was found again in an analysis we made of data from the study of Lewis *et al.* (1966). Eight subjects at each extreme of the field-dependence dimension were picked from their total group of forty-six college students. Considering frequency of dream reports in a home dream diary these subjects kept, seven of the eight most field-dependent subjects and only one of the eight most field-independent subjects were found to be 'non-reporters'—that is, failed to recall dreams. Recent evidence from studies using rapid eye movement and Stage-1 EEG sleep as indicators of dreaming makes it entirely clear that everyone dreams a number of times each night (Aserinsky and Kleitman, 1953; Dement and Kleitman, 1957). A lack of dream reports is therefore indicative of a failure to recall dreams rather than a failure to dream.

The hypothesis that the failure of field-dependent persons to remember their dreams is, in part at least, a function of repression, is being tested in a study Donald Goodenough, Helen Lewis, Arthur Shapiro and I are carrying out. This study is making use of a technique Helen Lewis and I developed in an earlier preliminary study (Witkin and Lewis, 1965). The technique consists of creating an important psychological event for the person just before he goes to sleep and obtaining his subsequent dreams by awakening him during each period of rapid eye movement and Stage-1 EEG. The pre-sleep event we use consists, on some occasions, of viewing an emotionally charged film; on other occasions, viewing a neutral film; and on still other occasions, an encounter with another person through the medium of suggestion. The results of the preliminary study showed, first of all, that the pre-sleep event often found expression in the subject's subsequent dreams in a clearly identifiable way. Further, reports from subjects that they had been dreaming, but could not remember the dream, occurred more often on awakenings following the exciting pre-sleep event than on awakenings following the neutral pre-sleep event. We anticipated this outcome on the premise that the exciting pre-sleep event, by 'charging' subsequent dreams, would make these dreams better 'candidates for repression' and so reduce dream recall. In the study Goodenough, Lewis, Shapiro and I are now doing we are following this same procedure of pre-sleep stimulation, using field-dependent and field-independent persons as our subjects. It is our expectation that field-dependent persons will be more likely to 'lose' dreams charged by an exciting pre-sleep experience. Such an outcome

[5] Personal communication from Harriet Linton.

would lend further support to the view that field-dependent persons tend to use repression as a typical mode of defence.

Summary of indicators of differentiation

Reviewing the evidence considered to this point, a tendency towards a more global or more articulated cognitive style has been shown to be associated with differences in body concept, in sense of separate identity and in nature of defences. It is now our view that the characteristics which make up the contrasting constellations described may be conceived as diverse manifestations of more developed or less developed psychological differentiation. Thus, we consider it more differentiated if, in his perception of the world, the person perceives parts of the field as discrete and the field as structured. We consider it more differentiated if, in his concept of his body, the person has a definite sense of the boundaries of the body and of the interrelation among its parts. We consider it more differentiated if the person has a feeling of himself as an individual distinct from others and has internalised, developed standards to guide his view of the world and of himself. We consider it more differentiated if the defences the person uses are specialised. It is our view that these various characteristics, which we have found to cluster together, are not the end-products of development in separate channels, but are diverse expressions of an underlying process of development towards greater psychological complexity. 'Level of differentiation' is a concept which encourages us to look across psychological areas and provides a basis for thinking about self-consistency in individual psychological make-up.

The level of differentiation at which a person functions may be assessed in different areas. For clinical evaluation one or several areas may be considered. It is perhaps best assessed through the person's cognitive style where, as noted earlier, objective experimental means of evaluation may be used. In this sense a person's cognitive style, in the articulated-global dimension, may be considered a 'tracer element'. Certainly, assessment of psychological differentiation need not be limited to the cognitive sphere. It may also be assessed effectively, for example, in the area of the body concept, by means of the figure-drawing sophistication-of-body-concept scale which I described earlier. In our own work, when we want to make a rapid assessment with regard to differentiation we use the Embedded-Figures Test and Figure-Drawing Test, both of which are easily administered and scored, but time permitting, we like to use the Rod-and-Frame Test as well. If the Wechsler has been given, we use the score for the block-design subtest, which, as we saw, is very similar in its requirements to the tests of field-dependence and is in fact a good test of field-dependence.

REFERENCES

ANDRIEUX, C. (1955) 'Contribution à l'étude des différences entre hommes et femmes dans la perception spatiale', *L'Année Psychol.*, 55, 41–60.

ASERINSKY, E., and KLEITMAN, N. (1953) 'Regularly occurring periods of eye motility and concomitant phenomena during sleep', *Science*, 118, 273.

AXELROD, S., and COHEN, L. D. (1961) 'Senescence and embedded-figures performance in vision and touch', *Percept. mot. Skills*, 12, 283–8.

BENNETT, D. H. (1956) 'Perception of the upright in relation to the body image'. *J. ment. Sci.*, 102, 487–506.

BERTINI, M. (1961) 'Il tratto difensivo dell'isolamento nella sua determinazione dinamica e strutturale', *Contributi dell'Istituto di Psicologica*, 25.

CHATEAU, J. (1959) 'Le test de structuration spatiale TIB. I.', *Le Travail humain*, 22, 281–97.

COHEN, J. (1957) 'The factorial structure of the WAIS between early adulthood and old age', *J. consult. Psychol.*, 21, 283–90.

COHEN, J. (1959) 'The factorial structure of the WISC at ages 7–6, 10–6, and 13–6', *J. consult. Psychol.*, 23, 285–99.

CRUTCHFIELD, R. S., WOODWORTH, D. G., and ALBRECHT, R. E. (1958) Perceptual performance and the effective person, *U.S.A.F. W.A.D.C. Technical Note*, no. 58–60, Lackland Air Force Base, Texas.

DAWSON, J. L. M. (1963) 'Psychological effects of social change in a West African community', unpublished doctorial dissertation, University of Oxford.

DEMENT, W., and KLEITMAN, N. (1957) 'The relations of eye movements during sleep to dream activity: an objective method for the study of dreaming', *J. exp. Psychol.*, 53, 339–46.

EPSTEIN, L. (1957) 'The relationship of certain aspects of the body image to the perception of the upright', unpublished doctoral dissertation, New York University.

FRANKS, C. M. (1956) 'Différences déterminées par la personalité dans la perception visuelle de la verticalité', *Rev. Psychol. appl.*, 6, 235–46.

GOODENOUGH, D. R., and KARP, S. A. (1961) 'Field dependence and intellectual functioning', *J. abnorm. soc. Psychol.*, 63, 241–6.

KARP, S. A. (1963) 'Field dependence and overcoming embeddedness', *J. consult. Psychol.*, 27, 294–302.

KONSTADT, N., and FORMAN, E. (1965) 'Field dependence and external directedness', *J. Personal. soc. Psychol.*, 1, 490–3.

LEWIS, H. B., GOODENOUGH, D. R., SHAPIRO, A. and SLESER, I. (1966) 'Individual differences in dream recall', *J. abnorm. Psychol.*, 71, 52–9.

LINTON, H. B. (1955) 'Dependence on external influence: correlates in perception, attitudes, and judgement', *J. abnorm. soc. Psychol.*, 51, 502–7.

MESSICK, S., and DAMARIN, F. (1964) 'Cognitive styles and memory for faces', *J. abnorm. soc Psychol.*, 69, 313–18.

SCHAFER, R. (1954) *Psychoanalytical Interpretation in Rorschach Testing*, Grune & Stratton.

SCHONBAR, R. A. (1964) 'Some dimensions of sensitivity of recallers and non-recallers of dreams', in Dream Research and Theory, Symposium presented at the Post-Graduate Center for Mental Health.

SILVERMAN, A. J., COHEN, S. I., SHMAVONIAN, B. M., and GREENBERG, G. (1961) 'Psychophysical investigations in sensory deprivation: the body-field dimension', *Psychosom. Med.*, **23**, 48–61.

WINESTINE, M. C. (1964) 'Twinship and psychological differentiation', unpublished Doctoral Dissertation, New York University.

WIT, O. C. (1955) 'Sex differences in perception', unpublished Master's Thesis, University of Utrecht.

WITKIN, H. A., and LEWIS, H. B. (1965) 'The relation of experimentally induced pre-sleep experiences to dreams: a report on method and preliminary findings', *J. Amer. Psychoanal. Assoc.*, **13**, 819–49.

WITKIN, H. A., DYK, R. B., FATERSON, H. F., GOODENOUGH, D. R., and KARP, S. A. (1962) *Psychological Differentiation*, Wiley.

WITKIN, H. A., LEWIS, H. B., HERTZMAN, M., MACHOVER, K., MEISSNER, P. B., and WAPNER, S. (1954) *Personality through Perception*, Harper.

4

J. *Kagan*   Developmental studies in
                                reflection and analysis*

The varied and murky phenomena implied by the word cognition
range from the unrestrained racing of images and words to the more
orderly, goal-directed sequence of mediated steps that are activated by
the desire to solve a problem or acquire a new cognitive structure.
This chapter restricts itself to the latter domain of cognitive events,
specifically to the processes of stimulus classification and hypothesis
selection. Three sequential operations typically occur when a person is
confronted with a problem—an initial categorisation of the relevant
information, storage of the coded categorisation and, finally, the im-
posing of transformations (formal algorithms or mediational elabora-
tions) upon the encoded data. The nature of the categorisation, transformation or elaborative mediation is governed, of course, by the nature
of the problem. Students of cognitive development have generally
assumed that the striking differences among the intellectual products
of children of different ages or among children of the same age were
attributable primarily to differences in the availability of vocabulary,
possession of deductive or inductive rules and mediational diversity. In
essence, the superior intellectual performance of older, in comparison to
younger, children has been ascribed to the greater knowledge repertoire of the older children. This supposition is intuitively attractive and
empirically verified. It is not surprising, therefore, that psychologists
have not seriously entertained the possibility that other factors may
contribute to age and individual differences in the form and quality of

* Reprinted from A. H. Kidd and J. E. Rivoire, Eds, *Perceptual Development in Children*, New York, International Universities Press, 1966, pp.
487–505, 517–22.

cognitive products. Specifically, there has been a tendency to ignore the relevance of differences in two aspects of information processing—differences in the degree of stimulus analysis that precedes initial coding, and the degree of reflection attendant upon classification and hypothesis selection. It now appears that children and adults have clear preference hierarchies with respect to these two variables. The empirical work described in this essay is an inquiry into the significance of these two variables that are so intimately involved in the initial classification phase of problem solving, the phase during which external information is given its first symbolic coding, and the best possible solution sequence is selected.

To preview the heart of the chapter, we have discerned two stable dimensions upon which children and adults are distributed. The first is called reflection–impulsivity and describes the degree to which the child reflects upon alternative classifications of a stimulus or alternative solution hypotheses in situations in which many response possibilities (i.e. classifications or solution hypotheses) are available simultaneously. In these situations some children have a fast conceptual tempo; they impulsively report the first classification that occurs to them or carry out the first solution sequence that appears appropriate. The reflective children, on the other hand, characteristically delay before reporting a classification or carrying out a solution hypothesis. They actively consider the alternatives available to them and compare their validity. The reflective child behaves as if he cared that his first response be as close to correct as possible.

The reader is urged to withhold any premature tendency to stereotype the reflective child as excessively cautious or frightened, and the impulsive child as daring, divergent or creative. The evidence to be presented does not allow such a glib evaluative template to be placed upon this class of behaviour. We enjoin the reader to be reflective, and to withhold evaluation of the 'goodness' of this predisposition until all the evidence has been considered.

A second dimension, called visual analysis, describes the child's tendency to analyse complex stimuli into their component parts. Some children fractionate a stimulus into small subunits; others label and react to a larger stimulus chunk. Analysis is relatively independent of reflection, and each of these variables contributes variance to a variety of cognitive products.

This line of inquiry was originally stimulated by an observation that piqued our curiosity because it did not agree with contemporary ideas concerning modal classification and conceptualisation habits among normal subjects. Specifically, we found that when adult subjects were asked to select, from a large array of human figures, 'a group of figures that went together on some conceptual basis', a sizeable number grouped these paper figures on the basis of a shared objective element that was a component part of the total stimulus (e.g. 'These three men go together because *they have no hair*', or 'These people are all *holding an object in their hands*'). We called this class of concepts *analytic* because the basis for the grouping always involved a differentiated component of a set of diverse stimuli. What was more surprising however, were the behavioural characteristics of the men who preferred this class of concepts to the more popular conceptual categories of abstract-inferential or thematic. The men who preferred analytic concepts were behaviourally more independent, more concerned with intellectual mastery, slightly more intelligent, more desirous of social recognition and displayed more spontaneous sudomotor activity at rest than men who did not report many analytic concepts (Kagan, Moss and Sigel, 1963). This cluster of attributes elicited cognitive dissonance, for we would have thought that ambitious, bright, independent men would prefer elegant, abstract concepts (i.e. happy soldiers, poverty-stricken people, creative artists) to the more stimulus-bound concepts classified as analytic.

Most of the work during the last four years has involved school-age children and has attempted to amplify our understanding of the significance of the analytic conceptual response and to discover its immediate and historical antecedents. The results indicate that spontaneous analytic concepts are the product of the joint action of the two more fundamental variables of reflection and visual analysis.

There is, at present, more information on the stability and significance of the reflection–impulsivity dimension than there is on the variable of visual analysis. The data are persuasive in indicating that the child's tendency to reflect on alternative responses (in situations where several alternatives are available simultaneously) generalises across varied problem situations, and shows remarkable intraindividual stability over periods ranging from two to twenty months. The operational definition of the reflection variable is response time in problem situations in which the subject is presented with a standard stimulus and an array containing the standard and five to ten highly similar variants. The child is required to select the one stimulus in the array that is identical to the standard. There is typically a negative correlation between response time and number of errors (i.e. incorrect selections) in these problem situations. Children who delay before offering their first answer make fewer errors. The adjective 'reflective' is most descriptive of the child who has long response times and few errors.

REFLECTION AND ANALYSIS: MEASUREMENT AND
DEVELOPMENTAL CHANGES

This section describes the test situations used most frequently with children to assess the reflection and analysis variables, and the relations among the major variables derived from these tests.

Conceptual style test (CST)

This test consists of thirty stimuli, each illustrating line drawings of three familiar objects. The child is asked to select two pictures that are alike in some way and to state the reason for his grouping. The items were constructed so that an analytic concept (i.e. a concept based on similarity in an objective element that was a differentiated component of only two of the stimuli) competed with an indifferential-abstract or thematic concept. The analytic concept typically was a less obvious conceptual association to the stimulus card than an inferential or thematic concept. The two major variables derived from this test were the number of analytic concepts and the average response time to concept selection. Fig. 4.1 illustrates three stimuli from this test.

The most common analytic concept to the watch–man–ruler item was: 'The watch and ruler have numbers'; to the zebra–shirt–striped-shirt item: 'These two have stripes'; to the house–match–pipe item: 'The house and pipe have smoke coming from them'. These concepts were called analytic because the numbers, stripes and smoke were objective, differentiated components of the total stimulus.

Delayed recall of designs (DRT)

In this test a simple design was presented for five seconds. This standard test was then removed, and after fifteen seconds an array of eight, nine or ten stimuli was presented. The S selected the one design that was identical to the standard. The major variables derived were number of errors (a secondary distinction was made between major and minor errors) and average response time. Fig. 4.2 illustrates a sample item.

Matching familiar figures (MFF)

This task was basically similar to the DRT, but illustrated familiar objects rather than geometric designs and, unlike DRT, contained no memory requirement. The S was shown a picture (the standard) and six similar stimuli, only one of which was identical to the standard. The S selected the one stimulus that was identical to the standard. The standard and variations were always available to the subject. The

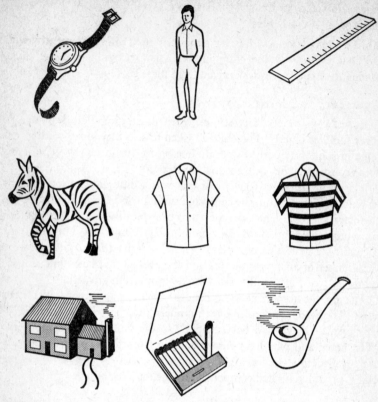

Fig. 4.1 Sample items from CST

major variables scored were number of errors, and average response time to first selection. Fig. 4.3 illustrates a sample item.

Haptic-visual matching (HVM)

In this task, the child first explored with his fingers a wooden form (approximately three inches square) to which he had no visual access. He was allowed an unlimited time to explore the form, and when he withdrew his hands, he was presented with a visual array of five stimuli, one of which illustrated the form he had explored haptically. The twenty-item test contained geometric forms as well as familiar objects and yielded three variables: errors, response time and palpation time (i.e. time S devoted to tactual exploration of the wooden form). Fig. 4.4 illustrates a sample item.

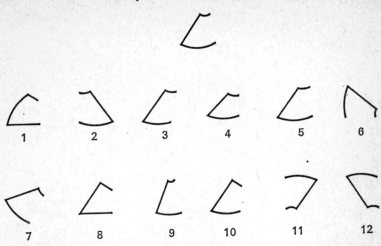

Fig. 4.2 Sample item from DRT

Visual analysis

This task assessed the degree to which the child attached a new label to component parts of a visual stimulus while associating the new label with the whole stimulus pattern. This task was regarded as a measure of a visually analytic attitude. The stimuli were designs that contained three distinct components: background, figural form and element. The background component was a repetitive pattern; the figural component referred to the shape into which the discrete elements fell. That is, the elements were small, discrete geometric forms that traced out the figural pattern. Fig. 4.5 illustrates a sample item.

The design in the upper left corner of the illustration was the stimulus to which the child associated a nonsense syllable. The semi-circles were the background components, the triangles were the element components, and the 'staircase' pattern was the figural component.

In the administration of this task, the child first learned four different nonsense syllables to each of four different complex designs. When the child reached criterion (eight consecutive correct trials) he was given a response-transfer task. In this transfer task he was shown separate illustrations on the background element and figural components, each without any perceptual support from the other two aspects of the original design. Thus, with reference to Fig. 4.5, the child would be shown the semicircles, the triangles or the 'staircase' and asked to apply the correct nonsense syllable. The transfer task contained two illustrations of each of the three components for each of the four designs (twenty-four items in all). During the transfer series the four

Fig. 4.3 Sample item from MFF

nonsense syllables, which were printed on cards, were always available to the child to insure that incorrect labelling of the separate components would not be due to forgetting of the newly acquired labels. After a short recess, a second set of four different designs was presented, and the child was asked to perform a similar task. The major variables derived from these tasks were number of ground, figural and element components labelled correctly on each task.

The five tests described above have been administered to children in grades 1 to 4 [ages six to nine] from a variety of schools (a minimum of fifty boys and fifty girls at each grade level). Figs. 4.6, 4.7 and 4.8 illustrate the changes in errors, response time, and level of visual analysis over these four grades.

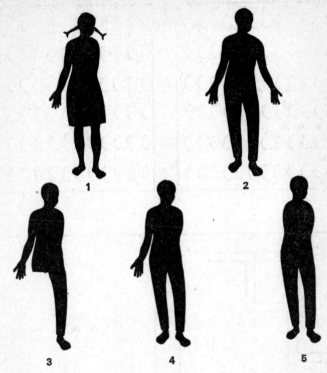

Fig. 4.4 Sample item from HVM

The developmental trends indicate that, with age, there is a linear increase in analytic concepts on the CST, a decrease in errors and an increase in response time on DRT, MFF and HVM. The visual-analysis data are more complex, but provocative. There is a marked increase, with age, in correct labelling of the figural component, accompanied by poorer recognition of the background components. Moreover, with age, boys have higher recognition scores for ground and element components than do girls, suggesting that the boys are visually more analytic.

Since the DRT, MFF and HVM tasks are easier for older children, and the older children make fewer errors, the correlation between response time and age suggests that a disposition favouring reflection over alternative solution hypotheses grows stronger as the child matures. Supplementary data from other studies support this conclusion.

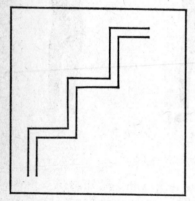
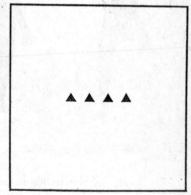

Fig. 4.5 Sample item from visual analysis task

RELATIONSHIPS AMONG RESPONSE TIME, RECOGNITION ERRORS AND
VERBAL ABILITY

The three perceptual recognition tasks (DRT, MFF and HVM) were similar in their psychological requirements, and all yielded the two variables of recognition errors and response time. In almost every sample studied there has been a negative relationship between frequency of recognition errors and average response time (i.e. the latency between presentation of the array of alternatives and the child's first selection), the coefficients typically ranging between −0.30 and −0.60. There was also a negative, but lower, relation between recognition errors and verbal ability (mean score on three verbal subtests of the WISC: vocabulary, information and similarities). The relation between

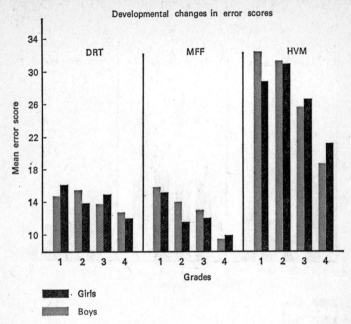

Fig. 4.6 Developmental changes in error scores

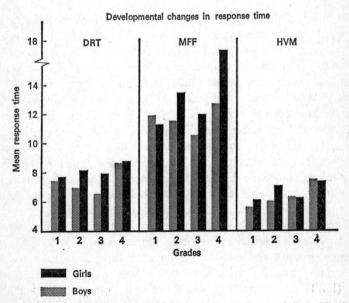

Fig. 4.7 Developmental changes in response time

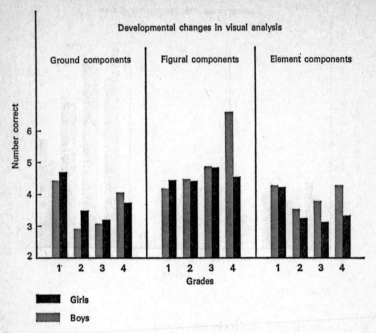

Fig. 4.8 Developmental changes in visual analysis

errors and verbal ability was typically lower for boys than for girls. Response time to these tasks, however, was independent of verbal ability, the correlations typically falling below 0·20. Thus, the reflection–impulsivity dimension appeared to be relatively orthogonal to the traditional construct of verbal intelligence. The moderate relation between recognition errors and verbal skills, in girls especially, suggests that the basic cognitive processes implied by the phrase 'high verbal intelligence' (e.g. richer verbal resources, greater self-confidence, problem-solving skills, stronger motivation to perform with competence) have some relevance for accuracy in perceptual recognition tasks among school-age children. Multiple correlation coefficients with recognition errors as the criterion and verbal ability and response time as the two predictors have yielded coefficients in the seventies.

There was remarkable consistency of recognition-error scores across the three tasks (coefficients typically ranged from 0·30 to 0·60 for different groups), and even higher intertask consistency for response times across the three tasks. Moreover, average response time on one task (DRT, for example) predicted not only response time but also errors on a second recognition task (MFF or HVM). Finally, both recognition errors and response time on DRT were highly stable over short (nine weeks) and long (seventeen months) periods. In sum, response time appears to be a critical conceptual variable; it shows generality over tasks, stability over time, and is relatively independent of verbal skills. The occurrence of recognition errors is a more complex variable, for it is related both to response time and to the multiple factors associated with verbal skills.

PSYCHOLOGICAL CORRELATES OF ANALYTIC CONCEPTS

Numerous studies early in the research attempted to explore the psychological correlates of analytic concepts on the CST (Kagan, Moss and Sigel, 1963; Kagan *et al.*, 1964; Lee, Kagan and Rabson, 1963). The early work on reflective and analytic attitudes used the CST because we were not yet aware of the role of the fundamental variables of response time and visual analysis. We realised only recently that the production of analytic concepts is a joint function of these two variables. Analytic concepts are most likely to occur when the child pauses to consider alternative conceptual groupings on the CST and has a penchant for analysing visual stimuli into smaller components. This section summarises some salient characteristics of children who report a large number of analytic concepts, a response disposition that involves the reflection–impulsivity dimension.

It will be recalled that the frequency of analytic concepts increased with age and this disposition showed stability over a one-year period (r ranged from 0·47 to 0·73).

An impressionistically consistent cluster of characteristics was possessed by seven- to ten-year-old boys who reported many analytic concepts. These boys were less distractible in the class-room, less likely to display task-irrelevant gross motor behaviour on the playground or in a restrictive laboratory setting and less likely to report many incorrect solutions. They were more likely to become involved in sedentary tasks requiring long periods of concentration, more likely to prefer intellectual vocations that required motoric passivity (e.g. scientist, writer), and typically produced more complete drawings of objects. One of the most objective demonstrations of the relationship between motoric restlessness and analytic attitude was contained in the positive association between analytic concepts and regular, non-variable respiratory rhythms during episodes of rest and episodes when the boy was attending to simple visual or auditory stimuli (Kagan and Rosman, 1964). Moreover, boys with many analytic concepts demonstrated greater cardiac deceleration when asked to attend to external stimuli. Cardiac deceleration and regular respiration rates have been shown to be reliable indexes of the degree to which a person invests attention in external stimuli (Lacey, 1959). It appears, therefore, that young boys who prefer analytic concepts are more capable of sustained attention to visual inputs than less analytic youngsters.

Analytic concepts were positively associated with long response times to the CST and DRT and with correct labelling of the element components in the visual analysis task, but negatively related to recognition errors on the DRT. Moreover, children who produced large numbers of analytic concepts, in contrast to those with few concepts, manifested earlier acquisition (in a standard concept-formation task) of concepts requiring visual analysis. Examples of such concepts are 'objects with a missing leg', and 'objects with a black band around them'. However, the analytic child did not show easier acquisition of concepts that did not require visual analysis (Lee, Kagan and Rabson, 1963). Finally, there was a moderate relationship, among girls, between rejection of traditional sex-role interests and analytic concepts. There was no such relationship among boys.

Study of all the data gathered so far suggests the following interpretation of analytic concepts on the CST. To almost every item on the CST the most obvious way of grouping two pictures involves a thematic relation between the pair (see Fig. 4.1). For example, the compelling associational tendency to the item illustrating a wrist watch, a man and a ruler is to link the watch and the man functionally (e.g. the man wears the watch). The pre-potent association to the house with smoke coming from the chimney, the matches and the pipe is a functional link between the matches and pipe. If the child is to produce an analytic concept he must suppress these initially strong, culturally popular associations, and reflect on alternative groupings. He must display response uncertainty. If, in addition to the tendency to reflect over alternative responses, he also has a disposition favouring visual analysis, he is likely to produce an analytic concept. The capacity to delay in the service of reflection, together with a predisposition to visual analysis, appear to be the critical determinants of analytic concepts.

PSYCHOLOGICAL CORRELATES OF RECOGNITION ERRORS AND
RESPONSE TIME

The early work with the CST led quickly to an appreciation of the variable of reflection in problems presenting multiple-answer possibilities. This realisation prompted the investigations with the DRT, and later with the MFF and HVM tasks. It was noted earlier that recognition errors and response time on DRT were highly stable over time and were correlated with errors and response time on the MFF and HVM. Recognition errors and response times differ in their patterns of relations in several respects. First, response time was typically orthogonal to verbal ability for both sexes, whereas error scores usually had a low but significant negative correlation with verbal skills. Moreover, visual-analysis scores (i.e. correct labelling of figure and element components) were negatively related to recognition errors, but not to response time. Finally, response time usually manifested more consistent intertask generality and greater stability over time than the error scores. In one elaborate study, the average response time to 108 tachistoscopic exposures (six different pictures) was positively related to response time on MFF (average $r=0.40$). We have coined the phrase 'conceptual tempo' to describe the connotative meaning we assign to the reflection variable. Some children consistently spew out the first reasonable hypothesis that occurs to them without pausing to reflect on its probable validity. Their strategy of problem solving has a shotgun character; the child fires a fusillade of answers in the hope that one will be correct, or, perhaps, because he needs immediate feedback from the environment to inform him of the quality of his performance. This child contrasts with one who characteristically pauses to consider the differential validity of several hypotheses. This child behaves as if he had a strong desire to be as correct as possible on his first attempt, and he is able to tolerate the ambiguity and tension inherent in the period of silence that is an inevitable concomitant of response selection. Two qualifications are in order. These general statements about the significance of long response times apply only to those problem situations in which all the alternatives are available simultaneously (either in visual form as in the DRT, or as mental images).[1] These conclusions do not apply to problems for which the child has no immediate solution hypothesis (e.g. What is the cube root of 810?), or to situations in which the child is so afraid of failure that he is reluctant to offer any answer. We believe that our test situations minimise the latter possibility, but are exploring ways of detecting the excessively fearful child who may show long response times. We are currently working on a method to detect two small groups of subjects for whom the above generalisations about response times may not always apply. There is, on the one hand, a small group of bright subjects who can have relatively fast response

[1] The assumption that response time is a sensitive index of response uncertainty was well demonstrated in a recent study by Morin and Forrin (1963).

times on easy tasks (like DRT) but make few errors. These children do not have fast response time on the MFF because this task is more difficult than the DRT. It is crucial to use tasks that are of optimum difficulty for each age level to guarantee that fast response times typically lead to high error scores. A second anomalous group, also small, contains children whose long response times result from extreme fear. These children may have high error scores, for they are not reflecting upon alternative possibilities during the long delay. They fail to respond quickly because they have no idea what to say and are afraid of offering any answer. It is likely that elimination of children who show both excessively long response times and high error scores will permit us to understand with greater clarity the antecedents of the reflection variable.

When recognition errors or response time on DRT or MFF were used as indexes of the reflection–impulsivity dimension, an impressionistically consistent set of relationships to other behaviours emerged. Impulsive children (i.e. high errors and fast response times) showed a marked increase in errors of commission on a serial learning task (i.e. reporting words not originally present on the list) after being told that their performance on the serial learning task was inadequate. The more impulsive the child prior to the learning task, the greater his increase in errors of commission following this threat.

There is much similarity between recognition errors on DRT, HVM or MFF, and orthographic errors in reading. One might expect these two classes of errors to be related in young children learning to read. In a recently completed study of 130 first-grade children we found a strong positive relationship between errors in recognising three-letter words (i.e. big, dog, cat, nap) and errors on DRT, MFF or HVM. However, there was a minimal relationship between the accuracy of recognition of single letters and errors on DRT, MFF or HVM. To illustrate, the correlation for sixty-five boys between HVM errors and word errors was 0·47 ($p < 0.001$); the correlation with single-letter errors was only 0·19. It appears that the tendency to read *log* for *dog*, *cat* for *pot*, or *eat* for *ear* is related to a disposition towards impulsive selection of hypotheses, even when the child has mastered the individual graphemes of his language.

It should be noted, finally, that recognition errors and response times are not influenced appreciably by the degree of acceptance or warmth displayed by an examiner. A carefully controlled experiment in which examiner rapport was manipulated (warm *v.* impersonal, cold approach to the child) did not allow rejection of the null hypothesis (Kagan *et al.*, 1964).

THE SIGNIFICANCE OF VISUAL ANALYSIS

Systematic work on visual analysis has only recently begun, and less information is available on the significance of this variable. As noted earlier, there is a developmental shift in preferred perceptual focus. First-grade children initially recognise the solitary background components with greater accuracy than second-, third- or fourth-grade children. The older children are more accurate in recognising the solitary figural components. Second, accurate recognition of the element components was associated with early recognition of tachistoscopically presented scenes that contained incongruous elements. This is a reasonable association, for a disposition towards visual analysis should facilitate early recognition of pictures that contain one or two incongruous elements (e.g. person in a woman's dress smoking a pipe; living-room with a tree). Finally, recognition of figural and element components was associated with low error scores on DRT, MFF and HVM, and with analytic concepts on CST. But these visual-analysis variables were orthogonal to response times and verbal skills.

DISCUSSION AND SUMMARY

The accumulated evidence from a dozen investigations of children in the first four grades is remarkably univocal in its message. Reflection over alternative solution possibilities and visual analysis are fundamental cognitive dispositions that are independent of each other and of the richness of the child's language repertoire. Moreover, each of these dimensions influences the occurrence of the more complex cognitive products of analytic conceptual groupings (on CST) and recognition errors (on DRT, MFF or HVM). The complementary role of visual analysis and reflection in predicting infrequent recognition errors is reasonable, for in order to select the correct variant on the first attempt one must analyse each stimulus into its components, inhibit the immediate reporting of initial hypotheses, and evaluate alternative solution possibilities. A reflective disposition displays a stability over time and a generality across tasks that is unusual for psychological attributes, and tempts one to conclude that this response tendency must be a basic component of the individual's behavioural organisation.

The points of contact between these two dispositions and basic theory and research in intellectual processes are not yet clear. Witkin and his colleagues (1962) have been concerned with the dimension of field-independence and have used performance on the Embedded Figures and Spatial Orientation Tests as the operational indexes of this variable. We have found no strong relation between reflection and solution time on

Witkin's version of the Embedded-Figures Test (Kagan *et al.*, 1964). But reflective children offer far fewer incorrect solution hypotheses prior to achieving solution. We have not assessed the relation between visual analysis and field-independence, but expect it to be moderately positive.

Basic theory in intellectual development has been concerned mainly with the growth of mediational systems and the acquisition of operations (or transformation rules) that allow more complex deductive and inductive reasoning. Both European and American investigators have been fascinated by the behaviour of cognitive structures, how they are born, grow and die. They have been indifferent to those processes that mark the beginning and end of a problem-solving sequence, namely, the initial processing of external information and the characteristics of the response classes involved in the overt reporting of a completed cognitive product. The growing interest in information processing in both adult and child should amplify our understanding of these aspects of mental activity.

Antecedents of reflection–impulsivity

A search for the historical and immediate antecedents of a reflective versus impulsive attitude should consider at least three possibilities, none of which is mutually exclusive of the others. These three are constitutional predispositions, involvement in the task and anxiety over task competence. There is some evidence favouring the idea that excessive motor restlessness and distractibility at age eight have their anlage in congenital deficit resulting from minimal and subtle brain damage during the peri-natal or early post-natal period. Since the extremely impulsive boys in our studies were also excessively restless and distractible, it is possible that these children suffered subtle cerebral damage early in life. It is possible, of course, that biological variables, unrelated to central nervous system deficit, predispose some infants and pre-school children to hyperactivity and impulsive reactions. Schaefer and Bayley (1963) have found that extremely active one-year-old infants were minimally attentive to intellectual problems at five and six years of age. The Fels longitudinal study has yielded similar results. Ratings of hyperkinesis during ages three to six were inversely correlated with ratings of involvement in intellectual activity during adolescence and adulthood (Kagan and Moss, 1962). Moreover, ratings of hyperactivity during ages four through eight were negatively related to analytic concepts among ten-year-old boys (Kagan *et al.*, 1964). This relationship suggests that signs prognostic of the development of an impulsive conceptual attitude may be manifest early in development.

In sum, there are tantalising scraps of evidence from several laboratories that lend some credibility to the idea that children who are extremely active during the opening years of development are more likely to be conceptually impulsive during the school years than those who are motorically more quiescent. We are now conducting an intensive longitudinal study of a group of infants who were seen first at eight weeks of age and who are thirteen months old at the time of this writing. Preliminary analyses indicate marked stability of the attributes of *motor activity and duration of sustained attention to external stimuli* over this forty-eight-week period, with the activity and attention variables inversely correlated with each other.

A second class of factors that might influence reflection deals with the degree of involvement in the task. A child with high standards of performance should be more likely to reflect on alternative hypotheses and more likely to want his first answer to be correct than a child who is minimally concerned with the quality of his performance. We have found that girls who rejected traditional feminine interests were more reflective than girls with traditional feminine standards. There is a positive relation, among girls, between degree of rejection of sex-typed activities and involvement in intellectual mastery (Kagan and Moss, 1962), and this relation furnishes indirect evidence for the proposition that reflective girls may have been more highly involved in our tasks.

A final hypothesis deals with the child's anxiety over his ability to perform adequately in tasks like DRT or MFF. Let us assume that most children have a desire to do well on these tests and to convince the examiner that they are able to perform adequately. Let us look closely at the psychology of the inter-personal situation the moment the examiner presents the problem to the child. The child who is anxious about his ability to perform adequately should be less able to tolerate the period of silence that must occur if he is to reflect over various hypotheses. He may fear that his failure to respond immediately will be interpreted as an indication of his inadequacy and he may be predisposed to offer an answer quickly. The confident child, on the other hand, should be more able to tolerate the delay between presentation of the problem and the offering of a solution. The fact that children show increased response times with age suggests that reflection gains strength with development. It is difficult to determine, however, whether this increased penchant for reflection is the product of greater confidence, a stronger need to avoid reporting incorrect answers, the ability to generate more solution possibilities, or, perhaps, variables we have not yet recognised.

Our current belief, held with only moderate confidence, is that a child's position on the reflection–impulsivity dimension can be the result of either constitutional or experiential factors, with the former most relevant for children at the extreme end of the impulsivity continuum.

Methodological implications

Responses to all psychological tests are, first of all, cognitive responses. The interpretation of an inkblot, the telling of a story to a TAT picture, or the selection of an answer on a multiple-choice test all involve the selection of one best response from a set of alternatives. The reflection–impulsivity dimension should affect the manner in which external information is classified and organised, and the content and form of the final response. It is reasonable to expect that production of motivational content variables on selected 'personality tests' (e.g. aggressive or sexual imagery to inkblots or pictures) may be the partial result of tendencies towards impulsivity or reflection. For example, there is a marked association between the production of ink-blot imagery that would be coded as aggressive or sexual in content and the production of a response containing movement components. Movement responses characteristically require longer response times than non-movement responses and typically require analysis of a component of the total stimulus. It is likely, therefore, that reflective children will produce more movement responses and, by so doing, also report a percept that has motivational content. It is reasonable to defend the idea that a penchant for reflection is one critical determinant of an 'aggressive' inkblot interpretation.

A second implication for method concerns certain factor-analytic approaches to understanding intellectual functioning. Group-administered tests of mental abilities do not obtain response-time data and, therefore, cannot evaluate the reflection–impulsivity variable. If this disposition is as critical as these data suggest, it is unwarranted to assume that one can discover the basic factors of mental activity through factor analysis of these scores.

Implications for problem solving

A second set of implications concerns problem-solving efficiency and the gradual establishing of permanent attitudes towards problem solving. In problems with alternate routes to solution, reflection and evaluation of the validity of solution sequences are critical for eventual success. The child who does not reflect upon the probable validity of alternative-solution sequences is likely to follow through on the first idea that occurs to him. This strategy is more likely to end up in failure than one which involves reflection. The impulsive child who reaches a cul-de-sac in a problem-solving sequence, and recognises that he has not solved the problem, is likely to become more anxious than he was initially. As a result of the increased anxiety his selection of a second solution path is likely to be impaired and the probability of success attenuated. This maladaptive cycle may become entrenched with time, and after four or five years of experiencing the sequence: problem $\longrightarrow$ impulsive selection of invalid solution $\longrightarrow$ failure $\longrightarrow$ anxiety $\longrightarrow$ selection of second solution $\longrightarrow$ failure, etc., the child may gradually withdraw from problem situations, and apathy and hostility may become characteristic reactions towards intellectual situations.

We do not wish to paint the reflective child as necessarily the better or brighter child. It is likely that efficient learning and creative problem solving will occasionally be facilitated by a reflective approach, occasionally by an impulsive approach. Indeed, a recent study (Lee, Kagan and Rabson, 1963) demonstrated this last point clearly. Some of the academic contents children must master require reflection and analysis, for instance, mathematics and the physical sciences. But maximal productiveness and mastery of principles in aspects of the arts, social studies and humanities may be hampered by an excessively reflective orientation. New pedagogical procedures should acknowledge this interaction between the preferred strategy of the learner and the material to be acquired and tailor the presentation of materials to the psychological requirements of the task and the cognitive predisposition of the learner.

REFERENCES

KAGAN, J., and MOSS, H. A. (1962) *From Birth to Maturity: a study in psychological development*, Wiley.

KAGAN, J., and ROSMAN, B. L. (1964) 'Cardiac and respiratory correlates of attention and an analytic attitude', *J. exp. child Psychol.*, 1, 50–63.

KAGAN, J., MOSS, H. A., and SIGEL, I. E. (1963) 'Psychological signficance of styles of conceptualisation in basic cognitive processes in children', *Monogr. Soc. Res. Child Devel.*, 28, no. 2.

KAGAN, J., ROSMAN, B. L., DAY, D., ALBERT, J., and PHILLIPS, W. (1964) 'Information processing in the child', *Psychol. Monogr.*, 78, no. 578.

LACEY, J. I. (1959) 'Psychophysiological approaches to the evaluation of psychotherapeutic process and outcome', in E. A. Rubenstein and M. B. Parloff, eds. *Research in Psycho-Therapy*, National Publishing Co., pp. 160–208.

LEE, C. L., KAGAN, I., and RABSON, A. (1963) 'The influence of a preference for analytic categorisation upon concept acquisition', *Child Devel.*, **34**, 433–42.

MORIN, R. E., and FORRIN, B. (1963) 'Response equivocation and reaction time', *J. exp. Psychol.*, **66**, 30–6.

SCHAEFER, E. A., and BAYLEY, N. (1963) 'Maternal behavior, child behavior and their intercorrelations from infancy through adolescence', *Monogr. Soc. Res. Child Devel.*, **28**, no. 3.

WITKIN, H. A., DYK, R. B., FATERSON, H. F., GOODENOUGH, D. R., and KARP, S. A. (1962) *Psychological Differentiation*, Wiley.

5

F. A. Haddon and
H. Lytton

Teaching approach and the development of divergent thinking abilities in primary schools*

SUMMARY. This research was designed to evaluate the effects of differing teaching approaches on divergent thinking abilities, the hypothesis being that informal, progressive teaching would promote these abilities more than formal, more subject-centred teaching. Two hundred and eleven children, 11 to 12 years old of all ability levels, were tested, half coming from 'Formal' and half from 'Informal' primary schools which were matched for verbal reasoning quotient (VRQ) and socio-economic background. The results showed that pupils from the Informal schools were significantly superior in divergent thinking abilities. The difference in means often reached the 0·01 level of significance and was in no case in the unpredicted direction. The hypothesis was thus confirmed.

A subsidiary hypothesis—that the correlation between VRQ and divergent thinking abilities would decrease as the VRQ of each sub-group rose—was also supported. As expected, these correlation values were generally higher in the Informal schools.

I. INTRODUCTION

Despite the attention which 'creativity' has received as a fashionable topic for research there is, as yet, as Vernon (1964) and Hudson (1966) point out, no clear evidence for the assumption that high scorers on tests of 'divergent thinking' in Guilford's terminology, will be particularly fertile in creative original production in their own life situation. Nor is there evidence for the converse, that high scorers on

* Reprinted from *British Journal of Educational Psychology*, **38**, 1968, 171–80.

tests of 'convergent thinking' alone, will lack such creativity. The best way of looking at this question probably is to regard high scores on divergent thinking tests as an indication of lack of anxiety about non-conformist responses, a necessary, but not a sufficient condition for creative work. To avoid undue claims, we have used the term 'divergent thinking', rather than 'creativity' throughout.

As Guilford has shown in his many studies (summarised in Guilford, 1956) divergent abilities can be distinguished factorially from convergent abilities which have hitherto formed the main component of general ability tests. It is important to explore divergent abilities since they hold some promise of providing new insights into cognitive functioning. Tests of these abilities may provide a welcome supplement to 'intelligence tests' as we have so far known them, and indicate the type rather than the level of future performance (Hudson, 1966). This model of cognitive abilities implies that divergent and convergent thinking are complementary aspects or different styles of intellectual functioning.

Whilst a great deal has been written on the guidance of creative ability, very little work appears to have been published investigating the effects of particular school situations. Torrance does hint briefly at the effects of school orientation towards learning (Torrance, 1962) and Hasan and Butcher (1966) report his view to the effect that the success of predominantly divergent thinkers is directly related to the degree of freedom and permissiveness and the lack of authoritarian discipline within a school. Vernon (1964), in a review of creativity and intelligence, also comments: 'I strongly suspect some schools do much more to stimulate and foster, or else to inhibit, creative talent than others.' Sears and Hilgard (1964) quote Spalding (1963) as finding strong negative relations between the expression of creativity in elementary-aged children and teacher behaviour characterised as formal group instruction, using shame as a punishment technique, whilst Sears (1963) found positive correlations between creativity and teachers' use of the technique of rewarding children by personal interest in their ideas rather than by evaluation.

The research reported here was concerned with evaluating the effects of contrasted Formal and Informal schools upon performance on tests of divergent thinking abilities. It was felt that teaching approach might be a variable affecting the degree of divergency exhibited in children's thinking. Two other aspects have also been examined. First, the relationship between IQ and performance on divergent tests has been looked at in some detail. Secondly, the relationship between performance on divergent tests and peer popularity has been compared with the relationship between VRQ and peer popularity in each of the schools used.

II. BASIC HYPOTHESIS AND RESEARCH DESIGN

It is generally accepted that abilities and personality characteristics are, to a large extent, moulded by environmental influences such as family and school. Since the school, however, is only one factor in the development of a child's personality, the basic structure of which has very largely been laid down by the time the child arrives there, measurable differences between school and school are likely to be small. The basic hypothesis is that some differences in divergent thinking abilities can, nevertheless, be detected between comparable children who have spent formative years in contrasted environments such as different primary schools provide. Schools may differ in many ways, one of which is the degree of formality or informality which permeates the approach to learning. The two types of schools which have been contrasted here are the Formal, or traditional, school which places emphasis upon convergent thinking and authoritative learning and the Informal or progressive school, where the emphasis is upon self-initiated learning and creative activities. It was predicted that children from the Formal school will have lower mean scores on 'divergent' tests than children from the Informal school, which, it was thought, encourages the growth of personality traits associated with divergency.

A further area of interest was the relation between IQ or VRQ (verbal reasoning quotient) and measures of divergent thinking. It was thought that given a high general cognitive potential, development along either convergent or divergent lines may receive considerable emphasis at the expense of the other, but that the Informal school, more than the Formal school, would develop both convergent and divergent thinking in line one with the other. Conversely, when intelligence is limited, VRQ and divergent thinking ability are likely to display greater correlation. In other words, the differentiation of divergent from convergent abilities is likely to show itself more clearly at higher than at lower levels of general intellectual ability (whether measured via convergent or divergent abilities). This prediction is in accordance with Yamamoto's (1965) findings. To summarise the predictions: (1) Mean scores on divergent tests would be significantly higher in the Informal schools than in the Formal schools. (2) Correlation between VRQ and divergent thinking abilities would decrease as the mean VRQ and mean divergent tests scores of sub-groups rose, but the values obtained would throughout be higher in the Informal school.

The tests

Full details of the tests and the system of scoring, adapted from that used by Torrance for the Minnesota Tests of Creative Thinking, are given in the Appendix. Briefly, the tests were:

The non-verbal or 'Iconographic' Tests

1. Circles (Torrance, 1962).
2. Vague shape of dots (developed from Torrance, 1962, Picture Construction task).
3. Block-printing (New test).

The Verbal Tests

4. Uses for a shoe-box (modified from Uses for a Can, Torrance, 1962).
5. Problems which might arise in taking a bath (Torrance, 1962, Common Problems).
6. Imaginative stories (Torrance, 1962).
7. The camping expedition, a disguised sociometric test (New test).

From each test two scores were obtained, one of which was Originality (except for Test 2—see Appendix). The total for each test was the total of the two component scores.

The subjects and schools

The schools used were selected after consultation with lecturers from a college of education who were familiar with the area, and after advice from a local inspector of schools. Two pairs of contrasted primary schools matched for socio-economic background were chosen. A and C are the Formal, B and D the Informal schools. Schools A and B are in a predominantly middle-class urban area, the mean VRQ being 106·5 and 103·5, respectively. Schools C and D draw their children from a more mixed social background in a different urban area, the mean VRQ being 96·1 and 98·3, respectively. The mean VRQ of the Formal schools combined (A and C) is 101·75, and that of the Informal schools (B and D) 101·14.

The tests were administered to all the children eligible for transfer to secondary schools the following term. In all, 211 children, 11–12 years old, were tested and the whole ability range in the schools was covered.

There were several advantages in choosing to administer the tests to children within a few days of completing their primary education:

(i) Such children had been subjected to the effect of their particular school for the maximum amount of time.

(ii) Selection for secondary education had already taken place, so that the children were not concerned about possible effects upon their future schooling.

(iii) IQs (or VRQs) for all the children were made available by the Chief Education Officer. These were based on Moray House Verbal Reasoning Test No. 72, which was used throughout the County as part of the selection procedure for allocation to secondary education.

III. RESULTS AND DISCUSSION

Comparisons between two types of school

The results of the tests are set out in Table 5.1. Each component was marked separately and the component scores combined to obtain a test score for each child. Mean scores for the group were calculated from these.

TABLE 5.1. *Comparison of mean test scores (raw scores)*

	Formal schools			Informal schools			t-value of dif- ference Com- bined means	P
	A Mean	C Mean	Com- bined mean A+C	B Mean	D Mean	Com- bined mean B+D		
VRQ	106·50	96·1	101·75	103·50	98·30	101·14	0·31	N.S.
Test 1	12·00	9·1	10·55	15·55	10·10	12·80	3·07	<0·01
2	5·72	5·92	5·82	7·48	7·52	7·50	5·48	<0·01
3	7·50	4·88	6·19	9·05	11·64	10·35	6·50	<0·01
4	4·98	6·58	5·78	6·86	7·62	7·25	2·11	<0·05
5	10·56	10·08	10·32	15·20	8·41	11·81	1·61	N.S.
6	12·46	12·50	12·48	14·75	13·54	14·15	2·51	<0·05
N	54	50	104	59	48	107		

N for Test 3—(numbers reduced on account of practical testing difficulties).

| | 29 | 25 | 54 | 35 | 25 | 60 | | |

The results in Table 5.1 in general confirm the main prediction of significantly higher scores being obtained from the Informal schools. Even in Test 5, where the difference does not reach statistical significance at the 0·05 level, the direction of the difference is in line with the other results. There is, of course, no appreciable difference in mean VRQ between the two groups of schools.

The Iconographic Tests—numbers 1, 2 and 3—all show highly significant differences between the two groups. This is not unexpected. It is reasonable to suppose that the effect of the different approaches will show to its maximum here, in that no child will be handicapped by having to respond in writing. This not only allows the less able child to make a response but applies particularly to the boys who often seem either unable or reluctant to express themselves in writing with the same fluency as girls of similar age. Conversely, one would expect lesser differences between the two groups on the Verbal tests. This is generally true again, Tests 4 and 6 showing a difference of means significant at the 0·05 level, whilst Test 5 just fails to reach this level.

TABLE 5.2. *Comparison of mean scores of test components (standard scores)*

Component	Tests from which obtained	Formal schools means	Informal schools means	't' value of difference	P
Fluence	6	7·26	7·67	1·78	N.S.
Flexibility	1, 4, 5	57·31	61·39	2·62	<0·01
Originality	1, 4, 5, 6	61·61	70·10	2·71	<0·01
Fit of concept	2	3·26	3·81	3·12	<0·01
Elaboration	2	2·58	3·69	5·30	<0·01

Having confirmed the main prediction, further analyses were made. The component raw scores which were used for the previous table were changed to standard scores with a mean of 20 and a standard deviation of 5 to make them comparable. It was then possible to extract the component scores from each test to obtain a total component score for Originality, etc., for the whole battery. The results are shown in Table 5.2. Scores for Test 3 were not included here because only 50 per cent of the children were tested.

An alternative way of looking at the results is shown in Table 5.3, in which the scores were added to give mean scores for Iconographic Tests, Verbal Tests, and all Divergent Tests. Comparisons are made over different ranges of VRQ. Results from Test 2 were not included in these calculations since the test was scored in a somewhat experimental manner.

The results again gave a clear indication of the superiority of the Informal schools in performance on the tests. It seemed important next to examine the differences between the two types of school over high and low ranges of VRQ. Whilst it is recognised that the VRQ is in some ways an unsatisfactory indication of general intelligence because it samples too narrow a range of intellectual abilities, nevertheless, considerable importance is attached to this index and to the abilities it measures, and it usually carries considerable weight in selection procedures. If, as has been claimed, the Informal schools are fostering the development of divergent thinking abilities, then one would expect a greater difference between the two types of school over the higher ranges of VRQ where there is greater intellectual potential. Conversely, over the lower ranges of VRQ, the expected differences would be less. Table 5.3 compares the two types of school over the range VRQ 100 and above, and VRQ below 100, respectively.

TABLE 5.3. *Comparison of mean scores over various ranges of VRQ (standard scores)*

	Formal schools means	Informal schools means	't' value of difference	P
Over full range of VRQ:				
VRQ	101·75	101·14	0·31	N.S.
Iconographic	18·96	21·29	4·16	<0·01
Verbal	19·50	20·72	2·71	<0·01
All Tests	38·34	41·87	4·15	<0·01
VRQ 100 and above				
VRQ	113·47	110·57	1·88	N.S.
Iconographic	20·18	22·37	2·88	<0·01
Verbal	20·29	21·97	3·18	<0·01
All Tests	40·36	44·18	3·62	<0·01
VRQ below 100:				
VRQ	88·59	89·11	0·32	N.S.
Iconographic	17·59	19·92	3·11	<0·01
Verbal	18·61	19·13	0·76	N.S.
All Tests	36·06	38·92	2·41	<0·05

The results shown in the lower part of Table 5.3 support the main hypothesis, but the prediction of greater differences with higher VRQs is borne out only as regards the Verbal, not the Iconographic tests. It is worth noting that for VRQs above 100 the differences are in the reverse direction to the differences on the divergent tests, yet in spite of this, the Informal schools achieve results which are significantly superior.

The evidence from correlations

The main prediction with regard to correlation, it will be recalled, was that the correlation between VRQ and divergent thinking abilities would decrease as VRQ rose. This is demonstrated by Table 5.4 which used the combined data from the four schools. The results here are in agreement with Yamamoto (1965) who reports 'a consistent decrease in the size of correlation as the IQ level of sub-groups became higher' (although the values quoted by him are considerably smaller in both the school systems used for his investigations than the values obtained here). In the lower half of Table 5.4 the data have been regrouped on the basis of total scores on the tests of divergent thinking.

TABLE 5.4. *Correlation of VRQ and divergent thinking tests*

All schools. Sub-groups based on VRQ ranges

	N	r
Full range of VRQ 70–135	211	0·480
VRQ 115 and above	35	0·076
VRQ 100 and above*	115	0·164
VRQ below 100	96	0·512

* This includes the category VRQ 115 and above.

All schools. Sub-groups based on divergent thinking scores

Mean Divergent Thinking score =40	N	r
Full range	211	0·480
Divergent score 40 and above	103	0·230
Divergent score below 40	108	0·440

These findings strongly confirm the view that convergent thinking and divergent thinking are two complementary aspects of intellectual ability in general (styles of functioning). They separate from each other, each attaining a more clearly independent status of its own, at higher levels of ability, and they overlap more closely at lower levels, whether ability is measured by convergent or by divergent tests.

Within this general concept of a diminishing relationship at higher levels of ability, a subsidiary hypothesis was that the correlation would be somewhat higher in the Informal schools. It was argued that in these schools, because of their particular approach to learning, the link between the two aspects would be maintained to a greater extent. The idea is more forcibly expressed by saying that formal education will tend to destroy this connection by putting a premium on convergent thinking and conformist behaviour. Table 5.5 explores this connection over various VRQ groupings.

TABLE 5.5. *Correlations between VRQ and divergent thinking tests*

VRQ	N	Formal schools			N	Informal schools		
		Icono-graphic *r*	Verbal *r*	All Tests *r*		Icono-graphic *r*	Verbal *r*	All tests *r*
Full range 104		0·335	0·418	0·454	107	0·379	0·618	0·560
115 and above 22		−0·041	−0·011	−0·050	13	0·018	0·026	0·036
100 and above* 55		−0·051	0·159	0·059	60	0·204	0·483	0·366
Below 100 49		0·245	0·576	0·487	47	0·367	0·578	0·548

* This includes the category 115 and above.

The evidence in this table is quite convincing in its support of the hypothesis. In every instance the value of *r* is higher in the Informal schools. This is especially noticeable in the range VRQ 100 and above, which suggests that formal education fails to develop latent ability to think along divergent lines among the most able children.

It is interesting to compare these results with the outcome of a pilot study in Birmingham (Kellmer Pringle and McKenzie, 1965) which involved two contrasted primary schools selected on criteria similar to those used in this study. The object of the research was to examine teaching methods as a factor influencing the degree of rigidity in problem solving. The definition of rigidity as 'the inability to re-structure a field in which there are alternative solutions to a problem in order to solve that problem more efficiently', is almost a negative definition of divergency and it might have been expected that the Informal school would have shown significantly less rigidity among its pupils. In fact, no overall difference was found, but since the comparison was made on the degree of set found in performance on one arithmetic test, this is hardly sufficient evidence for any definite con-clusion to be drawn.

Sociometric analysis

Considerable attention has been given in America to the social relation-ships of creative individuals—in our terminology, those who do well on tests of divergent thinking abilities. The general view seems to be that such children are subjected to pressure to conform and to conceal their divergent characteristics. It is suggested that the creative child will be lacking in popularity and that social pressures may well be a factor inhibiting the development of divergent abilites (Torrance, 1962).

However, it was felt that the qualities associated with the divergent personality—fluency, flexibility and sensitivity—might well be qualities which make for good social relationships in a society in which originality was valued, and that there could, therefore, be a positive relationship between popularity and divergent personality. Test 7 was included in the battery to explore this connection. It was expected that any correlation found would be low, but that the values would be higher in the Informal schools. The argument here was that in so far as a school is able to transmit its cultural values, those values should be reflected in the general appreciation of the individuals who exhibit them in action. As a corollary to this, the correlation between VRQ and popularity should show a higher value in the Formal schools.

Table 5.6 sets out these correlations. These have been calculated on a school by school basis because the value of sociometric status as expressed here varies according to the number of children in the class, and so it was not possible to combine the schools for comparisons. Spearman's rank order correlation has been used.

TABLE 5.6. *Rank order correlation coefficients between VRQ and sociometric status, and between divergent thinking scores and sociometric status*

School	N	VRQ range	VRQ and sociometric status	Divergent thinking and sociometric status
A. Formal	33	135—100	0·137	−0·128
C. Formal	50	126—70	0·337	0·279
B. Informal	47	135—85	0·058	0·363
D. Informal	37	131—61	0·462	0·382

There is partial support for the prediction, but two values require some discussion. In School A the top class contained only children of VRQ 100 and above. The probable result of this is to give a much lower value for both correlations. However, the important point here is not so much the value of the coefficients as the relationships between them. VRQ has a positive correlation with sociometric status, whereas divergent test scores have a negative one—as they did in Getzels' and Jackson's study.

The second point to discuss is the values obtained from School D. The three other schools all show the predicted direction in the differences between the two values. This is not only reversed in School D but the values themselves are the highest obtained. This school is a particularly delightful one to visit and gives one the impression of friendly informality combined with high standards of work and behaviour. It may be that the ethos of this school ensures esteem for both types of ability and thus makes for popularity of both high convergent and high divergent thinkers, who indeed are often the same children.

The overall results suggest that the school ethos as formulated by the head and the staff plays an important role in determining the children's values during the primary stage. This would seem to explain the inter-school differences in our investigations.

IV. CONCLUSIONS

The analysis of the test results provided considerable evidence in support of the chief hypothesis. This was, to repeat it briefly, that the Informal schools provide an environment which develops qualities of personality that result in a high level of divergent thinking ability. This has been supported by comparisons of mean test scores classified in a variety of ways. The means from the Informal schools have in most cases been significantly higher than those from the Formal schools. In those cases where the difference in means has not reached the level of statistical significance the direction of the difference has confirmed the general trend. In *no* case has there been a difference in the un-predicted direction.

The evidence from correlations was again in support of the contention that the Informal school succeeded in developing more of the divergent potential, since the correlation coefficients between VRQ and divergent test scores were consistently higher in the Informal schools. The general hypothesis of a decrease in the correlation value as both the VRQ and the divergent ability level of sub-groups rose was also confirmed.

The results from the sociometric analysis are inconclusive, but there is some indication that there is a positive connection between divergent ability and peer popularity in the Informal schools. This differentiation appears to increase if the lower VRQs are excluded (Schools A and B).

This study has not been comparing good *versus* bad schools, but good schools which operate with a somewhat different emphasis. It is certainly not permissiveness which is the distinguishing criterion of Informality as opposed to Formality. The most striking difference lies in the degree of emphasis laid upon self-initiated learning. Behind this emphasis in the Informal schools and fundamental to its success, lies the pattern of inter-personal relationships within the school. One's impression in the Informal school is of a relaxed, friendly atmosphere in which children move freely, both within the classroom and in the school generally. Particularly noticeable is the freedom of access to the libraries and the extent to which children work in them unsupervised. The Formal schools are not unfriendly but one senses a tighter rein and a firmer directive. Class work is more in evidence.

The investigation has shown that the optimum development of divergent thinking abilities is related to a certain teaching approach. As to what lies at the roots of this relationship we can only speculate. But it would seem that it is based on the teacher's confidence in the child's ability to think adventurously and in new directions, which in turn, will determine the child's estimation of himself and of his abilities. If the teacher can enter into the child's thinking, if she is prepared to let work develop in unexpected directions according to the child's needs and interests, if she can find and express genuine pleasure in the child's efforts, then self-initiated learning can be developed. It is in this climate that divergent thinking abilities are seen to flourish.

V. REFERENCES

ANDERSON, J. E. (1960) 'The nature of abilities'. In E. P. Torrance, ed., *Education and Talent*, Univ. of Minnesota Press, p. 9–31.
GETZELS, J. W., and JACKSON, P. W. (1968) *Creativity and Intelligence*, John Wiley.
GUILFORD, J. P. (1956) 'The structure of intellect', *Psychol. Bull.*, **53**, 267–93.
HASAN, P., and BUTCHER, H. J. (1966) 'Creativity and intelligence: a partial replication with Scottish children of Getzels' and Jackson's study', *Brit. J. Psychol.*, **57**, 129–35.
HUDSON, L. (1966) *Contrary Imaginations*, Methuen.
KELLMER PRINGLE, M. L., and MCKENZIE, I. R. (1966) 'Teaching method and rigidity in problem solving', *Brit. J. Educ. Psychol.*, **35**, 50–9.
SEARS, P. S., and HILGARD, E. R. (1964) 'The teacher's role in the motivation of the learner', in *Theories of Learning and Instruction*, 63rd N.S.S.E. Yearbook, Univ. of Chicago Press.
SPALDING, R. (1963) *Achievement, Creativity and Self-Concept Correlates of Teacher-Pupil Transactions in Elementary Schools*, Univ. of Illinois (U.S. Office of Education Co-operative Research Project No. 1352) (mimeographed).

TORRANCE, E. P. (1962) *Guiding Creative Talent*, Prentice-Hall.
VERNON, P. E. (1964) 'Creativity and intelligence', *Educ. Res.*, **6**, 163–9.
YAMAMOTO, K. (1965) 'Effects of restriction of range and test, unreliability on correlation between measures of intelligence and creative thinking', *Brit. J. Educ. Psychol.*, **35**, 300–5.

VI. APPENDIX: THE TESTS OF DIVERGENT THINKING ABILITIES AND SCORING PROCEDURES

Unless otherwise indicated, the tests are all taken from the Minnesota Tests of Creative Thinking (Torrance, 1962). The scoring procedures are adapted from the same source. The titles of the Minnesota tests are given in brackets.

Test 1—The Circles Test (Circles and Square Task)
Scoring—Flexibility: one point for each category of response.
Originality: one point for each response outside listed common responses.

Test 2—The Vague Shape of Dots Test (Derived from Picture Construction Task).
Scoring—Elaboration: one point for each new idea added to the initial response.
Fit of concept: this was the new category of score which attempted to score for sensitivity to the qualities of the stimulus on a scale of 1–5 points.

Test 3—The Block-printing Test (New test)
In this test the children were given an ink pad and a small block of wood, 2-in × 1¾-in × ½-in and a booklet of absorbent paper. They were required to discover how many different kinds of mark they could make and to use these as they liked. (There were twenty-six possible types of mark.)
Scoring—Flexibility: one point for each category of mark discovered, e.g., long edge print, short-side print, etc.
Originality: one point for each image, each pattern, each textural experiment or for making letters or figures.

Test 4—Uses for a shoe-box (Unusual Uses)
Scoring—Flexibility: one point for each category of response.
Originality: on the following basis: twelve or more children giving responses, score 0; six to eleven children giving responses, score 1; three to five children, score 2; two children, score 3; one child, score 4.

Test 5—Problems that might arise in taking a bath (Common Problems)
Scoring—Flexibility: one point for each response. (In this test each response constituted a new category.)
Originality: As for Test 4.

Test 6—Imaginative Stories (Imaginative Stories)

Scoring—Fluency: points awarded for length on a scale of 1–3.

Originality: one point for each of the following characteristics if they appeared at all: Description, vividness, indication of feelings, personal involvement, original solution or ending, orignal plot or setting, humour, inventive language, other original twists not covered by previous categories.

The scripts were scored by three judges, two of whom were unaware which schools were classed as Formal and Informal. The scores were then averaged for Fluency and Originality.

Test 7—The Camping Party Test (New test)

This was a simple sociometric test disguised as another test of divergent thinking ability. A simple sociometric status was obtained by counting the number of nominations to join the expedition which each child received. This information was not obtained for all the children who were tested since in three of the schools used, the children of lower ability were spread through other classes from which they were extracted for testing purposes. This meant that they were unable to receive a proper number of nominations.

6

H. *Lytton and*
A. *C. Cotton*

Divergent thinking abilities in secondary schools[*]

SUMMARY. In a previous study of primary schools, children in 'informal' schools scored higher on tests of divergent thinking than children in 'formal' schools. A parallel study of two 'informal' and two 'formal' secondary schools failed to yield a similar result. Some possible explanations of this finding are put forward.

Convergent ability was shown to be more closely related to social class than divergent ability.

I. INTRODUCTION

In an earlier experiment Haddon and Lytton (1968) found that children in two primary schools rated as 'informal' (stressing child-initiated learning) did better on five out of six divergent tests than children from two schools rated as 'formal' (stressing traditional learning). The present experiment, using the same tests, took the investigation from the primary field into the secondary, and there attempted to verify the hypothesis of a differential effect of differing school climates. In addition it investigated the inter-relationships between divergent tests, verbal reasoning tests and social class.

Two secondary modern schools and two grammar schools were chosen; within each pair of schools socio-economic background was very similar and the mean VRQs showed no significant difference. The 143 children (97 boys and 46 girls) tested were fourteen years old and

* Reprinted from *British Journal of Educational Psychology*, 39, 1969, 188–90.

in their third year in the school. By consensus among college or department of education lecturers, and local authority inspectors, one grammar school and one secondary modern were allotted to the 'formal' category, and the other pair to the 'informal' category. However, it was noted at the time the tests were given (and not only after the results were known) that the schools did not differ markedly in overall climate. The difficulty here is that teaching approach in a secondary school is uniform for a department rather than for the school; a department may be 'formal' or 'informal' without this permeating the whole school. The experiment was persevered with, as it was impossible to find better contrasted schools that were at the same time matched for socio-economic background.

The tests used were those described in Haddon and Lytton (1968).

II. RESULTS

(a) Types of school

The results of the divergent thinking tests did not reproduce the sharp differentiation that was noted in the earlier investigation in primary schools (Table 6.1). There were only two significant differences: the Imaginative Stories Test in the predicted direction and the Incomplete Circles Test in the opposite direction.

Since the tests (except for Test 2, which had been adapted from its previous version) were scored in exactly the same way as in the earlier study it is of interest to note the movement of raw scores from age eleven to fourteen. The only test for which a marked increase in scores occurred was Test 6 ('Imaginative stories'); all the others showed only slight increases or decreases. It is possible that this reflects the drop in divergent productivity that Torrance (1965) noted around thirteen years.

(b) Relationships between divergent thinking tests, verbal reasoning tests and social class

With the present population the overall VRQ/Divergent Test correlation over the full VRQ range was much lower (0·17) than in the earlier study, but far from increasing with the lower VRQ group, the correlation for this group practically vanished and, in actual fact, became negative (Table 6.2). The correlation between the verbal and non-verbal divergent tests (0·43) was satisfactorily higher than the correlation between VRQ and divergent tests, thus providing some justification for considering divergent and convergent thinking as

TABLE 6.1. *Comparison of mean test scores (raw scores)*

| | Formal schools | | | Informal schools | | | Differ. of combin'd means | 't' for difference |
							Informal –formal	Combin'd means
	A Mean	C Mean	Combin'd Mean A and C	B Mean	D Mean	Combin'd Mean B and D		
VRQ	118·4	103·8	111·13	118·8	105·3	112·05	0·82	N.S.
Test 1	12·97	11·89	12·35	10·41	10·97	10·78	—1·57	2·612*
Test 2	17·40	17·44	17·43	17·10	16·85	16·94	—0·49	N.S.
Test 3	7·96	6·67	7·20	6·86	8·07	7·65	0·45	N.S.
Test 4	12·21	10·38	11·13	10·68	10·09	10·29	—0·84	N.S.
Test 5	12·68	11·59	12·03	11·22	10·81	10·95	—1·08	N.S.
Test 6	15·22	15·72	15·52	21·45	16·40	18·14	2·62	2·72*
N	32	47	79	22	42	64		

* Significant at 1 per cent level.

Test 1: Incomplete circles. Test 4: Uses for shoe-box.
Test 2: Vague shape of dots. Test 5: Problems in taking a bath.
Test 3: Block printing. Test 6: Imaginative stories.

TABLE 6.2. *Correlation of VRQ and divergent thinking tests*

All schools. Sub-groups based on VRQ ranges

	N	r
Full range of VRQ (87–137)	143	0·170
VRQ 116 +	43	0·037
VRQ 101 +*	114	0·141
VRQ 100 and below	29	—0·058

*This includes category VRQ 116 +

All schools. Sub-groups based on divergent test ranges

	N	r
Full range	143	0·170
Divergent score 40·5 +	72	0·207
Divergent score 40·4 —	71	0·040

separable, though complementary aspects of intellectual functioning. But the study did not support the 'threshold theory' that convergent and divergent thinking become differentiated mainly at higher levels of general cognitive ability.

The correlation of social class (determined by father's occupation) with VRQ (0·58) was considerably higher than with total divergent test scores (0·26) suggesting that these latter tests are less dependent on environmental influences.

III. CONCLUSIONS

The negative result of the comparison between the 'types' of schools may be due to the lack of contrast between the schools, but it may also be that the effects of a more flexible approach to learning are not reflected in the performance of 14-year-olds in these divergent tests, perhaps because of the limitations of the tests (cf. Walker, 1967). The result should therefore not be interpreted as a negative verdict on 'informal' schools, but it illustrates the difficulty of this kind of investigation in the more complex secondary school organisation.

The low correlations between VRQ and divergent tests suggests that these are two distinguishable aspects of intellectual ability. *Convergent* ability seems to be more subject to the influence of social class than divergent ability.

IV. REFERENCES

HADDON, F. A., and LYTTON, H. (1968) 'Teaching approach and the development of divergent thinking abilities in primary schools', *Brit. J. Educ. Psychol.*, **38**, 171–80.
TORRANCE, E. B. (1962) *Guiding Creative Talent*, Prentice-Hall.
TORRANCE, E. B. (1965) *Rewarding Creative Behavior*, Prentice-Hall.
WALKER, W. J. (1967) 'Creativity and high school climate', in Gowan, Demos and Torrance, eds., *Creativity: Its Educational Implications*, Wiley.

7

P. W. Jackson and
S. Messick

The person, the product, and the response: conceptual problems in the assessment of creativity*

The ultimate concern of the psychologist is the human mind and its inventions. Although there are many ways to describe man's mental complexity—and particularly to depict his cognitive strengths—the two terms 'intelligence' and 'creativity' seem to have the greatest summary power. It is this concentration of meaning that explains the endurance of these two words in the layman's language and their continued use in professional discussions.

Typically, efforts to distinguish empirically between the concepts of creativity and intelligence have concentrated on attempts to demonstrate that performance on tests requiring the production of unusual and remote responses is independent (to some extent) of performance on conventional tests of intelligence. But as Golann quite correctly points out in his recent review of studies of creativity,

'. . . these data are in a sense arbitrary: intelligence is not performance on a test; creativity is more than test performance or being judged as creative. What is needed for the understanding of the relationship between creativity and intelligence is not only data at the correlational level, but conceptual reorganisation as well' (Golann, 1963, p. 560).

The controversy created by some of the recent research studies of creativity seems to have focused attention not on unresolved conceptual problems but on the empirical specification of particular, and sometimes arbitrary, aspects of the creativity-intelligence distinction. Moreover, the interesting results obtained with tests of fluency and remote

*Reprinted from *Journal of Personality*, 33, 1965, 1–19.

associations have diverted our attention temporarily from the important task of considering other criteria, in addition to the production of unusual responses, essential to the total assessment of creativity.

THE EVALUATION OF INTELLECTUAL PERFORMANCE

The exercise of a person's cognitive powers is often the occasion for evaluation. People are continually being informed that they have done well or poorly on intellectual tasks, and the variety of forms these judgments may take is almost as great as the variety of behaviours being judged. The wide assortment of evaluative comments can be crudely classified, however, into two overlapping categories. On the one hand, there are those judgments having to do with the 'correctness' or 'rightness' of a person's response. These evaluations deal with the degree to which certain objective and logical criteria have been satisfied. On the other hand, there are judgments having to do with the worth or 'goodness' of a person's response. These evaluations deal with the degree to which certain subjective and psychological criteria have been satisfied. Although, as has been suggested, these two classes of evaluations overlap (and some kinds of behaviour satisfy both sets of criteria), the two are nonetheless distinguishable and the distinction between them has important implications for the conceptual separation of intelligent and creative responses.

In the simplest terms, the adjectives 'correct' and 'good' apply differentially to the terms 'intelligent' and 'creative'. Intelligent responses are correct; they satisfy objective criteria; they operate within the constraints of logic and reality and thus may be considered right or wrong, true or false. Creative responses, in contrast, are 'good'; they satisfy subjective criteria; although they may not necessarily be limited by the demands of logic and reality, they are responsive, as we shall see, to a wide variety of judgmental standards. Always, though, in the assessment of a response's creativeness or 'goodness' we are aware of the humanness required to make the judgment. As Santayana puts it, 'for the existence of good in any form it is not merely consciousness but emotional consciousness that is needed. Observation will not do, appreciation is required' (Santayana, 1896, p. 16).

The distinction being made here between the correct and the good is contained, at least implicitly, in many other discussions of the creative process. Guilford, for one, is particularly aware of it when he says, 'There are different bases or criteria by which a product is judged. One is its logical consistency with known facts. Another is its less-than-logical consistency with other experiences' (Guilford, 1957, p. 116).

Guilford goes on, however, to imply that logical criteria are applied primarily to scientific products whereas artistic products are evaluated by less-than-logical standards. In the present distinction no such separation between the evaluation of scientific and artistic products is implied. A piano solo may be as incorrect as the solution to a mathematical equation. A scientific theory may be as good as a great novel. The poet's attempt to write a Spenserian sonnet may be both incorrect and poor, as may the engineer's design for a bridge.

In many of the tests currently proposed to assess creative ability, the failure to differentiate between correct responses and good responses leads to unnecessary confounding. Take as an instance the Remote Association Test developed by Mednick (1963). In this test the S is presented with three words, such as 'rat', 'blue', and 'cottage', and is required to supply a fourth word to serve as a kind of associational link between the three stimulus words. For the example given the answer is 'cheese'. Now it is argued that this answer reflects a degree of creativity because it is 'remote' and 'useful', at least in the sense of meeting specified requirements. We would insist that the answer reflects an aspect of intelligence because it is correct. To further illustrate his point, Mednick maintains that the answer 7,363,474 to the question 'How much is 12 and 12?' is original but is not creative because it is not useful. What seems more important, however, is not that the answer lacks usefulness, but that in the absence of a special formal system to justify it, it is wrong. As we would use the term, there are no creative answers to the question, 'How much is 12 and 12?' The constraints of reality implied in the question only allow for correct or incorrect responses.

Mednick introduces the concept of usefulness because he realises, as do most researchers in this field, that the criterion of unusualness or originality is not enough. These qualities, as Guilford's work has so brilliantly demonstrated, do take us beyond the confines of correctness in evaluating cognitive performance. But, as Guilford and others also recognise, the identification of the unusual is, at best, a first step in trying to understand the good.

CREATIVE PRODUCTS AND APPRECIATIVE RESPONSES

Frequency and fit

No matter what other positive qualities it might possess, then, we generally insist as a first step that a product be novel before we are willing to call it creative. Indeed, the conjoining of novelty and creativeness is so deeply ingrained in our thinking that the two concepts are sometimes treated as synonymous. The result is that novelty often comes to be used as the most common and, in some of our current paper-and-pencil tests of creativity, the only measure of a product's creativeness.

The application of the criterion of unusualness requires a two-step operation: a comparison of the product in question with other products of the same class and a counting of those comparisons that yield similar or identical products. Further, if such a relative frequency criterion of unusualness is to be applied consistently, some standard must be established to decide how few is few.

The universe of objects with which the judged object is compared also requires definition. The judgment of unusualness is typically made not in terms of *all* other objects of a general class, such as all paintings in existence, but in terms of a greatly restricted subset. Thus, for example, when we say that a child's painting contains an unusual representation of three-dimensional space, our standard of comparison most frequently includes other paintings by children, and we would not make the same judgment if adult work were the standard. When we consider the potential populations against which the unusualness of a particular object might be judged, it becomes apparent that the relative infrequency of the object might alter so dramatically as we shift our frames of reference that the same product could be unique in one population and common in another. Clearly, the choice of an appropriate population or norm group against which to judge a creative work is of utmost importance in applying the standard of unusualness. In short, the infrequency of a response is relative to *norms*, which thus serve as a judgmental standard for evaluating unusualness.

Although the judgment of uniqueness or infrequency may be the logical first step in evaluating the creativeness of a product, if we proceeded no further, the total set of products considered creative by the first criterion alone would be a strange collection. It would include, among other things, all of the products that are simply bizarre or odd. Somehow the mere oddities must be weeded out. This task requires the application of a second criterion, *appropriateness*.

To be appropriate a product must fit its context. It must 'make sense' in light of the demands of the situation and the desires of the producer. Further, when products are complex, their internal elements must also blend together and be appropriate to each other. Thus, both internal and external criteria of appropriateness may be distinguished. Indeed, two separate critical stances arise from the relative emphasis on internal or external views of appropriateness.

The major role of the appropriateness criterion, as it is used here, is to help eliminate from the set of unusual products those that are simply absurd. As a criterion of creativeness, it is used conjointly with unusualness rather than independently, since appropriateness without unusualness would be merely a cliché. At fairly low levels of creative production—as, for example, in paper-and-pencil tests of divergent thinking—the criterion of appropriateness is not too difficult to apply. When a person is asked, for instance, to think of different uses for a common object such as a paper clip and he responds, 'Eat it', the inappropriateness of his response is obvious. When a person is asked to write captions for cartoons and responds by giving the names of colours, again there is little question about the inappropriateness of his reaction. Note, however, that both of these illustrative responses would probably be unusual, if not unique, in a statistical sense. In those cases where the product has to meet some 'reality tests' the application of the appropriateness criterion does not appear to be too difficult.

As products become more complex, however, and more responsive to the needs of the producer than to the demands of the situation, the determination of appropriateness also becomes more complex. There are times, of course, when the judgment is still fairly easy to make. It does not require much aesthetic training to realise that the meter of a poem beginning 'Death is here/Death is there/Death is lurking every-where...' is inappropriate to the theme being treated. Yet at higher levels of creation the entanglement of sense and nonsense can become so involved that the judgment of appropriateness requires a detailed examination by a highly trained person. Even then there is always the chance that the creator, who is often more aware of the demands that gave rise to his product than is the critic, will disagree with the judgment.

Thus, as the term is used in the judgment of creative products, appropriateness deals with much more than the logical fit of the product within its context or of the product's elements with each other (although this kind of fit would be the dominant question in many applications of the criterion). There are times, however, when a product violates conventional logic but somehow manages to hang together and to have a logic of its own. Thus, although the judgmental standard for evaluating appropriateness is the *context* of the response, this context must be interpreted psychologically as well as logically and should include the producer's intentions as well as the demands of the situation.

Finally, appropriateness is a continuous quality, not a discrete one.

It exists in degrees rather than completely or not at all. Considering its lower forms, we recognise the appropriateness of a product that is merely 'responsive'—that bears a clear relation to the environment or to the internal motivations of its producer. Considering its higher forms, we marvel at the way in which the product reflects not only the massive forces that went into its making, but the more subtle influences as well. At low levels of appropriateness we speak of a product as being 'about right', given its sources, the avowed purpose of its maker, and the like. At higher levels we speak of a product as being 'just right'. Indeed, at the very highest level of appropriateness we may experience almost a sense of recognition when we come upon the product. Things are so right they look almost familiar. One critic described such products as having 'the handprint of necessity upon them instead of the quickly tarnished sheen of the merely novel, the fetchingly precious, the different'.[1] When he comes upon these 'handprints of necessity', the viewer may sometimes feel as if his expectations have been fulfilled, whereas what has really happened is that the product has made him aware of what his expectations should have been.

The transcendence of constraint

Although unusualness and appropriateness may be necessary criteria for limiting the class of potentially creative products, are they sufficient for making required distinctions in quality and level within the class? Among the products that are considered to be both unusual and appropriate some are surely at a higher level of creative excellence than others. One property present in some products but absent, or less obvious, in others is the power to transform the constraints of reality. Some objects combine elements in ways that defy tradition and that yield a new perspective. They literally force us to see reality in a new way. These products involve a *transformation* of material or ideas to overcome conventional constraints. The question of how much transformation power a product has can serve, then, as a third criterion of creativeness. Just as the unusualness of a product is judged relative to norms and its appropriateness relative to the context, the transformation power of a product would be judged relative to the strength and nature of the *constraints* that were transcended.

The criterion of transformation is more difficult to define than are those of unusualness and appropriateness. At first glance it might seem to be nothing more than an extreme example of unusualness. But

[1] James Dickey, in *The New York Times Book Review*, 22 December 1963, p. 4.

it is unusualness with a difference; it is an aggressive unusualness that attacks conventional ways of thinking about things or of viewing objects. In its most dramatic forms a transformation involves a radical shift in approach to a subject or in handling material—the kind of shift, for example, caused by the introduction of the heliocentric theory or Freud's earliest propositions.

The difference between a merely unusual product and a transformation may be approached in another way. Things are often unusual in the purely quantitative sense—in the sense of being the most or the least, the largest or the smallest form of a pre-existing class of objects. (The objects and events described in the *Guinness Book of Superlatives* offer fine examples of this sort of unusualness.) Products that are unusual in this 'record-breaking' sense need not, and usually do not, qualify as transformations. Transformations are not merely improvements, however unusual, on pre-existent forms. Rather, they involve the creation of new forms.

The distinction just made between the concepts of transformation and unusualness requires, now, that a further distinction be made between an object that represents a transformation and one that is merely new. If transformation demanded only a new combination of elements, almost any unique collection of things, however derived, would qualify. Mechanical techniques for supplying these fortuitous combinations could be devised, as in the story of the popular writer who obtained the plots of his novels by spinning a set of wheels on which were written adjectives, nouns, verbs, and the like. Generally, however, these new combinations do not qualify as transformations because they are low in heuristic power. They terminate rather than generate thought. They are the occasion for surprise and laughter, but not for reflection and wonder.

The possibility just alluded to—that the presence of a transformation may be determined in part by its effect on the viewer—raises the interesting question of whether the other two response properties, unusualness and appropriateness, might also have distinguishable effects upon the person who experiences them. Are there, in short, types of aesthetic responses that somehow parallel the criteria of creativeness? This intriguing possibility occurred to us at approximately the stage in the development of criteria for creativeness to which the writing has progressed so far. Although recognising that the job of identifying the criteria was not complete, we decided to delay that task for a time while we attempted to distinguish among possible dimensions of aesthetic response and to relate them conceptually to dimensions of creative performance. In order to give the reader some idea of how the present scheme came into being, we will retrace in the exposition of our ideas the same path that was followed in their development. Thus, for a time, we will put aside the search for more criterion response properties and focus on how the criteria we have already discussed might strike the viewer. The development thus far is summarised in Table 7.1, which lists the three response properties of creative products and the judgmental standards associated with each.

TABLE 7.1

Response properties	Judgmental standards
Unusual	Norms
Appropriate	Context
Transformed	Constraints

The impact of the product

Confrontation with an unusual object or event characteristically evokes *surprise* in the viewer. The unusual is attention-getting, it 'catches our eye', its unexpectedness may shock or amaze us. By definition we cannot be prepared for it, except in a very general way. Therefore, the impact of first exposure creates surprise and requires a period of adaptation during which the unusual object or event is assimilated into the viewer's experience.

Reaction to the unusual, then, is at its maximum immediately upon exposure and diminishes rapidly thereafter. Though surprise may occur more than once in response to the same object, the second and subsequent exposures never quite match the impact of the first. Objects and events whose value is derived almost solely from their unusualness —such as freaks in side shows or *New Yorker* cartoons—rarely warrant continued viewing.

The quality of appropriateness calls forth in the viewer a reaction, which we will call *satisfaction*, that is akin to the general condition of comfort. This feeling of satisfaction would seem to have two major sources. First, there is the recognition that the demands of the creator, the material, and the milieu have been responded to and that, as was mentioned before, the response is not only right, but is 'just right'. There is thus a recognition of inevitableness about the product, given the context in which it is embedded. Second, there is the recognition that the product is not only 'right' but is complete or sufficient. The first source of satisfaction focuses on the qualitative aspects of appropriateness (i.e., on how *well* the demands are met), the second source of satisfaction focuses on what might be considered the quantitative aspects of appropriateness (i.e., on how *completely* the demands are met). The satisfied viewer's answer to the first criterion is 'just right', his answer to the second is 'enough'.

Products embodying a transformation are likely to be *stimulating* to the viewer. The primary value of such products resides in their power to alter the viewer's conventional way of perceiving or thinking about his world. Whereas confrontation with the unusual requires the viewer to assimilate the product, to make it part of his world, confrontation with a transformation requires that he revise his world. The new element is not only the product itself but the changed environment which has been caused by the product. Metaphorically, a transformation is something like a stone dropped in water. To a person standing on shore the object of interest is not the stone, which quickly disappears from sight, but rather the waves it produces. A transforming object invites the viewer to move out, intellectually, in new directions. A transforming product stimulates the viewer to consider its consequences.

In review, then, the first three criteria of creativeness—unusualness, appropriateness, and transformation—may possibly be the source of three types of aesthetic responses, which may be summarised by the key words: surprise, satisfaction, and stimulation. The possibility that different types of aesthetic responses might be isolated gives rise to two important questions which can only be posed here. First, can the aesthetic responses themselves be used to indicate the presence of the qualities that give rise to them? Can we, for example, take the reaction of surprise to be sufficient evidence for the existence of unusualness? Clearly, the answer to this question has extremely important implications for the assessment of creativity. The second question is whether the aesthetic responses are unique to the viewer of the creative product or whether they also appear in the creator himself. Obviously the creator also judges his own product, yet his judgment need not and clearly does not always agree with the verdict of an 'external' judge. Before questions such as these can be examined, however, it is necessary to return to the criteria of creativeness and to ask what else needs to be added to the three that have already been suggested.

The coalescence of meaning

The properties of unusualness, appropriateness, and transformation in varying combinations characterise a large proportion of those things we are willing to call creative. Further, these criteria are applicable to products stemming from very divergent sources, from the scientist and philosopher as well as from the craftsman and artist. Yet despite the power of these criteria there is another important quality that does not seem to be covered by them. This quality, which appears in some of the most highly creative products and which serves as our fourth criterion, deals with the property of *condensation*.

As was mentioned previously, novelty wears out quickly. The history of fad and fashion is, in essence, an elaborate documentation of the short life and relativity of unusualness. In striking contrast, however, to the ephemeral quality of the novel object is the endurance of the greatest creative achievements of man. These we continually seek to re-examine and re-experience. Although the criteria of appropriateness and transformation may partially explain this endurance, something additional seems to be involved.

Products that warrant close and repeated examination are those that do not divulge their total meaning on first viewing. These products offer something new each time we experience them, whether a great work of art or a highly developed scientific theory. They have about them an intensity and a concentration of meaning requiring continued contemplation.

Because confusion and disorder also compel the viewer's attention (as he tries to make sense out of what he sees), it is necessary to distinguish between condensation on the one hand and chaotic complexity on the other. The chief difference would seem to involve the unity and coherence of meaning derived from the condensation as compared with the unrelated and irrelevant meanings derived from disorder. An assortment of debris gathered in a junkyard and the ordered arrangement of the same material by an artist serves to illustrate the distinction being made here. Any meaning derived from the random assortment of junk is fortuitous and is obtained either from a chance association between the elements or from irrelevant associations that the material might stimulate in the viewer. By contrast, the ordered arrangement, if it is worthy of artistic notice, contains more meaning than can be understood at first glance. The colour and shape of the objects, their texture, their spatial location, and their original function all combine to enhance their aesthetic appeal.

In the highest forms of creative condensation the polar concepts of simplicity and complexity are unified. That which at first glance appears simple turns out on closer inspection to possess only *apparent* simplicity. Conversely, that which at first appears to be complex is found to embody a hidden simplicity that binds together the many complex elements. Some of the more successful poems of Robert Frost and some of the paintings of Klee and Miro illustrate well the use of the simple to represent the complex. The reverse situation, that in which initial complexity cloaks a hidden simplicity, occurs frequently in musical works, where repeated listening is often required before the major themes and their variations become apparent.

The condensation achieved by a creative product summarises essences, and the summary may be expanded and interpreted in a multiplicity of ways—intellectually or affectively, in terms of image or idea. It may be interpreted differently by different viewers or by the same viewer on different occasions. This multiplicity of interpretation and the extensiveness of the expansions generated by the condensation are an indication of its summary power, and an appraisal of *summary power* provides a important judgmental standard for the evaluation of creative condensation.

Parenthetically, it might be noted that the latter two response criteria of transformation and condensation are closely related to the two main mechanisms of the dream work in psychoanalytic theory (Freud, 1955). Thus, the present formulation includes elements that, from a psycho-analytic point of view, illustrate the role of primary process in creative activity (Pine, 1959; Tauber and Green, 1959).

Before leaving this discussion of condensation, two additional points need to be mentioned. The first deals with the increased ambiguity and complexity of the criteria of creativeness as we go from unusualness to condensation, the second deals with their developmental interdependence. At this point the meaning of unusualness appears to be more clearly demarcated than the meaning of condensation, and this is partly because condensation is just a more complex concept than unusualness. Indeed, each of the four criteria, in the order presented here, seems to be more complex than the last. As it is used here, the term complex could be partially translated as meaning 'obscure and complicated', but we wish to stress a more derivative connotation, namely, 'difficult to make judgments of'. We recognise that difficulty in judgment is a conse-quence of complexity rather than its meaning, but such a distinction is unimportant in the present context. The important point is that judg-ments of condensation and transformation will be more difficult to make than judgments of unusualness and appropriateness; there will be more differences in viewpoint, and agreement will be more difficult to reach even within schools of thought. This implies that judges will have to know more, or do more, or take more time when judging the criteria of transformation and condensation than they will when applying the other two criteria. In this judgmental sense, then, condensation and transformation are more complex than unusualness and appropriateness.

In addition to this progression in complexity, the four criterion response properties of creativeness are also ordered with respect to developmental interdependence. Each of the four criteria, from unusualness to condensation, is applied in turn conjointly with the previous ones, so that in this sense each is dependent on the ones that precede it. This sequential requirement is only partial, however, in the interdependence of transformation and condensation. The transformations of a creative product must be appropriate and unusual; the condensation must also be appropriate and unusual, but it may not always represent a transformation. If we accept unusualness and appropriateness as necessary properties for a product to be considered creative, then the hierarchical ordering of transformation and condensation provides an additional basis, along with degrees of variation within each of the response dimensions, for distinguishing levels of creative attainment within the class of creative products.

Having added a fourth response property, condensation, we return to a consideration of aesthetic responses to examine the possible effect of this new criterion upon the viewer. So far our hypothetical viewer has been surprised by unusualness, satisfied by appropriateness, and stimulated by transforming qualities of creative products. The question now is how will he react when he confronts a product of high condensation, one that exists on many levels of meaning. The definition of the criterion itself almost contains a description of the experiencing viewer. A condensed product is an object worthy of pondering; it should be examined slowly, carefully, and repeatedly. In a word, the viewer is called upon to *savour* a condensation. The surprise, the satisfaction, and the stimulation that characterise responses to other criteria of creativeness are present as well in the response to a condensation, but there is an important difference. In the reaction to a condensation these other responses are enduring and somewhat intensified. Surprise occurs not only on the first encounter, but also on subsequent ones as new and unusual aspects of the product are discovered; satisfaction deepens with repeated exposure as the appropriateness of each element in the product is more fully revealed; stimulation is enriched as each new reaction to the product builds on those that have preceded it. It is this continued freshness of the product and of the viewer's response to it that makes it an object worthy of savouring.

With the addition of condensation to the list of response properties and of savouring to the list of aesthetic reactions, we complete our discussion of creative products and appreciative responses (see Table 7.2 for an outline of the development thus far). One further point needs to be made explicit, however: just as the criterion response properties are relative to judgmental standards, so are the aesthetic responses.

TABLE 7.2

Response properties	Judgmental standards	Aesthetic responses
Unusualness	Norms	Surprise
Appropriateness	Context	Satisfaction
Transformation	Constraints	Stimulation
Condensation	Summary power	Savouring

The degree and character of surprise is a function of the norms of expectation in much the same manner as is unusualness. Similarly, satisfaction is relative to the context, stimulation to the nature and strength of the constraints, and savouring to summary power.

PERSONAL QUALITIES AND COGNITIVE STYLES

Among psychologists, creativity has frequently been thought of as a single dimension or at least as a unified cluster of traits, resembling —and to some extent overlapping with—general intellectual ability. Some researchers, particularly factor analysts such as Guilford, have isolated a set of cognitive factors related to different aspects of intellectual production, but the relation of these factors to creative production is less well delineated. Other investigators have argued that creative behaviour depends as much on personality as on cognitive power, and they have accrued evidence to show that the highly creative person is more impulsive, makes greater use of fantasy processes, is more tolerant of ambiguity, and so forth, than is his less creative peer.

At the level of everyday experience it is recognised that creative expression of the highest quality tends to come from people who limit their efforts to a single mode of expression. The great scientist is generally not also the great poet, the great painter is not also the great dancer, and even the great composer is not also the great conductor. Moreover, in the eye of the public, personality characteristics tend to be associated with a *medium* of expression rather than with the level of expression or any other features of creative production. Thus, in terms of personality characteristics, the outstanding poet looks more like the incompetent poet than he does like the outstanding scientist, who, in turn, looks more like his less competent colleagues than he does like the superb composer. Both the professional view and the public view, therefore, acknowledge that the maker of creative products looks different from his fellow men, but there is little agreement on the form this difference takes. Is the difference chiefly cognitive or does it involve personality components as well? Is the difference linked to a mode of expression entailing, as it were, a way of life, or is it more closely related to stylistic qualities of the products themselves? Each view of the creative process implies a position about the nature of the creator, which in turn helps to determine the types of variables emphasised in the assessment of creativity.

Within the present context there is a set of personal qualities that may be considered to match, so to speak, the response properties used as criteria of creativeness. The present view is not meant to imply that trait names should be used as labels in characterising people. An answer to that question depends on such matters as the dominance of the trait in question, its distribution in the population, and so on. Rather, we wish to suggest a relation between personal qualities and properties of the creative response.

The question of whether personal qualities are necessary for the production is still another matter. Do personal qualities 'cause' the appearance of the creative criteria? Might an infrequent or appropriate response occur by chance or must it always occur as the result of a particular human condition? Again, the view taken here does not prejudge the answer to this question, although it does imply that the consistent production of creative responses cannot occur by chance and, further, that the 'cause' of such a phenomenon entails psychological as well as social and environmental influences.

In the present view the person who consistently produces infrequent or unusual responses is thought of as being highly *original*. The relativity of the judgments of unusualness would also affect the judgment of personal originality. Persons whose responses look quite unusual when judged against one standard and who would, therefore, be thought of as original, might lose the halo of originality when the judgmental norms are changed. The personal quality of originality is an attainment, in the sense that it is inferred from the repeated production of unusual responses. In addition, there are several personal qualities that are predisposing to originality, that increase the likelihood of unusual responses but do not guarantee them. These predisposing characteristics include intellectual abilities, cognitive styles, motives, and values. For example, ideational fluency, impulse expression, and cognitive styles of tolerance of unreality, tolerance of inconsistency, and the like would appear to be likely candidates for predisposing the individual towards originality (Barron, 1955).

The production of an appropriate response would seem to be

accomplished most easily by a person who is highly *sensitive* to the demands of his environment and to the subtleties of the material with which he is working. His sensitivity may result from a conscious *analysis* of the relations between elements, but it need not. There is some evidence that at least in some fields the most sensitive people cannot articulate their awareness with any degree of precision. Their sensitivity is *intuitive*; the person who behaves intuitively is sensitive to cues that cannot be identified verbally. Thus, both an analytic attitude and an intuitive attitude could serve as predisposing cognitive styles for sensitivity.

Transformation involves the transcending of traditional boundaries and limitations. Personal qualities that would seem to contribute to the production of transformations are of two sorts, cognitive and non-cognitive. Relevant cognitive qualities are those that deal with the stability and the fluidity of conceptual systems, intellectual categories, and the like. The production of transformations reflects *flexibility* and calls for qualities not unlike those involved in breaking a 'set' —as in the Luchins water-jar experiment. In perceptual terms this type of intellectual fluidity would be reflected in the ability to perceive objects in their own right—independent of their symbolic representation, their stereotyped function, or their relatedness to the immediate needs of the viewer. This kind of perceptual freedom has been given the label 'allocentric perception' by Schachtel (1959). At the cognitive and ideological level, this flexibility has been called 'openmindedness' by Rokeach (1960).

The non-cognitive qualities that contribute to the production of a transformation include a playful attitude towards reality and a willingness to expose (even to flaunt) ideas, attitudes, and objects that violate tradition. An attitude of playfulness, a desire to toy with reality is important because it would appear that most transformations come as a discovery on the heels of many trials. Thus to some extent transformations involve an element of 'luck', but it is the kind of luck that cannot occur without the predisposing attitudes that lead to experimentation and other forms of intellectual play. No single adjective adequately summarises the personal qualities that contribute to the production of transformations. The word that comes closest to describing the cognitive qualities and one that at least does not do violence to the non-cognitive qualities is the adjective *flexible*.

Just as a condensation may often contain a paradoxical union of simplicity and complexity, so does the production of the condensation call for a fusing of contradictory personal qualities. There is first the coalescence of personal and universal concerns with the strangely paradoxical result of losing in self-awareness while gaining in total awareness. Although the product may bear the marks of its maker, his personal needs and interests have been consumed, as it were, by the more abstract relevance of the product itself. Second, there is the intimate interplay, even fusion, of thought and feeling that contributes to a condensation. Even the most 'logical' production—such as an elegant mathematical solution to a problem—demands an openness to thoughts and feelings that are only dimly perceived and that may be incapable of precise logical statement. Third, there is an alternate blending of working style, a cyclic pattern of patience and passion, of reflection and spontaneity, a continual shifting from total acceptance of one's ideas and actions to a critical rejection of them. In a very useful discussion of the creative process, Erich Fromm (1963) distinguishes between two phases of productive behaviour. According to Fromm, the first phase is essentially feminine in quality. It is the birth-giving phase, the moment of conception. Following this, a more masculine phase occurs during which the creator must hone and polish his work to ready it for social judgment. In this second phase irrelevances and superfluities are eliminated, the uniqueness of the work is more sharply defined, and its content is more effectively expressed. The central theme underlying the production of a condensation involves, then, the unification of things that are normally thought of as separate or at least distinguishable—producer and product, personal and universal concerns, cognitive and affective processes, masculine and feminine styles of work.

The complexity of condensations and the personal qualities from which they emerge do not seem to permit the use of a single adjective to describe the person who is most apt to produce condensations. Yet, in the interests of symmetry and as a mnemonic device for summarising the conceptual scheme presented here, we searched for a word that would come close to capturing both the substance and the sense of our description. The word that in our opinion does the most justice to what has been said about the producer of condensations is *poetic*. Webster's *New World Dictionary* describes a poem, and thus indirectly a poet, as 'expressing facts, ideas, or emotions in a style more concentrated, imaginative, and powerful than that of ordinary speech'. The terms 'concentrated', 'imaginative', and 'powerful' are relevant here and apply of course to many products that would not be commonly thought of as poems. It is this more global referent of poetic qualities that we imply when we characterise people who create effective condensations as poetic. The categories are summarised in Table 7·3.

The creative person, his product, and the world's response to it combine to form the drama of human invention. The transaction among these three elements is intimate and our understanding of any one enhances our understanding of the other two. However, though at present far from it, social science must work towards a conceptualisation

TABLE 7.3

Predisposing cognitive styles	Personal qualities	Response properties	Judgmental standards	Aesthetic responses
Tolerances of incongruity, of inconsistency, etc.	Original	Unusualness	Norms	Surprise
Analytic and intuitive	Sensitive	Appropriateness	Context	Satisfaction
Openminded	Flexible	Transformation	Constraints	Stimulation
Reflective and spontaneous	Poetic	Condensation	Summary power	Savouring

that serves to unify the psychological, aesthetic, and social aspects of this phenomenon. It is not enough, of course, to offer pious hopes for a future ecumenical council whose job it will be to unify these divergent views of the creative process. Two kinds of preparatory work are necessary before such a grand design is sought. First, we must add greater detail to early attempts at unification—such as the one presented here. The present scheme, at best, is an incomplete outline that must be elaborated more fully if its potential contribution is to be realised. Second, we must initiate empirical studies that will give weight to these efforts at theory, thus preventing them from deteriorating into mere word games.

In the final analysis, however, it is well to remember that theories of creativity are themselves creative products. As such, they must abide by the same laws as those they are designed to unearth. A realisation of this fact should temper our zeal in advocating any single prescription for how best to proceed. The day on which we are certain about how to construct a theory of creativity will also be the day on which we are certain about how to construct a poem.

REFERENCES

BARRON, F. (1955) 'The disposition toward originality', *J. abnorm. soc. Psychol.*, 51, 478–85.

FREUD, S. (1955) *The Interpretation of Dreams*, New York, Basic Books.

FROMM, E. (1963) 'The creative attitude', in H. Anderson, ed., *Creativity and Its Cultivation*, Michigan State Univ. Press.

GOLANN, S. E. (1963) 'Psychological study of creativity', *Psychol. Bull.*, 60, 548–65.

GUILFORD, J. P. (1957) 'Creative abilities in the arts', *Psychol. Rev.*, 64, 110–18.

MEDNICK, S. A. (1963) 'The associative basis of the creative process', in M. T. Mednick and S. A. Mednick, eds., *Research in Personality*, Holt, Rinehart & Winston.

PINE, F. (1959) 'Thematic drive content and creativity', *J. Pers.*, 27, 136–51.

ROKEACH, M. (1960) *The Open and Closed Mind*, New York, Basic Books.

SANTAYANA, G. (1896) *The Sense of Beauty*, Scribner's.

SCHACHTEL, E. G. (1959) *Metamorphosis*, New York, Basic Books.

TAUBER, E. S., and GREEN, M. R. (1959) *Prelogical Experience*, New York, Basic Books.

8

J. P. *Guilford*   Creativity*

I discuss the subject of creativity with considerable hesitation, for it
represents an area in which psychologists generally, whether they
be angels or not, have feared to tread. It has been one of my long-
standing ambitions, however, to undertake an investigation of creativity.
Circumstances have just recently made possible the realisation of that
ambition. But the work has been started only within the past year.
Consequently, if you are expecting answers based upon new empirical
research you will be disappointed. What I can do at this time is to
describe the plans for that research and to report the results of considerable thinking, including the hypotheses at which my students and
I have arrived after a survey of the field and its problems. The research
design, although not essentially new, should be of some interest.
I will also point out some implications of the problems of creativity in
vocational and educational practices.

SOME DEFINITIONS AND QUESTIONS

In its narrow sense, creativity refers to the abilities that are most
characteristic of creative people. Creative abilities determine whether
the individual has the power to exhibit creative behaviour to a noteworthy degree. Whether or not the individual who has the requisite
abilities will actually produce results of a creative nature will depend
upon his motivational and temperamental traits. To the psychologist,
the problem is as broad as the qualities that contribute significantly to

* Reprinted from *American Psychologist*, 5, 1950, 444–54.

creative productivity. In other words, the psychologist's problem is that of creative personality.

In defining personality, as well as other concepts preparatory to an investigation, definitions of an operational type are much to be preferred. I have often defined an individual's personality as his unique pattern of traits. A trait is any relatively enduring way in which persons differ from one another. The psychologist is particularly interested in those traits that are manifested in performance; in other words, in behaviour traits. Behaviour traits come under the broad categories of aptitudes, interests, attitudes, and temperamental qualities. By aptitude we ordinarily mean a person's readiness to learn to do certain types of things. There is no necessary implication in this statement as to the source of the degree of readiness. It could be brought about through hereditary determination or through environmental determination; usually, if not always, by an interaction of the two. By interest we usually mean the person's inclination or urge to engage in some type of activity. By attitude we mean his tendency to favour or not to favour (as shown objectively by approach-withdrawal behaviour) some type of object or situation. Temperamental qualities describe a person's general emotional disposition: for example, his optimism, his moodiness, his self-confidence, or his nervousness.

Creative personality is then a matter of those patterns of traits that are characteristic of creative persons. A creative pattern is manifest in creative behaviour, which includes such activities as inventing, designing, contriving, composing, and planning. People who exhibit these types of behaviour to a marked degree are recognised as being creative.

There are certain aspects of creative genius that have aroused questions in the minds of those who have reflected much about the matter. Why is creative productivity a relatively infrequent phenomenon? Of all the people who have lived in historical times, it has been estimated that only about two in a million have become really distinguished (Giddings, 1907). Why do so many geniuses spring from parents who are themselves very far from distinguished? Why is there so little apparent correlation between education and creative productiveness? Why do we not produce a larger number of creative geniuses than we do, under supposedly enlightened, modern educational practices? These are serious questions for thought and investigation. The more immediate and more explorable problem is a double one: (1) How can we discover creative promise in our children and our youth? and (2) How can we promote the development of creative personalities?

NEGLECT OF THE STUDY OF CREATIVITY

The neglect of this subject by psychologists is appalling. The evidences of neglect are so obvious that I need not give proof. But the extent of the neglect I had not realised until recently. To obtain a more tangible idea of the situation, I examined the index of the *Psychological Abstracts* for each year since its origin. Of approximately 121,000 titles listed in the past twenty-three years, only 186 were indexed as definitely bearing on the subject of creativity. The topics under which such references are listed include creativity, imagination, originality, thinking, and tests in these areas. In other words, less than two-tenths of one per cent of the books and articles indexed in the *Abstracts* for approximately the past quarter century bear directly on this subject. Few of these advance our understanding or control of creative activity very much. Of the large number of textbooks on general psychology, only two have devoted separate chapters to the subject during the same period.

Hutchinson (1931), reviewing the publications on the process of creative thinking to the year 1931, concluded that the subject had hardly been touched by anyone. Markey (1935), reviewing the subject of imagination four years later, reported very little more in the way of a fundamental contribution to the subject.

Some of you will undoubtedly feel that the subject of creative genius has not been as badly neglected as I have indicated, because of the common belief that genius is largely a matter of intelligence and the IQ. Certainly, that subject has not been neglected. But, for reasons which will be developed later, I believe that creativity and creative productivity extend well beyond the domain of intelligence.

Another important reason for the neglect, of course, is the difficulty of the problems themselves. A practical criterion of creativity is difficult to establish because creative acts of an unquestioned order of excellence are extremely rare. In this respect, the situation is much like that of a criterion for accident proneness which calls for the actual occurrence of accidents. The accidental nature of many discoveries and inventions is well recognised. This is partly due to the inequality of stimulus or opportunity, which is largely a function of the environment rather than of individuals. But if environmental occasions were equal, there would still be great differences in creative productivity among individuals.

There are, however, greater possibilities of observing individual differences in creative performance if we revise our standards, accepting examples of lower degrees of distinction. Such instances are more numerous. But even if we can detect and accept as creative certain acts of lower degrees of excellence, there are other difficulties. Creative people differ considerably in performance from time to time. Some writers on the subject even speak of rhythms of creativity. This means that any criterion, and probably any tests of creativity as well, would show considerable error variance due to function fluctuation. Reliabilities of tests of creative abilities and of creative criteria will probably be generally low. There are ways of meeting such difficulties, however. We should not permit them to force us to keep foot outside the domain.

Another reason for the oversight of problems of creativity is a methodological one. Tests designed to measure intelligence have fallen into certain stereotyped patterns, under the demands for objectivity and for scoring convenience. I do not now see how *some* of the creative abilities, at least, can be measured by means of anything but completion tests of some kind. To provide the creator with the finished product, as in a multiple-choice item, may prevent him from showing precisely what we want him to show: his own creation. I am not opposed to the use of the multiple-choice or other objectively scorable types of test items in their proper places. What I am saying is that the quest for easily objectifiable testing and scoring has directed us away from the attempt to measure some of the most precious qualities of individuals and hence to ignore those qualities.

Still another reason for the neglect of the problems of creativity is to be found in certain emphases we have given to the investigations of learning. For one thing, much learning research has been done with lower animals in which signs of creativity are almost non-existent. For another thing, learning theory has been generally formulated to cover those phenomena that are easiest to order in logical schema. Learning theorists have had considerable difficulty with the behaviour known as insight, to which creative behaviour shows much apparent relationship (Wertheimer, 1945). It is proper to say that a creative act is an instance of learning, for it represents a change in behaviour that is due to stimulation and/or response. A comprehensive learning theory must take into account both insight and creative activity.

THE SOCIAL IMPORTANCE OF CREATIVITY

There is general recognition, on the part of those outside the academic fold, at least, of the importance of the quest for knowledge about creative disposition. I can cite recent evidences of the general interest in the discovery and development of creative talent. Large industries that employ many research scientists and engineers have held serious meetings and have had symposia written about the subject (Kettering, 1944). There is much questioning into the reasons why graduates from the same institutions of higher learning, with high scholastic records and with strong recommendations, differ so widely in output of new ideas. The enormous economic value of new ideas is generally recognised. One scientist or engineer discovers a new principle or develops a new process that revolutionises an industry, while dozens of others merely do a passable job on the routine tasks assigned to them.

Various branches of the government, as you all know, are now among the largest employers of scientific and technical personnel. These employers, also, are asking how to recognise the individuals who have inventive potentialities. The most common complaint I have heard concerning our college graduates in these positions is that while they can do assigned tasks with a show of mastery of the techniques they have learned, they are much too helpless when called upon to solve a problem where new paths are demanded.

Both industry and governmental agencies are also looking for leaders. Men of good judgment, planning ability, and inspiring vision are in great demand. How can leaders with imagination and vision be discovered? Can such qualities be developed? If those qualities can be promoted by educational procedures, what are those procedures?

We hear much these days about the remarkable new thinking machines. We are told that these machines can be made to take over much of men's thinking and that the routine thinking of many industries will eventually be done without the employment of human brains. We are told that this will entail an industrial revolution that will pale into insignificance the first industrial revolution. The first one made man's muscles relatively useless; the second one is expected to make man's brain also relatively useless. There are several implications in these possibilities that bear upon the importance of creative thinking. In the first place, it would be necessary to develop an economic order in which sufficient employment and wage earning would still be available. This would require creative thinking of an unusual order and speed. In the second place, eventually about the only economic value of brains left would be in the creative thinking of which they are capable. Presumably, there would still be need for human brains to operate the machines and to invent better ones.

SOME GENERAL THEORIES OF THE NATURE OF CREATIVITY

It is probably only a layman's idea that the creative person is peculiarly gifted with a certain quality that ordinary people do not have. This conception can be dismissed by psychologists, very likely by common consent. The general psychological conviction seems to be that all individuals possess to some degree all abilities, except for the occurrence of pathologies. Creative acts can therefore be expected, no matter how feeble or how infrequent, of almost all individuals. The important consideration here is the concept of continuity. Whatever the nature of creative talent may be, those persons who are recognised as creative merely have more of what all of us have. It is this principle of continuity that makes possible the investigation of creativity in people who are not necessarily distinguished.

The conception that creativity is bound up with intelligence has many followers among psychologists. Creative acts are expected from those of high IQ and not expected from those of low IQ. The term 'genius', which was developed to describe people who distinguish themselves because of creative productivity, has been adopted to describe the child with exceptionally high IQ. Many regard this as unfortunate, but the custom seems to have prevailed.

There is much evidence of substantial, positive correlations between IQ as measured by an intelligence test and certain creative talents, but the extent of the correlations is unknown. The work of Terman and his associates is the best source of evidence of these correlations; and yet, this evidence is not decisive. Although it was found that distinguished men of history generally had high estimated IQs, it is not certain that indicators in the form of creative behaviour have not entered into those estimations (Cox, 1926). It would be much more crucial to know what the same individuals would have done on intelligence tests when they were children. Terman's study of the thousand children of exceptionally high IQs who have now reached maturity does not throw much light on this theory. Among the group there is plenty of indication of superior educational attainment and of superior vocational and social adjustment. On the other hand, there seems to be as yet little promise of a Darwin, an Edison, or a Eugene O'Neill, although the members of the group have reached the age level that has come to be recognised as the 'most creative years.' The writers on that study recognise this fact and account for it on the basis of the extreme rarity of individuals of the calibre of those whom I have mentioned (Terman and Oden, 1947). It is hoped that further follow-up studies will give due attention to criteria of a more specifically creative character.

When we look into the nature of intelligence tests, we encounter many doubts concerning their coverage of creative abilities. It should be remembered that from the time of Binet to the present, the chief practical criterion used in the validation of tests of intellect has been achievement in school. For children, this has meant largely achievement in reading and arithmetic. This fact has generally determined the nature of our intelligence tests. Operationally, then, intelligence has been the ability (or complex of abilities) to master reading and arithmetic and similar subjects. These subjects are not conspicuously demanding of creative talent.

Examination of the content of intelligence tests reveals very little that is of an obviously creative nature. Binet did include a few items of this character in his scale because he regarded creative imagination as one of the important higher mental functions that should be included. Revisions of the Binet scale have retained such items, but they represent only a small minority. Group tests of intelligence have generally omitted such items entirely.

The third general theory about creativity is, in fact, a theory of the entire personality, *including* intelligence. I have defined personality as a unique pattern of traits, and traits as a matter of individual differences. There are thousands of observable traits. The scientific urge for rational order and for economy in the description of persons directs us to look for a small number of descriptive categories. In describing mental abilities, this economy drive has been grossly overdone when we limit ourselves to the single concept of intelligence. Furthermore, the term 'intelligence' has by no means achieved logical or operational invariance and so does not satisfy the demand for rational order.

We do not need the thousands of descriptive terms because they are much interrelated, both positively and negatively. By intercorrelation procedures it is possible to determine the threads of consistency that run throughout the categories describing abilities, interests, and temperament variables. I am, of course, referring to the factorial conception of personality. From this point of view, personality is conceived geometrically as a hypersphere of n dimensions, each dimension being a dependable, convenient reference variable or concept. If the idea of applying this type of description to a living, breathing individual is distasteful, remember that this geometric picture is merely a conceptual model designed to encompass the multitude of observable facts, and to do it in a rational, communicable, and economical manner.

With this frame of reference, many of the findings and issues become clarified. The reason that different intelligence tests do not intercorrelate perfectly, even when errors of measurement have been taken into account, is that each test emphasises a different pattern of primary abilities. If the correlations between intelligence test scores and many types of creative performance are only moderate or low, and

I predict that such correlations will be found, it is because the primary abilities represented in those tests are not all important for creative behaviour. It is also because some of the primary abilities important for creative behaviour are not represented in the test at all. It is probably safe to say that the typical intelligence test measures to a significant degree not more than a half-dozen of the intellectual factors (Jones, 1949). There are surely more intellectual factors than that. Some of the abilities contributing to creative success are probably non-intellectual; for example, some of them are perceptual. Probably, some of the factors most crucial to creative performance have not yet been discovered in any type of test. In other words, we must look well beyond the boundaries of the IQ if we are to fathom the domain of creativity.

DEVELOPMENT OF CREATIVITY

Before referring to the experimental design and to more specific hypotheses concerning the nature of creativity, I will venture one or two opinions on the general problem of the development of creativity. For I believe that much can be done to encourage its development. This development might be in the nature of actual strengthening of the functions involved or it might mean the better utilisation of what resources the individual possesses, or both. In any case, a knowledge of the functions is important.

We frequently hear the charge that under present-day mass education methods, the development of creative personality is seriously discouraged. The child is under pressure to conform for the sake of economy and for the sake of satisfying prescribed standards. We are told by the philosophers who have given thought to the problem that the unfolding of a creative personality is a highly individual matter which stresses uniqueness and shuns conformity. Actually, the unfolding of the individual along the lines of his own inclinations is generally frowned upon. We are told, also, that the emphasis upon the memorising of facts sets the wrong kind of goal for the student. How serious these charges are no one actually knows. We have very little experimental evidence that is decisive one way or the other and such evidence is hard to obtain.

Charles Kettering (1944) one time commented upon a survey in which it was found that a person with engineering or scientific training had only half the probability of making an invention compared with others. His comment was that an inventor should be defined as 'a fellow who doesn't take his education too seriously'. If the results of that survey represent the actual situation, either creative individuals do not seek higher education in engineering and science, or that kind of education has negative transfer effects with respect to inventiveness.

Many of us teachers assert that it is our main objective to teach students how to think, and this means also to think constructively. Certainly, if we succeeded in this objective, there should be much evidence of creativeness in the end product. I am convinced that we do teach some students to think, but I sometimes marvel that we do as well as we do. In the first place, we have only vague ideas as to the nature of thinking. We have little actual knowledge of what specific steps should be taken in order to teach students to think. Our methods are shotgun methods, just as our intelligence tests have been shotgun tests. It is time that we discarded shotguns in favour of rifles.

We all know teachers who pride themselves on teaching students to think and yet who give examinations that are almost entirely a matter of knowledge of facts. Please do not misunderstand me. I have a strong appreciation of knowledge of facts. No creative person can get along without previous experiences or facts; he never creates in a vacuum or with a vacuum. There is a definite place for the learning of facts in our educational system. But let us keep our educational objectives straight. Let us recognise where facts are important and where they are not. Let us remember, too, that the kinds of examinations we give really set the objectives for the students, no matter what objectives we may have stated.

The confusion of objectives is illustrated by the following incident. The story was told by a former dean of a leading Midwestern University. An old, experienced teacher and scholar said that he tried to encourage originality in his students. In a graduate course, he told the class that the term paper would be graded in terms of the amount of originality shown. One school teacher in the class was especially concerned about getting a high mark in the course. She took verbatim notes, continuously and assiduously, of what the learned professor said in class. Her term paper, the story goes, was essentially a stringing together of her transcribed lecture notes, in which the professor's pet ideas were given prominent place. It is reported that the professor read the term papers himself. When the school teacher's paper was returned, the professor's mark was an A, with the added comment, 'This is one of the most original papers I have ever read'.

Before we make substantial improvement in teaching students to think, in my opinion we will have to make some changes in our conceptions of the process of learning. The ancient faculty psychology taught that mental faculties grow strong by virtue of the exercise of those faculties. We all know from the many experiments on practice in memorising that exercises in memorising are not necessarily followed by improvement of memory in general. We all know that exercises in perceptual discriminations of certain kinds are not followed by improvement of perceptual discriminations in general (Thorndike and Woodworth, 1901). Thorndike and others concluded that the study of courses in high-school curricula did not necessarily result in a general improvement in intellect, but that the increases in test scores could be attributed to learning of a more specific nature (Broyler *et al.*, 1927; Thorndike, 1924). Following this series of experiments the conclusion has often been that learning consists of the development of specific habits and that only very similar skills will be affected favourably by the learning process.

In view of the newer findings concerning primary abilities, the problems of formal discipline take on new meaning, and many of the experiments on the transfer of training will have to be re-examined and perhaps repeated with revised conditions. The experiments just cited do justify the rejection of the concepts of a general memory power, a general perceptual-discrimination power, and perhaps, also, rejection of the concept of a single power called intellect. These findings are in harmony with factorial theory. But the other alternative to the idea of formal discipline is not necessarily a theory of specific learning from specific practice.

There is certainly enough evidence of transfer effects. Experiments should be aimed to determine whether the instances of positive, zero, and negative transfer effects conform in a meaningful way to the outlines of the primary abilities. The work of Thorndike and others that I have just cited does, in fact, actually throw some light on this question. Although this aspect of their findings is usually not mentioned, they reported that high-school students' experiences in numerical, verbal, and spatial types of courses—arithmetic and book-keeping, Latin and French, and manual training—were associated with relatively greater gains in numerical, verbal, and spatial types of tests, respectively.

A general theory to be seriously tested is that some primary abilities can be improved with practice of various kinds and that positive transfer effects will be evident in tasks depending upon those abilities. At the present time some experiments of this type are going on in the Chicago schools under the direction of Thelma Gwinn Thurstone (Thurstone, 1948). In one sense, these investigations have returned to the idea of formal discipline. The new aspect of the disciplinary approach is that the presumed functions that are being 'exercised' have been indicated by empirical research.

FACTORIAL RESEARCH DESIGN

The general outline of the design for a factor-analysis investigation is familiar to many of you. It has been described before but needs to be emphasised again (Thurstone, 1948). The complete design involves a number of steps, not all of which are essential but all of which are highly desirable if the investigator is to make the most efficient use of his time and to achieve results of maximum value. The major steps will be mentioned first, then more details concerning some of them.

One first chooses the domain of his investigation. It may be the domain of memory abilities, visual-perceptual abilities, reasoning abilities, or the domain of introversion-extraversion.

One next sets up hypotheses as to the factors he expects to find in that domain. His preparatory task of hypothesis formation goes further. It includes the framing of several alternative hypotheses as to the more precise nature of each factor. This is necessary as the basis for transforming each factor hypothesis into the operational terms of test ideas. He then constructs tests which he thinks will measure individual differences in the kind of ability, or other quality, he thinks the factor to be. He will want to include in the test battery some reference tests that measure already known factors. One reason for this is that the new tests will almost inevitably also measure to some extent factors that have previously been established, such as verbal comprehension, number facility, and visualisation. If such variance is probably going to appear in more than one new test in the battery, it is best to have that variance clearly brought out and readily identifiable. Another reason is that it is possible, after all, that one or more of the hypothesised factors will turn out to be identifiable with one or more of the known factors. The possibility of this identification must be provided for by having the suspected, known factors represented in the battery.

The test battery is administered to a sample of adequate size from a population of appropriate qualifications. Certain kinds of populations are better for bringing out variances in some common factors and other kinds are more suitable for other purposes. There should be relative homogeneity in certain features that might be correlated with the factors, such as sex, age, education, and other conditions. Some thought should be given to whether tests should be speed tests or power tests or something between the two. Some consideration should also be given to the most appropriate type of score for each test.

Factors are extracted and their reference axes are rotated into positions that are compelling because of the nature of the configuration of test vectors in the hyperspace. The psychological nature of each factor is surmised by virtue of the kinds of tests that have substantial variance attributable to that factor in contrast to tests which lack that variance.

In many respects, the complete factor-analysis design has properties parallel to those of a good experiment. In both, we begin with hypotheses. In both, some conditions are held constant while others are varied. In both, the measured outcomes point towards or away from the hypotheses. One important difference is the possibility of a statistical test of significance of the measured result for the experiment but not for the factor analysis. Confidence in the latter case depends upon the compellingness of the factor structure and the repeated verification of a result.

As an illustration of this analogy to an experiment, I will cite the factorial study of the well-known figure-analogies test. In the Army Air Forces research results, the figure-analogies test exhibited variances in three factors denoted as reasoning I, II, and III (Guilford, 1947). They were thus designated because they were peculiar to a number of reasoning tests, but their more precise natures were obscure. Examination of what one does in solving a figure-analogies item suggests several possible psychological functions or activities. First, one has to grasp correctly the relation between figure one and figure two. This suggests an ability to see a relationship between two objects. Second, one must observe the properties of the third figure. Then, one has to see what kind of a fourth figure it takes to satisfy the same relationship between figure three and figure four. Having decided upon the kind of figure needed, one has to find it among four or five that are supplied in the multiple-choice item. This is a kind of classifying act. There is still another possibility. The mislead responses may be so reasonable that considerable discrimination may be needed to select the best figure for the purpose. Considering the figure-analogies item from a more holistic point of view, there may be a primary ability involved in seeing that there is an identity of two relationships when the elements related are different. Or, there may be a general reasoning-by-analogy ability. Transposability of relations may be a key function here. Thus, we have several hypotheses as to the functions involved. There could be others. For every one of them we also have the further question as to whether the ability implied is restricted to the visual perception of figures or whether it is more general, extending to word meanings, numbers, and sounds. And if it is general, what are its limits?

To seek answers by factorial methods, one would construct special tests, each limited, if possible, to one kind of act implied by each hypothesis. One would also vary the kind of material in each type of test to explore the scope of generality. The answeres to the hypotheses (for each hypothesis is in reality a question) would be to find that the loading for each factor would rise with some of the variations and fall with others as compared to its loading in the traditional figure-analogies test. We would hope to find the changes in factor loadings so marked that we would not feel seriously the lack of t tests or F tests.

The question of the sources of factor hypotheses calls for some comment. In a domain in which there have already been factorial studies, the previous results are always suggestive. This makes it appear that the factorist merely moves from hypotheses to hypotheses. This is quite true. It is a fundamental truth of all scientists, no matter what their methods. Some hypotheses are merely better supported and more generally accepted than others at the time. There is enough uncertainty left in many a hypothesis to invite further investigation. That is what makes science interesting. That is what I think Kettering meant when he stated that the inventor is one who does not take his education (or knowledge) too seriously.

In a personality domain in which there has been little previous illumination of the underlying variables, other sources of hypotheses must be sought. The critical-incident technique of Flanagan (1949) would be one useful exploratory approach. Incidentally, one might say that this method has been used informally in connection with creative people from the 'Eureka' episode of Archimedes down to modern times. The literature includes many descriptions of creative events. It would be more correct to refer to these historical reports as anecdotes, however, rather than critical incidents, since they suffer from most of the weaknesses of anecdotes. Where modern writers have attempted to interpret them psychologically, the interpretations have been quite superficial. They abound with vague concepts such as 'genius', 'intuition', 'imagination', 'reflection', and 'inspiration', none of which leads univocally to test ideas. In the writings of those who have attempted to give a generalised picture of creative behaviour, there is considerable agreement that the complete creative act involves four important steps.

According to this picture, the creator begins with a period of preparation, devoted to an inspection of his problem and a collection of information or material. There follows a perid of incubation during which there seems to be little progress in the direction of fulfilment. But, we are told, there *is* activity, only it is mostly unconscious. There eventually comes the big moment of inspiration, with a final, or semi-final, solution, often accompanied by strong emotion. There usually follows a period of evaluation or verification, in which the creator tests the solution or examines the product for its fitness or value. Little or much 'touching up' may be done to the product.

Such an analysis is very superficial from the psychological point of view. It is more dramatic than it is suggestive of testable hypotheses. It tells us almost nothing about the mental operations that actually occur. The concepts do not lead directly to test ideas. In attempting to distinguish between persons with different degrees of creative talent, shall we say, for example, that some individuals are better incubators than others? And how would one go about testing for incubating ability? The belief that the process of incubation is carried on in a region of the mind called the unconscious is of no help. It merely chases the problem out of sight and thereby the chaser feels excused from the necessity of continuing the chase further.

It is not incubation itself that we find of great interest. It is the nature of the processes that occur during the latent period of incubation, as well as before it and after it. It is individual differences in the efficiency of those processes that will be found important for identifying the potentially creative. The nature of those processes or functions will have to be inferred from performances of the individuals who have been presented with problems, even though the creator is largely unaware of them.

SPECIFIC HYPOTHESES CONCERNING CREATIVE ABILITIES

The hypotheses that follow concerning the nature of creative thinking have been derived with certain types of creative people in mind: the scientist and the technologist, including the inventor. The consensus of the philosophers seems to have been that creativity is the same wherever you find it. To this idea I do not subscribe. Within the factorial frame of reference there is much room for different types of creative abilities. What it takes to make the inventor, the writer, the artist, and the composer creative may have some factors in common, but there is much room for variation of pattern of abilities. Some of the hypotheses mentioned here may apply also to areas of creative endeavour other than science, technology, and invention, but others may not. Included in the list of primary abilities that may contribute to creative efforts of these special groups are the reasoning factors, but I shall restrict mention here to other possible thinking factors that are more obviously creative in character.

First, there are probably individual differences in a variable that may be called *sensitivity to problems*. How this variation among individuals may come about will not concern us at this time. Whether it is best regarded as an ability or as a temperament trait will not concern us, either. The fact remains that in a certain situation one person will see that several problems exist while another will be oblivious to them.

Two scientists look over a research report. There are generally acceptable conclusions, but there is one minor discrepancy in the results. One scientist attributes the discrepancy to 'experimental error'. The other feels uneasy about the discrepancy; it piques his curiosity; it challenges him for an explanation. His further thinking about the matter develops into a new research project from which highly important findings result. Such an incident was reported by Flanagan (1949); it could be found duplicated many times.

There are questions as to the generality of such a variable. Is the supposed sensitivity restricted to a certain kind of situation or a certain kind of problem? Is it a perceptual quality as well as a thought quality? Could it be a general impressionability to the environment? Is it our old friend 'curiosity' under a new name? Is it an ability to ask questions? Is it a general inhibition against closure? There may be other hypotheses just as pertinent. Each one suggests possible tests of individual differences.

Examples of possible tests follow. One might present the examinee with a short paragraph of expository material and instruct him to ask as many questions as he can that are suggested by the statements, with relatively liberal time allowed. A large part of the scientist's success depends upon his ability to ask questions, and, of course, to ask the right questions. In another test, one might name common household appliances, such as a toaster, or articles of clothing, such as trousers, and ask the examinee to list things that he thinks are wrong or could be improved. As a perceptual test, one might present pictures of objects or forms that are conventional and regular except for minor irregularities. Can the examinee detect the unusual features or will he overlook them? A third possibility is in the form of what we have called a 'frustration test', merely because it is somewhat frustrating to many who have tried it. Contrary to the usual test practice, no task instruction is given: only items, and the very general instruction 'do something which each item; whatever you think should be done'. Each item is of a different type. One or two examinees have refused to do anything with the test.

There is very likely a *fluency* factor, or there are a number of fluency factors, in creative talent. Not that all creators must work under pressure of time and must produce rapidly or not at all. It is rather that the person who is capable of producing a large number of ideas per unit of time, other things being equal, has a greater chance of having significant ideas. There have been previous results yielding several verbal-fluency factors but I have insufficient time to acknowledge those studies properly here. It is probable that there are a number of fluency factors, non-verbal as well as verbal, yet undiscovered. There is a general problem to be investigated, apart from creativity, whether many of the primary thinking abilities have both a power and a speed aspect somewhat independent of each other. Some work of Davidson and Carroll (1945) suggests this in a result with regard to one of the reasoning factors.

One kind of fluency test would consist of asking the examinee to name as many objects as he can in a given time, the objects having some specified property; for example, things round, things red, or things to eat. In another test, the ideas might be more complex, as in naming a list of appropriate titles for a picture or for a short story. Still more demanding and also more restricting would be the task of naming exceptions to a given statement. Fluency of inferences may be tested by providing a hypothetical statement to which the examinee is to state as many consequences or implications as he can in a limited time. The statement might be: A new invention makes it unnecessary for people to eat; what will the consequences be? This type of test has been previously proposed by several investigators.

The creative person has *novel* ideas. The degree of novelty of which the person is capable, or which he habitually exhibits, is pertinent to our study. This can be tested in terms of the frequency of uncommon, yet acceptable, responses to items. The tendency to give remote verbal associations in a word-association test; to give remote similarities in a similies test; and to give connotative synonyms for words, are examples of indications of novelty of ideas in the category of verbal tests.

The individual's *flexibility* of mind, the ease with which he changes set, can possibly be indicated in several ways by means of tests. Although there have been disappointments in the attempt to establish a common factor of this type (Guilford, 1947), the concept of flexibility and of its probable opposite, rigidity, will not be downed. In conjunction with some of the fluency tests, there may be opportunities to obtain some indications concerning flexibility. Does the examinee tend to stay in a rut or does he branch out readily into new channels of thought? Tests whose items cannot be correctly answered by adhering to old methods but require new approaches, in opposition to old habits of thinking, would be pertinent here. Certain types of puzzles fit this requirement fairly well, for example, a problem in which the examinee cannot succeed without folding the paper on which he writes, and the idea of doing so must come from him.

Much creative thinking requires the organising of ideas into larger, more inclusive patterns. For this reason, we have hypothesised a *synthesising ability*. As a counterpart to this, one might well expect an *analysing ability*. Symbolic structures must often be broken down before new ones can be built. It is desirable to explore many kinds of both synthesising and analysing activities, in both perceptual and conceptual problems, in order to determine the existence of such factors and their numbers and whether they cut across both perceptual and conceptual areas.

From Gestalt psychology comes the idea that there may be a factor involving *reorganisation* or *redefinition* of organised wholes (Wertheimer, 1945). Many inventions have been in the nature of a transformation of an existing object into one of different design, function, or use. It may be that this activity involves a combination of flexibility, analysis and synthesis, and that no additional hypothesis of redefinition is really needed, but the possibility must be investigated.

There is a possibility of a dimension of ability that has to do with the degree of *complexity* or of intricacy of conceptual structure of which the individual is capable. How many interrelated ideas can the person manipulate at the same time? The scientist must often keep in mind several variables, conditions, or relationships as he thinks out a problem. Some individuals become confused readily; they can keep only one or two items of structure delineated and properly related. Others have a higher resistance to confusion—a greater span of this type. Such an ability might be identifiable with the hypothesised synthesising factor, but the study should make possible a separation of the two if the distinction is real.

Creative work that is to be realistic or accepted must be done under some degree of evaluative restraint. Too much restraint, of course, is fatal to the birth of new ideas. The selection of surviving ideas, however, requires some *evaluation*. In this direction there must be a factor or two. The evaluations are conceivably of different kinds, consequently the kinds of possible tests are numerous. In a paragraph of exposition, we may ask the examinee to say whether every underlined statement is best classified as a fact, a definition, or a hypothesis. He will, to be sure, need some preliminary instruction in these distinctions. In another test, we can present him with a stated problem, then ask him which of several items are relevant to its solution and which ones are not. In still another test, we can give a problem and several alternative solutions, all correct. The examinee is to rank the solutions in the order of degree of excellence or fitness.

The hypotheses mentioned, as was stated earlier, refer more

specifically to a limited domain of creative thinking more characteristic of the scientist and technologist. Even so, this entails a factorial study of substantial proportions. Similar studies will need to be made in the domains of planning abilities, in order to anticipate abilities more characteristic of the economic, the political, and the military leader. Still other restricted domains will need to be investigated to take care of the writer, the graphic artist, and the musical composer.

The question will inevitably arise, 'How do you know your tests are valid?' There are two answers to this question. The first is that the factorial study of the tests is in itself one kind of validation. It will determine which tests measure each factor and to what extent. That is a matter of internal validity or factorial validity. It answers the question, 'What does the test measure?' The second answer will be in terms of which factors are related to the creative productivity of people in everyday life. That calls for the correlation of factor measures with practical criteria. I feel very strongly that only after we have determined the promising factors and how to measure them are we justified in taking up the time of creative people with tests. If a certain factor we discover turns out not to be related to creative production, we have made a bad guess, but we will have discovered a new factor that may have some other practical validity. If a certain factor is not related to the criteria of creative productivity, the tests which measure it uniquely will also prove to be invalid for predicting these criteria. It is better to fail in the validation of a single factor measure than to fail in the validation of a half-dozen tests. If we make a study of the practical validity of every creative test we can think of before it is analysed, we are bound to exert considerable wasted effort of our own and of our examinees. This statement, incidentally, applies to the validation study of any test.

Creative productivity in everyday life is undoubtedly dependent upon primary traits other than abilities. Motivational factors (interests and attitudes) as well as temperament factors must be significant contributors. Hypotheses concerning these factors in connection with creative people might be fruitful starting points for factorial investigations. The design of the research would be much the same as that described for creative abilities.

SUMMARY AND CONCLUSIONS

By way of summary, it can be said that psychologists have seriously neglected the study of the creative aspects of personality. On the other hand, the social importance of the subject is very great. Many believe that creative talent is to be accounted for in terms of high intelligence or IQ. This conception is not only inadequate but has been largely responsible for the lack of progress in the understanding of creative people.

The factorial conception of personality leads to a new way of thinking about creativity and creative productivity. According to this point of view, creativity represents patterns of primary abilities, patterns which can vary with different spheres of creative activity. Each primary ability is a variable along which individuals differ in a continuous manner. Consequently, the nature of these abilities can be studied in people who are not necessarily distinguished for creative reasons. Productivity depends upon other primary traits, including interests, attitudes, and temperamental variables.

It is proposed that a fruitful exploratory approach to the domain of creativity is through a complete application of factor analysis, which would begin with carefully constructed hypotheses concerning the primary abilities and their properties. It is suggested that certain kinds of factors will be found, including sensitivity to problems, ideational fluency, flexibility of set, ideational novelty, synthesising ability, analysing ability, reorganising or redefining ability, span of ideational structure, and evaluating ability. Each one of these hypotheses may be found to refer to more than one factor. Some hypothesised abilities may prove to be identical with others or accounted for in terms of others. At any rate, these hypotheses lead to the construction of tests of quite novel types, which is a promising condition for the discovery of new factors. The relation of such factors to practical criteria of creative performance will need to be established. It is likely that the tests have been aimed in the right direction.

Once the factors have been established as describing the domain of creativity, we have a basis for the means of selecting the individuals with creative potentialities. We also should know enough about the properties of the primary abilities to do something in the way of education to improve them and to increase their utilisation. These ends certainly justify our best efforts.

REFERENCES

BROYLER, C. R., THORNDIKE, E. L., and WOODYARD, E. (1927) 'A second study of mental discipline in high schools', *J. educ. Psychol.*, **18**, 377–404.

COX, C. M. (1926) *Genetic Studies of Genius*, vol. ii, Stanford University Press.

DAVIDSON, W. M., and CARROLL, J. B. (1945) 'Speed and level components in time-limit scores', *Educ. and psychol. Meas.*, **5**, 411–35.

FLANAGAN, J. C., *et al.* (1949) *Critical Requirements for Research Personnel.* Pittsburgh, American Institute for Research.

GIDDINGS, F. H. (1907) *Elements of Sociology.* New York, Macmillan Co.

GUILFORD, J. P. (ed.) (1947) *Printed Classification Texts*: Army Air Forces Aviation Psychology Research Program, Report No. 5. Washington D.C.: Government Printing Office.

HUTCHINSON, E. D. (1931) 'Materials for the study of creative thinking', *Psychol. Bull.*, **28**, 392–410.

JONES, L. V. (1949) 'A factor analysis of the Stanford-Binet at four age levels', *Psychom.*, **14**, 299–331.

KETTERING, C. F. (1944) 'How can we develop inventors?' in a symposium on *Creative Engineering.* New York, American Society of Mechanical Engineers.

MARKEY, F. V. (1935) 'Imagination', *Psychol. Bull.*, **32**, 212–36.

TERMAN, L. M., and ODEN, M. H. (1947) *The Gifted Child Grows Up.* Stanford University Press.

THORNDIKE, E. L. (1924) 'Mental discipline in high school studies', *J. educ. Psychol.*, **15**, 1–22, 83–98.

THORNDIKE, E. L., and WOODWORTH, R. S. (1901) 'The influence of improvement in one mental function upon the efficiency of other functions', *Psychol. Rev.*, **8**, 247–61, 384–95, 553–64.

THURSTONE, L. L. (1948) 'Implications of factor analysis', *Amer. Psychologist*, **3**, 402–8.

WERTHEIMER, M. *Productive Thinking*, Harper, 1945.

SECTION 2

Personality dimensions and attainment

What role does a child's personality as described by his scores on a personality test have in determining how well he does at school? In recent years a great deal of research has been carried out in this area; but the results have often been conflicting. In the study reported here, Professor H. J. Eysenck, one of the most prolific and influential writers on personality, joins forces with D. Cookson, a child guidance specialist, in a comprehensive attempt to resolve the outstanding issues. They examine the variation in school children's scores on various attainment tests with respect to sex differences (S) and two personality measures—Neuroticism (N) and Extraversion (E).

Eysenck and Cookson analyse the relationships between the variables they studied, by two statistical methods: correlation coefficients computed for each pair of variables, and the more powerful technique of analysis of variance. It is not necessary to be fully conversant with this latter method to appreciate the results they obtained: but a few words of explanation about two of the technical terms which occur frequently in the article, interaction and linearity, may be of help. (Those *who wish to follow the analysis through in greater detail may also like to consult one of the books on statistics in the booklist on p. 406.)*

Eysenck and Cookson's conclusions regarding interaction *between variables and the* linearity of *their relationships can be understood from an examination of the tables which they present. For the analysis of variance these contain mean values of children's attainment scores in different subgroups of the total samples. Thus, when the conclusion is drawn that N has no significant effect on Verbal Reasoning, but has a significant interaction with E with respect to this test, this effect can be clearly seen in Table 9.2 for males. The bottom row of the table shows little variation in mean verbal reasoning scores for three levels of neuroticism (98·79, 97·39 and 97·90), but inside the table the neurotic extraverted boys can be seen to have a lower verbal attainment score than the stable extraverted boys (95·48 compared to 101·21). In other words, although in the total sample there is no overall relationship between N and Verbal Reasoning (VR), among the extraverted boys the two variables N and VR are related. In such a situation we say that extraversion and neuroticism interact with respect to verbal reasoning. N and VR would similarly be said to interact if they were related to each other in the total sample but were not related to each other among the extraverted boys. In fact, whenever the relationships differ significantly between a total sample and a subgroup interaction is said to occur.*

The question of the linearity of the relationships can also be understood by an examination of the tables of mean values. A linear relationship is shown when the mean attainment scores increase proportionately with a personality test score; a U-shaped relationship is shown when attainment is highest for both high and low mean values of a personality variable and lowest for the middle value. Most of the tables show a moderate effect of this kind for attainment and neuroticism. For example, in Table 9·2, groups of girls with the highest and lowest N scores have slightly higher mean attainment scores (100·30 and 102·06) than those with the intermediate N score (99·24).*

Besides using analysis of variance to arrive at their conclusions Eysenck and Cookson also align their study with those of other people by presenting the correlation coefficients between all the measures they employed. It is this use of different techniques of analysis on data collected from a very large sample of children which makes their study particularly valuable. It also represents the all too rare occurrence of a theoretician combining forces with someone professionally concerned with children to tackle a major research problem.*

J. BYNNER

9

H. J. Eysenck and D. Cookson

Personality in primary school children*

Ability and achievement

SUMMARY. Scores of some 4,000 eleven-year-old boys and girls on the JEPI were analysed in relation to performance on scholastic and ability tests at the primary school leaving age. Analysis by correlation and analysis of variance methods revealed that extraverted boys and girls are scholastically superior to introverted ones, the regression being linear: that stable boys and girls did only marginally better than unstable ones, the regression being somewhat curvilinear; that interaction effects between N and E only occurred in conjunction with sex, unstable extraverted girls doing unexpectedly well, unstable extraverted boys unexpectedly poorly. Grammar school entrance proportions favoured extraverted and stable boys and girls, and disfavoured 'liars' on the L scale. Personality determined performance on ability/achievement tests more closely in the case of girls than of boys. The results suggest the importance of personality variables, particularly extraversion/introversion, in the attempt to predict scholastic success; it seems likely that introverts are 'late developers' as compared with extraverts, but in the absence of proper follow-up studies this conclusion remains speculative.

I. INTRODUCTION

There has been a resurgence of interest in recent years in the investigation of temperamental variables in relation to scholastic achievement. The discovery that intellectual ability is only one of the determinants of achievement is not of course all that recent, but the lack of suitable

* Reprinted from British Journal of Educational Psychology, 39, 1969, 109–22.

personality tests seemed to channel most research efforts into the cognitive field. The growth of dimensional theories of personality, together with the availability of inventories for the measurement of some at least of these dimensions, has changed the picture, and now we have quite a large series of studies comparing the intellectual status and the scholastic achievements of introverts and extraverts, or stable and unstable children and students. Cattell *et al.* (1966) have gone as far as to suggest that ability, temperament and motivation all contribute something like 25 per cent to the achievement variance, and such far-reaching claims are certainly worth investigating. However, such studies as have been reported have often seemed to give contradictory results; the same personality variable (e.g., extraversion) might correlate positively or negatively with achievement in different samples. Such contradictions lower one's faith in the validity of the findings, and require explanation.

One obvious hypothesis which would serve to integrate much of the evidence available is related to the concept of the 'late developer'; if introverts, say, develop more slowly than do extraverts, then superiority of achievement in extraverts during the first few years of schooling might turn into inferiority during later years. Evidence in favour of this hypothesis is in data available, and comes out quite clearly even in such early pioneering studies as that of MacNitt (1930). This author studied 964 junior and high school pupils aged thirteen and upwards, using a specially constructed introversion inventory; he analysed their average school marks in English, Mathematics, Social Science, Physical Science and Foreign Languages and came to the following conclusion: 'Those tending towards extraversion receive on the average higher marks than the introverts in Grades VII and VIII; slightly higher marks in Grades IX and X; and lower marks in Grades XI and XII.... Those in the introverted group seem to increase their school marks on the average through the various grades, the extraverts' marks remaining on the average approximately the same. . . . In general, there is a substantial relationship between introversion-extraversion and average school marks' (pp. 131–2). Taking Social Science as an example, we find correlations with introversion to be −0·331 in the youngest group, −0·192 in the middle group, and +0·380 in the oldest; for English the figures are −0·379, −0·127, and +0·043. Physical Science reaches a value of +0·489 for the oldest group, an interesting finding in virtue of Hudson's (1966) suggestion of a relationship between introverted personality traits and preference for science; in line with this possibility is the fact that achievement in foreign languages remains obstinately negative, with a value of −0·494 in the oldest group. Not too much should be made of these values, but they do suggest (1) a strong relationship, changing in time, between personality (specifically introversion-extraversion) and scholastic achievement, and (2) a differential direction of this relationship, with introversion predisposing pupils towards scientific achievement, and extraversion predisposing them towards linguistic achievement.

A similar inversion over time appears in the more recent work of S. B. G. Eysenck (1965), who correlated JEPI scores on extraversion with intelligence test scores; this correlation turned from positive at age 11 (0.22 for girls, 0.27 for boys) to negative at age 14 for girls (-0.25) and at age 15 for boys (-0.10). Intelligence and achievement are of course two different concepts, but it should be remembered that intelligence tests in schools are often highly contaminated with knowledge, and are thus measures of Vernon's *v-ed* factor rather than of *g*. Other recent studies, mostly using either the Junior Minnesota Personality Inventory (MPI) or Eysenck Personality Inventory (EPI), or else the Cattell scales, have also tended to find positive correlations between achievement and intelligence, on the one hand, and extraversion, on the other (Jones, 1960; Morrison *et al.*, 1965; Ridding, 1967; Rushton, 1966; Savage, 1966); the children investigated were on the whole quite young. Thus, the evidence, while not unanimous, does seem to support the superiority of extraverted children in the primary school and at the beginning of the secondary school.

As regards the other main personality dimension studied in several researches, emotionality or neuroticism, the findings tend to suggest that among children high N scores are associated with poor performance (Butcher *et al.*, 1963; Callard and Goodfellow, 1962; Hallworth, 1961; Lunzer, 1960; Entwistle and Cunningham, 1968). These generalisations tend to break down when attention is turned to university students (Holmes, 1960; Furneaux, 1962; Lynn, 1959; Kelvin *et al.*, 1965); these tend to excel when high on introversion and on neuroticism. However, students are clearly a very unusual and highly selected sub-group, and should not necessarily be expected to show similar relations between personality and achievement to school children who tend to be quite unselected. Students must, by definition, have passed successfully through a long series of tests, weeding out those whose N component acted as a hindrance rather than as a motivational variable. In school children no such weeding-out process is likely to have taken place.

In view of the considerable amount of agreement which has become apparent in the relation between personality and achievement, it may seem superfluous to carry out and report yet another study of a similar kind. There are several reasons for believing that such a study might produce useful results; these reasons are related to certain weaknesses in design characteristic of several past studies. These may be briefly listed. (1) Boys and girls may show quite different regressions of achievement or ability on personality variables, yet very little attention has in fact been paid to this point. (The recent study of Entwistle and Cunningham, 1968, supports this argument, and emphasises the need for treating the sexes separately.) (2) Sampling has not always been very thorough; usually just one or two schools have been used, although it is known that schools often differ profoundly from each other, and may give rise to quite different relationships in characteristics measured. (3) Statistical treatment has usually been very simple; mostly product-moment correlation coefficients have been reported. The underlying assumption of linear regression may not be justified; no tests for curvilinearity have been reported in most of the studies consulted. (4) The personality variables studied have usually been treated in isolation; this is not justified unless it can be shown that no interaction is in fact taking place. Suppose that neurotic introverts and stable extraverts do particularly well on achievement tests; simple tests against N or E separately will not disclose any significant correlations. There are too many examples of such interaction in the experimental literature (Eysenck, 1967) to allow us to dismiss this possibility as fanciful. Some form of zone analysis is clearly called for.

It is with these thoughts in mind that the experiment reported here was initiated; the set-up and the analysis were dictated by the hope that more detailed study of such factors as sex or personality interaction might reveal interesting new facts additional to the expected positive correlation between achievement and extraversion, and the equally expected negative correlation between achievement and neuroticism. Our achievement variables contain, in addition to intelligence (verbal reasoning), the English and Mathematics papers of the 11 + examination and the success or failure of the pupil to gain access to a grammar school: this seemed of some interest in view of the prevailing lack of knowledge of the degree to which personality may influence selection. Reading ability is another achievement which is of obvious importance in connection with school work, and was consequently included.

II. THE STUDY

Subjects

All schools in Staffordshire with fourth-year junior children were asked to take part in the research. Of those that agreed to do so, 206 with about 6,000 fourth-year children participated in all parts of the study and a further 55 with some 1,500 children participated to a more limited degree. In all about 77 per cent of all the 9,750 children in the age group were involved to some extent and all types of rural and urban areas within the county were well represented. At the time the research was done the children ranged in age from 10 years 9 months to 11 years 9 months, and all children in this age group from each school that took part were included.

General procedure

The measuring techniques and instruments used in the research were investigated in a pilot study, but the carrying out of all parts of the main investigation, all scoring and all recording and dispatching of result was left entirely to the individual schools, each of which received a detailed manual of instructions and information.

The data were collected during May, June and July, 1966, and the schools were allowed to administer the tests, etc., at any convenient times during this three months period, although certain stipulations were made regarding conditions of testing and the order in which various tests were to be carried out.

Main measuring techniques and instruments

The Junior Eysenck Personality Inventory. The most important measuring instrument for the purpose of the present analysis is the Junior Eysenck Personality Inventory (S. B. G. Eysenck, 1965), which was designed to measure the personality dimensions, neuroticism or emotionality and extraversion/introversion, and which also has a Lie scale.

The children were asked to read the instructions on the test form, and additional oral explanations, mainly for the benefit of the duller children, were also given. They were not allowed to talk to each other about the questions, and no help was given with reading or in explaining the meanings of words or phrases. Teachers were asked to exclude those children who were unable to read the inventory.

The completed forms were checked to make sure no child had left out any item or had made some other error.

Abilities and achievements. Already available were the results of two Moray House tests of verbal reasoning, one of Mathematics and one of English, taken six months earlier as part of the secondary selection procedure. For each test obtained marks are converted to 'quotients', which are standard scores with a mean of 100 and a standard deviation of 15. It was also known whether or not a child had qualified for a grammar school place.

Reading level was measured by the Schonell Graded Word Reading Test (Schonell and Schonell, 1960) which is administered individually. Only the obtained score, which is the number of words correctly read, was used in the analysis, although it is usually converted to a reading age when the test is used by schools.

Personality ratings. The four personality traits for which the teachers made ratings were: emotional stability, perseverance, sociability and impulsiveness. For each trait there were five scale categories, ranging from 1 (highest) to 5 (lowest), and each category was accompanied by a description of children's behaviour or attributes considered most relevant to that level. The teachers were given the rough proportions of children expected in different categories, with a view to obtaining approximately normal distributions. Every child was rated on one trait before any child was rated on the next.

Family background. Information on size of family and ordinal position in the family was obtained from the children. The classification of occupations used (Central Advisory Council for Education, 1954) is based on the Registrar-General's classification into social classes and has five categories, ranging from professional and managerial occupations (1) to unskilled occupations (5). Teachers were asked to find out from each child the occupation of his father or guardian.

Teachers rated the degree of interest in their child's progress shown by parents on a four-point scale from 1 (highest level of interest) to 4 (lowest). With each scale category was a description of parental attitudes considered appropriate at that level.

Summary of main variables

Junior EPI	Extraversion (E)
	Neuroticism (N)
	Lie scale (L)
Abilities and achievements	Verbal reasoning (Tests 70 and 71)
	Mathematics
	English
	Reading
	Grammer School pass/fail

Personality ratings   Emotional Stability
                                    Perseverance
                                    Sociability
                                    Impulsiveness
Family Background   Size of family
                                    Ordinal position in family
                                    Occupational classification
                                    Parental interest in child's progress.

Method of analysis

On the basis of the distributions of N, E and L scores, a sample was selected for the purpose of an analysis of variance. As a first step all children with L scores over 8 were excluded. An attempt was then made to divide the two distributions (E and N) into thirds, in such a manner that a maximum number of cases should be included in each of the resulting 9 groups, for both sexes. The two sets of scores finally adopted were as follows: Low N, 0–11. Average N, 12–17, High N, 18–24. Low E, 0–15. Average E, 16–18. High E 19–24. In this way we obtained, for the two sexes separately, 9 groups of children showing all possible combinations of low, average or high N, and low, average or high E. The number of cases in each of the 2 × 9 cells was 160, as a minimum, up to 182, as a maximum; the actual number used varied according to the availability of the achievement scores for the particular children involved. Thus the total number in a given analysis was never smaller than 2,880, and never larger than 3,276. In any particular analysis the number of children in each cell was of course kept constant. The reason for the marked variation in numbers was of course that if one child failed to complete his English test say, then 17 other children had to be dropped from the analysis in order to keep numbers in the cells equal. While these analyses of variance constitute the main part of our results, correlational analyses were also carried out on rather larger numbers in order to obtain data from non-selected groups; the analysis of variance group is of course highly selected, although preserving in its main features the characteristics of the total population.

III. RESULTS

Verbal reasoning

Two tests of verbal reasoning were given, VR 70 and VR 71; both were very similar and both are relatively orthodox measures of verbal intelligence. For the purpose of simplicity we shall refer to the scores on these tests as measures of intelligence, without wishing to beg any of the many questions raised by this term. An analysis of variance was carried out on the data from VR 70; these, it will be remembered, formed a $2 \times 3 \times 3$ design, with 2 sex groups, 3E groups and 3N groups. The means for these various groups are given in Table 9.1. Sex, as expected, produces significant differences (girls higher) at better than the 0·01 level of probability. E produces even more significant differences (p<0·001), with the more extraverted having higher scores; this effect seems to be linear. N produces effects which are barely significant (p<0·05); the most stable having slightly higher scores than the other two groups. None of the interactions are significant; thus the main effects can be evaluated without regard for possible cross-influences.

TABLE 9.1 *Scores on VR 70*

	Male				Female			
	N –	A	N+	All	N –	A	N+	All
I	92·98	91·43	92·19	92·20	94·64	90·98	94·94	93·52
A	96·55	92·60	94·09	94·41	98·20	95·43	95·80	96·48
E	97·73	99·05	92·92	96·57	101·54	99·34	100·18	100·35
All	95·75	94·36	93·07	94·39	98·13	95·25	96·98	96·78

I = introverts. A = ambiverts. E = extraverts. N – = stable. A = average.
N + = emotionally unstable.

Results for VR 71 are shown in Table 9.2. Sex again plays a very significant part (p<0·001), as does E (p<0·001), but N is not significant. However, the N × E interaction is significant (p<0·05), as is the S × N × E interaction (p<0·01). The sex and E differences go in the same direction as before, i.e., girls and extraverts are superior. The significant interactions appear to originate with the emotional extravert groups; for the girls, this group is the second highest (score 103·90), while for the boys this group is near the bottom (score 95·48). A similar difference actually appears in VR 70 also (100·18 as compared with 92·92), but is below the level of significance. This group occupies the position of psychopaths and prospective criminals in Eysenck's scheme (1964, 1967) and it seems possible that for boys (whose criminal propensities are well known to be much higher than those of girls) this combination of personality traits is more lethal, and interferes more with the massed practice involved in traditional intelligence tests

(Eysenck, 1959), than in girls. However, before seeking too earnestly for an explanation of the finding it might perhaps be wise to replicate the findings itself; the failure of the interactions to achieve significance in the VR 70 study suggests caution in accepting the results as necessarily genuine. Some support is given by the significant sex × E interaction found by Entwistle and Cunningham (1968) in their work with thirteen-year-old school children.

TABLE 9.2. *Scores on VR 71*

	Male				Female			
	N−	A	N+	All	N−	A	N+	All
I	95·80	94·45	95·09	95·11	98·78	94·25	98·31	97·11
A	99·35	95·46	103·15	99·32	101·96	99·64	98·68	100·09
E	101·21	102·26	95·48	99·65	105·44	103·84	103·90	104·39
All	98·79	97·39	97·90	98·03	102·06	99·24	100·30	100·53

Mathematics

The results of the mathematics examination fail to show any difference between the sexes; the often documented superiority of males in dealing with figures apparently just makes good their inferiority in the verbal reasoning tests. (This explanation can be tested by looking at the English marks of the two sexes, where the girls should be very superior according to this hypothesis.) No differences are apparent, either, for N as a main effect, but E is again involved in producing marked differences in achievement (p<0·001) N × E × S and S × N × E interactions are both significant at the p<0·01 level. The detailed results are given in Table 9.3.

TABLE 9.3. *Scores on mathematics test*

	Male				Female			
	N−	A	N+	All	N−	A	M+	All
I	91·08	90·79	91·70	91·19	92·93	87·88	92·76	91·22
A	96·28	91·81	100·11	96·06	95·81	94·46	93·59	94·62
E	98·52	99·32	92·96	96·93	99·85	98·36	97·60	98·60
All	95·29	93·98	94·92	94·73	96·20	93·60	94·65	94·81

The interaction effects are again mainly due to the extraverted, emotional children; the girls in this group do well, the boys poorly, compared to their colleagues in the other groups. It may be surmised that this result is either due to lower intelligence in the male subgroup, or else to the reactive inhibition produced in the examination-taking situation when confronted with massed practice on relatively monotonous material.

English

The results for this test are given in Table 9.4; as far as sex is concerned they bear out our expectation that girls would be very superior to boys ($p < 0.001$). The other results are identical with those found in the Mathematics paper; N is significant, E highly significant ($p < 0.001$), and the $N \times E$ and $S \times N \times E$ interactions are significant at the 0.01 level. Extraverts do better than ambiverts or introverts, and the interaction seems largely due to the emotional/extravert group, with the girls having good scores and the boys bad ones.

TABLE 9.4. *Scores on English Test*

	Male				Female			
	N−	A	N+	All	N−	A	N+	All
I	90·85	90·63	92·23	91·23	95·71	92·48	96·67	94·95
A	95·71	91·76	100·89	96·12	98·44	97·78	95·87	97·36
E	97·53	99·21	92·49	96·41	103·42	101·28	100·62	101·77
All	94·70	93·87	95·20	94·59	99·19	97·18	97·72	98·03

Reading

The reading test score again shows the familiar pattern with girls superior ($p < 0.001$) and extraverts superior ($p < 0.001$); N shows a significant main effect ($p < 0.05$) and a very significant interaction with E ($p < 0.001$.) The detailed results are shown in Table 9.5. The N main effect would appear to be a curvilinear one, with N+ and N− groups having higher scores than A (average) groups. This effect is in fact universal in all our tests, although it is not usually significant; inspection of the VR tests and the Mathematics and English will demonstrate this general tendency quite clearly. It would be idle to speculate at this point about the possible reasons for this curvilinear trend which in any case, while statistically significant over such a large number of children, is effectively very weak and of little practical importance.

TABLE 9.5. *Scores on Reading Test*

	Male				Female			
	N–	A	N+	All	N–	A	N+	All
I	54·29	54·70	61·01	56·67	58·77	59·42	63·16	60·45
A	66·15	59·75	62·17	62·69	65·94	64·15	63·53	64·54
E	67·08	66·56	66·87	66·84	71·38	70·09	70·57	70·68
All	62·51	60·34	63·35	62·07	65·37	64·55	65·76	65·23

Grammar school entrants: proportions

Table 9.6 lists the proportions of grammar school entrants for the different personality configurations. Both E and N are highly significant (p<0·001), while sex and all interactions are non-significant. Extraversion is a favourable sign for grammar school selection (particularly among the girls, it would appear) and neuroticism/emotionality is an unfavourable sign (again the differences are somewhat larger among the girls than among the boys). The differences are not only statistically significant, but they are clearly of practical importance; the low E—high N girls send 9 per cent to the grammar school, the high E—low N girls 25 per cent. It would be idle to deny the importance in this connection of personality traits, even though some of the variance is presumably mediated through the connection between E and ability/achievement.

TABLE 9.6. *Proportions of grammar school entrants in different groups*

	Male				Female			
	N–	A	N+	All	N–	A	N+	All
I	0·1538	0·1264	0·1593	0·1465	0·2198	0·0934	0·0934	0·1355
A	0·1758	0·1209	0·1264	0·1410	0·2198	0·1319	0·1209	0·1575
E	0·2088	0·1593	0·1923	0·1868	0·2527	0·2637	0·2308	0·2491
All	0·1795	0·1355	0·1593	0·1581	0·2308	0·1630	0·1484	0·1808

Correlational analysis

Product-moment correlations were computed between variables discussed above, for altogether 2,162 girls and 1,869 boys. The correlations are given in Table 9.7: values for boys are set out below the leading diagonal of the matrix, values for girls above. The values in the two halves are reassuringly similar, showing that conclusions can with confidence be drawn from them, and that what is true of boys is equally true of girls. With numbers as large as these, correlations in excess of 0.04 would be statistically significant, although of course not much psychological importance would be attributed to such very low coefficients.

Age has been included in the table for the sake of interest, although of course the variance was very small. Nevertheless, there is a slight positive correlation with E and a slight negative one for N, both in line with the general age trend as set out in the Manual of the JEPI. Age also shows a very slight positive relationship with reading, but an even slighter negative one with intelligence and achievement tests: these are replicated from one group to the other, and must therefore be considered significant statistically. However, the practical importance of these slight values is almost certainly nil, and we will disregard them.

Extraversion, as expected from the analyses of variance, shows positive correlations with the intelligence and achievement tests, ranging from 0.23 to 0.19 for the boys, and from 0.22 to 0.19 for the girls. Neuroticism gives smaller but still highly significant correlations with intelligence and achievement tests, ranging from −0.06 to −0.11 for the boys, and from −0.06 to −0.11 for the girls. The L scale, interestingly enough, also correlates very significantly with intelligence and achievement tests, values ranging from −0.12 to −0.16 for the boys, and from −0.13 to −0.17 for the girls. L does not correlate significantly with E, but does correlate significantly with N (−0.28 and −0.29 respectively for boys and girls); hence one variable could be used as a suppressor variable for the other. Even without doing this, it is clear that the contributions of N and L are additive.

The reading, verbal reasoning, Mathematics and English tests all correlate quite highly together and obviously form the nucleus of a 'scholastic aptitude' factor; all these tests show almost identical relationships with E, N and L. The correlation between VR 70 and VR 71 is of course artificially high because it is more of the nature of a reliability coefficient. Grammar school entrance is positively correlated with the scores on this scholastic aptitude factor, but the correlations are much lower than those between the tests; they range from 0.48 to 0.69, thus leaving over half the variance to be attributed to non-scholastic factors. Personality features appear to play some part in this; entrants are more likely to be extraverted (0.08 and 0.07 respectively, for boys

TABLE 9-7. *Intercorrelations of selected tests*

	1	2	3	4	5	6	7	8	9	10
1 Age		0·06	-0·03	-0·04	0·06	0·05	-0·05	-0·03	-0·05	-0·01
2 E	0·07		-0·21	-0·03	0·22	0·19	0·18	0·19	0·19	0·07
3 N	-0·03	-0·19		-0·29	-0·06	-0·11	-0·11	-0·11	-0·10	-0·09
4 L	-0·06	-0·03	-0·28		-0·17	-0·15	-0·15	-0·13	-0·15	-0·08
5 Reading	0·06	0·23	-0·06	-0·16		0·77	0·74	0·70	0·76	0·48
6 VR 70	-0·05	0·19	-0·11	-0·15	0·77		0·94	0·88	0·85	0·68
7 VR 71	-0·05	0·19	-0·11	-0·14	0·74	0·94		0·90	0·84	0·69
8 Maths.	-0·04	0·20	-0·11	-0·12	0·70	0·87	0·89		0·82	0·64
9 English	-0·04	0·19	-0·10	-0·15	0·81	0·90	0·89	0·82		0·61
10 Grammar school	-0·01	0·08	-0·09	-0·07	0·48	0·67	0·68	0·63	0·65	

(Boys lower part, girls upper part of matrix.)

and girls) and non-neurotic (−0·09 for both sexes). In addition low scores on the L scale seem to be regarded with favour; correlations of −0·07 and −0·08 are found. These correlations are not very high, suggesting that personality as measured contributes only something like 3 per cent to the selection process. This, however, is probably an underestimate; when the figures are corrected for attenuation, as perhaps they ought to be for this purpose, the figure would become somewhat more respectable. Even then, of course, we cannot correct for chance factors in the selection process which probably assume quite a considerable importance, together with home influences and other causes not subject to measurement in this experiment. We would estimate that of the child-contributed variance to the entrance selection procedure, personality factors measured by the JEPI contribute something like 5 per cent to 10 per cent. Such estimates are of course difficult to justify without much more knowledge of all the factors active in the selection process, but they may serve as a base-line on which future research can improve.

Psychological significance

The statistical significance of many of the data reported should not blind us to the fact that with such large numbers of children even quite small differences appear significant, and that, even though these differences appear equally with boys and girls, and are hence replicable, yet their psychological and practical importance may be small. What is required is some yardstick to assess the general importance of observed differences, rather than a measure of statistical significance. A difference in IQ of one point may significantly discriminate between two very large groups, but would be dismissed as unimportant. Where does psychological importance begin, and how can it be indexed? The most obvious index would seem to be some adaptation or other of the method of standard scores, i.e., an indication of the strength of the observed difference in terms of the total variance. In Table 9.8 we have set out, for boys and girls separately, the ratio of observed differences between extraverts and introverts on various tests to the standard deviation of these tests. It will be seen that for boys this ratio is never below one-third, and exceeds one-half in the case of the reading test; for girls the ratio is in all cases but one in excess of one-half. Thus, if we consider the SD of IQ to be 15, the differences between extraverted and introverted boys would amount to something like 6 points, that between extraverted and introverted girls to something like 8 points. These differences are certainly not unimportant from the psychological point of view, and are larger than the sex differences usually reported, and considered of some interest.

TABLE 9.8. *Ratio of observed differences of SDs of tests for extraverts v. introverts*

	Boys	Girls
VR 70	0·34	0·52
VR 71	0·33	0·52
Mathematics	0·40	0·50
English	0·38	0·47
Reading	0·55	0·55

It is clear that for girls the ratios given in Table 9.8 are larger than they are for boys. No explanation is offered for this phenomenon, which in any case may not be replicated in future research; until such replication is reported not too much importance should be attached to this difference. Entwistle and Cunningham (1968) have reported tentatively a similar suggestion.

IV. DISCUSSION

To what extent may our sample be regarded as representative? With respect to verbal intelligence and achievement in Mathematics and English our 1,869 boys and 2,162 girls are not far removed from the national average of 100; the figures are given below in Table 9.9. There is a slight inferiority, but it is too small to give much concern.

TABLE 9.9. *Mean scores on VR 70, Maths and English Papers*

	Boys	Girls
VR 70	98·25	98·35
Maths.	98·19	98·20
English	97·75	97·62
(N)	(1,869)	(2,162)

With respect to personality we would perhaps expect considerable agreement between the figures from this sample and the standardisation data on extraversion; the actual figures bear this out. Boys score on the average 17·42, girls 17·42; this compares with standardisation figures of 17·69 and 17·32 respectively. Variances too are almost identical. In so far as the standardisation sample may be regarded as a proper national sample, so far can we regard our present group as representative. With respect to L we would of course expect our present sample to have lower scores, because high scores were in fact excluded; the means for our group are 3·86 and 3·86 compared with standardisation means of 4·79 and 5·49. Variances are slightly lower, but it is the drop in means which is important and relevant. Concurrent with this drop in L scores, and not unexpected because of the usual negative correlation between L and N, is a rise in N scores. For our group the means are 12·70 and 12·63; these figures should be compared with the standardisation means of 11·10 and 11·83. Variances are slightly reduced, but the important and relevant figure is the difference in means. Our sample is obviously not representative, containing fewer 'liars' (high L scorers) and more 'neurotics' (high N scores). This slight failure to be representative is the price we have to pay for excluding potentially invalid inventories with high lie scores: it is impossible to be sure whether our choice was or was not a reasonable one. In any case the deviation from proper sampling norms is only a marginal one; it is unlikely that any of our main conclusions has been much affected by it.

These conclusions may be listed as follows:

1. Extraverted boys and girls do better scholastically and on verbal reasoning tests than do introverted boys and girls; the relation is linear on the whole, and may be expressed by a product moment correlation coefficient of 0·20 or thereabouts.

2. Emotional boys and girls do only slightly less well than do stable ones, and the significance of N as a main effect is marginal. The relation is curvilinear, with high N and low N children doing better than those with average N.

3. Interaction effects between E and N seem to be related to sex: emotional extraverts do well in the female group, but badly in the male group. This result is partly in line with the findings of Entwistle and Cunningham (1968).

4. Sex differences are apparent in the English paper, but neither in VR nor in Mathematics; the superiority of the girls in English is equalled by their superiority in Reading.

5. Grammar school entrance proportions favour extraverted and stable boys and girls; instability is actually a worse prognosticator for girls than for boys.

6. E scores determine performance of girls more closely than performance of boys.

7. 'Liars' on the L scale tend to be rejected from grammar school entrance; this would of course lower the observed relation between low N scores and acceptance, because of the known negative correlation between N and L. The figures might be more impressive had not very high 'liars' been excluded from the analysis.

These findings present us with some difficult and complex questions. To what extent can we find answers to the casual question implicit in much of what we have said—does intelligence 'cause' extraverted behaviour, or does extraversion 'cause' children to do well in school? We do not believe that our data enable us to answer this type of question, and indeed we are not certain that the question is a meaningful one as phrased. Further research of a more detailed and experimental kind is obviously called for. It is more easily possible to partial out intelligence scores from the personality-achievement correlations, but we have not done this because of doubts about the VR tests being even reasonably pure measures of Burt's 'innate mental ability'; their very high correlations with the achievement tests suggest that scholastic achievement makes such a large contribution to VR scores as to make the task of partial correlation analysis of doubtful value. An exception to this general rule is presented by the grammar school entrance data: here clearly we must try and estimate the influence of personality variables when the influence of ability/achievement is held constant, without however wishing to argue necessarily that the causal sequence goes along this direction. An analysis was undertaken, but will not be reported in detail; it revealed in essence that for most groups the admission rate was governed by ability/achievement, but that introverted boys (but not girls) were accepted more frequently than their VR scores would suggest, and that neurotic boys were selected more frequently, and neurotic girls less frequently, than would be expected on the basis of their VR scores. We do not find it easy to explain these findings. We will come back to these points in a later paper.

Our findings challenge comparison with the Entwistle and Cunningham (1968) paper, which is the only one of those quoted which based its findings on a really adequate number of cases. Working with a sample of 1,472 girls and 1,523 boys aged thirteen, these authors found a significant, negative, linear correlation between N and school achievement ($r = -0.16$); our own figure is slightly lower and there is a suggestion of curvilinearity in the analysis of variance. Possibly the differences are due to the differences in age of the two samples; possibly the curvilinearity is an artefact of the special selection process used to find equal-sized groups for our analysis of variance. In any case there is agreement on the detrimental effect of N school children, as far as school achievement is concerned. Entwistle and Cunningham failed to find a correlation between school achievement and E 'because a distinct sex difference produces an overall non-linear relationship. Extraverted girls and introverted boys tend to be more successful in school work than children with the opposite personality characteristics.' We did find a very significant relationship approximating the value of $r=0.2$ between E and school achievement for both sexes; according to our hypothesis of the introvert 'late developer', this difference between the two investigations would be explained by the age difference between the two samples. Had a fifteen-year-old sample been tested we would have predicted an actual inversion of our results, with introverts superior to extraverts. There may of course be a sex difference in the point of cross-over from E-superiority to I-superiority; Entwistle and Cunningham's data suggest that this point may occur earlier for boys than for girls (but see S. B. G. Eysenck, 1965). Our data agree with Entwistle and Cunningham in suggesting that extraversion is a more positive influence towards school achievement in girls than in boys, although our data emphasise an $E \times N$ interaction which does not appear in their data; in ours, of the emotional girls it is the extraverted one that does *best*, while of the emotional boys it is the extraverted one that does *worst*. There is no overall curvilinear regression of school achievement on E, for boys and girls together, or for each sex separately, as in their Fig. 2. This interaction effect ($N \times E$) may also be a function of age, disappearing as the children get older.

It is clear that Entwistle and Cunningham are right when they say that we are dealing with 'complex inter-relationships about which we still know all too little'. The reason why the problem is a difficult one is clearly related to the differential influence of age and sex on personality and achievement; this makes essential use of very large groups of children, and the coverage of different ages. The present study may serve as an introduction to the analysis of eleven-year-old children, while the Entwistle and Cunningham one serves the same purpose for thirteen-year-old children. A study of fifteen-year-olds would give us an even better perspective, but of course all this would still only be cross-sectional; what is most urgently needed is a good follow-up study, on large numbers of children, taking into account school achievement and intelligence, as well as personality and home background. The advantage we now have is simply that we can frame more clear-cut hypotheses than was possible a few years ago; we are certainly still very far from having any firm answers to our questions.

Some hypotheses have already been suggested by Entwistle and

Cunningham, and by us in a previous section; here we wish merely to point out that the testing of such hypotheses demands a much more analytic approach than has been customary. Eysenck's attempt to make use of the Yerkes-Dodson law in relating achievement in school to N demands for its verification some measure of the *difficulty level* of the school work involved, as this is a crucial parameter of the law in question; what is more, this difficulty level may differ from school to school, or even from class to class, and will almost certainly differ from pupil to pupil. Without measuring these aspects of difficulty level no proper assessment of the value of the theory is possible. Again, motivation is an important variable which is frequently neglected, although it plays a crucial role in the complex of hypotheses which we are considering (Eysenck, 1964); it might with advantage be measured along the lines suggested by Entwistle (1968). Possibly some of the observed differences between extraverts and introverts, and their relation to age, reflect differences in response to social motivation; this may be stronger in the primary school, to give way gradually to intrinsic scholastic motivation. This shift in turn may occur earlier in England than in the USA, where schools are reputed to present a 'softer' option than in England; this may account for the later cross-over between achievement and extraversion in the work of MacNitt (1930) than in that of Eysenck (1965). Some attempt to measure this variable of 'formal work' will have to be made if we wish to test adequately any of the theories which suggest themselves. Complexity in the data does not preclude scientific analysis, but it does demand corresponding complexity of analysis, theory and measurement.

ACKNOWLEDGEMENTS. We are most grateful to the many primary school teachers in Staffordshire who supplied the bulk of the research data; for such whole-hearted co-operation, often involving much effort and many hours of work, they deserve every praise. We are also grateful to the Staffordshire County Council Education Committee for permission to carry out the research and to numerous members of the Health and Education Departments for valuable advice and indispensable assistance. The Maudsley and Bethlem Research Fund gave support to the study.

V. REFERENCES

BUTCHER, H. J., AINSWORTH, M. E., and NESBITT, J. E. (1963) 'Personality factors and school achievement—a comparison of British and American children', *Brit. J. Educ. Psychol.*, 33, 276–86.
CALLARD, M. P., and GOODFELLOW, C. L. (1962) Three experiments using the

Junior Maudsley Personality Inventory. Neuroticism and Extraversion in school boys as measured by JEPI', *Brit. J. Educ. Psychol.*, 32, 241–51.

CATTELL, R. B., SEALY, A. P., and SWENEY, A. P. (1966) 'What can personality and motivation source trait measurements add to the prediction of school achievement?' *Brit. J. Educ. Psychol.*, 36, 280–95.

CENTRAL ADVISORY COUNCIL FOR EDUCATION (1954) *Early Leaving: A Report of the Central Advisory Council for Education*, H.M.S.O.

ENTWISTLE, N. J. (1968) 'Academic motivation of school attainment', *Brit. J. Educ. Psychol.*, 38, 181–8.

ENTWISTLE, N. J. and CUNNINGHAM, S. (1968) 'Neuroticism and school attainment—a linear relationship?' *Brit. J. Educ. Psychol.*, 38, 123–32.

EYSENCK, H. J. (1959) 'Personality and problem solving', *Psychol. Rep.*, 5, 592.

EYSENCK, H. J. (ed.) (1964) *Experiments in Motivation*, Pergamon Press.

EYSENCK, H. J. (1964) *Crime and Personality*, Routledge and Kegan Paul.

EYSENCK, H. J. (1967), *The Biological Basis of Personality*, Springfield, C. C. Thomas.

EYSENCK, S. B. G. (1965) *Manual of the Junior Eysenck Personality Inventory*, University of London Press.

FURNEAUX, W. D. (1962) 'The psychologist and the university', *Universities Quart.*, 17, 33–47.

HALLWORTH, H. J. (1961) 'Anxiety in secondary school children', *Brit. J. Educ. Psychol.*, 31, 281–91.

HOLMES, F. J. (1960) 'Predicting academic success in a general college curriculum', *I.P.A.T. Information Bull.*, No. 4.

HUDSON, J. (1966) *Contrary Imaginations*, Methuen.

JONES, H. GWYNNE (1960) 'Relationship between personality and scholastic attainment', *Bull. Brit. Psychol. Soc.*, 40, 42.

KELVIN, R., LUCAS, C., and OJHA, A. (1965) 'The relationship between personality, mental health and academic performance in university students', *Brit. J. Soc. Clin. Psychol.*, 4, 244–53.

LUNZER, E. A. (1960) 'Aggressive and withdrawing children in the normal school', *Brit. J. Educ. Psychol.*, 30, 119–23.

LYNN, R. (1959) 'Two personality characteristics related to academic achievement', *Brit. J. Educ. Psychol.*, 29, 213–17.

MACNITT, R. D. (1930) *Introversion and Extraversion in the High School*, Boston, R. G. Badger, The Gorham Press.

MORRISON, A., MACINTYRE, D., and SUTHERLAND, J. (1965) 'Teachers' personality ratings of pupils in Scottish primary schools', *Brit. J. Educ. Psychol.*, 35, 306–19.

RIDDING, L. W. (1967) 'An investigation of the personality measures associated with over and under achievement in English and arithmetic', *Brit. J. Educ. Psychol.*, 37, 397–8.

RUSHTON, J. (1966) 'The relationship between personality characteristic and scholastic success in eleven-year-old children', *Brit. J. Educ. Psychol.*, 36, 178–84.

SAVAGE, R. D. (1966) 'Personality factors and academic attainment in junior school children', *Brit. J. Educ. Psychol.*, 35, 91–2.

SCHONELL, F. T., and SCHONELL, F. E. (1960) *Diagnostic and Attainment Testing*, Oliver & Boyd.

SECTION 3
Social relationships

The first article in this section is an extract from Moreno's classical work on sociometry, Who Shall Survive? This extract sets out to show some of the ways in which groups function. It is somewhat more restrained in tone than most of the book, where Moreno's personal philosophy and value judgements come through so strongly that the value of sociometry as an objective means of social measurement seems at times subordinate. The philosophy which this book reflects is a global and Utopian one and is inextricably linked with the aims of measuring social relationships. This emphasis on social relationships in terms of the group, while reflected in most work on the behavioural sciences today, was a definite novelty when Moreno's original work was published. Here you have a portion of a work produced by a man who founded a science.

The second article is much more narrow in scope and restricted in aim. The vast aims of Moreno's work are replaced by a specific problem of social relationships. What happens when children at the eleven-plus are taken from their groups in the primary schools and rearranged in new groups in the secondary schools? This article attempts to show

how teachers rank students in a grammar school, and how the students rank one another. It deals with the concepts of differentiation and polarisation, the culture of the school and the culture of the anti-group. When the students arrive from the primary school, they are usually keen and eager to please, as they have been used to occupying star roles in their respective primary schools. However, as they progress up the school some of them must meet disappointment, a violation of their accustomed role, and Lacey tries to show some of the effects of streaming, the development of an anti-group culture and so on.

The third article, like the second, is very much classroom-based. Even so, Staines starts off with a consideration of the theoretical considerations involved in the theory of Self. He stresses the complexity of the concept of Self, considering how the individual builds up his self-picture from the comments of others and from his own experiences, and how what the child perceives of self is translated into what the child conceives to be self. The theory of the threefold self is considered, where the subject's conception of himself, his conception of what others think of him and his conception of what he ought to be, are all different aspects of the 'truth'.

From this theoretical discussion, Staines concludes that the self is largely a learned structure—postulating that teachers are likely to be very influential in the forming of their pupils' self-pictures. He maintains that personality characteristics are vitally important in this area, attempting to demonstrate that such elements of the self-image as self-confidence and self-acceptance can be changed, depending upon the teaching methods used. This is achieved while still pursuing the usual goals of the classroom, and, to a very large extent, depends upon the comments of the teacher.

V. J. LEE

10

J. L. *Moreno*   Organisation and
                        conduct*

*The first two paragraphs below are from Moreno's book (pp. 219–20);
they explain the context in which Moreno's work, described in the following pages, was carried out.*

The community in which the study was made is near Hudson, New
York; it is the size of a small village, between 500 and 600 persons; it is a
closed community; it has a unisexed population; the girls are still in their
formative age and remain in Hudson for several years until their training
has been completed; they are sent in from every part of New York State
by the courts.

The organisation is dual, consisting of two groups, staff members and
students. There are sixteen cottages for housing purposes, a chapel, a school,
a hospital, an industrial building, a steam laundry, a store, an administration
building, and a farm. The housemother has the function of the parent; all
meals are cooked in the house under the direction of a kitchen officer; the
girls participate in the household in different functions, as waitresses,
kitchen helpers, cooks, laundresses, corridor girls.

We have often followed with our eyes birds, groups of birds in spring,
and watched how they were aligned, one in front, two or three following, then a big bunch close together, then thinning out to three or four,
one or two following alone and one or two still more by themselves, on
the sides. We often wondered by what kind of rules these groupings
are governed. Probably a social instinct drives them to travel in groups.
But we wondered whether the arrangement they produce within these
groupings is influenced by mechanical forces only, speed of flying,

* Reprinted from *Who Shall Survive?* New York, Beacon House, 2nd
edition, 1953, pp. 380–92.

endurance, and so on, or whether attractions and repulsions among the individual birds have a part in producing the formation.

It is certainly so with people. When we observe adolescents at play on the grounds we see how three or four are anxiously trying to keep pace with one who is running ahead, one walking with another arm in arm, two or three scattered, each alone. And if we watched the same group daily, we could ascertain that this arrangement is not accidental, it is repeated at least over a certain period of time in much the same formation until, perhaps, one gets tired of the other and new attachments develop and a new leader comes to the front.

One contrasting element, a coloured child among white children, for instance, produces in general an attitude of interest and sympathy. Eventually the other children may become indifferent towards her but rarely do they become hostile. It is different, however, if the numbers change. If three, four, five or more coloured enter into a group of twenty to thirty white individuals, the emotional attitude tends generally to change. Each of the coloured is sensitive to what happens to the other through the actions of the white group and they are inclined to form into a gang spontaneously. But if the two races are about equal in numbers, hostilities are always ready to be let loose; sympathy and indifference are rarer.

The following incident illustrates such a situation developing in a cottage group. Into C13, which had twenty-nine white girls, an Indian girl, WI, was placed. She became a pet of the housemother and of the girls. Later two half-Indian girls were assigned to the group. The attitude of the group towards the first Indian girl became critical. They were less attentive to her in play and more seldom defended her in quarrels. When the new Indian girls were scolded by the housemother, WI felt it as an affront to herself as well as to them. The three developed gradually a unity of attitude. The white girls began to feel themselves as a group apart from the Indian girls and became less intimate with them. The minority group, however, were the first to become sensitive to the changed situation. When a fourth Indian girl, SN, was placed into the group, she had to be removed from it due to the difficulties among the girls. Contrasting elements appear to have a stimulating effect up to a certain point, but become an irritating factor if this point is overstepped. A sociometric test at this date revealed the Indian girls in a gang formation, rejected by the white and rejecting them in return. The *saturation point* for Indian members seemed to be reached. Soon afterwards it absorbed readily a foreign-born Polish girl and a Russian Jewish girl. This infers that a group can be saturated for one contrasting element and still be able to adjust easily to other contrasting elements. The structural organisation of the group and the degree of differentiation the group has attained indicate its status in respect to saturation for different contrasting elements.

The problem of adjusting contrasting racial and nationality elements into one group appeared to be more difficult in *home* groups than in other collectives. Since the members must live in such close proximity contrasting nationality and racial characteristics are felt more strongly and meet with greater resistance. The saturation point for Negroes and Indians within the same white group was higher in work and play groups than in home groups. Members with different nationality and racial characteristics prove often to be a stimulus for competition and progress for a group. The stimulus appears of greater advantage in work and cultural groups than in home groups. We recognised the need of a balanced distribution of the different races and nationalities within each group and within the community as a whole: that is, the necessity to develop a racial quotient. It appears that one factor in the racial quotient will be found to be dependent upon the criterion of the given collective.

Just as contrasting nationality and racial elements affect group organisation and conduct, other contrasting elements, as sex, have to be considered. If, within a population of 500 to 600 white girls who have lived segregated from the normally organised community, suddenly a group of men appear and reside for a time, a switching of the emotional interest of the girls from their own sex to the men takes place. It can be said that the tele (*or* group spirit) is 'bored' with unisexed attachments only and runs avidly into this new outlet. When a few men reside permanently in such a community they become centres of 'sexual currents' and pampered due to the excessive amount of attention they receive. Another situation develops in Hudson where a group of sixty coloured girls are placed in two cottages of the community. These coloured girls provide a new direction for emotional interest, and under the circumstances a therapeutic advantage to the community in this respect.

In any community there are certain groupings which develop, the organisation of which is influenced by forces coming from within. Home and work groups as they are formed in Hudson result from forces coming exclusively from within the community. But in any community certain groupings develop, the organisation of which is influenced by forces coming from without. We see an instance of this kind in existence in what we may call a 'dual' organisation within a state institution: on the one hand, the group of inmates, and on the other, the group of staff members. 'This is an inmate', or 'This is a member of the staff'. Inevitably a different group attitude of each group towards the other develops, around each of these two criteria. The more the attempt is made to melt these two groupings into one, into a monistic organisation, as, for instance, in Hudson, the more the community gains the character of a large, a huge family. It is then, at least for the time being, as if the children have changed their parents, as if the state has taken them into its parenthood. In this spirit, even the commitment loses its hard character as it can be said that all children are 'committed' to live with their own parents up to a certain age as long as they are minors.

We have already shown that groups with a population of both sexes have an organisation which grows and that the developmental level of a social group can be recognised from the degree of differentiation within its structure. Just as an individual can be 'socially retarded', a whole group can be 'socially retarded'; it may have an organisation corresponding to a developmental level lower than generally found at its age level. Again, we have observed group organisations which were broken up because one set of members within it tended towards producing structures of lower differentiation. On the other hand, group organisation can be 'socially premature' when the organisation of the group is characteristic for a developmental level beyond that of the organisation commonly found at its age level. The development of differentiation demonstrates a different pattern if the population of the group is unisexed. The homosexual current flowing between the members is not counteracted, as in mixed groups, by a heterosexual current.

Through the sociometric test we were able to determine when children begin to develop their own societies and at what age levels these associations gained such an emotional effect upon their members that their conduct is determined more and more by these influences and less and less by the influences coming from the mixed adult–children groups. It appears that the critical age in the adult–child relation begins around the eighth year and that about this time the *child–child relations* within children's associations become more highly organised and less dependent upon the adult.

The cases of isolation which develop from the eighth year to the period of pubescence are not simply isolated, forgotten, left out individuals as found at the kindergarten level but result at least partly from different causes. One set of children is attached to and more affected by the adult group, their family or teachers; another set of children is attached to or more attentive to a group of children. There is also a third set of children. They fall *between* the two social groups which are fundamentally related to every growing individual. They belong to both groups, but not fully to either. This sociometric position seems to mark the beginning of isolation of many individuals who eventually crystallise either apart from both groups, as in schizophrenic conditions, or develop an attitude of aggression. That these isolates finally prefer the boy-gang to the family-gang is due to the fact that whereas their aggression towards the family usually ended in failure, the aggression towards the boy-gang occasionally met with the satisfaction of dominating it. The isolated aggressor has an easier chance here. It is the outcome of such developments which we could study on a large scale in Hudson. Through sociometric tests we found that only 19 per cent of the population was attached to and more easily influenced by adults, while 70 per cent of the population was attached to and more easily influenced by their peers; 11 per cent remained little influenced by either group, isolated.

These facts suggested a difficult therapeutic problem within the community. The staff of adults, housemothers and teachers and others directly in contact with the girls, in all about eighty persons, appeared unable to touch emotionally the larger part of the population. It appears that this fact is the chief reason why the staff of institutions are often forced to resort to rigid discipline and particularly to inflicting punishment if they want to impress their will upon a population the majority of which escapes their spontaneous influencing. In Hudson, if the housemothers, teachers, and others want to impress their will upon the 70 per cent who escape them, they have to resort to the strategy of using the 19 per cent as tools, intermediaries, to reach the 70 per cent. But we have learned through our sociograms that these 19 per cent are often not the key individuals for the majority. They often live within their cottage group in close affiliation with the housemother, segregated and rejected by many of their peers. They emulate the domineering attitude of a housemother which does not stir the rest of the group towards cooperation. And this is the case the more the group gravitates in its conduct in a direction determined by emotional trends, tending towards the development of adolescent gangs.

THE PSYCHOLOGICAL HOME

The family is a complex social group. It consists of two groupings each with a different criterion. The one grouping, composed of the man and the woman, is a sexual grouping. The relation between the man and woman is the dominant factor. It had been started by the two persons alone and existed before children came into it. It had been started without intending to take additional members into it, or at least without knowing whom they might be who would enter into it. The second grouping, composed of the father, the mother and the children, is a monastic grouping, monastic because the spirit of the monastery prevails in this group. The monastery was a revolt against the first grouping. It cut itself off from the matrix and emulated methodically the other portion of the family. Another revolt against the family structure is the communistic attempt to divorce the nurturing of the offspring from their procreators. In this case the second portion of the group is cut away and the original remains. These revolts suggest that the two portions are of different origin and may not always have been together. Group two is probably a further differentiation after a totemistic pattern and it can be assumed that the recognition of consanguinity of father and child aided in melting the two portions into one. The psychological experience of parenthood and the distinction of being a parent derived from it must have been enormous and is to this day. It was somewhat shattered when man learned that his individual contribution to the child is negligible compared to the racial heritage of his kind.

The cottage groups in institutions are more simply organised than is the family. The father–mother situation is not present. Only the second, the monastic portion is left, a unisexed group, or a mixed group with a housemother or a housemother and a housefather, but all unrelated to one another. There is no element of blood-relation binding them one to another. It is an 'experimental home'.

It is difficult for girls who come to a community like Hudson to feel at home as all legitimate motives for such attitude are at first missing: the natural bond feeling as in a successful family group; the feeling of individual liberty and possession; and the feeling of permanent arrangements and objectives. But as we know from observation the importance for children of adolescent age to produce attachment to a nucleus of persons who offer protection and a stimulus for emotional and intellectual progress, it is equally crucial for us to know in what this 'psychological' home which some girls develop and others do not, consists. Is there any possibility to measure this? No girl develops this feeling if she is repulsed by the members of the group who, in turn, do not produce in her any motive for staying with them. 'Home' quality is a nucleus of attractions and repulsions and if the repulsive tendency dominates, the home feeling is wanting.

Every individual gravitates towards a situation which offers him as a personality the highest degree of spontaneous expression and fulfilment and he continuously seeks for companions who are willing to share with him. The psychological home is his goal. This home idea may be identical with his actual home group or it may be related to one or more persons outside towards whom he is attracted. It may even be nothing but a vague notion within his mind. Still it may be sufficient to influence his attitude and conduct in his actual home group. The continued existence of a home depends upon the interest its members have for each other. Any home, to function successfully, must have the support of some portion of the group. The only permanent feature, the only invariable in any home structure, is a configuration of relations, a psychosocial nucleus. The larger the membership of the home group the more important it becomes to determine, from the point of view of its continued existence and of its influence upon the conduct of its members, which members gravitate to persons outside.

An illustration may be taken from one of the cottage groups in Hudson. Cottage 8 has thirty-one members. At the time of the first sociometric test its housemother held the affection, sufficiently to direct their conduct continuously, of Kathryn, May, Grace, Marion, Mafalda, Anna, Jane, Bertha, Felma, Kathleen, Gail and Dorothy. Four of these girls, Marion, Anna, Jane, and Kathleen held strong positions within the group. Marion is attracted to and holds the affection of six girls and five of these are different ones from those the housemother holds: Alice, Sylvia, Gladys, Merline and Lucille. Anna is attracted to and holds the affection of three: Bertha, Jane and Kathleen, whom the housemother holds too, and Laura and Helen, two others, so that she strengthens the bonds of the housemother to these three and further extends her relationship to the latter two. Jane holds the affection of two key individuals, Anna and Marion. Kathleen holds Felma, Anna, Kathryn, May and Grace, all girls whom the housemother holds, and two others, Eva and Letitia. Two girls have a direct personal bond to the housemother only, but not to other girls, Gail and Dorothy. Six girls remain isolated from both housemother and other girls: Lillian, Violet, Louise, Virginia, Marie and Sarah. Four girls, Norma, Edith, Eileen and Charlotte, are bound together into a gang outside the influence of other girls or of the housemother. Thus ten girls remain outside the psychological nucleus of twenty-one girls in the cottage group C8. These ten are evidently indifferent towards the group and the housemother and gravitate towards persons outside the group. The psychological nucleus of the cottage can be described as a chain leadership with the housemother in the centre and twelve girls around her. It is obvious that if by circumstances, either through parole, illness, or reassignment, six of these twelve should leave the cottage at one time the housemother would be faced with a dilemma, the psychological nucleus would be shattered, and the group threatened with disintegration.

In other cottage groups the home nucleus varies in its structure. In C1 with a low membership of twenty, we see the nucleus limited to the housemother and fourteen girls, each strongly related to her but weakly related to one another; further, three girls remain isolated, three unchosen and rejected. In C3 the nucleus revolves around one girl, the housemother remains outside the nucleus, more like a housekeeper. The reason why a large number of these girls who remain unattached to either housemother or girls do not run away is that they have *nowhere to run to*, or else various objectives make the school still more attractive to them than any place they have previously known.

An important factor is the amount of emotional energy each member spends or is able to spend in his home group. This becomes the more obvious the larger the home group, especially to the member who is anxiously interested or responsible in holding the group together, the housemother. The question is how great or small the capacity of the housemother is to hold her girls; how many girls have no attachment to the housemother of the cottage or to another individual able to encourage and adjust her to the group. From this point of view, if a cottage were to have a population of ten girls and five of them remained unintegrated, the group would be worse off than if the population were twenty-five in which the same number were not integrated because the larger the number of girls in a cottage the greater is the opportunity for all eventually to find some agent connecting her with the group. The measure of a housemother's expansiveness is not simply the number but also the personalities of the girls she can hold. Certain girls might require but a minimum of exertion on her part, while for others a maximum of exertion may be called for. The length of time she requires to build up a relation may differ greatly from one girl to another. The ideal principle would be not to assign any new child to any group which has even one member still unintegrated. It is necessary to ascertain accurately the expensiveness of the housemother, as upon it depends the kind of training necessary to increase this capacity and to devise techniques to supplement and substitute natural forces.

We see the natural mother, however large her family, turning her attention to the most helpless, the last-born. This suggests that a housemother should divert her attention to the new child as soon as she comes into her group. The natural mother, when she has one child more disadvantaged, crippled, or backward, transfers to this one an exceptional love and continuously suggests the same spirit to the other members of the family. This procedure leads often to the spoiling of the child and its overdependence upon the mother, but there is a sound principle in it which can be applied to many housemother–child situations.

It suggests that the housemother should not only pay attention to the new child herself, but observe one of the older girls to whom the child is singularly drawn and place upon this girl responsibility in behalf of the child. She has to learn the function of inner assignment in a group, to release numerous functions to the older girls, to turn her attention always to the weakest spot in the group, to assign one girl to another, two girls to a third, a group to a leader and never allow it to happen that one girl is privileged. Instead, she should encourage the development of new centres all the time, as in general, the very limitations she has towards the girls the superior girl-leader has also towards her followers. Such a leader has, just as an adult, a limited capacity to absorb and to respond to love and demands upon her affections. It has often been reported that large families have a greater number of delinquents than small families. This can in large measure be accounted for by the limited emotional expansiveness of man and by his limited aptitude for emotional absorption. Even a natural mother becomes a 'technical' mother as soon as she has to leave one or two of her children to themselves while she performs other duties which call her away from them or because she has so many children that she cannot be attentive to all. This becomes still more obvious in our cottage groups. We see our housemothers unaware of the natural limitations of their emotional expansiveness, getting restless, nervous, irritable, apparently without reason, but behind it is always the same cause, the feeling of her inferiority to play up to all the demands and calls upon her and consequently her attempt to cover up the deficiencies in her cottage through various subterfuges. She may become supersensitive to criticism, quick-tempered when she had not been so before, and use the very slang of the girls in order to impress them quickly. This kind of conduct may delay the housemother's progress in creating a relation or break down in a moment the work of months and affect by indirection her relation to the friends and followers of the severely scolded girl. Other housemothers may try to get away from their limitations through a policy of *laissez-faire*, watching the surface routine of the cottage only. This is another declaration of insufficiency, another example of the technical mother, leaving an emotional vacuum in so many spots of her group unchecked by bonds between herself and the girls or between the girls themselves.

But if the housemother feels that her cottage is her permanent home and the girls with whom she lives her children, she will make an effort to inject all her love and abilities into the situation. If her primary interests are outside the institution, she will be less efficient than the task of a housemother demands and exhaust all her resources.

A special problem in adjustment is represented by the new girl and the new housemother. The more introverted the organisation of a group, the harder is it for an individual to break into it and find adjustment in it, and the more the group will be inclined to develop a feeling of difference and distinction from other groups and correspondingly every individual of this group, a feeling of difference and distinction in respect to individuals of other groups in the given community. When a housemother leaves and a new one replaces her, we see the new housemother beginning with great enthusiasm but soon thereafter becoming hysterical, unsure of herself, anxious for approval and before she reaches the end of this phase, showing fatigue, discouragement, depression. She sees no way out except by giving up the position as outside her aptitude or by following some form of routine. It is necessary to develop a housemother gradually by giving her during the first six months of practice a small number of girls not exceeding the size of a normal family and including not more than one or two children who are especially difficult. When this procedure is not followed and the 'limit' of the housemother (or of anyone in a similar position) is surpassed by force, the performance of this person deteriorates or she simply becomes ill.

There is another factor which determines group reaction towards the new housemother and the new girl. It is the *preserving* influence of group organisation upon the conduct of its members. When, due to increased influx of population a cottage had to be filled beyond its normal capacity, the number of complaints of girls about other girls increased. It reminds us of the old argument that overpopulation leads to war. It seemed natural that the greater the number of girls who have to be accommodated within the same number of rooms the greater can be the opportunity for frictions. We calculated, if overcrowding has an effect upon the conduct of the group, then we should be able to improve the conduct of the group through reducing the number of its members. We had occasion to test this when in C4 five girls were assigned to other groups or paroled within a few days. The number of disciplinary cases dropped immediately. However, when we applied a similar test to C3 and reduced the number of its members below normal capacity, the number of disciplinary cases failed to drop. An analysis of C4 showed that the five girls who had been assigned or paroled from it reduced, on one hand, the overflow to normal capacity and, on the other, removed girls who, while they did not occupy any key-positions within the group, injected a restlessness into it, either because they were anxious to be paroled soon or because they wanted to be assigned to another cottage. But when we analysed C3 we found that we had cut out of its structure girls who were well adjusted within it and hence we had not helped the remainder of the group. In other words, we learned that a *mechanical* reduction of a large cottage group to a smaller one does not necessarily have a therapeutic effect: it depends primarily upon which individuals are cut out and what group organisation remains. C4 had a more highly differentiated structure; the reassignment of the five girls was a necessary operation; the number of disciplinary cases dropped. But in C3 the structure was so undifferentiated that, as it appeared, no reassignment would have substantially aided immediately.

Apparently it is the preserving influence (upon the conduct of its members) of group organisation which is responsible for these reactions. C3 and C4 have as groups a *historical* development. As the number paroled from or newly entering into a cottage group in the course of one year is approximately one-fourth of its population, four years go by before a complete population turnover takes place in a cottage. All individuals who have passed through the group have left their mark according to their position in it. At any time incoming girls meet with an established organisation built not only by the members who are present, but by those who have left a surviving effect upon the group organisation. They are also met by what may be called the *survival* of social and psychological impressions which *predispose* the attitude of the group towards them. This phenomenon preserves the group against any radical innovations the newcomer may seek to impose suddenly. It is a group's *social defence mechanism*. Groups which last over a period of years develop a definite character. The organisation of any such group will explicitly reveal it and this, in turn, will be very suggestive as to what persons should or should not be assigned to it.

It has become evident to us that perhaps the chief factor in the growth of group organisation is this survival of the impress of several layers of older structures and conditions. We see, for instance, a housemother conducting a group; her method has been to show affection and to attach the girls to herself personally. She leaves the cottage and is replaced by a housemother whose method is impersonal and who puts each of the girls into a plan which she has designed. If the former housemother was successful, the new one cannot break the spell of her influence upon the group overnight. This influence may be reflected not only in the individual girl's reactions, but more than that, in the interrelations among the girls. Old structures give way only gradually to new structures.

Similarly the personality of every individual who has been a member of a particular group may leave impressions which survive long after he has departed. We see this illustrated over and over again in certain situations arising within families. Yet we pay one-sided attention to the problem in adjustment it so frequently causes. When a son marries, we pay attention to his problem of adjustment in the new relationship but little attention to the problem arising through the change in the old family organisation he has left. The complaint of the mother that no one is able to fill his place now that he has left is a popular suggestion of the survival effect of an individual after departure from a group. Many disturbances within the group arise due to such *negative* reasons. The interrelations which are cut out of the group structure by his leaving are not at once replaced.

11

C. Lacey

Some sociological concomitants of academic streaming in a grammar school*

A great deal is now known about the macro-sociology of secondary education in this country. Recent studies[1] focusing on selection for entry and on the performance in secondary schools of pupils with various social and psychological characteristics, have sketched in the major dimensions of the problem. This paper, on the other hand, which is an early report on one aspect of the research in the sociology of education, being undertaken at Manchester University,[2] is an attempt to lay bare some of the micro-sociological mechanisms within one school and dwells primarily on processes of differentiation and sub-culture formation. It must therefore be seen against the background of well-established findings in the field. The paper contains three sections:

1. A description of some of the sociological characteristics of boys entering the school.

* Reprinted from *British Journal of Sociology*, 14, 1966, 245–62.

[1] See, for example, J. E. Floud, A. H. Halsey and F. M. Martin, *Social Class and Education Opportunity*, Heinemann, 1957; J. W. B. Douglas, *Home and School*, MacGibbon & Kee, 1963; Central Advisory Council for Education's Report of 1954, *Early Leaving*, HMSO.

[2] This is the first report on research financed by a grant from the Ministry of Education to the Department of Sociology and Social Anthropology in the University of Manchester. A team of three research associates (Mrs Audrey Lambart, Mr David Hargreaves and myself) was appointed to undertake research in different schools. The work of the team was co-ordinated by Drs R. Frankenberg and V. G. Pons and owes a great deal to the interest of Professors M. Gluckman, P. Worsley and Dr A. H. Halsey of Oxford University, who acted as consultant to the scheme.

2 (*a*) A descriptive analysis of some aspects of the developing informal structure of one class in the school, with particular reference to two case studies.

(*b*) An attempt to establish a model which describes the passage of pupils through the school.

3. An attempt to verify the model through the use of quantitative indices—in particular, the concepts of differentiation and polarisation which are developed in section 2 (*b*).

The overall aim is to provide a picture of the stratification and subsequent sub-culture development, associated with academic streaming.

SECTION I. THE INTAKE

The grammar school is a highly selective institution. To start with, therefore, it is important for us to investigate the ways in which this selection affects the composition of the newly recruited first-year classes. It is only possible to talk about subsequent sub-cultural development if the initial characteristics of the group are clear.

The particular factors that will concern us here are:

1. The way selection restricts the intake to a particular type of student.
2. The way selection isolates the successful candidate from his fellow pupils and friends at his junior school.

1. Though not completely conclusive, the evidence gathered supports my contention that the new intake to a grammar school will consist largely of eleven-year-olds who have been accustomed to playing what I have called 'best pupil' role in their junior schools, and are, in their new environment, often separated from their former school friends. The extent to which this is true in any grammar school will, of course, depend on a large number of factors, such as the percentage of grammar school places available and the number and the size of junior and grammar schools in the catchment area.

It is useful to look at Hightown Grammar School[3] as an illustration of the way the selection process works.

The Local Education Authority of Hightown sends about 15 per cent of its eleven-year-olds to grammar schools each year. This clearly

[3] Hightown is a pseudonym for the town in which the school is located and I therefore refer to the school itself as Hightown Grammar School. I conducted eight months' full-time and ten months' part-time fieldwork in the school. In all I have been associated with this school and others in the area for $3\frac{1}{2}$ years.

does not imply that 15 per cent of the pupils in *any* junior school in the town will find themselves in the same grammar school. There are six grammar schools in Hightown and these are specialised in a number of ways; there are two Roman Catholic grammar schools (one for boys and one for girls) which serve the separate RC education system in Hightown and the surrounding area; and four LEA grammar schools (two for girls and two for boys) which draw their pupils almost exclusively from Hightown. For non-Catholic, eleven-year-old boys in Hightown there are then three possible grammar school avenues; entry to a direct grant school outside the town, Hightown Grammar School and Hightown Technical Grammar School. (A very small fraction attend public schools.)

The distribution of boys between these avenues is, however, complicated by the unequal reputation of the schools to which they have access. A few of the most able boys compete successfully for places in direct grant schools, the bulk of the most able enter Hightown Grammar and the remainder enter Hightown Technical Grammar.

Table 11.1 shows that the boys entering Hightown Grammar are selected from a large number of junior schools, and that the selection test tends to scoop a few pupils from each school. Over half the boys come from schools that send six or less pupils. Evidence from a variety of sources (junior school reports, autobiographies and the statements of junior school teachers etc.) clearly shows that these contingents include the vast majority of top scholars, team leaders, school monitors, head boys and teachers' favourites. In short they are the 'best pupils'.

TABLE 11.1. *1962 intake to Hightown Grammar classified according to size of junior school contingents*

Mean size = 3·5 boys per contingent

	Size of contingents				
	1–3	4–6	7–9	10–12	Total
Number of junior schools	24	5	4	2	35
Number of pupils	42	25	30	21	118

2. The relative isolation of pupils from their former schoolmates is only partially illustrated in Table 11.1. When the boys arrive at Hightown Grammar they are divided at random into four classes. These classes are also House Groups. The pupils in them remain together for prayers, school meals and registration as well as lessons.

A more comprehensive picture of the degree of isolation of the first-year boy, on his arrival at Hightown, must therefore take into account the effect of the school organisation. In order to do this I used 'friend-ship choice' questionnaires, from which it was possible to extract the number of boys who had friends in their first-year classes who had attended the same junior school as themselves. This showed that 58 boys out of 118 questioned had no friend from the same junior school in their class. Thus almost half of the first-year intake spend the great majority of their time at school in a class in which they are isolated from their previous friends.

It can be seen from the foregoing analysis that any batch of new boys assembling at Hightown Grammar School are likely to make up a highly selected and homogeneous group. The annual intake being about 120, they represent under 4 per cent of their age group in the community and all are boys who have ostensibly been selected on the basis of their sex, religion and academic achievement. Only the direct grant grammar schools are more selective; their pupils are likely to have achieved a higher academic standard and to find themselves even more isolated from their junior school friends.

The homogeneity of the intake and the relative isolation of indi-vidual new boys from their junior school friends are both important factors affecting patterns of behaviour in the first-year classes. The first-year pupils show a high degree of commitment to the school. School uniform is rigidly adhered to; caps and blazers are proudly dis-played, school functions and clubs are attended disproportionately by first-year boys. Their behaviour in the classroom is characterised by eagerness, cooperation with the teacher and a high degree of competi-tion among themselves. 'Please sir, Willy Brown is copying my sums' is a remark that could only come from a first-year boy. I once tried to measure the response rate to a narrative and question-and-answer lesson given by a History teacher. So many responded to each question that I could not record them. As the tension mounted boys who did not know the answers looked around apprehensively at those who did. These were in a high state of excitement and they smiled triumphantly at those who did not know the answers; they stretched their arms and bodies to the utmost as they eagerly called 'sir', 'sir', 'sir', every time the master glanced in their direction. When the master said 'All right, Green, you tell us', there were quiet sighs and groans as those who had not been called upon subsided into their seats. The whole performance was repeated as soon as the next question was asked.

During such spells the desire to participate was so great that some boys would put up their hands and strain for notice, even though they had no idea of the answer. And, if asked to give the answer, they would either make a gesture suggesting that they had suddenly forgotten, or else subside with an embarrassed and confused look, to the jeers and groans of the rest of the class who would then redouble their efforts to attract attention.

The type of enthusiasm characteristic of a first-year class was occasionally found in second- or third-year forms but there were a number of observable differences. The second and third forms were more likely to 'play dead' and to allow five or six people to 'do all the work'; and, even if the master succeeded in getting a larger proportion to participate, there was always a residue of boys who hardly participated or who only did so by giving obviously wrong or funny answers. Finally there was the possibility that the form would use any excitement of this kind to sabotage the lesson or to play the fool. For example, a boy will stretch so hard that he falls out of his desk, another will accidentally punch the boy in front as he puts up his hand and the form's 'funny man' will display his wit in response to an ambiguous question—sometimes isolating the teacher from the class by referring to a private class joke.

First-year forms are thus widely regarded by teachers as the easiest and most rewarding to teach. They are typically allocated to young inexperienced masters or to masters who have difficulty with discipline. Misdemeanours are largely the result of high spirits, over-eagerness or forgetfulness rather than conscious malice. Hopes are high and expectations as to school performance and subsequent careers are unrealistically rosy.

SECTION 2 (*a*). THE INFORMAL STRUCTURE—TWO CASE STUDIES

As soon as this highly selected first-year population meets at Hightown Grammar School and is allocated to the four first-year classes, a complex process of interaction begins. This process takes place through a variety of encounters. Boys talk and listen to each other, talk and listen to teachers, listen to conversations, notice details of accent, gesture, clothing, watch others at work and at play in various situations and in innumerable different permutations.

During the first few days much of this interaction appears to take place in a fairly random way influenced mainly by the physical and organisational arrangements. Soon, patterns of selection begin to emerge. Various initial interactions yield information and experience, which are retained by the individual and provide some basis for the interpretation and partial control of other interactions. This partial control is extremely important because it soon gives rise to a recognisable, although unstable and changing structure.

When I started observing the first-year classes in March 1963, the members of each class had only been together for about six months, but each class already had a definite structure of which the pupils clearly had detailed knowledge. When a master called a boy to read or answer a question, others could be seen giving each other significant looks which clearly indicated that they knew what to expect.

On one occasion, for example, a master asked three boys to stay behind after the lesson to help him with a task calling for a sense of responsibility and cooperation, the master called 'Williams, Maun and Sherring'. The class burst into spontaneous laughter, and there were unbelieving cries of 'What, Sherring?' The master corrected himself. 'No, not Sherring, Shadwell.' From the context of the incident, it was clear that Sherring's reputation was already inconsistent with the qualities expected of a monitor. On another occasion, Priestley was asked to read and the whole class groaned and laughed. Priestley, a fat boy, had been kept down from the previous year because of ill health (catarrh and asthma) and poor work. He grinned apprehensively, wiped his face with a huge white handkerchief and started to read very nervously. For a few moments the class was absolutely quiet, then one boy tittered, Priestley made a silly mistake, partly because he was looking up to smile at the boy who was giggling, and the whole class burst into laughter. Priestley blew his nose loudly and smiled nervously at the class. The teacher quietened the class and Priestley continued to read. Three lines later a marked mispronunciation started the whole class laughing again. This performance continued with Priestley getting more and more nervous, mopping his brow and blowing his nose. Finally, the master with obvious annoyance snapped, 'All right, Priestley, that's enough!'

This short incident, one of several during the day, served to remind Priestley of his structural position within the class and to confirm the opinions and expectations of the class and the teacher towards him. Priestley's behaviour was consistent with his performance in the examinations at the end of the Autumn term when he was ranked twenty-ninth out of thirty-three.

During this period of observation I also noticed the significance of the behaviour of another boy, Cready. Cready first attracted my attention because, although his form position was similar to Priestley's (twenty-sixth) he habitually associated with a strikingly different group. He behaved very differently in class, and had a markedly different reputation.

Cready was a member of the school choir and it so happened that the English master, whose classes I was observing, was also the music

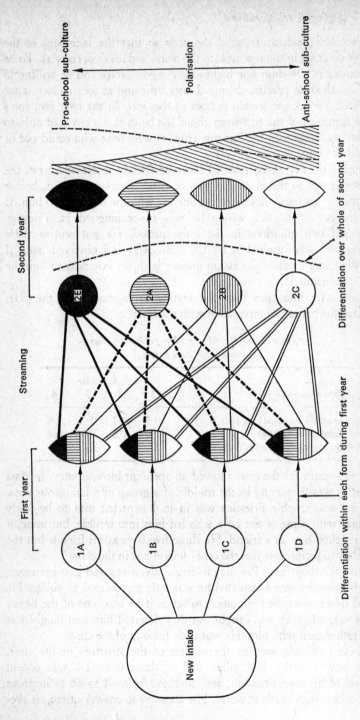

Fig. 11.1 Differentiation and polarisation association with the streaming that takes place at the end of the first year

teacher and he had arranged the class so that the members of the school choir sat in the row next to the piano and his desk (row 4). To be a member of the choir one had to have a good voice and be willing to stay in school to practise during dinner time and at four o'clock, once or twice a week for certain periods of the year. In the next two rows were members of the first-form choir. To be in this a boy had only to be willing to sing. In the last row (row 1) were boys who could not or would not sing.

During the first three lessons I observed Cready answered four of the questions put to the class. On two of these occasions he had, before putting up his hand, discussed the answer with the boy next to him. If Cready got an answer wrong he was never laughed at. Priestley answered two questions in the same period. He got one of these wrong and was laughed at by the class. Also as I observed later, if Priestley attempted to discuss an answer with the boy next to him, he was reprimanded.

Table 11.2 illustrates how the seating arrangements in the class affected the pattern of interaction with the teacher:

TABLE 11.2. *Record of teacher–pupil interaction—average for three lessons*

| | Row number | | | |
Type of interaction	1	2	3	4
Answers to questions (per boy)	0.5	0.7	1.3	3.6
Rebukes (per boy)	1.6	1.2	0.5	0.4
Questions from boys (totals)	3	1	2	10

A sociogram for the class showed an apparent inconsistency. In class Priestley was frequently in the middle of a group of mischievous boys. If there was trouble Priestley was in it. I expected him to be fairly popular with some of the boys who led him into trouble, but none of them picked him as a friend. He chose five boys as his friends but the only boy to reciprocate was the other Jewish boy in the class.

The other boys used Priestley to create diversions and pass messages, and because he was so isolated he was only too pleased to oblige. He could never resist the temptation to act as if he was 'one of the boys'. However, when he was caught out they deserted him and laughed at him rather than with him. He was truly the butt of the class.

These incidents, seen in the context of the structure of the class, show how Priestley had fallen foul of the system. He was not in control of his own situation, and anything he tried to do to improve his position only made it worse. His attempts to answer questions pro-

voked laughter and ridicule from his class-mates. His attempt to minimise the distress this caused, a nervous smile round the class, a shrug
of the shoulders; pretending either that he had caused the disturbance
on purpose or that he did not care, served to worsen his position with
the teacher.[4]

He compensated for his failure in class and lack of academic success
by learning the stocks and shares table of the *Financial Times* every
week. This enabled him to develop a reputation in a field outside the
sphere in which the school was competent to judge. He would emphasise the *real* importance of this in his future career and thus minimise
the effect of his scholastic failure. Even this did not improve his standing in the school, especially with the staff. It served only to explain his
laziness, his bad behaviour and lack of concern with school work.
'Oh Priestley, he is just biding his time with us, from what I hear his
future is assured anyway.' 'He is just lazy,' said the English master.

If I had had to forecast the future performance of these boys on the
evidence I would, of course, have expected Cready to do better in the
following examinations and Priestley if anything, worse:

Examination results:

		First-year exams				Second-year exams		
		Autumn	*Spring*	*Summer*		*Autumn*	*Spring*	*Summer*
Priestley	1A	29	30	26	2C	12	27	16
Cready	1A	26	10	10	2E	11	12	10

It is interesting to note the family background of these two boys.
Priestley is Jewish, second in a family of three and lives in an area of
expensive detached houses. His father is a clearance stock buyer.
Cready on the other hand lives on a council estate, is fourth out of six
in the family and his father is a quality inspector in an abrasives
factory.

Cready and Priestley do not, therefore, conform with the established
correlation between academic achievement and social class. Cready, a
working-class boy from a large family on a council estate, is making
good, while Priestley, an upper-middle-class boy from a smaller family,
is failing academically. However, this negative case highlights the point
I want to make; there was a measure of autonomy in the system of
social relations of the classroom. The positions of Cready and Priestley

[4] This pattern holds good for the other lessons I observed in this class.
However, I do not wish to imply that this relationship between seating,
class position and interaction is typical of the school as a whole. Other
classes have different patterns.

are only explicable in the light of an analysis of the system of social relations *inside* the classroom. This system is open to manipulation by those who are sensitive to its details. Hence Cready, who had all the major external factors stacked against him, was able to use the system of social relations to sustain and buoy himself up, while Priestley, despite all the advantages that he brought to the situation, had fallen foul of the system and was not only failing but also speedily losing any motivation to succeed in the sphere in which the school was competent to judge him.

I reiterate that this is not an attempt to disprove the general established trend but to highlight the fact that there are detailed social mechanisms and processes responsible for bringing it about, which are not completely determined by external factors. By studying these mechanisms it will be possible to add a dimension to our understanding of the general processes of education in our schools.

SECTION 2 (*b*). DIFFERENTIATION AND POLARISATION

It is important to discuss these processes in a more general way and set up a model which describes the passage of pupils through the grammar school. To do this, I will need to introduce two terms—'differentiation' and 'polarisation'.

By differentiation is meant the process of separation and ranking of students according to a multiple set of criteria which makes up the normative academically orientated, value system of the grammar school. This process is regarded here as being largely carried out by teachers in the course of their normal duties.

Polarisation on the other hand is regarded as a process taking place within the student body, partly as a result of differentiation but influenced by external factors and with an autonomy of its own. It is a process of sub-culture formation in which the school-dominated normative culture is opposed by an alternative culture which I will refer to as the anti-group culture. The content of the anti-group culture will, of course, be very much influenced by the school and its social setting. It may range from a folk music, CND group in a minor public school to a delinquent sub-culture in a secondary modern school in an old urban area. In Hightown Grammar School it fell between these extremes and was influenced by the large working-class and Jewish communities of Hightown.

There are a number of scales on which a master habitually rates a boy. For the purposes of the analysis I will consider two.

(*a*) Academic scale.

(*b*) Behaviour scale. This would include considerations as varied as general classroom behaviour and attitudes, politeness, attention, help-fulness, time spent in school societies and sports.

The two are not independent. Behaviour affects academic standards not only because good behaviour involves listening and attending but because a master becomes favourably disposed towards a boy who is well-behaved and trying hard. The teacher, therefore, tends to help him and even to mark him up. I have found in my own marking of books that when I know the form (i.e. good and bad pupils) I mark much more quickly. For example, I might partly read the essay and recognise the writing 'Oh, Brown. Let's see, he tries hard, good neat work, missed one or two ideas—7/10' or, 'This is a bit scruffy, no margin, not underlined, seems to have got the hang of it though. Who is it? Oh, Jones, that nuisance—5/10!'

There is another reason why good behaviour is correlated with academic achievement. A boy who does well and wishes to do well academically is predisposed to accepting the system of values of the grammar school, that is he behaves well. This is because the system gives him high prestige and it is therefore in his interest to support it; the membership of the choir illustrates this point. He is thereby sup-porting his position of prestige. On the other hand a boy who does badly academically is predisposed to criticise, reject or even sabotage the system, where he can, since it places him in an inferior position.[5]

A boy showing the extreme development of this phenomena may subscribe to values which are actually the inverted values of the school. For example, he obtains prestige from cheeking a teacher, playing truant, not doing homework, smoking, drinking and even stealing. As it develops, the anti-group produces its own impetus. A boy who takes refuge in such a group because his work is poor finds that the group commits him to a behaviour pattern which means that his work will stay poor and in fact often gets progressively worse.

The following extracts from an essay entitled 'Abuse' and written by a first-form boy for his housemaster, illustrates a development of anti-group values of an extreme nature for a first-year pupil.

> I am writing this essay about abuse in the toilets. . . . What they (the prefects) call abuse and what I call abuse are two different things altogether.
>
> All the people where I live say I am growing up to be a 'Ted' so I try to please them by acting as much like one as I possibly can. I go around kicking a ball against the wall that is nearest to their

[5] For a fuller exposition of this argument specifically related to delin-quency, see A. Cohen, *Delinquent Boys*, Collier-Macmillan, 1955.

house and making as much noise as I can and I intend to carry on doing this until they can leave me alone. . . . It seems to me the Grammar School knows nothing about abuse for *I would much rather be a hooligan and get some fun out of life than be a snob always being the dear little nice boy doing what he is told.*

In Section 1 we saw that at the beginning of the first year, the pupils constitute a relatively homogeneous and undifferentiated group. They are uniformly enthusiastic and eager to please, both through their performance of work and in their behaviour. The pupils who are noticed first are the good pupils and the bad pupils. Even by the Spring term some masters are still unsure of the names of quiet pupils in the undifferentiated middle of the classes they teach.

It is fairly rare for an anti-group to develop in the first year. Although one or two individuals may develop marked anti-group values, they are likely to remain isolates. In the 1962 first year, I was able to recognise only one, Badman, quoted earlier. He wished to be transferred to a secondary modern.

The more usual course of events associated with a marked degree of (relative) failure in the first year is for the child to display symptoms of emotional upheaval and nervous disorder and for a conflict of standards to take place. Symptoms that occurred in the first year intake of 1962 included the following:

Bursting into tears, when reprimanded by a teacher.
Refusal to go to school or to go to particular lessons, accompanied by hysterical crying and screaming.
Sleeplessness.
Bedwetting.
Truanting from certain lessons or truanting from school.
Constantly feeling sick before certain lessons.
One boy rushed to stage in assembly clutching his throat and screaming that he could not breathe.
Consistent failure to do homework.
High absence record.
Aggravation of mild epilepsy.

The fifteen cases recorded probably represent all the cases of major disturbance but a large number of the cases of minor disturbance probably never became known to the school.

The individual significance of these cases cannot be discussed here but their general significance is important to the model under discussion. We have seen that the 11+ selects the 'best pupils' from the top forms of the junior schools. These forms have been highly differentiated in preparation for the 11 + examination. The pupils have, in many cases, been 'best pupils' for some time and have internalised many of the expectations inherent in the position of 'best pupils'. Their transfer to the grammar school not only means a new environment, with all that such a change entails—for example, new class-mates, new teachers and new sets of rules—but also for many of them a violation of their expectations as best pupils. It is when this violation of expectations coincides with 'unsatisfactory' home backgrounds that the worst cases of emotional disturbance occur.

In the second year the process of differentiation continues. If streaming takes place between the first and second years as it did in the year group I am studying it helps speed the process and a new crop of cases of emotional disturbance occur. In the 1963 second year most of these cases were associated with boys who were failing to make the grade in the top stream and boys who were in the bottom half of the bottom stream. After six months in the second year this bottom stream was already regarded as a difficult form to teach because, to quote two teachers:

1. 'They are unacademic, they can't cope with the work.'
2. 'Give them half a chance and they will give you the run around.'

The true anti-group starts to emerge in the second year, and it develops markedly in the third and fourth years. It is in the third and fourth years that strenuous efforts are made to get rid of anti-group pupils. Considerable pressure is put on the Headmaster by the teachers that take the boys and the Head in turn transmits this to the Board of Governors. In most cases application to leave will also be made by the boy and his parents. However, the Board of Governors are often loath to give permission for a boy to leave or transfer for two reasons. (1) The governors are also the governors for the secondary modern schools in the area and cannot readily agree to passing on discipline problems from the grammar school to the secondary modern. (2) They are generally very suspicious of grammar school teachers and feel reluctant to risk an injustice to a pupil who is often a working-class boy.

However, there are some requests that cannot easily be refused, for example cases of ill health, family hardship or consistent truanting. There are also a number of cases of unofficial leaving. In these cases the boy has actually left school and taken a job but is still being marked as absent in the register. It is difficult to estimate accurately the extent of the total loss but in two years somewhere between ten and fifteen pupils left or were transferred from each year before taking 'O' level or reaching the age of sixteen.

A similar process can be observed in the sixth form and results in a crop of leavers in the first-year sixth. The extent to which differentiation develops and is internalised in the sixth is illustrated by the following remark made to the Economics master. He had just rebuked a boy in the Upper Sixth Modern and told him that unless he worked harder he would not pass Economics 'A' level: 'Well, the way I look at it is this: If some of the boys in the General[6] form can get it and they usually do, then I should be all right.'

SECTION 3

The indices developed in this part of the paper are prepared from two questionnaires completed by all members of the 1962 intake. One questionnaire was given at the end of the first year and one at the end of the second. The indices are designed to illustrate the processes of differentiation and polarisation.

On both occasions the boys were asked who had been their close friends over the last year. They were asked to restrict themselves to boys in the school and to six choices, unless they felt they definitely could not do so.

There was virtually no difference in the average number of choices *received* per boy in the four *unstreamed* first-year classes.

TABLE 11.3

1A	4·1 choices per boy	
1B	4·1 ,, ,, ,,	
1C	4·2 ,, ,, ,,	
1D	4·5 ,, ,, ,,	

When the boys were streamed on academic criteria at the end of the first year these same friendship choices were related to the new forms 2E 2A 2B 2C, see Table 11.4(*a*).[7]

Not only do the figures reveal striking differences but these differences are related to academic achievement. At the end of the first year, the higher up the academic scale a boy was placed, the more likely he was to attract a large number of friendship choices.

At the end of the second year the boys were asked the same question. The response was equally striking. Column (*b*) of Table 11.4 shows

[6] The general stream is the bottom stream in the sixth form.
[7] Approximately the top one-quarter of each first-year form went into 2E, the second quarter into 2A and so on.

that the year spent among a new class of boys has hardly changed the overall positions of 2E, 2A, and 2B, although the actual friendship choices for any one boy will have undergone considerable change. However, 2C has undergone a substantial change. The increase from 3·3 to 4·3 for 2C represents an increase of something like 30 choices, in a class of 30 boys. That the new popularity of the boys in 2C is brought about by the growth of a new set of norms and values or the beginnings of the anti-group sub-culture is demonstrated by Table 11.5. The boys of 2C have become popular for the very reasons that they were unpopular in their first year.

TABLE 11.4. *Average number of friendship choices received per boy after streaming: first year and second year*

	Average number of choices per boy in each class	
	(*a*) 1st year	(*b*) 2nd year
2E	4·8	5·0
2A	4·5	4·5
2B	3·9	3·9
2C	3·3	4·3

The boys of 2E and 2A who according to our hypothesis *should* be positively influenced by the academic grading, since they are successful in relation to it, show that it does in fact have a marked positive influence on their choice of friends (e.g. 2E make 24 choices into 2A, 13 choices into 2B and only 7 into 2C). There is no element in the organisation of the school that could bring this about.

TABLE 11.5. *Distribution of friendship choices according to class: second year 1963 (1962 intake at end of second year)**

Number in each class in brackets	2E	2A	2B	2C	Others	Total of choices made	% of choices in own class
2E (31)	96	24	13	7	11	151	63·2
2A (31)	28	94	16	6	14	158	59·5
2B (28)	20	17	63	23	20	143	45·6
2C (30)	9	4	18	92	13	136	67·2
TOTALS (of choices received)	153	139	110	128	58	588	

* Read across for choices made, down for choices received by each class.

In 2B a change takes place. Their choices into 2E and 2A have the expected form but there is an unexpectedly large number of choices into 2C, i.e. 23, more than into either 2E or 2A. Similarly, the boys of 2C show a marked tendency to choose their friends outside 2C, from 2B rather than 2E and 2A. There must be a basis, other than the school-imposed academic values, on which these friends are chosen. This alternative set of norms and values I have already referred to as the anti-group sub-culture.

Table 11.6 shows that in the second year academic achievement is related to social class. To some degree this a problem of working-class and middle-class culture.[8] That this is not the whole answer, is demonstrated by reminding ourselves of Table 11.4(*a*) and (*b*) where it is clearly demonstrated that this anti-group development took place

TABLE 11.6. *Distribution of the sons of non-manual workers between the four second-year streams*

	Non-manual/manual ratio	Ratio
2E	18/14	1·3
2A	18/13	1·4
2B	13/14	0·9
2C	8/23	0·3

between the ends of the first and second year. If it were solely a social class phenomena it would have been apparent at the end of the first year.

This analysis is confirmed by another set of data which is in many ways complementary to the first. In the second year questionnaire I asked 'What boys do you find it difficult to get on with?' Once again I allowed them to put up to six names unless they felt they could not possibly confine themselves to six. This time, however, many boys refrained from putting any names down and only a few put six. Enough names were mentioned to establish a pattern of unpopularity. Once again the largest number of choices were made into the informants own class.

The number of choices made into other forms was always less than 7 with one notable exception—2C received 26 from 2E, 9 from 2A and 20 from 2B and so received the highest number of unpopularity choices, 97 compared with 53 for 2E which is the next highest.

[8] See D. N. Holly, *British Journal of Sociology*, June 1965, for analysis of the effect of social class on performance in a comprehensive school.

TABLE 11.7. *Distribution of choices of unpopular boys: second year, 1963*

	2E	2A	2B	2C	*Others*	*Prefects*	Total of choices made	*Average number of choices received*
2E	38	4	4	26	3	0	75	1·71
2A	5	33	1	9	22	1	51	1·45
2B	7	4	24	20	1	0	56	1·14
2C	3	4	3	42	3	6	61	3·23
TOTALS (of choices received)	53	45	32	97	29	7	243	

The preponderance of choices into 2C is explained by the anti-group development in 2C. These boys are now regarded as bullies and 'tough eggs' who in Badman's terminology would rather be hooligans and have a good time than be nice little boys. They are aggressive, loud-mouthed and feared by many who are successful in terms of the dominant school norms.

An expectation that is considerably altered by academic streaming is the school-leaving age. Boys who are successful will expect to continue after 'O' level at fifteen or sixteen into the sixth form.

At the end of the first year the boys were asked 'At what age would you like to leave school?'

The results demonstrate the overall optimism of the first year. Only 25 per cent wanted to leave at the end of the fifth year, 75 per cent desiring a sixth-form career. In practice only something like 50 per cent ever achieve this. When the figures were broken down into the second-year classes they reveal, even so, considerable foresight.

Even the relatively low value of 2E compared with 2A is fairly

TABLE 11.8. *Average age at which the boys in each class would like to leave school*

	Before streaming at end of first year	*After streaming at end of second year*
2E	17·4	17·4
2A	17·7	17·3
2B	17·3	17·4
2C	17·0	16·7

realistic in that since 2E take the GCE at the end of four years compared with the normal five for 2A, B and C, many will expect to
complete their sixth-form career at 17½ compared with the normal
18½. The fact that at this stage in their school career they had not been
told officially that they would be going into 2E in the following year
only marginally affects the situation because by this time the process of
structuring and differentiation had gone on sufficiently for most boys
to know whether they would go into 2E or not. In the same questionnaire 28/32 of the boys who eventually went into 2E indicated that 2E
was the second-year class of their choice.

By the end of the second year, the averages of the desired leaving
age revealed a number of puzzling features.

2E remained the same while the average age for 2A fell below 2B.
2B's average in fact increased to the same level as 2E, 2C's average
value decreased, but not as much as one might expect. The situation
has been complicated by an additional factor which I have called
'streaming reaction'.

When the top seven or eight boys from each of the first year house-
groups are put into 2E it is fairly obvious that most of them are not
going to be able to maintain a high position in the form. In fact
Table 11.9 shows that only two were able to maintain their position,
the rest were all placed lower in 2E than in their first-year class.
This was less marked in 2A with only sixteen boys doing less well.
It was reversed in 2B and 2C.

TABLE 11.9. *Examination performance before streaming compared
with examination performance after streaming*

	Number of boys who were placed higher in second year than in first year	Same	Number of boys who were placed lower in second year than in first year
2E	0	2	28
2A	7	4	16
2B	17	2	6
2C	15	0	2

The depressing effect of streaming reaction on the Express form is
unlikely to influence their estimates of the length of their school
careers to any great extent, because all the E stream are expected to go
into the sixth form and they are told this constantly throughout the
year. A typical remark would be, 'All of you will be expected to go
on into the sixth form and *many* of you will I hope go on to university'.

Streaming reaction is very marked in the E stream but it takes on a different form (see later).

2C is also affected by its polar position. It is not much to a boy's credit to have got a higher place in the class if that class is 2C. Masters discussing 2C with me put it bluntly. 'There is not one boy in the class who has any sort of academic ability. In fact most of them shouldn't be in the school at all. It's not fair on them and it's not fair on the school.' Remarks of this sort were frequently made while talking to me in front of the class and were obviously audible to the front rows of boys, as well as to myself. The low prestige of 2C therefore minimised the correcting effects of streaming reaction, with respect to leaving age.

It was in 2 A and B that streaming reaction had its maximum effect. The relative positions of the two forms were for a long while ambiguous, since the head had not made it clear. Some masters thought that 2A and 2B were on the same level, others that 2A was better than 2B. Only one master thought that 2B was academically better than 2A but it is significant that he was able to make the mistake and hold to it for a considerable length of time.

In these two classes then, streaming reaction was a major factor in affecting the length of time that the boys wanted to stay at school.

TABLE 11.10. *Personal estimate of success in second year*

	Regarded the past year as a success	Couldn't say	Regarded the past year as unsuccessful
2E	19	1	11
2A	24	—	7
2B	21	—	7
2C	24	2	4
TOTALS	88	3	29

Another demonstration of 'streaming reaction' is shown by the personal assessment of success table. The boys were asked 'Do you consider that the past year at school has been a success?'

The difference between 2A and 2B is not significant but the difference between 2E and 2C is, especially when one considers the way in which the staff assess the 'success' of the two forms in tackling academic tasks. This difference can only be accounted for by the past experience of the two groups, the different sets of standards they have acquired and the way in which their new experiences measure up to those standards. This is confirmed by an analysis of the experience of the eleven boys who regarded themselves as unsuccessful in 2E. On average, they dropped sixteen places in their second-year exams compared with their first-year exams. On average the rest of the class dropped eight places. During the year two of these boys had been considerably emotionally disturbed. Crying in lessons, crying before school and refusing to come to school. A third went through a similar period and his father wrote to the school complaining that 'the boy is utterly demoralised'. The only other category of boys to yield so large a number of disturbed cases in the second year was the bottom of 2C!

TABLE 11.11. *Estimate of length of time spent on homework before and after streaming*

	Estimated average time spent on homework each night: first year	Estimated average time spent on homework each night after streaming: second year
2E	1 hr 3 mins	2 hrs 0 mins
2A	1 hr 4 mins	1 hr 43 mins
2B	1 hr 10 mins	1 hr 18 mins
2C	1 hr 1 min	1 hr 7 mins

Finally Table 11.11 shows another area of activity that is affected by streaming. The boys were asked to estimate the average length of time spent on homework each evening. Streaming has given rise to distinctly different climates of expectation with relation to homework. Although there is considerable overlap in the estimates given by individual boys in the four classes (which of course deserves further analysis), the table does give a convincing demonstration of another aspect of the process of differentiation.

CONCLUSION

In this article I have attempted to develop a model which describes the internal processes of a grammar school in terms of sub-culture formation, differentiation and polarisation. The indices presented in the last section are an early attempt to verify quantitatively some of the impressionistic data of Section 2. The research is, however, still continuing and a great deal of the material already collected is still at an early stage of analysis.

It is expected that material, yet to be collected, as well as that already in the pipeline, will clarify and modify this early formulation. Nevertheless the evidence presented here seems to indicate that the relationship between the internal organisation[9] and development of pupil sub-cultures[10] is an important factor in the process of education that warrants careful examination in further research.

[9] B. Jackson, *Streaming: an Education System in Miniature*, Routledge, 1964.
[10] See J. S. Coleman, *Adolescent Society*, Collier-Macmillan, 1961.

NOTE The substance of this article appears also in *Hightown Grammar: The School as a Social System* (Manchester University Press, 1970) from which the diagram appearing on p. 155 is taken.

12

J. W. Staines　　The Self-picture as a factor in the classroom*

SUMMARY. 1. A theoretical analysis of the concept of the Self shows it to be a learned structure, growing mainly from comments made by other people and from inferences drawn by children out of their experience in home, school and other social groups. Amongst the people likely to be most influential in determining the Self-picture are teachers. Two hypotheses were formulated: that it is possible to distinguish reliably between teachers in normal classrooms in respect of the frequency and kind of comments they make with reference to the Self; and that it is possible to teach so that, while aiming at the normal results of teaching, specific changes can be made in the Self-picture.

2. The results of the investigation indicated that:

(a) The first hypothesis was supported. Marked differences occurred between teachers in the frequency of Self-reference in their comments, particularly in their positive or negative comments on the child's performance, status and Self-confidence or potency.

(b) The second hypothesis was also supported. One teacher studied the Self-ratings of his class and tried to teach so that certain Self-ratings were changed. A small number of changes occurred in Self-traits, but statistically significant changes were found in two dimensions of the Self, certainty and differentiation. Both changes were interpreted as indicating greater psychological security.

(c) A control class taught by a teacher regarded as typically 'sound' and having no awareness of the Self-picture as an outcome of education showed significant decreases in certainty about the Self and in differentiation. The uncertainty spread throughout the Self and was significantly greater

* Reprinted from *British Journal of Educational Psychology*, **28**, 1958, 97–111.

than that of the experimental group. Both changes were interpreted as leading to a marked psychological insecurity. These changes, usually indicative of poor adjustment, were the unsought and unnoticed concomitant outcomes of normal methods aimed at securing the usual academic results.

(*d*) Standardised tests showed that both classes made about the same gains in some aspects of English and Arithmetic over the experimental period.

(*e*) The analysis of the Self into categories and dimensions and the use of a Self-rating scale appear to provide a useful method of discriminating between teachers according to the Self-reference of their words and of their methods of managing situations in the classroom.

I. INTRODUCTION: THE EMPIRICAL AND THEORETICAL IMPORTANCE OF THE SELF-PICTURE

The importance of the Self in psychological thinking has both empirical and theoretical foundations. Self-reference is frequent in the conversation of adults, and classroom data show that this is also true of children. Clinical records stress the importance of the Self-picture and of Self-acceptance and rejection. From such evidence it appears that the Self is empirically a matter of prime importance in that a great deal of behaviour is concerned with maintaining and enhancing the established pattern of the Self as it appears to the person, as he thinks it ought to be, and as he thinks other people believe it to be. Most psychological theorists introduce the Self or a related concept in considering motivation, and writers on personality postulate the Self as the integrating factor in personality. Cattell (1950) calls it the fourth factor in the economy of the personality, 'the keystone of personality' integrating Id, Ego and Super-Ego into 'one dynamic structure or unified sentiment'. Lewin (1935) sees the Self as an inner, relatively permanent structure, giving consistency to the personality. Stagner (1951) believes that the Self-image contributes stability to the personality, while Murphy (1947) has claimed that no part of behaviour is free of the Self.

If the Self is so closely related to the empirical data of behaviour and to the theoretical aspects of personality, it is important for education and for the teacher. This is particularly so since the Self is both an outcome of education and, once it has developed, a condition of subsequent learning. Such educational relevance should lead to an investigation of the conditions under which the Self develops, the methods by which it is changed, the limitations upon change once it has developed, and the effect of a particular kind of Self-picture upon learning.

II. THEORETICAL CONSIDERATIONS

The notion of the Self is highly complex. It is primarily perceptual, 'a learned perceptual system which functions as an object in the perceptual field' (Raimy, 1948). It is built from many perceptual experiences. The child learns about his Self from his own experiences and from the behaviour of others. From the teacher who says: 'John, go to the back. You're one of the big ones', the boy learns about himself and about himself-in-relation-to-others, as well as something of the social expectations centred on that aspect of his physique. He learns that he can run faster than some others, that he can read well or that he cannot sing. Gradually, the raw perceptual materials of the Self are transformed by the manufacturing processes of the mind, so that the Self also becomes conceptual. Memory images and other kinds of mental structures, notably concepts, are developed. The Self, as known to the individual, is thus both perceptual and conceptual.

One method of analysis of this complex Self-structure is to see the Self in three levels or phases, each level having a number of sectors or categories. The first level is the Cognised or Known Self which comprises all those characteristics of the individual that he recognises as part of the 'Me'. Whether or not these correspond to objective reality or to what others think about him does not matter. The Cognised Self is what the individual perceives and conceives himself to be. The second level of the Self, called the Other Self, is what the person believes others think of him: 'The teacher thinks I'm no good at English.' The third level is the Ideal Self, part wish, part 'ought', the standard to be reached: 'I ought to be more careful of detail.' These elements of the Self are of supreme importance for behaviour since many of the individual's actions are ordered by his constant efforts to maintain and enhance these various aspects of the Self-picture.

The categories are those aspects of the Self which individuals commonly report on. The most obvious are physical characteristics and skills of various kinds. Others appearing in conversations and in such clinical records as Rogers (1951) include traits, attitudes and interests, values, wants, and goals, status and role, in-groups and philosophy of life. Each of these categories appears in all three levels of the Self-picture. The individual has, for example, a picture of his physique as part of the Cognised Self, a belief that others see his physique in a certain way and a wish that it were something else.

In addition to the levels and categories, the data require the postulation of dimensions. A dimension is a direction in which people may vary, and at least nine major dimensions may be distinguished.

Individuals may be placed along a continuum of Self-awareness, from the person who, through momentary preoccupation with a task, is little aware of himself to the person who is continually and painfully self-conscious. This is the dimension of salience. Differentiation means the degree to which the person distinguishes the various levels and categories within the Self. He may have his concept of his status differentiated in great detail but his values category may be relatively undifferentiated. Potency is the sense of confidence a person develops in his own adequacy. The dimension of integration concerns the development of a hierarchy in the levels and categories so that the person can predict his behaviour, knowing that he will not be the victim of rash impulses and that he can trust himself in conflict situations. Insight is the degree to which the Self-picture corresponds to reality. Stability refers to Stagner's contention that the Self must be stable in order to give a consistent basis for personality and action. People will vary in their resistance to change and in their willingness to accommodate the Self-picture to new data. Self-acceptance is the name given to a continuum whose limiting points are an unreal over-valuation of the Self and Self-rejection. Between them lies the optimal region of Self-acceptance which occurs when the Cognised and Ideal Self are close together: 'I am like this and happy to be this way.' Concomitance of Cognised and Other Self is also a sign of Self-acceptance: 'I am like this and others think so too.' When this occurs, the Ideal Self loses the tyrannical quality that Horney (1942) finds in neurotics. The real dimension refers to the number of identifications which a person makes with ideas, groups, institutions and objects. Finally, people differ in the degree of certainty with which they can report on what they are like. Position on the dimension of certainty should change with age and development of the Self-picture.[1]

III. THE FIRST HYPOTHESIS AND EMPIRICAL PROCEDURES

The Self-structure develops in response to environmental stimuli. Since teachers are an important aspect of the child's environment, it is likely that they have some effect on the child's Self-picture. A number of questions arise. What part do teachers play in the development of the Self-picture? Can teachers change the child's Self-picture if they try to do so? If they can, what methods of teaching produce what kinds of Self-picture? Is it possible to distinguish between teachers in the

---

[1] For a full description of categories and dimensions, see J. W. Staines (1954) 'A Sociological and Psychological Study of the Self-Picture and Its Importance in Education', unpublished Ph.D. Thesis, University of London.

frequency and kind of comment which they make about the child's Self? An investigation was planned to answer this last question, and to show what effects, if any, followed deliberate teaching for change in the Self-picture.

The research followed the traditions established by Lewin (1939), more fully developed by Anderson and his colleagues (1946) and followed with modifications by Bales (1951) and Withall (1948), of seeing a class as a group and attempting to record and analyse data from teacher–child and child–child interaction. Their data on the educational outcomes of the interaction between personalities in the atmosphere of the classroom were sufficiently reliable to show that classroom situations are much more complex than was suspected and are producing other than orthodox lesson outcomes.

Observation of a number of teachers showed that the data of Self-reference were likely to provide a tentative answer to the investigation. Teachers made frequent comments on the child's Self: 'You're better at sums than you are at spelling', 'Let Rosemary come to the front— she's only small', 'We expect more from you because you're older', and so on. Some teachers make such remarks more frequently than others. An hypothesis was formulated: that teachers may be reliably distinguished by the frequency of their use of words and kinds of situational management which, in the opinion of competent judges, are likely to mould the Self.

To test this hypothesis, two problems had to be solved, how to gather and how to order the data. Two pairs of teachers, one pair in the Junior and one in the Infants' school, agreed to participate in the investigation although they did not know its purpose until all the data had been collected. They permitted the investigator to copy down and classify all that was said and to interview the children at any time. The pairs of teachers were comparable in experience and were rated by their respective head teachers as similar in proficiency. The classes were similar in numbers of boys and girls, in age, in intelligence, and in social class as judged from fathers' occupations. The children were mainly working class.

The times spent in observation of lessons are recorded in Table 12.2.

The preponderance of Arithmetic and English in the lessons observed reflects the importance attached to these subjects in the Junior school, and the Infants' school periods were chosen to match. The children became accustomed to the presence of the observer in a preliminary period and quickly accepted him as part of the classroom set-up.

The data were classified in terms of the categories and dimensions of the Self, using a method of scoring with symbols, supplemented by the

TABLE 12.1. *Classes used in observation period*

Classes	Numbers		Age in months		IQ	
	Boys	Girls	Mean	Range	Mean	SD
Junior A	15	14	129	122–134	114·4	10·4
Junior B	16	15	128	123–134	112·8	10·1
Infants C	20	24	89	84–96	No tests used	
Infants D	26	17	87	84–100	in this depart-	
					ment.	

indicators, ' + ', ' − ', 'n', and 'ambi'; ' + ' meant that the effect of the comment or situation was thought to be positive, ' − ' implied a probable negative effect, and 'n' stood for neutral. 'Ambi' indicated that

TABLE 12.2. *Minutes of observation for various lessons*

Class	Arithmetic	English	Social studies	Nature study	Music	Handwork
A	100	105	30	—	—	15
B	97	87	51	—	—	15
C	86	100	30	—	20	15
D	105	100	—	30	—	15

the effect was likely to be positive for some and negative for other children. The following are examples of the scoring in two of the categories:

1. Physique

(*a*) 'Jack, you're tall. Help me with this.' Score Ph. + since the teacher values tallness and Jack sees his height as a valued possession.

(*b*) 'Marie has the best complexion for Cinderella. We'll have her.' Score Ph. ambi, since Marie is chosen from a group of volunteers and the comment is positive for Marie, negative for the others.

(*c*) 'You won't do for the queen—you're not tall enough.' Score Ph. − because the child feels her physique is not valued.

(*d*) 'You're taller than the others. You're just right for this part.' Score Ph. o since a marked comparison with others is made, and positive, negative and ambivalent judgements are included. Interview evidence showed the importance of this kind of situation.

2. Performance

Comments on performance may be positive, negative or ambivalent. They may build up the child's Self-picture as able to do things, break it down or be ambivalent in their effects. Skills may bring the correct answer or performance with no comment from the teacher. The child sees himself as able by his success, or incompetent because of failure. A correct answer is scored Sk. +. Failure by silence, slowness or the wrong answer is scored Sk. −. In comments other than the routine 'Yes', 'You're good at...' 'Wrong'. 'You don't know your...', one score is given for the achievement or the failure and a second for status (St. + or St. −). That the teacher's comments are related by the child to his status in the eyes of the class was revealed by such comments as these made in interviews: 'They think I can't do it.' 'Everyone thinks how good you are.'

A comment by the teacher is sometimes followed by a class reaction: 'Good boy! Look at this everyone!' (Class approves). 'Wrong. Just look what Jack's done!' (Class laughs). Each element in the situation is scored, skill, status for the teacher's comment and status for the reaction of the class Sk. ambi is scored when a comment makes possible a positive as well as a negative Self-picture and it is impossible to determine which occurs: 'Who's right? Hands up those right.' Some children are right, some wrong. Hierarchy in skills is used when the teacher's comments tend to make the child see himself as better in one skill than another, so leading to greater differentiation: 'You're better at English than Arithmetic.'

Similar methods of scoring were used for other dimensions and categories. The potency is the score total of all scores relating to the child's confidence in any aspect of himself. It is got by subtracting the negative from the positive Self-reference comments. The salience score is the total of all Self-ratings together with the Self-orientation total. The latter comments refer to the person as a whole rather than to any category; 'You're a fine one, you are.' Incisions are interruptions by the teacher in the child's own sequences of purpose and achievements, usually by way of unnecessary directions. The Self-direction category includes those comments which give the child an opportunity to see himself as a purposing, planning individual. A classification for classroom management distinguishes two modes, direct and indirect. Direct management is any routine command by the teacher. The indirect method is illustrated by co-operative relationships between the teacher and the class. It will help to form the child's concept of himself as causal. Level of aspiration is related to the Ideal Self. Task-oriented comments are those with no salience or Self-reference.

Treatment of data. The material was rated by the writer (Judge X) and two school counsellors with three years' training in Psychology at Sydney University. When the data was divided into units by each judge, agreement on the units between Judges X and Y and X and Z was above 90 per cent and this was held to indicate sufficient accuracy. Units where agreement was not finally reached after discussion were eliminated. The remaining units were rated for categories and dimensions. After two months, a page was taken at random from the records and re-marked by Judges X and Y with a re-test reliability for X of 94 per cent and for Y of 92 per cent.

A survey was made of the ratings for the various teachers, a total found for each teacher, and the score in each category and dimension represented as a percentage of the total. Many of the differences between the scores of the teachers were very small and are not reported here because of lack of space.[2] Table 12.3 gives the categories where the differences are greatest or of most interest. Table 12.4 shows an analysis of the data for the dimensions. Many of the differences between the teachers were found by chi-squared to be significant at the 1 per cent or 5 per cent level,[3] but because of the small numbers in many categories comparisons were made simply on the basis of observed scores.

In general, the Infants' teachers used more Self-references than the Junior teachers. B differs considerably from A, and very widely from C and D in the categories of the Self. In the dimensions, salience scores will, by definition, closely parallel the total scores, and with this sample of teachers, differentiation does also. Wide individual differences between teachers are evident in the totals for both salience and differentiation, but not in the percentages. It is in the potency dimension, however, that the most striking difference occurs. Scores in the other three dimensions show small differences, largely because of the method of scoring the data. If all positive scores are regarded as acceptance scores, and all negative scores as rejection, then the characteristics of the teachers and the classroom atmospheres are very different indeed.

IV. DISCUSSION OF RESULTS

The Junior teachers are most alike where scores are small. In categories and dimensions where scores are large, these teachers differ widely,

[2] For full details of methods of scoring and results, see Staines, *loc. cit.*
[3] Between A and B: 1 per cent level, Sk. −, Status +, Status −, Self-direction. Incisions, direct Classroom Management. 5 per cent level, Skill +, Values.
Between C and D: 1 per cent level, Performance total, Status −, Incisions, Self-orientations, Traits. 5 per cent level, Skills −, Status total.

TABLE 12.3. *Categories showing most marked differences between teachers*

Performance	A	B	Performance	C	D
Skill +	107	73	Skill +	64	76
Skill −	19	50	Skill −	15	37
Total	141	129	Total	79	113
Status			*Status*		
Positive (+)	70	30	Positive (+)	71	67
Negative (−)	14	48	Negative (−)	24	63
Total	84	78	Total	95	130
Values			*Values*		
Responsibility	5	0	General	8	1
General	5	0	Total	12	5
Total	11	2			
Wants			*Physique*		
Level of aspiration	11	7	Total	16	1
Self-direction	85	14			
Incisions	1	14	*Wants*		
			Level of aspiration	15	22
Classroom management			Self-direction	24	20
Direct	11	33	Incisions	8	36
			Classroom management		
			Direct	34	40
			Traits		
			Negative (−)	7	25
			Self-orientation		
			Total	9	35

particularly in the performance and status categories, in the four major dimensions—areal, salience, differentiation and potency—in Self-direction and in direct classroom management, that is, in the giving of orders rather than opportunities for seeing oneself as purposing, choosing and causal.

Teacher A. The pattern is clear-cut. Teacher A is particularly strong in positive emphasis on skills and makes few negative comments. The status category shows the same pattern. He is outstanding in the opportunity he offers children for Self-determination—an important

TABLE 12.4. *Scores on dimensions of Self and on frequency of each dimension as a percentage of total of units*

Dimensions	Junior A Raw score	Junior A % of total	Junior B Raw score	Junior B % of total	Infants' C Raw score	Infants' C % of total	Infants' D Raw score	Infants' D % of total
1. Salience	372	96·7	317	98·3	383	91·9	481	96·2
2. Differentiation	371	96·5	313	97·0	380	90·2	475	95·0
3. Potency +	290	75·4	130	40·3	223	53·5	217	43·4
−	54	14·0	160	49·6	93	22·3	205	41·0
4. Integrity	1	0·3	—	—	—	—	—	—
5. Insight	5	1·3	2	0·6	3	0·7	1	0·2
6. Acceptance	1	0·3	—	—	3	0·7	1	0·2
7. Rejection	—	—	5	1·6	4	1·0	2	0·4

feature if, as Murphy (1947) suggests, the Self develops best where there is opportunity for Self-direction. He puts more stress on values than do two of the others. In the dimensions of salience, potency and differentiation, Teacher A's scores suggest that he is likely to make the child Self-aware—to teach him, as Kilpatrick (1941) suggests, that 'It is I who am doing it'. It will be a positive, Self-accepting salience. His emphasis is strongly on differentiation so that children may see their strengths and weaknesses more accurately and in greater detail, making for more adequate adjustment. A's score on the potency dimension is significant. Teachers B and D give confidence with one hand and take it away with the other. Teacher A gives most (score 290) and takes least (score 54).

Teacher B. The pattern here is also clear-cut but very different. In the performance category, B makes fewer positive and many more negative comments than A. In the status category, although the totals are approximately the same as A's (A 84, B 78), the constituents are strikingly different. The pattern of the performance category is repeated in having a smaller number of positive and a greater number of negative comments. The pattern occurs again when B makes less effort than A to hold up a level of aspiration, although the difference in scores is not great. He gives very few opportunities for Self-direction. The effect of this on the Self-picture must be magnified by the repetition of incisions. The absence of Self-choice and the interference with the child's goal-directed or purposive sequences are complementary.

In the dimensions, B is widely different from the other teachers. The amount of salience is less. There is less differentiation and a tendency to use the wholistic approach with children ('You're no good...'). Totals for the potency dimension are widely different from those of the other teachers, as are the positive (score 130) and negative (score 160) constituents. This teacher shows less positive development of confidence or Self-potency than the others and, at the same time, more negative effects. He gives least and takes most.

The infants' teachers are slightly more alike than are the Junior teachers, particularly in In-group comments, values, attitudes and interests, and in the salience and differentiation dimensions.

Teacher C. This teacher comments on the physique of children more often than the other teachers, and is the only one to draw comparisons at this point. Her comments on skills are more positive than negative. She prefers positive to negative comment on status and places more emphasis on Traits than the Junior teachers, but not so much as Teacher D. She gives little opportunity for Self-direction and, as might be expected, her classroom management is largely direct. In dimensions, her outstanding score is in potency, where there is a tendency to build up the child's confidence (score 223), with only a small score for negative comments (93).

Teacher D. Teacher D stresses performance on the positive side and negative comments are less frequent than Teacher B's, and more than A's and C's. Status comments are greater than for the other three teachers, but are chiefly negative. This is also true for traits. The opportunity that she gives for Self-direction is slight and her scores for incisions and salience are highest of all. The differentiation score is high. The potency score, got by algebraically totalling the high positive score (217) and the high negative score (205), is very low. If her effect on the Self-picture were predicted from this evidence it would seem that Teacher D tends to make children highly Self-aware in many categories, but not particularly confident in any aspect of themselves.

In summary, the teachers' comments overwhelmingly stress performance and status. It is inevitable that where the stress is on performance, it should also be on status; but the latter category is also evident independently in the verbal material, although not distinguished in the scores. The psychological significance of such emphasis on status may be argued from its numerical preponderance, but the writer feels from his experience with teachers and students that it is largely overlooked by teachers. They are, indeed, careful to avoid most of the obvious status aspects where the child's feelings are involved and are usually considerate of them. But material taken in a number of interviews with the children suggests that, much more frequently than teachers believe, the ordinary run-of-the-day comments on success and failure, and incidents where a child is casually preferred to another for what seems to the teacher an unimportant task or role, may be fraught with status possibilities and intense emotional content. While no claim is made that these unnoticed situations are always significant for all children, it is reasonable to conclude that the teachers who most frequently invoke status situations and make relevant comments are most likely to modify the child's Self-picture in this direction.

How effective is this method of distinguishing teachers? It would seem to separate them on what competent judges believe are likely to be the effects of their words and situational management on a number of categories and dimensions. These categories and dimensions are held to be central aspects of the Self and it is useful to know that teachers differ so widely in relation to them. A second obvious conclusion from the scores is that teachers do not develop to any significant degree many of the other important educational outcomes to which subject matter and teaching methods may be closely geared, and which might be drawn into the Self in order to be most effectively related to behaviour.

The point at which this method of investigation is least effective is in gauging the effect upon the child of the various verbal and situational interactions. Categorisation of what a teacher says, while indicating a prevailing classroom atmosphere, gives no clue as to how effective it really is in forming the Self-picture. Teacher D, for instance, uses reproof much more frequently than any other teacher and each reproof is rated St. — . Yet the observer could not say what effects her words had. Interviews showed that some children had a 'water-off-a-duck's-back' attitude towards her but that others were much more sensitive to her flow of personal comment. In an attempt to discover whether the different teaching styles and aims would lead to changes in the Self-picture, the second part of the investigation was carried out.

V. THE SECOND HYPOTHESIS AND EMPIRICAL PROCEDURES

The hypothesis was formulated that teachers who differ in the frequency of their Self-referential comments would produce significantly different

Self-pictures. If this were so, it would follow that classroom situations would produce educational outcomes other than the traditional skills, knowledges and appreciations.

To test this hypothesis it was decided to use the two Junior teachers previously observed, since they differed widely in certain known aspects, particularly in the opportunities they gave children for Self-direction, in their attitudes towards children's skills and their care for preserving status. Teacher A was more likely than Teacher B to produce socially desirable changes in the Self-picture as he was interested in children and their problems. Accordingly, class A was chosen as the experimental group, class B as the control. Such a design would show whether Teacher A's methods would support the hypothesis, while the results from Teacher B's class could supply additional confirmatory evidence.

The subjects

Though the two classes were matched for age, intelligence and socio-economic class, they were not equal in attainments. The experimental group had a greater number of children whose achievement scores on standardised tests were low, although eight of them were the most intelligent children in either class. Both classes were tested with a Self-rating card test[4] to measure the phases and categories of the Self-picture before and after the experimental teaching period.

The experimental teaching methods

The teaching period for the experiment was twelve weeks. Teacher A rated his class on the categories in the card test for each phase of the Self, and compared his ratings with the children's Self-ratings in order to decide what treatment might be given to each child. In doing so he became familiar with the general concepts used in the analysis of the Self and accepted the idea that these could be used as ends of the teaching process. He planned his methods so that situations could be arranged in which the child would be led by the teaching methods to see himself in various ways. These would include seeing himself as a planning, purposing, choosing individual, responsible and accountable, for these are basic aspects of the healthy socialised Self. The child should test his purposes by carrying them through, see himself as adequate and causal and, at the same time, differentiate his relative strengths and weaknesses. Particular attention was to be paid to preserving his status. At the same time the syllabus for entrance to grammar school was to be covered without interfering with the

4 See Staines, *loc. cit.*, for details of construction and validation.

prospects of the candidates. For the Ideal Self, the teacher planned to hold up a suitable level of aspiration, either directly and by commendation or indirectly by allusion and suggestion. The teacher also planned to convey his judgements which make up the child's Other Self in such a way that the child would be unlikely to reject them as incongruous with the Self-picture he already had.

Provision was made for teaching methods relevant to the child's place on the dimensions of the Self. The Areal Self for each child could be increased by identification with more objects, values, ideas and people. For the over-self-conscious child (high in salience), treatment was to include a reduction in comments referring specifically to the Self, an increase in Alper's task-involved (1946) comments and in Ruger's (1910) technique of the 'scientific attitude,' and care with the use of such simple situations as the public display of work. Differentiation was related to the avoidance of 'whole' comments such as 'Good' and 'You're hopeless', and to an emphasis on seeing various characteristics more accurately. Adequacy or potency was to be built up by success and appreciation and by the teacher's care for the child's status. Accepting behaviour by the teacher was thought to be the best way of teaching Self-acceptance.

The experimental period began at the end of the first month of the school term when the card test was administered for the first time. After twelve weeks, the test was re-administered and the data analysed for significant differences between the classes. To understand the results, it is necessary to make brief explanatory comments on the instructions given for the card test. In a pilot study, children were given the Self-ratings in the form of 66 cards and asked to place them in heaps or columns labelled Not True, Neither True nor Untrue, True, and Not Sure. The children asked for finer gradings. For instance, of two cards that could be placed in the 'True' column, one might be 'more true than the other'. Accordingly, ratings were made in Columns 1, 2, 3 for Untrue items, 4, 5, 6 for Neither true nor untrue, 7, 8, 9 for True and 10 for Not sure. Columns 1 (Most untrue of me), 5, and 9 (Most true of me) contained items about which the children were most certain.

VI. RESULTS

The first of two ways of considering results is to ask what differences there were between the two groups at the end of the period.

The percentage frequencies of children's rankings of various items as 'Most true of me' served as the basis of the calculation. Six items of the card test showed differences between the classes at the 1 per cent level and 5 per cent level. At the 1 per cent level were 'I try to see fair play', 'Good at games'. 'Willing to have a try at things no matter how hard they are', and 'Like hobbies'. At the 5 per cent level were a greater willingness to admit cheating, and an item testing Self-direction. All the differences were in favour of the experimental class. Teacher A believed of the item relating to cheating that the greater freedom in his class and the rational approach led children to admit it more freely. In the item testing Self-direction ('Make up my own mind'), little change had taken place in the experimental class, but a major one had occurred in the control class. Teacher B's methods were characterised by incisions and a great deal of direction in classroom management and were likely to produce widespread uncertainty and insecurity. The effects of his methods appear in significant differences between the classes in the responses to this item. The hypothesis is thus supported in relation to a limited number of characteristics.

The second method of estimating the results of the experiment is concerned with the dimensions.

Highly significant differences were found between the initial and final scores of the experimental class and also between the final scores of the two classes in the dimensions of certainty and differentiation. For the certainty dimension, the evidence is found in the movement towards or away from the rating 'Not sure' and is presented in Table 12.5 as the total numbers of cards placed by each class in the 'Not sure' category (column 10), for each level of the Self. That is, the twenty-nine children in the experimental class had placed a total of 123 cards in this category in the first test and 72 in the second test. This change is interpreted as an increase in the certainty as to what the Self really was.

TABLE 12.5. *Uncertainty scores (Column 10) at the beginning and end of the experimental period*

	Test 1			Test 2		
	Self	Ideal Self	Other Self	Self	Ideal Self	Other Self
Experimental	123	159	385	72	34	149
Control	370	89	582	448	300	932

When the significance of the figures for the various levels of the Self is tested by chi-squared technique, Teacher A shows a significant decrease in 'Not sure' scores for the Self, Ideal Self and the Other Self. The class gained significantly in certainty about the boundaries of the Self. Equally significant statistically, and numerically much greater, is the increase in scores in the 'Not sure' rating in the control group. Starting with a significantly greater degree (1 per cent level) of uncertainty than the experimental group in the Self and Other Self, after the 'settling-down' period of one month, this group increased its uncertainty over its own initial score and over the experimental group in all three levels of the Self. Particularly striking are the figures for the Ideal Self and the Other Self.

Differentiation

The figures for differentiation are found by taking the scores for 'Least true' and 'Most true' ratings (Table 12.6). A movement towards the middle ranges and away from the extreme points on the scale is differentiation. A movement towards the extremes, Columns 1 and 9, indicates a tendency to see oneself as black or white, and an inability to make moderate judgements of the various aspects of the Self.

TABLE 12.6. *Differentiation of the self at the beginning and end of the experimental period*

	Test 1		Test 2	
	Most true	*Least true*	*Most true*	*Least true*
Experimental	621	299	522	288
Control	340	191	357	209

There is a significant decrease (1 per cent level) for the experimental group for 'Most true', and a small non-significant decrease in 'Least true'. The control group shows a slight non-significant increase for both columns. It is clear that the experimental group has moved significantly away from 'Most true' and, to a lesser degree, from 'least true'. Since the numbers in 'Not sure' have also decreased significantly, the movement from all three must be in the direction of the middle ranges towards greater differentiation. The control group not only failed to move away from 'Most true' and 'Least true', but actually increased these numbers slightly. When these two totals are added to the flight to the 'Not sure' column, it can be seen to what degree the middle ranges are depleted. It indicates how little these children, compared with the experimental group, can see themselves with either certainty or moderation. If it is true that insecurity is marked by rigidity, then the scores on the differentiation dimension reinforce the conclusion drawn from the uncertainty scores. The hypothesis is thus very strongly supported.

One further line of evidence must be considered. Both classes used for the investigation were scholarship classes. Teacher A believed that, while working on the lines of the experiment, he could still secure the necessary academic results. No check was kept on scholarship results, but standardised tests for word recognition and mechanical arithmetic were given at the beginning and end of the experimental period. The results appear in Table 12.7.

TABLE 12.7. *Mean scores on standardised tests before and after the experimental period*

	Test 1		Test 2	
	Vernon Word Recognition	Mechanical Arithmetic	Vernon Word Recognition	Mechanical Arithmetic
Experimental	108·4	119·8	111·8	141·1
Control	127·0	130·1	129·5	145·0

The experimental teaching can be seen to have improved attainments while achieving those changes in the Self-picture detailed above. The methods used with the control group, while securing slightly less improvement, produced the very maladjustment changes in certainty and differentiation indicated earlier. This is further support for the second hypothesis in the investigation.

VII. DISCUSSION

These results have implications related to both teaching goals and methods, and a number of points may be briefly discussed: new light has been thrown on the variables operating in the learning situation; these are now seen to be related inevitably to adjustment; they occur in every classroom but can be controlled by appropriate teaching methods; they are the product of group situations as well as of individual attention and they can be controlled within the present examination framework.

The experiment has shown the existence of additional variables in the learning situation other than the skills, knowledge, attitudes and appreciations commonly expected as the outcomes of teaching. The measuring instrument evolved shows that changes have occurred in the Self-picture, in the Ideal Self, in the Other Self, and in the attitudes to each of these aspects. Awareness of such variables is important for learning theory and for practical teaching. Learning experiments, as well as practical teaching situations, show many conflicting results, some of which are undoubtedly due to the presence of unrecognised factors in the learning set-up. The next step in the investigation of the problems of learning is the isolation of other variables that contribute to the unpredictability of learning situations. This experiment has shown that the Self-picture is probably one such variable. Changes occur in this as an outcome of learning situations and the Self-picture must be recognised as a hitherto unnoticed factor occurring in every learning situation. Furthermore, since any learning becomes a condition of subsequent learning, the kind of Self-picture that is learnt becomes a factor to be controlled in both experimental and practical teaching situations.

The experiment has shown that good and poor adjustment are linked with the goals and teaching methods of the typical classroom. The changes that occurred in the Self-picture are usually accepted as symptoms of good and poor adjustment. Teacher A, using the free methods indicated, and stressing the aspects of the Self-picture discussed above, is able to make his pupils more sure of what they are like and more accepting of what they are, more able to differentiate themselves and to see themselves with moderation as well as with certainty, more certain of what they want to be like and more aware of what judgements they think others make of them. Such changes are accepted as the marks of good adjustment, and Teacher A clearly produces these characteristics in his children. Teacher B's data shows that typical high-pressure teaching, with vigorous personal emphasis, with great stress on correctness and on the serious consequences of failure, and with constant emphasis on the passing of examinations, can lead to significantly greater signs of insecurity. It is shown further that this insecurity spreads, not only through the items of the Self, but through the Ideal and Other Self, that is, through all the aspects of one major integrational factor of personality. Clinical evidence, of course, shows that this does happen, but the appearance and spread of insecurity in the Self have not hitherto been recorded in the ordinary classroom situation. In the light of this information, the educational significance of the Self becomes clearer and both teaching goals and teaching methods should be modified.

The educational significance of the Self is reaffirmed when it is realised that changes in the Self-picture are an inevitable part of both outcomes and conditions of learning in every classroom, whether or not the teacher is aware of them or aiming for them. They occur, as in A's class, where the teacher deliberately included them in his teaching goals and adapted his methods accordingly, and they occur in B's class where the teacher aimed at orthodox goals and was ignorant of these correlative factors. Since both classes were reasonably typical and both teachers recognised by their headmasters as competent teachers, it is reasonable to generalise and expect such factors to operate in all classrooms.

It is also clear from the experiment that teaching methods can be adapted so that definite changes of the kind sought for will occur in the Self. The Self can be deliberately produced by suitable teaching methods. In this experiment a start has been made in the task of relating aspects of teaching methods to categories, levels and dimensions of the Self.

One of the conditions for producing the Self-picture as an outcome of education is that it is, and always will be produced in group situations. It can, of course, be produced in the special group situation of two, the teacher giving individual attention to the child, but in this experiment the normal group situation was always present. This makes the problem of obtaining the Self-picture relevant to normal classroom conditions where group situations must always hold.

Finally, the Self is relevant to classroom situations in another very important way. It was produced in this experiment in the normal conditions of teaching for examination results. Both classes were scholarship classes and it was agreed that any experimental conditions under which class A worked should not endanger the scholarship prospects of the children. On standardised tests in reading and number, Teacher A produced slightly greater mean improvement in his class. If it is objected that a teacher cannot spend his time teaching for an improved Self-picture and better adjustment because of examination pressure, here is some evidence that at least equally good academic results may be got while improving adjustment. In other words, it is possible for a teacher to conceive his educational goals in the wider terms of the Self-picture and to secure these while attaining the necessary academic standards. On the negative side, it is likely that Teacher B, conceiving his goals in academic terms and ignorant of the concomitant outcomes, laid the child open to failure in the future because he failed to strengthen the child's Self-picture. A changed emphasis thus became feasible, from subject-matter goals to goals expressed in terms of the Self, for in this way both academic and adjustment goals become attainable.

These points suggest that, because the Self is an ubiquitous factor in all learning experiences, its presence should be recognised and its importance stressed by all teachers, and its controlled development made a major teaching aim. But since the psychology of the Self has been little emphasised in courses on educational psychology and not at all by traditional practice in schools, it is certain that few teachers are aware of its importance. The implications for pre-service and in-service training are clear, but much more research must be done in the field. Two lines of investigation are likely to be fruitful. The first concerns the persistence of the pattern of the Self-picture emerging from each class. How long do such Self-pictures persist under similar conditions? What is the effect upon later learning of a child spending a second year with either A or B? Could A reverse B's pattern of Self-picture or would B, in the child's most formative years, undo A's constructive work? Do the answers differ for different 'types' of personalities? Should care be taken to prevent a child experiencing two successive teachers like B? The second line of investigation concerns the range of the curve of teachers on which A and B would be placed if the experiment were extended to include more teachers. Would B be an extreme type and A be near the norm? Or is B near the norm and A atypical? Only a wider investigation can answer such questions.

ACKNOWLEDGEMENTS. I wish to acknowledge with gratitude the grant in 1952 of a Fellowship from the Imperial Relations Trust Fund which made this investigation possible, and to express my appreciation of the help and guidance of Dr C. M. Fleming, Reader in Education at the University of London Institute of Education. I am grateful also to the New South Wales Department of Education which granted me leave for the period of study, and to the Education Officers, heads and teachers of public and private schools in England who allowed me to gather the data.

VIII. REFERENCES

ALPER, T. G. (1946) 'Task-orientation *vs* ego-orientation in learning and retention', *Amer. J. Psychol.*, 59, 236–48.

ANDERSON, H. H., and BREWER, J. E. (1946) 'Studies of teachers' class-room personalities, *II*', *Appl. Psychol., Monogr.*, 8, Stanford University Press.

BALES, R. F. (1951) *Interaction Process Analysis: a method for the study of small groups*, Addison-Wesley Press.

BRUNER, J. S. (1951) 'Personality, dynamics and perceiving', in J. S. Blake, G. V. Ramsay, ed. *Perception, an Approach to Personality*, New York, Ronald Press.

CATTELL, R. B. (1950) *Personality, a Systematic, Theoretical and Factual Study*, McGraw-Hill.

HORNEY, K. (1942) *Self Analysis*, Norton.

KILPATRICK, W. H. (1941) *Selfhood and Civilisation, a Study of the Self-Other Process, Bureau of Publications*, Teachers' College, Columbia.

KLUCKHOHN, F. R. (1953) 'Dominant and variant value orientations', in C. Kluckhohn, and H. A. Murray, ed., *Personality*. London, Jonathon, 1949; revised edition, 1953.

LEWIN, K. (1935) *Dynamic Theory of Personality*, McGraw-Hill.

LEWIN, K., LIPPITT, R., and WHITE, R. K. (1939) 'Patterns of aggressive behaviour in experimentally created social climates', *J. Soc. Psychol.*, 10, 271–300.

MURPHY, G. (1947) *Personality, a Biosocial Approach to Origins and Structure*, Harper.

RAIMY, V. C. (1948) 'Self-reference in counseling interviews', *J. Consulting Psychol.*, 12, 3.

ROGERS, C. R. (1951) *Client-Centred Therapy: its current practice, implications and theory*, Houghton Mifflin.

RUGER, H. A. (1910) 'The psychology of efficiency', *Arch. Psychol.*, 15.

STAGNER, R. (1951) 'Homeostasis as a unifying concept in personality theory', *Psychol. Review*, 58, 2–17.

WITHALL, J. (1948) 'The development of a technique for the measurement of social-emotional climates in class-rooms'. *J. Exper. Educ.*, 18.

WOOLF, W. (1946) *The Personality of the Pre-School Child*, New York, Grune and Stratton.

SECTION 4

Motivation and attitudes

In this section we move in a steady progression from hard theory about the origins of human behaviour to practical attempts to modify it. The unifying theme and major emphasis of all the articles presented is the modifiability of human behaviour. When considering the statistical treatment of the results in Harrison's paper, it may be useful to re-read the Introduction to Section 2 of this book.

We start with an abridged version of Hebb's classic article in which he pleads for a move away from the notion of specific drives like hunger and thirst as the springs of human action. This article was one of the first to argue that psychological hypothesising about motivation needed to take neurophysiological knowledge into account. His 'optimal level of stimulation' concept has this quality as well as providing a means of reconciling the views of many other motivation theorists. In J. McV. Hunt's first article we see an attempt to apply Hebb's theorising to children's behaviour and its educational implications become readily apparent. His 'incongruity-dissonance' concept suggests that mild difficulty and stress have motivating properties, whereas too much *difficulty causes disruption and breakdown of learning. McV. Hunt's second article takes the argument further into the classroom—this time introducing his concept of 'intrinsic motivation'. He maintains that a task is intrinsically motivating if its level of complexity is just a little ahead of the complexity of previously mastered tasks. By careful structuring of the teaching situation for different children at different stages of development teachers can 'pull' children along towards greater feelings of competence and higher levels of achievement. Swift's article emphasises the social context of the learner. He provides a comprehensive review of studies relating social class to achievement and concludes that it is the attitudes and values of the social and family background from which the learner comes which determine the strength of his achievement motivation.*

With the introduction of the term 'attitudes' we move further in the direction of behaviour modification. A prerequisite for research on influences on attitudes is a method of measuring them, and in the articles by Harrison and Barker Lunn we see different approaches to the problem. Harrison constructs Likert scales to measure his four attitude dimensions. This means that he assigns a score of 1 to 5 to each of the five response categories (Strongly Agree . . . Strongly Disagree) for each item and obtains a total score for the scale by adding together these individual scores for all the items comprising the scale. Barker Lunn constructs ten scales to measure children's attitudes to various aspects of their school, their teacher and other children. She derives items for the scales from statements made by children in group discussions, and then applies factor analysis to the children's responses to these items to identify separate clusters of correlated items. Each cluster can be identified with an attitude dimension, and she constructs attitude scales to measure each dimension. Although she mentions the use of different scaling criteria ('Factor' and 'Guttman') for selecting the items for the scales, in each case the children's scale scores are obtained by adding together their 'positive' responses to the full set of items in the scale. Both papers report relationships between children's attitude-scale scores and other variables. In the case of the Harrison study, hypotheses are investigated which relate to Swift's views on the characteristics of culturally disadvantaged children who do well at school. Barker Lunn presents correlations showing relationships between many of her attitude scales and measures of children's ability and school achievement.

Finally, we turn to behaviour change via attitude change, in a health education study on discouraging children from smoking. Watson takes three different ways of presenting information on the dangers of smoking and compares their effects on children's attitudes to smoking, their knowledge of its association with illness and their smoking behaviour.

Several points stand out in this section. First, that important contributions to effective teaching can be made by motivation theory derived both from work in the psychological laboratory and from direct observations of human behaviour. Secondly, the study of the learner's social background together with the attitudes to learning transmitted to him by his family, emphasises the need for a general educational strategy operating both in and out of the classroom. Thirdly, the evaluation of such a strategy requires sound methods of assessing children's behaviour and attitudes, and experiments to find out which are the best ways of influencing them.

J. BYNNER

13

D. O. *Hebb*　　Drives and the CNS
(Conceptual nervous
system)*

It is just as well to be explicit about the use of the terms motivation
and drive. 'Motivation' refers here in a rather general sense to the
energising of behaviour, and especially to the sources of energy in a
particular set of responses that keep them temporarily dominant over
others and account for continuity and direction in behaviour. 'Drive'
is regarded as a more specific conception about the way in which this
occurs: a hypothesis of motivation, which makes the energy a function
of a special process distinct from those Stimulus-Response or cognitive
functions that are energised. In some contexts, therefore, 'motivation'
and 'drive' are interchangeable.

The main line of descent of psychological theory, as I have recently
tried to show (1953), is through associationism and the stimulus-
response formulations. Characteristically, stimulus-response theory has
treated the animal as more or less inactive unless subjected to special
conditions of arousal. These conditions are first, hunger, pain, and
sexual excitement; and secondly, stimulation that has become associated
with one of these more primitive motivations.

Such views did not originate entirely in the early ideas of nervous
function, but certainly were strengthened by them. Early studies of the
nerve fibre seemed to show that the cell is inert until something happens
to it from outside; therefore, the same would be true of the collection of
cells making up the nervous system. From this came the explicit theory
of drives. The organism is thought of as like a machine, such as the
automobile, in which the steering mechanism—that is, stimulus-

* Reprinted (abridged) from *Psychological Review*, 62, 1955, 244–7,
250–4.

response connections—is separate from the power source, or drive. There is, however, this difference: the organism may be endowed with three or more different power plants. Once you start listing separate ones, it is hard to avoid five: hunger, thirst, pain, maternal, and sex drives. By some theorists, these may each be given a low-level steering function also.

Now it is evident that an animal is often active and often learns when there is little or no drive activity of the kinds listed. This fact has been dealt with in two ways. One is to postulate additional drives— activity, exploratory, manipulatory, and so forth. The other is to postulate acquired or learned drives, which obtain their energy, so to speak, from association with primary drives.

It is important to see the difficulties to be met by this kind of formulation, though it should be said at once that I do not have any decisive refutation of it, and other approaches have their difficulties, too.

First, we may overlook the rather large number of forms of behaviour in which motivation cannot be reduced to biological drive plus learning. Such behaviour is most evident in higher species, and may be forgotten by those who work only with the rat or with restricted segments of the behaviour of dog or cat. (I do not suggest that we put human motivation on a different plane from that of animals [Brown, 1953]; what I am saying is that certain peculiarities of motivation increase with phylogenesis, and though most evident in man can be clearly seen with other higher animals.) What is the drive that produces panic in the chimpanzee at the sight of a model of a human head; or fear in some animals, and vicious aggression in others, at the sight of the anaesthetised body of a fellow chimpanzee? What about fear of snakes, or the young chimpanzee's terror at the sight of strangers? One can accept the idea that this is 'anxiety', but the anxiety, if so, is not based on a prior association of the stimulus object with pain. With the young chimpanzee reared in the nursery of the Yerkes Laboratories, after separation from the mother at birth, one can be certain that the infant has never seen a snake before, and certainly no one has told him about snakes; and one can be sure that a particular infant has never had the opportunity to associate a strange face with pain. Stimulus generalisation does not explain fear of strangers, for other stimuli in the same class, namely, the regular attendants, are eagerly welcomed by the infant.

Again, what drive shall we postulate to account for the manifold forms of anger in the chimpanzee that do not derive from frustration objectively defined (Hebb and Thompson, 1954)? How account for the petting behaviour of young adolescent chimpanzees, which Nissen (1953) has shown is independent of primary sex activity? How deal with the behaviour of the female who, bearing her first infant, is terrified at the sight of the baby as it drops from the birth canal, runs away, never sees it again after it has been taken to the nursery for rearing; and who yet, on the birth of a *second* infant, promptly picks it up and violently resists any effort to take it from her?

There is a great deal of behaviour, in the higher animal especially, that is at the very best difficult to reduce to hunger, pain, sex, and maternal drives, plus learning. Even for the lower animal it has been clear for some time that we must add an exploratory drive (if we are to think in these terms at all), and presumably the motivational phenomena recently studied by Harlow and his colleagues (Harlow, 1953; Harlow *et al.*, 1950; Butler, 1953) could also be comprised under such a drive by giving it a little broader specification. The curiosity drive of Berlyne (1950) and Thompson and Solomon (1954), for example, might be considered to cover both investigatory and manipulatory activities on the one hand, and exploratory, on the other. It would also comprehend the 'problem-seeking' behaviour recently studied by Mahut and Havelka at McGill (unpublished studies). They have shown that the rat which is offered a short, direct path to food, and a longer, variable and indirect pathway involving a search for food, will very frequently prefer the more difficult, but more 'interesting' route.

But even with the addition of a curiosity-investigatory-manipulatory drive, and even apart from the primates, there is still behaviour that presents difficulties. There are the reinforcing effects of incomplete copulation (Sheffield *et al.*, 1951) and of saccharin intake (Sheffield and Roby, 1950; Carper and Polliard, 1953), which do not reduce to secondary reward. We must not multiply drives beyond reason, and at this point one asks whether there is no alternative to the theory in this form. We come, then, to the conceptual nervous system of 1930 to 1950.

About 1930 it began to be evident that the nerve cell is not physiologically inert, does not have to be excited from outside in order to discharge (Hebb, 1949, p. 8). The nervous system is alive, and living things by their nature are active. With the demonstration of spontaneous activity in CNS it seemed to me that the conception of a drive system or systems was supererogation.

For reasons I shall come to later, this now appears to me to have been an oversimplification; but in 1945 the only problem of motivation, I thought, was to account for the *direction* taken by behaviour. From this point of view, hunger or pain might be peculiarly effective in guiding or channelling activity but not needed for its arousal. It was not surprising, from this point of view, to see human beings liking intellectual work, nor to find evidence that an animal might learn something without pressure of pain or hunger.

The energy of response is not in the stimulus. It comes from the food, water, and oxygen ingested by the animal; and the violence of an epileptic convulsion, when brain cells for whatever reason decide to fire in synchrony, bears witness to what the nervous system can do when it likes. This is like a whole powder magazine exploding at once. Ordinary behaviour can be thought of as produced by an organised series of much smaller explosions, and so a 'self-motivating' CNS might still be a very powerfully motivated one. To me, then, it was astonishing that a critic could refer to mine as a 'motivationless' psychology. What I had said in short was that any organised process in the brain is a motivated process, inevitably, inescapably; that the human brain is built to be active, and that as long as it is supplied with adequate nutrition will continue to be active. Brain activity is what determines behaviour, and so the only behavioural problem becomes that of accounting for *in*activity.

It was in this conceptual frame that the behavioural picture seemed to negate the notion of drive, as a separate energiser of behaviour. A pedagogical experiment reported earlier (Hebb, 1930) had been very impressive in its indication that the human liking for work is not a rare phenomenon, but general. All of the 600-odd pupils in a city school, ranging from six to fifteen years of age, were suddenly informed that they need do no work whatever unless they wanted to, that the punishment for being noisy and interrupting others' work was to be sent to the playground to play, and that the reward for being good was to be allowed to do more work. In these circumstances, *all* of the pupils discovered within a day or two that, within limits, they preferred work to no work (and incidentally learned more arithmetic and so forth than in previous years).

The phenomenon of work for its own sake is familiar enough to all of us, when the timing is controlled by the worker himself, when 'work' is not defined as referring alone to activity imposed from without. Intellectual work may take the form of trying to understand what Robert Browning was trying to say (if anything), to discover what it is in Dali's paintings that can interest others, or to predict the outcome of a paperback mystery. We systematically underestimate the human need of intellectual activity, in one form or another, when we overlook the intellectual component in art and in games. Similarly with riddles, puzzles, and the puzzle-like games of strategy such as bridge, chess, and *go*; the frequency with which man has devised such problems for his own solution is a most significant fact concerning human motivation.

It is, however, not necessarily a fact that supports my earlier view, outlined above. It is hard to get these broader aspects of human behaviour under laboratory study, and when we do we may expect to have our ideas about them significantly modified. For my views on the problem, this is what has happened with the experiment of Bexton, Heron, and Scott (1954). Their work is a long step towards dealing with the realities of motivation in the well-fed, physically comfortable, adult human being, and its results raise a serious difficulty for my own theory. Their subjects were paid handsomely to do nothing, see nothing, hear or touch very little, for twenty-four hours a day. Primary needs were met, on the whole, very well. The subjects suffered no pain, and were fed on request. It is true that they could not copulate, but at the risk of impugning the virility of Canadian college students I point out that most of them would not have been copulating anyway and were quite used to such long stretches of three or four days without primary sexual satisfaction. The secondary reward, on the other hand, was high: $20 a day plus room and board is more than $7,000 a year, far more than a student could earn by other means. The subjects then should be highly motivated to continue the experiment, cheerful and happy to be allowed to contribute to scientific knowledge so painlessly and profitably.

In fact, the subject was well motivated for perhaps four to eight hours, and then became increasingly unhappy. He developed a need for stimulation of almost any kind. In the first preliminary exploration, for example, he was allowed to listen to recorded material on request. Some subjects were given a talk for six-year-old children on the dangers of alcohol. This might be requested, by a grown-up male college student, fifteen to twenty times in a thirty-hour period. Others were offered, and asked for repeatedly, a recording of an old stock-market report. The subjects looked forward to being tested, but paradoxically tended to find the tests fatiguing when they did arrive. It is hardly necessary to say that the whole situation was rather hard to take, and one subject, in spite of not being in a special state of primary drive arousal in the experiment but in real need of money outside it, gave up the secondary reward of $20 a day to take up a job at hard labour paying $7 or $8 a day.

This experiment is not cited primarily as a difficulty for drive theory, although three months ago that is how I saw it. It *will* make difficulty for such theory if exploratory drive is not recognised; but we have already seen the necessity, on other grounds, of including a sort of exploratory-curiosity-manipulatory drive, which essentially comes down to a tendency to seek varied stimulation.

For psychological purposes there are major changes in recent ideas of nervous function. One concerns the single cell, the other an 'arousal' system in the brain stem. This arousal system is synonymous with a general drive state. The drive is an energiser, but not a guide; an engine but not a steering gear. These are precisely the specifications of activity in the arousal system. Also, learning is dependent on drive, according to drive theory and this too is applicable in general terms —no arousal, no learning; and efficient learning is possible only in the waking, alert, responsive animal, in which the level of arousal is high.

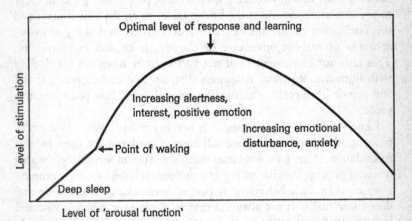

FIG. 13.1. *Level of 'arousal function'*

Consider the relationship of the level of stimulation to the level of arousal (Fig. 13.1). When arousal or drive is at a low level, a response that produces increased stimulation and greater arousal will tend to be repeated. This is represented by the rising curve on the left. But when arousal is at a high level, as at the right, such responses will tend to be disrupted, perhaps because the occurrence of other irrelevant responses is facilitated. Thus there will be an optimal level of arousal for effective behaviour.

From this notion we have a significant behavioural conception, namely that the same stimulation in mild degree may attract (by prolonging the pattern of response that leads to this stimulation) and in strong degree repel (by disrupting the pattern and facilitating conflicting or alternative responses).

The significance of this relation is in a phenomenon of the greatest importance for understanding motivation in higher animals. This is the *positive attraction of risk taking*, or mild fear, *and of problem solving*, or mild frustration, which was referred to earlier. Whiting and Mowrer (1943) and Berlyne (1950) have noted a relation between fear and curiosity—that is, a tendency to seek stimulation from fear-provoking objects, though at a safe distance. Woodworth (1921) and Valentine (1930) reported this in children, and Woodworth and Marquis (1947) have recently emphasised again its importance in adults. There is no doubt that it exists. There is no doubt, either, that problem-solving situations have some attraction for the rat, more for Harlow's (1953) monkeys, and far more for man. When you stop to think of it, it is nothing short of extraordinary what trouble people will go to in order to get into more trouble at the bridge table, or on the golf course; and the fascination of the murder story, or thriller, and the newspaper accounts of real-life adventure or tragedy, is no less extraordinary. This taste for excitement *must* not be forgotten when we are dealing with human motivation. It appears that, up to a certain point, threat and puzzle have positive motivating value, beyond that point negative value.

I know this leaves problems. It is not *any* mild threat, *any* form of problem, that is rewarding; we still have to work out the rules for this formulation. Also, I do not mean that there are not secondary rewards of social prestige for risk taking and problem solving—or even primary reward when such behaviour is part of lovemaking. But the animal data show that it is not always a matter of extrinsic reward; risk and puzzle can be attractive in themselves, especially for higher animals such as man. If we can accept this, it will no longer be necessary to work out tortuous and improbable ways to explain why human beings work for money, why school children should learn without pain, why a human being in isolation should dislike doing nothing.

One other point before leaving Fig. 13.1: the low level of the curve to the right. Emotion is persistently regarded as energising and organising (which it certainly is at the lower end of the scale, up to the optimal level). But the 'paralysis of terror' and related states do occur. As Brown and Jacobs (1949, p. 753) have noted, 'the presence of fear may act as an energiser . . . and yet lead in certain instances to an increase in immobility'. Twice in the past eight months, while this address was being prepared, the Montreal newspapers reported the behaviour of a human being who, suddenly finding himself in extreme danger but with time to escape, simply made no move whatever. One of the two was killed; the other was not, but only because a truck driver chose to wreck his truck and another car instead. Again, it is reported by Marshall (1947), in a book that every student of human motivation should read carefully, that in the emotional pressure of battle no more than 15 to 25 per cent of men under attack even fire their rifles, let alone use them efficiently.

Tyhurst's (1951) very significant study of behaviour in emergency and disaster situations further documents the point. The adult who is told that his apartment house is on fire, or who is threatened by a flash flood, may or may not respond intelligently. In various situations, 12 to 25 per cent did so; an equal number show 'states of confusion, paralysing anxiety, inability to move out of bed, "hysterical" crying or screaming, and so on'. Three-quarters or more show a clear impairment of intelligent behaviour, often with aimless and irrelevant movements, rather than (as one might expect) panic reactions. There seems no doubt: the curve at the right must come down to a low level.

Now back to our main problem: If we tentatively identify a general state of drive with degree of arousal, where does this leave hunger, pain, and sex drives? These may still be anatomically separable, as Stellar (1954) has argued, but we might consider instead the possibility that there is just one general drive state that can be aroused in different ways. Stellar's argument does not seem fully convincing. There are certainly regions in the hypothalamus that control eating, for example; but is this a *motivating* mechanism? The very essence of such a conception is that the mechanism in question should energise *other* mechanisms, and Miller, Bailey, and Stevenson (1950) have shown that the opposite is true.

But this issue should not be pressed too far, with our present knowledge. I have tried to avoid dogmatism in this presentation in the hope that we might try, for once, to see what we have in common in our views on motivation. One virtue of identifying arousal with drive is that it relates differing views (as well as bringing into the focus of attention data that may otherwise be neglected). The important thing is the fact that at low levels of stimulation an increase of drive intensity may be rewarding, whereas at high levels it is a decrease that rewards.

Obviously these are not explanations that are being discussed, but possible lines of future research; and there is one problem in particular that I would urge should not be forgotten. This is the cortical feedback to the arousal system, in physiological terms: or, in psychological terms: the *immediate drive value of cognitive processes*, without intermediary. This is psychologically demonstrable, and *has* been demonstrated repeatedly.

Anyone who is going to talk about acquired drives, or secondary motivation, should first read an old paper by Valentine (1930). He showed that with a young child you can easily condition fear of a caterpillar or a furry animal, but cannot condition fear of opera glasses, or a bottle; in other words, the fear of some objects, that seems to be learned, was there, latent, all the time. Miller (1951) has noted this possibility but he does not seem to have regarded it very seriously, though he cited a confirmatory experiment by Bregman; for in the same passage he suggests that my own results with chimpanzee fears of certain objects, including strange people, may be dealt with by generalisation. But this simply will not do, as Riesen and I noted (1943). If you try to work this out, for the infant who is terrified on *first* contact with a stranger, an infant who has never shown such terror before, and who has always responded with eager affection to the only human beings he has made contact with up to this moment, you will find that this is a purely verbal solution.

Furthermore, as Valentine observed, you cannot postulate that the cause of such fear is simply the strange event, the thing that has never occurred before. For the chimpanzee reared in darkness, the first sight of a human being is of course a strange event, by definition; but fear of strangers does not occur until later, until the chimpanzee has had an opportunity to learn to recognise a few persons. The fear is not 'innate' but depends on some sort of cognitive or cortical conflict of learned responses. This is clearest when the baby chimpanzee, who knows and welcomes attendant A and attendant B, is terrified when he sees A wearing B's coat. The role of learning is inescapable in such a case.

The cognitive and learning element may be forgotten in other motivations, too. Even in the food drive, some sort of learning is fundamentally important: Ghent (1951) has shown this, Sheffield and Campbell (1954) seem in agreement, and so does the work of Miller and his associates (Berkun, Kessen and Miller, 1952; Miller and Kessen, 1952; Miller, 1953) on the greater reinforcement value of food by mouth, compared to food by stomach tube. Beach (1939) has shown the cortical-and-learning element in sex behaviour. Melzack (1954) has demonstrated recently that even pain responses involve learning. In Harlow's (1953) results, of course, and Montgomery's (1953), the cognitive element is obvious.

These cortical or cognitive components in motivation are clearest when we compare the behaviour of higher and lower species. Application of a *genuine* comparative method is essential, in the field of motivation as well as of intellectual functions (Hebb and Thompson,

1954). Most disagreements between us have related to so-called 'higher' motivations. But the evidence I have discussed today need not be handled in such a way as to maintain the illusion of a complete separation between our various approaches to the problem. It *is* an illusion, I am convinced; we still have many points of disagreement as to relative emphasis, and as to which of several alternative lines to explore first, but this does not apply fundamental and final opposition. As theorists, we have been steadily coming together in respect of ideational (or representative, or mediating, or cognitive) processes; I believe that the same thing can happen, and is happening, in the field of motivation.

REFERENCES

BEACH, F. A. (1939) 'The neural basis at innate behavior. III. Comparison of learning ability and instinctive behavior in the rat', *J. comp. Psychol.*, **28**, 225–62.

BERKUN, M. M., KESSEN, MARION L., and MILLER, N. E. (1952) 'Hunger-reducing effects of food by stomach fistula versus food by mouth measured by a consummatory response', *J. comp. physiol. Psychol.*, **45**, 550–4.

BERLYNE, D. E. (1950) 'Novelty and curiosity as determinants of exploratory behavior', *Brit. J. Psychol.*, **41**, 68–80.

BEXTON, W. H., HERON, W., and SCOTT, H. T. (1954) 'Effects of decreased variation in the sensory environment', *Canad. J. Psychol.*, **8**, 70–6.

BROWN, J. S. 'Problems presented by the concept of acquired drives', in *Current Theory and Research in Motivation: a symposium*, University of Nebraska Press, pp. 1–21.

BROWN, J. S. and JACOBS, A. (1949) 'The role of fear in the motivation and acquisition of response', *J. exp. Psychol.*, **39**, 747–50.

BUTLER, R. A. (1953) 'Discrimination learning by rhesus monkeys to visual-exploration motivation', *J. comp. physiol. Psychol.*, **45**, 95–8.

CARPER, J. W., and POLLARD, F. A. (1953) 'Comparison of the intake of glucose and saccharin solutions under conditions of caloric need', *Amer. J. Psychol.*, **66**, 479–82.

GHENT, LILA (1951) 'The relation of experience to the development of hunger', *Canad. J. Psychol.*, **5**, 77–81.

HARLOW, H. F. (1953) 'Mice, monkeys, men, and motives', *Psychol. Rev.*, **60**, 23–32.

HARLOW, H. F., HARLOW, MARGARET K., and MEYER, D. R. (1950) 'Learning motivated by a manipulation drive', *J. exp. Psychol.*, **40**, 228–34.

HEBB, D. O. (1930) 'Elementary school methods', *Teach. Mag.* (Montreal), **12**, 23–6.

HEBB, D. O. (1949) *Organisation of behavior.* Wiley.

HEBB, D. O. (1953) 'On human thought', *Canad. J. Psychol.*, **7**, 99–110.

HEBB, D. O. and RIESEN, A. H. (1943) 'The genesis of irrational fears', *Bull. Canad. Psychol. Ass.*, **3**, 49–50.

HEBB, D. O. and THOMPSON, W. R. (1954) 'The social significance of animal studies', in G. Lindzey, ed., *Handbook of Social Psychology.* Addison-Wesley, pp. 532–61.

MARSHALL, S. L. A. (1947) *Men Against Fire.* New York, Morrow.

MELZACK, R. (1954) 'The effect of early experience on the emotional responses to pain', unpublished doctor's dissertation, McGill University.

MILLER, N. E. (1951) 'Learnable drives and rewards', in S. S. Stevens, ed., *Handbook of Experimental Psychology*, Wiley, pp. 435–72.

MILLER, N. E. (1953) 'Some studies of drive and drive reduction', paper read at Amer. Psychol. Ass., Cleveland, September.

MILLER, N. E., BAILEY, C. J., and STEVENSON, J. A. E. (1950) 'Decreased "hunger" but increased food intake from hypothalamic lesions', *Science*, **112**, 256–259.

MILLER, N. E., and KESSEN, MARION L. (1952) 'Reward effects of food via stomach fistula compared with those via mouth', *J. comp. physiol. Psychol.*, **45**, 555–64.

MONTGOMERY, K. C. (1953) 'The effect of activity deprivation upon exploratory behavior', *J. comp. physiol. Psychol.*, **46**, 438–41.

NISSEN, H. W. (1953) 'Instinct as seen by a psychologist', *Psychol. Rev.*, **60**, 291–4.

SCHLOSBERG, H. (1954) 'Three dimensions of emotion', *Psychol. Rev.*, **61**, 81–8.

SHEFFIELD, F. D., and CAMPBELL, B. A. (1954) 'The role of experience in the "spontaneous" activity of hungry rats', *J. comp. physiol. Psychol.*, **47**, 97–100.

SHEFFIELD, F. D., and ROBY, T. B. (1950) 'Reward value of a non-nutritive sweet taste', *J. comp. physiol. Psychol.*, **43**, 471–81.

SHEFFIELD, F. D., WULFF, J. J., and BACKER, R. (1951) 'Reward value of copulation without sex drive reduction', *J. comp. physiol. Psychol.*, **44**, 3–8.

STELLAR, E. (1954) 'The physiology of motivation', *Psychol. Rev.*, **61**, 5–22.

THOMPSON, W. R., and SOLOMON, L. M. (1954) 'Spontaneous pattern discrimination in the rat', *J. comp. physiol. Psychol.*, **47**, 104–7.

TYHURST, J. S. (1951) 'Individual reactions to community disaster: the natural history of psychiatric phenomena', *Amer. J. Psychiat.*, **107**, 764–9.

VALENTINE, C. W. (1930) 'The innate bases of fear', *J. genet. Psychol.*, **37**, 394–419.

WHITING, J. W. M., and MOWRER, O. H. (1943) 'Habit progression and regression

—a laboratory study of some factors relevant to human socialization', *J. comp. Psychol.*, 36, 229–53.

WOODWORTH, R. S. (1921) *Psychology*, New York, Holt.

WOODWORTH, R. S., and MARQUIS, D. G. (1947) *Psychology*, 5th edn., New York, Holt.

14

J. McV. Hunt   Experience and the
development of motivation:
some reinterpretations*

A recent issue of the *Saturday Evening Post* carried a cartoon that
some of you may have noted. It depicts a boy entering his house,
perhaps from school, where his father is sitting with his paper. The boy
appears to be fixing his father with an accusing glare. The punch line
reads, 'Somebody goofed, I'm improperly motivated'.

This cartoon depicts the vantage point from which I have been
examining what we think we know about the relation between
experience and motivation. When a child's behaviour fails to fit the
standards somebody in our society holds for him, it is pretty well agreed
among us who are supposed to be experts on human nature that
'somebody goofed'. And that somebody is usually considered to be a
parent.

The question is: what is the proper formula? If one examines the
accruing evidence relevant to what has been the dominant conception
of the experiential sources of motivation, one can hardly escape the
conclusion that this conceptual scheme needs some revisions. If we
based our child-rearing entirely on our dominant theory of motivational
development, we would probably goof as often and as badly as
run-of-the-mill parents.

Today I wish, first, to remind you of three of the most basic and
general of the propositions in that theory of motivation which has
been dominant for the past thirty to forty years. These are propositions
which, although stated in somewhat varied forms, have been shared
by both psychoanalysts and academic behaviour theorists. Secondly,
I wish to cite evidence which calls these propositions into question,

*Reprinted from *Child Development*, 31, 1960, 489–504.

and thirdly, to suggest, tentatively, three new interpretative principles which appear to me to be congruent with a large number of facts and which have interesting implications.

Our conceptions of motivation have traditionally been concerned with three large questions: (*a*) Why does an organism or person become active? (*b*) Why does the organism or person act one way rather than another? and (*c*) How do you get the organism or person to change his behaviour to something conceived to be more desirable or appropriate?

THE DOMINANT THEORY

Drive

According to our dominant theory, it is claimed, first of all, that 'all behaviour is motivated', and that the aim or function of every instinct, defence, action, or habit is to reduce or eliminate stimulation or excitation within the nervous system. It is not easy to state when this view was first presented. Signs of it appear in the seventh chapter of Freud's *Interpretation of Dreams* in 1900, and the idea is full-blown in his paper entitled *Instincts and their Vicissitudes* in 1915. The idea also appears in Woodworth's *Dynamic Psychology* (1918), where the term *drive* was first introduced into the glossary of American psychology. The idea was full-blown in Dashiell's *Fundamentals of Objective Psychology* (1928).

Although Freud (1915) believed that the source of motivation lay outside the domain of psychology in physiology, American psychologists, untroubled by such limits to their domain, have gone on to answer the first question concerning what motivates organisms to become active by saying that they are *driven*. Organisms have been conceived to be driven, first by those so-called primary inner stimuli which arise from homoeostatic imbalances or needs. With no shame whatsoever, psychologists have long cited the evidence from the work of such physiologists as Claude Bernard (1859) and his successors, and especially of Walter B. Cannon (1915), and also of the psychologist Curt Richter (1927) to document this answer. Organisms are driven, second, by various forms of intense and painful external stimulation. It has been assumed that these two forms of stimulation arouse an inner state of excitement which has usually been called *drive*.

It is also assumed, as the proposition that 'all behaviour is motivated' implies, that the organism would be inactive unless driven by either inner or outer stimuli. Freud (1915) has been highly explicit about this assumption, and the assumption lies implicitly behind the notion of conditioned or learned drive in behaviour theory and behind the traumatic notion of anxiety in psychoanalysis. It is obvious, of course, that animals and people are sometimes active when it is hard to see how either homoeostatic drive or painful external stimulation could be operative. It is then assumed that some of the weak, innocuous stimuli present must have been associated in the past with either painful stimuli or homoeostatic needs. In such a way the weak stimuli which are present must have acquired the capacity to arouse the drive, often now called anxiety by psychologists as well as psychoanalysts, and it is such acquired or conditioned drive that is conceived to activate the organism.

Such conditioned drive or anxiety has been well demonstrated in the laboratory. Before World War II, Miller (1941, 1948) at Yale showed that rats which had been repeatedly shocked in a white box would, when later returned to the white box, make an effort to escape. Moreover, in the course of these efforts, they could be got to learn new skills such as that of turning a wheel to open a door. Rats which had not been shocked in the white box made no such efforts to escape. In another demonstration, Solomon and Wynne (1953) have shown that dogs which have experienced a tone or a buzzer paired a few times with a subtetanising shock will run away from that tone or buzzer for hundreds of trials, with the average reaction time of starting continuing to decrease through 600 such trials. In my own work (Hunt, 1941) rats fed irregularly in infancy ate more than their litter-mate controls and sometimes (Hunt 1947) hoarded food in adulthood after a period without food. Here, as I conceived it, the cues of hunger were conditioned to intense hunger excitement during the infantile experience. In adulthood the conditioned hunger drive facilitated the rate of eating and, sometimes, hoarding.

Such work has demonstrated that this notion of conditioned drive or anxiety, which goes back to the work of Bechterev (1913) and Watson and Raynor (1920), has a solid basis in reality. But in what has been the dominant theory of motivation, as epitomised by Freud's (1926) later traumatic theory of anxiety, and by the Hull (1943) and Dollard–Miller theory of acquired drives (Miller and Dollard, 1941; Dollard and Miller, 1950), conditioning is conceived to be the only way in which an organism can become fearful of innocuous stimuli.

Habit

Habit has been the answer to the second question concerned with why an animal or person acts one way rather than another. The organism is controlled by the habits which have served to reduce drive in the past when that organism was in the presence of the inner and outer drive stimuli, and the cue stimuli impinging upon him at any given moment now. Under the term *habit*, I am including psychoanalytic modes, which have supposedly been fixated during infancy in the course of either too much gratification or too much frustration, and I am including also ego-defences, or anxiety equivalents, and cathexes, as well as the instrumental responses and traits commonly investigated in psychological laboratories.

Changing behaviour has been conceived to be a matter of motivating the organism with either punishment or homoeostatic need to make the desired behaviour which can then be reinforced by arranging for it to reduce the drive aroused by the punishment or the need. Although the conditions and conceptions of psychotherapy in the clinic differ considerably from the conditions and conceptions of the behaviour theorist investigating learning in laboratory animals, in either case it is conceived that motivation is a necessity, and motivation means changing the emotional or drive conditions which are quite extrinsic to either the instrumental behaviour or the cognitive, informational processes concerned.

This dominant theory has been a conceptual edifice of large dimensions and of considerable detail. It has provided a plausible account of both personality development and social motives. The experimental facts of homoeostasis and of conditioned drive and fear are sound. Nevertheless, it has become more and more evident in the past ten years that some of the basic assumptions of this dominant theoretical scheme and some of the explanatory extrapolations contradict facts and call for reinterpretation.

REINTERPRETATIONS

Is all behaviour motivated?

The first of the assumptions to be called into question is the one that *all behaviour is motivated* and that *organisms become inactive unless stimulated* by homoeostatic need or painful stimulation or conditional stimuli for these. A large variety of observations contradict this assumption and imply spontaneous molar activity. Beach (1945) has reviewed the observations of play in the young to show that playful activities are most likely to occur when either young animals or children are homoeostatically satisfied and also comfortably warm. The very occurrence of either homoeostatic need or strong external stimulation stops play and turns the young animal or child to activities calculated to relieve such stimulation. Berlyne (1950, 1955) has shown that well-fed and watered rats will explore areas new to them if given only the opportunity. Montgomery (1953) moreover, has shown that hunger and thirst tend to limit the exploratory behaviour of rats rather than facilitate it, and Montgomery and Monkman (1955), as well as others, have shown that conditioned fear inhibits exploration. Harlow, Harlow, and Meyer (1950) have demonstrated that well-fed monkeys will learn to un-assemble a three-device puzzle with no other drive and 'no other reward than the privilege of unassembling it'. In another study Harlow (1950) found two well-fed and well-watered monkeys worked re-peatedly at unassembling a six-device puzzle for ten continuous hours, and they were still showing what he characterised as enthusiasm for their work on the tenth hour of testing. From his observations of the human child, moreover, Piaget (1952) remarks repeatedly on the en-thusiastic and repeated performance of such emerging skills as the release of a toy, sitting up, standing, etc.

Such evidences of spontaneous behaviour, which is unmotivated in the traditional sense, have led to the naming of such new motives as a curiosity drive by Berlyne (1955), an exploratory drive by Montgomery (1951), and exteroceptive and curiosity drives by Harlow (1953). I would like to object that merely naming such drives explains nothing. If we continue we shall be revisiting McDougall's (1915) practice of postulat-ing a separate drive for almost every variety of activity. Let us stop with noting that such observations do contradict our assumption that organisms will become inactive unless driven by homoeostatic needs and painful stimuli, and give up this ancient Greek notion that living matter is inert substance to which motion must be imparted by extrinsic forces. We can then embrace the thermodynamic conception of living things as open systems of energy exchange which exhibit activity in-trinsically and upon which stimuli have a modulating effect, but not an initiating effect.

This notion of activity being intrinsic in living tissue is receiving support from studies of organ systems as well as studies of molar or-ganisms. The EEG, for example, shows that brain cells are con-tinuously active (Jasper, 1937; Prosser, 1934). In sleep the slow waves of large amplitude are taken to imply that large numbers of cells are firing synchronously, and the effect of waking and stimulation and exciting the brain-stem-reticular formation is to asynchronise this firing which shows in rapid waves of low magnitude (Lindsley, 1957).

Granit (1955) points out that the spontaneous firing of retinal cells increases with dark adaptation and thereby functions to prevent the de-afferentisation of visual cortex with darkness. Twenty years ago, this spontaneous firing was considered, at worst, to be due to some failure of experimental control, or at best, noise in the channel of information. Recently, the Laceys (1958) have found spontaneous fluctuations of sudomotor activity and cardiac activity which they also see as functioning in the control of the organism's relations with its environment. Especially intriguing is their notion that the carotid sinus mechanism functions as a feedback loop which participates in the directing of attention inward or outward by inhibiting or facilitating receptor inputs. But the point of mentioning these evidences of spontaneous activities of organ systems here is merely to help inter for good the notion that activity of living systems requires homoeostatic need or painful external stimulation and to foster the idea that to live means to be active in some degree.

Reinforcement

This idea of activity being intrinsic in living organisms has implications for our conception of reinforcement. It makes it unnecessary to see an activity as a matter of either reducing or avoiding stimulation which is implied in the assumption that organisms become inactive unless stimulated. This is a second fundamental assumption of the dominant theory which has been shared by psychoanalysts and behaviour theorists alike.

On the one hand, there is still a place for drive reduction. It is clear that under conditions of homoeostatic need and painful stimulation, and perhaps under circumstances when the conditions of stimulation are changing with too great rapidity, both animals and persons learn techniques and strategies leading to gratification or reduction in external stimulation. The evidence that led Thorndike to formulate the 'law of effect' is as convincing as ever. Moreover, in association with reductions of homoeostatic needs, animals and men may also learn cathexes or emotional attachments. The facts referred to are those highly familiar in secondary reinforcement (Hull, 1943; Pavlov, 1927).

On the other hand, the facts implying that organisms show spontaneous molar activity also imply that, when animals and human beings have been living under conditions of low and unchanging stimulation for a time, increases of stimulation become reinforcing. Butler has shown that rhesus monkeys will learn quite complex discriminations with the only reward being a peek through a glass window (Butler, 1953) at the things in the next room or a few seconds of auditory experience (Butler, 1957). Berlyne (1950) has shown that, the greater the variety of stimulation in an area which rats are permitted to explore, the longer they continue their explorations.

Especially important in this connection are the studies of human behaviour under conditions of minimal variation in stimulation. I refer to the studies of perceptual isolation by Bexton, Heron, and Scott (1954) at McGill and also the work of Lilly (1956). At McGill, college students were paid 20 dollars a day to do nothing. They lay for twenty-four hours a day on a comfortable bed. The temperature was optimal and constant. Eyes, ears, and hands were shielded to minimise stimulus variation. Few subjects could endure more than two or three days of such conditions. They developed a desire for variation which was almost overwhelming.

While interpreting such facts in terms of a multiple set of drives for curiosity, exploration, or stimulation will get us only to a redescription of them, Hebb's (1955) notion of an optimal level of activation—and, I would like to add, stimulus variation below which *increases* are reinforcing and above which *decreases* are reinforcing—is an integrative conception of fair magnitude. Moreover, the drive-reduction principle of reinforcement may be seen to be but half of this more general curvilinear principle.

But this is probably not the whole story. It looks as if there were, natively, both positive and negative forms of exciting stimulation. Sheffield, Roby, and Campbell (1954) have argued that the reinforcing effect of eating is not a matter of reduction of the hunger drive but rather a matter of the positive value of the consummatory act of eating. Moreover, Sheffield, Wulff, and Backer (1951) have shown that male rats will learn mazes to get to females in heat even when they are allowed only intromission but not allowed to continue coitus to the point of drive-reducing ejaculation. From the fact that Davis and Buchwald (1957) at Indiana have shown that showing pictures of nude women to college males increases excitement as shown by increased palmar conductance and the arrest of EEG-alpha, it is clear that such stimulation is exciting rather than excitement-reducing. Young (1955) has long emphasised the importance of the hedonic quality of experience for reinforcement, and he has shown that speed of running in rat subjects increases with the concentration of sucrose in the incentive drink.

The suggestion that the two forms of excitation, one positive and one negative, are built into organisms comes also from the work of Olds and Milner (1954). Electrical stimulation of the septal area is positively reinforcing, but electrical stimulation of the brain-stem reticular formation is negatively reinforcing. Perhaps, it is not without significance that the septal area is part of the old olfactory brain which has been considered to have an especially important part in the mediation of sexual and consummatory behaviour in mammals. At any rate, it looks as though certain types of stimulation may be positively reinforcing even though they be intense and exciting. This may mean that the curvilinear principle may be limited in its domain to strong stimulation via the exteroceptors when homoeostatic needs are minimised.

The suggestion of innate, positive and negative exteroceptive stimulation comes secondly from recent work by Harlow (1958). It has been customary to see an infant's cathexes or love for its mother developing as secondary reinforcement largely out of its feeding experiences. Freud (1905), of course, contended that the pleasure from stimulation of the oral erogenous zone furnished the experiential basis for both pleasure-sucking and maternal attachment, a contention which contradicted his most definitive formulations of drive theory (Freud, 1915). The fact that an infant must suck for its nourishment, according to libido theory (Freud, 1905, p. 587), merely guaranteed discovery of the pleasures of oral stimulation. Behaviour theorists have seen both sucking and love of mother as forms of secondary reinforcement deriving from the fact that the child satisfies its hunger by means of sucking the mother's breasts (Mussen and Conger, 1956, pp. 137ff.). Harlow (1958), however, has recently compared the degree of attachment of young monkeys to a wire mother-surrogate on which they nursed at a bottle with attachment to a padded and cloth-covered mother-surrogate on which they received nothing but the feel of softness. In terms of the amount of time spent on each of the two mother-surrogates, the monkeys showed more than ten times the attachment to the soft-padded surrogate as to the wire surrogate. When various fear-evoking stimuli were presented to the baby monkeys in their cages, it was to the padded and cloth-covered surrogate that the frightened infant monkey turned, not to the wire surrogate on which it had been nursed. Harlow argues from these findings that it is the sensory quality of softness which gives the reinforcement. His study suggests, moreover, that it is important to investigate the capacity for various kinds of stimuli for positive and negative reinforcement in the very young. Pratt (1954) cites a monograph by Canestrini (1913) on the sensory life of the newborn for an observation that certain stimuli are associated with decreases in the rate of the heart rate, and are therefore pleasant, while others are associated with increases in heart rate and are unpleasant.[1] In view of the finding by

---

[1] An examination of Canestrini's monograph shows that Pratt was mistaken in stating that Canestrini remarked upon decreases in heart rate being associated with pleasure, but some of his published kymograph records do indicate decreases in heart rate. It may well be that heart rate could serve as an indicator of the emotional value of various sensory inputs and these

Davis and Buchwald (1957) that seeing a picture of a nude female results in reduction of the heart rate of male college students, it is possible that this physiological indicator may provide a technique for determining the direction of the reinforcing effect of stimuli in the newborn. At any rate, what is suggested is that McDougall's (1915) old notion of natively positive and negative values for receptors inputs be re-examined.

Conditioned fear and anxiety

The third assumption that I wish to examine in the light of empirical evidence is the notion that fear and anxiety are *always* inculcated as a consequence of traumatic experiences of helplessness in the face of homoeostatic need or painful external stimulation. Note that I am not denying that such conditioned fears do exist, I am only questioning the word *always* . . . are always inculcated as a consequence of traumatic experiences.

The first relevant studies go way back to the 1920s. Harold and Mary Cover Jones (1928) attempted to test the claims of Watson (1928) and Watson and Raynor (1920) concerning conditioned fears. They exposed their subjects of various ages, ranging from early infancy to adult, to a large but sluggish and harmless bull-snake. Fear of the snake was exceedingly common among adults, teenagers, and latency-age children, but it was absent in children below three years of age. It began to appear among children older than three and was typical of children six and older. From the fact that the fear appeared at a younger age in those of higher intelligence than those of lower intelligence, the Joneses argued that fear of snakes is a response which comes automatically into the developing child's repertoire through maturation. This remains as an alternative hypothesis to that of conditioned fear.

A study by Frances Holmes (1935), which is seldom cited, calls both of these interpretations into question. Holmes compared the fearfulness of the children of lower-class background who were attending a day nursery, with the fearfulness of children of upper-class background who were attending a private nursery school. She got her fear scores by indicating that the child could get some attractive toys with which to play by going into the dark room adjacent to the examining room, or by taking them off a chair situated beside that of a strange

---

might be tested for their reinforcement values. I am indebted to Dr William Gerler for reading this monograph carefully to check my own impression of Canestrini's text.

woman dressed in a large floppy black hat and a long grey coat, or by climbing along a plank some three feet off the floor. If the child started immediately for the toys, he got a score of one for that item. If he hesitated but ultimately went ahead on his own, he got a score of two. If he would go only if accompanied by the examiner, the score was three. If he refused to go at all, the score was four. There were seven such situations. The results show that the fear scores of the lower-class children averaged only about half the size of those for the upper-class children, and the fear scores for boys were lower than those for girls. Yet it would be the lower-class children who had experienced the more homoeostatic need and painfully rough treatment than the upper-class children, and the boys had probably experienced more painful experiences than the little girls. That intelligence is not the factor is shown by the fact that the fear scores showed a correlation of only about $+0.2$ with mental age, and the differences were still significant when intelligence was partialled out. Something besides either conditioned fear or the correlation between fear and intelligence is required to make these results comprehensible.

Recently, evidence even more contradictory to the notion of conditioned fears has been coming from the work of Seymour Levine. Levine, Chevalier, and Korchin (1956) have compared the adult behaviour of rats shocked and rats petted daily from birth to their twentieth day with the adult behaviour of rats left continuously in their nest with their mothers. When he started this work, Levine expected to find that the shocked animals would show traumatic effects of their shock experiences in heightened emotionality and damaged capacity to learn adaptive responses. On the contrary, the shocked animals, along with the handled animals gained weight faster than those left in the nest (Levine, 1957a and b, 1958; Levine et al., 1956). Byron Lindholm, working with the writer, has repeated and confirmed this finding. Moreover, Levine's shocked and handled animals both showed less emotionality than those left continuously in the nest with their mothers, i.e., less emotionality in the sense that they defecated and urinated less frequently when placed in a strange situation. Finally, the shocked and handled animals, which have appeared alike in all of these experiments, learned an avoidance response more rapidly and drank more readily after eighteen hours without water than did the rats left in the nest with their mother.

Clearly these results on both human children and rats imply that fear and anxiety must sometimes have some other basis than that of being associated with painful stimulation. As many of you know, Hebb (1946, 1949) has formulated a radically different explanation of fear which may be termed either an incongruity or a dissonance theory.

The facts which suggested Hebb's conception came largely from observing chimpanzees being raised under controlled conditions at the Yerkes Laboratory. Fear, defined as withdrawal behaviour in response to the appearance of some object, does not appear in young chimpanzees until they are approximately four months old. Then, the objects feared are familiar objects in unfamiliar guise. Fear of strangers is an example. This appears spontaneously to the first stranger seen, so it cannot be based on associating strangers with painful stimulation. Fear of strangers does not appear in chimpanzees—or in children, I might add—who have always been exposed to a large number of persons. While the avoidance response is unlearned, the familiar, expected aspects of objects must be learned. The young animal must have established as residues of his experience cortical firing patterns (or cognitive structures—whichever term you like) from which new receptor inputs can be incongruous. Consider the kinds of objects regularly feared. They are, for instance, the familiar keeper or experimenter in strange clothes, the experimenter in a Halloween mask, a plaster cast of a chimpanzee head (which lacks, of course, the familiarly attached body), an anaesthetised chimpanzee infant (from which the familiar patterns of motion are absent). On the other hand, objects which have never entered into the young chimpanzee's life may be strange without evoking withdrawal. In other words, the feared object is one which excites receptors in a fashion which is incongruous with the central, sequential pattern of neural firing which has accrued as a residue of the chimpanzee or human infant's past experience. Until the central pattern has been learned, incongruous stimulation is impossible.

Such a conception can well account for Holmes' findings that lower-class children are less fearful than higher-class children and that boys are less fearful than girls even though both lower-class children and boys of nursery school age are likely to have had the wider experience with the sorts of situations used by Holmes to evoke fear. It may well be that being shocked and handled provides a variety of experience which leaves the rat pups which have been subjected to it less disturbed by such things as open fields and eighteen hours without water, but these effects may ultimately be found to be a matter of still another mechanism. It is too early to say.

Taking seriously this incongruity-dissonance conception of the genesis of fear leads to interesting reinterpretations of a great many of the motivational phenomena of child development. Consider these few. In considering separation anxiety, the incongruity principle makes it necessary to puzzle about how the absence of mother could be the conditional stimulus for the traumatising and helpless distress that has been supposed to have occurred in her absence. In considering fear of the dark, it also becomes unnecessary to puzzle about how the absence of light stimulation could so widely have been associated with painful stimulation. Multiple mothering need not be seen as a traumatising experience in the light of this conception, but rather as an innoculation against social shyness and fear. The timidity of the overprotected child and the social shyness of the rural mountain people get an explanation which has been difficult in terms of the theory of conditioned fear.

MOTIVATION IN TERMS OF THE INCONGRUITY-DISSONANCE PRINCIPLE

This introduction of the incongruity-dissonance principle concludes the three reinterpretations I wish to present today, but I do wish to call your attention to the pervasive character of this incongruity-dissonance principle. It appears to have great explanation power which figures, in one guise or another, in several systematic theories besides that of Hebb, all of which have been characterised as non-dynamic.

Hebb's (1949) theorising is physiological, at least in a verbal sense, in that he conceives the residues of past inputs to be stored in semi-autonomous, reverberating cerebral circuits which he terms *cell assemblies*. These cell assemblies are the neural analogue of concepts, and they get sequentially integrated into what he calls *phase sequences*. The sequential organisation in time provides for the subjective phenomenon of expectation. When markedly incongruous receptor inputs disrupt this sequential organisation, behaviour is changed and the process is felt as unpleasant emotion. Slight degrees of incongruity, which can readily be accommodated, lend interest and may provide attractive problems, but the larger ones are repelling and perhaps even devastating.

Piaget (1952, 1954) utilises very much the same incongruity notion to account for the development of intelligence and concepts in human children. In his system, the child comes at birth with certain sensory-motor coordinations which he terms *schemata*. Variation in stimulus situations calls for adaptive *accommodations* or changes in these schemata, which changes are *assimilated* or stored as residues. Piaget also finds limited incongruities between central schemata and receptor inputs to be interesting and facilitative of growth, but incongruities which extend beyond the child's capacity for accommodation instigate withdrawal or fear and even terror. In Piaget's theory the child's gestalt-like conceptions of reality (space, time, and number) are schemata which develop through a continuous process of accommodations and assimilations and become fixed or static only when the child's schemata come to correspond so well with reality that no further accommodations are required. Here agreement among people is dictated by reality.

Helson (1947, 1948) has called the residues of immediate past experience in the typical psychophysical experiment an *adaptation level*. Both he and McClelland (1953) have seen affective arousal to be a matter of the size of the discrepancy between receptor inputs and the adaptation level. Small discrepancies may be attractively pleasant, large ones repellingly unpleasant. As an example, some of you will readily recall having experienced the affective startle that comes when you have been set to pick up what you thought was a full pail, only to find it empty.

Festinger (1957) has recently written a book entitled *A Theory of Cognitive Dissonance* in which he shows that a discrepancy between belief about a situation and perception of that situation acts like a drive. The subject acts to reduce the *dissonance* by either withdrawing from the incredible situation or by changing his beliefs, and, not incidentally, he finds the dissonance highly unpleasant.

Rogers (1951) has described the basis for anxiety as discrepancy between the 'phenomenological field' and the perceived reality as represented by his two circles. Roger's phenomenological field, however, is not the perceptually-given phenomenal field of such German phenomenologists as Delthei and Husserl. It is rather the inferred storehouse of past experience and represented in the present by expectations, aspirations, self-concept, and the like. Thus, his conceptual scheme appears to fall within the domain of the incongruity-dissonance principle.

Kelly's (1955) *Psychology of Personal Constructs* also makes central use of this principle. The term *personal constructs* refers to the ways in which individuals construe and anticipate events. These each person derives from the way in which he has experienced such events in the past. When a person's constructions fail to predict events, this is disturbing, even anxiety-producing, and it motivates some kind of change, but the change may take place in defences against such change of constructs or in avoiding such events, or in the constructs themselves.

Perhaps, it is worth noting in closing that this incongruity-dissonance principle makes both motivation and reinforcement intrinsic to the organism's relations with its environment, intrinsic, if you will, to the organism's information-processing. It is as if the organism operated like an error-actuated, feedback system where the error is derived from discrepancy between receptor-inputs of the present and the residues of past experience which serve as the basis for anticipating the future. The dominant view of the past half century has seen both motivation and reinforcement as extrinsic to the information-processing. This has put a tremendous burden of responsibility for the management of affective motivation on parents, teachers, and all those in positions of authority and control. Visions of man completely controlled as exemplified by George Orwell's *1984*, are conceivable only by assuming that the extrinsic motivating forces of homoeostatic need and painful stimulation are completely dominant. In this light the terror of the baby chimp at seeing his keeper in a Halloween mask and the irritation of the believer when his beliefs are disconfirmed are perhaps symbols of hope. They may justify Abraham Lincoln's well-known dictum that 'you can fool some of the people all the time, and all the people some of the time, but you cannot fool all the people all the time'.

To return to the cartoon of the lad who was improperly motivated: Perhaps, the task of developing proper motivation is best seen, at least in nutshell form, as limiting the manipulation of extrinsic factors to that minimum of keeping homoeostatic need and exteroceptive drive low, in favour of facilitating basic information-processing to maximise accurate anticipation of reality.

REFERENCES

BEACH, F. A. (1945) 'Current concepts of play in animals', *Amer. Naturalist*, 79, 523–541.

BECHTEREV, V. M. (1913) *La Psychologie objective*, trans. N. Kostyleff, Paris, Alcan.

BERLYNE, D. E. (1950) 'Novelty and curiosity as determinants of exploratory behavior', *Brit. J. Psychol.*, 41, 68–80.

BERLYNE, D. E. (1955) 'The arousal and satiation of perceptual curiosity in the rat', *J. comp. physiol. Psychol.*, 48, 238–46.

BERNARD, C. (1859) *Leçons sur les propriétés physiologiques et les alterations pathologiques des liquides de l'organisme*, Paris, Ballière, 2 vols.

BEXTON, W. H., HERON, W., and SCOTT, T. H. (1954) 'Effects of decreased variation in the sensory environment', *Canad. J. Psychol.*, 8, 70–6.

BUTLER, R. A. (1953) 'Discrimination learning by rhesus monkeys to visual-exploration motivation', *J. comp. physiol. Psychol.*, 46, 95–8.

BUTLER, R. A. (1957) 'Discrimination learning by rhesus monkeys to auditory incentives', *J. comp. physiol. Psychol.*, 50, 239–41.

CANESTRINI, S. (1913) 'Uber das Sinnesleben des Neugebornen', in A. Alzheimer and M. Lewandowsky, eds., *Monogr. Gesamt. Neurol. Psychiat.* (Heft 5), Berlin, Springer.

CANNON, W. B. (1915) *Bodily Changes in Pain, Hunger, Fear, and Rage*, Appleton-Century.

DASHIELL, J. (1928) *Fundamentals of Objective Psychology*, Houghton Mifflin.

DAVIS, R. C., and BUCHWALD, A. M. (1957) 'An exploration of somatic response patterns: stimulus and sex differences', *J. comp. physiol. Psychol.*, **50**, 44–52.

DOLLARD, J., and MILLER, N. E. (1950) *Personality and Psychotherapy*, McGraw-Hill.

FESTINGER, L. *A Theory of Cognitive Dissonance*, Row, Peterson.

FREUD, S. (1900) 'The interpretation of dreams', in *The Basic Writings of Sigmund Freud*, trans. A. A. Brill, New York, Modern Library, 1938, pp. 179–548.

FREUD, S. (1905) 'Three contributions to the theory of sex', in *The Basic Writings of Sigmund Freud*, trans. A. A. Brill, New York, Modern Library, 1938, pp. 553–629.

FREUD, S. (1915) 'Instincts and their vicissitudes', in *Collected Papers*, vol. iv. Hogarth Press, 1950, pp. 60–83.

FREUD, S. (1926) *Inhibition, Symptom, and Anxiety*, trans. H. A. Bunker as *The Problem of Anxiety*, Norton, 1936.

GRANIT, R. (1955) *Receptors and Sensory Perception*, Yale University Press.

HARLOW, H. F. (1950) 'Learning and satiation of response in intrinsically motivated complex puzzle performance by monkeys', *J. comp. physiol. Psychol.*, **43**, 289–94.

HARLOW, H. F. (1953) 'Motivation as a factor in the acquisition of new responses. In *Current Theory and Research in Motivation: a symposium*, University of Nebraska Press, pp. 24–49.

HARLOW, H. F. (1958) 'The nature of love', *Amer. Psychologist*, **13**, 673–85.

HARLOW, H. F., HARLOW, M. K., and MEYER, D. R. (1950) 'Learning motivated by a manipulation drive', *J. exp. Psychol.*, **40**, 228–34.

HEBB, D. O. (1946) 'On the nature of fear', *Psychol. Rev.*, **53**, 259–76.

HEBB, D. O. (1949) *The Organization of Behavior*, Wiley.

HEBB, D. O. (1955) 'Drives and the CNS (conceptual nervous system). *Psychol. Rev.*, **62**, 243–54.

HELSON, H. (1947) 'Adaptation-level as frame of reference for prediction of psycho-physical data', *Amer. J. Psychol.*, **60**, 1–29.

HELSON, H. (1948) 'Adaptation-level as a basis for a quantitative theory of frames of reference', *Psychol. Rev.*, **55**, 297–313.

HOLMES, FRANCES B. (1935) 'An experimental study of the fears of young children', in A. T. Jersild and Frances B. Holmes, 'Children's fear', *Child Developm. Monogr.*, **20**, 167–296.

HULL, C. L. (1943) *Principles of Behavior*, Appleton-Century.

HUNT, J. MCV. (1941) 'The effects of infant feeding-frustration upon adult hoarding in the albino rat', *J. abnorm. soc. Psychol.*, **36**, 338–60.

HUNT, J. MCV., SCHLOSBERG, H., SOLOMON, R. L., and STELLAR, E. (1947) 'Studies on the effects of infantile experience on adult behavior in rats: 1. Effects of infantile feeding frustration on adult hoarding', *J. comp. physiol. Psychol.*, **40**, 291–304.

JASPER, H. H. (1937) 'Electrical signs of cortical activity', *Psychol. Bull.*, **34**, 411–81.

JONES, H. E., and JONES, MARY C. (1928) A study of fear. *Child Educ.*, **5**, 136–43.

KELLY, G. A. (1955) *The Psychology of Personal Constructs*, Norton.

LACEY, J. I., and LACEY, BEATRICE C. (1958) 'The relationship of resting autonomic activity to motor impulsivity', in *The Brain and Human Behavior*. Baltimore, Williams & Wilkins, pp. 144–209.

LEVINE, S. (1957a) 'Infantile experience and consummatory behavior in adulthood', *J. comp. physiol. Psychol.*, 50, 609–12.

LEVINE, S. (1957b) 'Infantile experience and resistance to physical stress', *Science*, 126, 405.

LEVINE, S. (1958) 'Noxious stimulation in infant and adult rats and consummatory behavior', *J. comp. physiol. Psychol.*, 51, 230–3.

LEVINE, S., CHEVALIER, J. A., and KORCHIN, S. J. (1956) 'The effects of shock and handling in infancy on later avoidance learning', *J. Pers.*, 24, 475–93.

LILLY, J. C. (1956) 'Mental effects of reduction of ordinary levels of physical stimuli on intact, healthy persons', *Psychiat. Res. Rep.*, no. 5, 1–9.

LINDSLEY, D. B. (1957) 'Psychophysiology and motivation', in M. R. Jones, ed., *Nebraska Symposium on Motivation*. University of Nebraska Press, pp. 44–105.

MCCLELLAND, D. C., ATKINSON, J. W., CLARK, R. A., and LOWELL, E. L. (1953) *The Achievement Motive*, Appleton-Century-Crofts.

MCDOUGALL, W. (1915) *An Introduction to Social Psychology*. Boston, Luce.

MILLER, N. E. (1941) 'An experimental investigation of acquired drives. *Psychol. Bull.*, 38, 534–5.

MILLER, N. E. (1948) 'Studies of fear as an acquirable drive: I. Fear as motivation and fear-reduction as reinforcement in the learning of new responses', *J. exp. Psychol.*, 38, 89–101.

MILLER, N. E., and DOLLARD, J. (1941) *Social Learning and Imitation*, Yale University Press.

MONTGOMERY, K. C. (1951) 'The relation between exploratory behavior and spontaneous alternation in the white rat', *J. comp. physiol. Psychol.*, 44, 582–9.

MONTGOMERY, K. C. (1953) 'The effect of the hunger and thirst drives upon exploratory behavior', *J. comp. physiol. Psychol.*, 46, 315–19.

MONTGOMERY, K. C., and MONKMAN, J. A. (1955) 'The relation between fear and exploratory behavior', *J. comp. physiol. Psychol*, 48, 132–6.

MUSSEN, P. H., and CONGER, J. J. (1956) *Child Development and Personality*, Harper.

OLDS, J. (1955) 'Physiological mechanisms of reward', in M. R. Jones, ed., *Nebraska Symposium on Motivation*, University of Nebraska Press, pp. 73–139.

OLDS, J., and MILNER, P. (1954) 'Positive reinforcement produced by electrical stimulation of septal area and other regions of the rat brain', *J. comp. physiol. Psychol.*, 47, 419–27.

PAVLOV, I. P. (1927) *Conditioned Reflexes*, trans. C. V. Anrep, Oxford University Press.

PIAGET, J. (1952) *The Origins of Intelligence in Children*, New York, International Universities Press.

PIAGET, J. (1954) *The Construction of Reality in the Child*, trans. Margaret Cook, New York, Basic Books.

PRATT, K. C. (1954) 'The neonate', in L. Carmichael, ed., *Manual of Child Psychology*, 2nd edn., Wiley, pp. 215–91.

PROSSER, C. L. (1934) 'Action potentials in the nervous system of the crayfish: I. Spontaneous impulses', *J. cell. comp. Physiol.*, 4, 185–209.

RICHTER, C. P. (1927) 'Animal behavior and internal drives', *Quart Rev. Biol.*, 2, 307–43.

ROGERS, C. R. (1951) *Client-centred Therapy*, Houghton Mifflin.

SHEFFIELD, F. D., ROBY, T. B., and CAMPBELL, B. A. (1954) 'Drive reduction versus consummatory behavior as determinants of reinforcement', *J. comp. physiol. Psychol.*, 47, 349–55.

SHEFFIELD, F. D., WULFF, J. J., and BACKER, R. (1951) 'Reward value of copulation without sex drive reduction', *J. comp. physiol. Psychol.*, 44, 3–8.

SOLOMON, R. L., and BRUSH, ELINOR S. (1956) 'Experimentally derived conceptions of anxiety and aversion', in M. R. Jones, ed., *Nebraska Symposium on Motivation*, University of Nebraska Press, pp. 212–305.

SOLOMON, R. L., and WYNNE, L. C. (1953) 'Traumatic avoidance learning: acquisition in normal dogs', *Psychol. Monogr.*, 67, no. 4 (whole no. 354).

THORNDIKE, E. L. (1913) *Educational Psychology*. Vol. i, *The original nature of man*, vol. ii, *The Psychology of Learning*. New York, Teachers Coll.

WATSON, J. B. (1928) *Psychological Care of the Infant and Child*. Norton.

WATSON, J. B., and RAYNOR, ROSALIE (1920) 'Conditional reactions', *J. exp. Psychol.*, 3, 1–4.

WOODWORTH, R. S. (1918) *Dynamic Psychology*, Columbia University Press.

YOUNG, P. T. (1955) 'The role of hedonic processes in motivation', in M. R. Jones, ed., *Nebraska Symposium on Motivation*, University of Nebraska Press, pp. 193–237.

15

J. McV. Hunt   ## Using intrinsic motivation to teach young children*

Teaching is important, but it is often best done not by the felt effort of giving young children information and criticism but by pulling them along by means of preparations in the environment.

Pulling children along by means of the prepared environment is based largely on what I like to call 'intrinsic motivation'. This is a form of motivation which is quite independent of pain avoidance, homeostatic needs and sex. It is a form of motivation which is inherent in the organism's information processing and action.

This form of motivation appears to have its origins in what the Russians call the 'orienting response'. This is that response of attending and arousal which is evoked by a change in the character of any particular kind of input.

As the very young child repeatedly encounters any given pattern of input, he acquires recognitive familiarity. This recognitive familiarity appears to have emotional significance. Early in life, it appears to be one of the first bases for attentional selection and probably for emotional attachment.

Recognition is important in providing the individual with a standard from which some new input can be novel. It also appears to provide the individual with a position of security which fits him to learn. When one is completely surrounded by the strange and complex, it is as difficult to learn as when one is completely surrounded by the boringly familiar.

In the human infant, the attraction of things newly recognised is

* Reprinted from *Educational Technology*, 11, 1971, 78–80.

probably in part responsible for what has been called pseudo-imitation: the tendency to imitate familiar vocalisations and activities. You can demonstrate this for yourself. Get a youngster who is about three and a half or four months old, and hold him as you talk to him. Say: 'You're a fine little baby, a very fine little baby,' in typical adult fashion. Then, find out from his mother the kinds of noises he has been making. Practice making these sounds until she agrees that they sound like the infant's. Then, look back at the infant and make these sounds that resemble his own: 'Ow-ow-ow-ow-ow-ow.' Note how his pupils widen, how his eyes open, how his mouth goes; and sometimes, you can get the child going, 'Ow-ow-ow-ow' back to you. You get conversation. You get a relationship, if you will. It is conversation without either semantics or syntax, but it is conversation, nevertheless.

In somewhat older children, one can demonstrate the next stage of intrinsic motivation. This is marked by interest in what is novel and of increasing complexity. The 'Ow-ow-ow-ow' routine has become boring. It will not elicit the pupils' widening, the eyes' widening, the response; but, if you know the child, you can modify the sounds he makes, and get the imitation back on the basis of a novel variation. Such a shift in interest from the familiar to the somewhat less familiar, and from there to the much less familiar, is probably exceedingly important in the process of learning language. It is this interest in the novel which presumably entices the child to begin to imitate patterns of speech which do not already belong in his repertoire.

The phenomenon of habituation plays an important role in the development of the interest in the novel and more complex. One can observe this very early in the development of an infant; one can see it all the way through life. This interest in the novel, the new and the more complex is really a kind of corollary of the habituation process. Repeated encounters with patterns lead first to recognition and then to boredom. Once this has occurred it is the new that becomes interesting.

But the infant's stance toward what is new changes as he encounters an increasingly wide variety of circumstances frequently enough to make them recognitively familiar. Once the infant has learned to recognise a variety of things, he almost looks as if he comes to a learning set. It is as if (and I say 'as if' with emphasis) he were saying to himself that, 'Things ought to be recognisable.' In this new stance, when he is presented with something novel, something still unrecognisable, he faces a task, the task of recognition. At the earlier stance, looking-time probably represented the hedonic value of the object. Now, looking-time is not merely a matter of the hedonic value of the thing looked at, because he has the task of making it recognisable. One can see this in adult behaviour. I have a cubistic painting of a falconer in my study. When my mother visited, she remonstrated, 'Joseph, how can you have an awful picture like that up there.' But in the meantime, she was looking at that picture—all the time. And she looked at it for 15 or 20 minutes at a stretch. I no longer look at it very long. It's old stuff. But it was as if she were trying to make this cubistic broken-pattern into some continuous, more familiar pattern. It is thus that, I argue, for infants who have reached the stage of interest in novelty, looking has become a task. It is no longer tied up with hedonic value, pure and simple. At the same time, once an infant begins to show intense interest in the novel, he also begins to show an interest in progressive complexity. One might even say that the child gets 'hooked' on increasing complexity.

In our culture, we are all, to some degree, hooked on complexity if we are free in our encounters with information and with opportunities for action. A parable: based on an experiment on rats by Dember, Earl & Paradise at the University of Michigan. They put rats into a figure-eight maze arranged with a door between the two circular compartments. The wall of one circle was painted solid; the other was painted with horizontal black and white stripes. The animals were put into the maze for an hour. The experimenters simply recorded, during the first hour of encounter, the proportion of time that each rat spent in each of the two circular compartments. No attempt was made to predict the part in which the rat would remain most of the time during this first encounter. But, after the rat had been in the maze once and was given a second exposure of an hour after an interval of twenty-four hours, the theory predicts that, if the rat changes in the compartment where he spends most of his time, *he will change from the less complex to the more complex one.* Those rats who made changes were all among those who preferred the compartment painted in the solid colour the first time, and then the one painted with the black and white stripes the second time. Of thirteen shifts, twelve were in the direction predicted. Do you see the point? Even at the level of rats, if one starts with a choice of the more complex of two circumstances, then there is no change to the simpler. But if the rat starts with a preference for the less complex of two sets of circumstances, he will change in a search for more complexity. This interest in complexity operates in the domain of action as well as in the domain of perception. The fascination which children show as they are learning such new skills as walking, climbing, etc., appears to be based on this interest in increasing complexity. It appears to me that this interest in increasing complexity of action is the basis for what Robert White, at Harvard, has called 'competence motivation'. One finds it at the adult level, also, for note that one finds it quite boring to play a favourite game with one less skilled than himself.

On the other hand, it is also true that it is no fun to be clobbered in that favourite game by someone who is far more skilled than one is. There is an optimum of complexity. As one becomes accustomed to a new increased level of complexity, there is no novelty in reverting back to the less complex. The interest in complexity is unidirectional. It is always in the direction of the more complex, and never in the direction of the less complex, except perhaps, under conditions of fatigue or illness. This is true for any domain, whether it be musical scores, crossword puzzles, motor skills, or competitions.

COMPLEXITY AND COMPETENCE MODELS

Very little research has been done on the search for complexity as a principle in the process of development. Yet, as I see it, this principle is the basis upon which one can motivate a continuous process of learning. In fact, it seems to me to account for what Froebel called 'growth motivation' and what John Dewey also referred to by this term. The complexity of the action and behaviour of another child as the model for imitation is an important factor in the child's interest in developing his own competence. As an infant arrives at a given stage where he can perform a given kind of action, then a somewhat more complex model of that action appeals to his interest. But the presentation of the next level of increased complexity requires a nice judgement. When the increase is too great, the child's increased interest in the model becomes a basis for frustration.

Obviously, one cannot always judge whether the model is too complex or not. It is highly important that the child should be free to take it or leave it according to his own inclinations. It is only when children face disapproval or the loss of love for failing to accept models that are beyond them that difficulty results. When the complex model does motivate, when the child is interested, this interest on the child's part is the best cue that the model is the right distance from the child's established competence.

LEARNING SETS

That repeated recognition leads to the notion that things should be recognisable is, I believe, a kind of 'learning set'. That repeated success in efforts to retain or to regain perceptual contact with interesting spectacles results in a kind of alertness is, I believe, another example of a 'learning set'. By 'alertness' I mean that, even in the first several months of infancy, if the environment is properly prepared so that the child can regain perceptual contact with the spectacles which interest him, it is as if he came to say to himself, 'If I do something, I can make something interesting happen.' One of the first learning sets that was ever observed in child development was the behaviour implying the notion that 'things have names'. This is based upon Ann Sullivan's report of Helen Keller at the pump in the incident where she learned the difference between water and cup. That was followed by a number of other distinctions, then came the behaviour in which Helen would touch various objects and put out her hand to have the words spelled into her hand. Another such learning set involves the assumption that things come in groups. It would also appear to me that many of Chomsky's linguistic rules are derived from encountering the same syntactic orders perceptually over and over. Little Darius, the son of an American anthropologist and his Iranian wife, at eighteen months says to his American grandmother 'Gama' with the accent on the first syllable, and to his Persian grandmother he says 'Gama' with the accent on the last syllable. He has acquired one of the supersegmental rules for each of the two languages, and he has managed this acquisition in the first year-and-a-half of his life.

Many of the strategies for getting and processing information appear to be 'learning sets'. These include the concrete operational strategies of Piaget in which the child is involved chiefly in thinking about what he has observed. They also involve the formal operational strategies, also of Piaget, that develop at about the beginning of adolescence and involve the creation of a logical grid, and thinking that directs observation and then interprets observation in terms of a formal system of logical possibilities. So long as children are at the level of concrete operations, discovery learning appears to be the method of teaching of choice. It does little good simply to lecture to students at this age. Once children have acquired formal operations, however, beginning with adolescence, it is quite sensible to teach by talking to them. But one can teach very little in this talking fashion until later adolescence, and, if a full repertoire of these learning sets and strategies for making sense of things have not yet developed earlier, one cannot teach them by lecturing, even in adolescence.

THE PROBLEM OF THE 'MATCH'

What I like to call 'the Problem of the Match' is highly important in the strategy of teaching. This problem of the match we have already encountered in the matter of getting a model for imitation which is not less complex than the level of competence that the child has already achieved, yet is not so complex as to be frustrating. *Frustration* and *disconfirmation* have always been major ways of inducing learning. They illustrate a principle of importance in this matter which I call the problem of the match. In educational circles, the match has been recognised by what has been termed 'readiness'. And 'readiness' has typically been conceived to be a preparation for learning that comes via that process of maturation controlled entirely by heredity. It is thus, that at six years of age, all children are presumed to be ready for school and ready to learn to read. The school itself commonly constitutes a fairly fixed set of environmental circumstances. All of the children in a given city are presumed to have approximately the same set of readiness, regardless of which side of the tracks they come from. It is clear, however, from comparisons of the linguistic and cognitive skills of children from the slums with the measures of linguistic and cognitive skills in children from the suburbs, that they differ markedly. Once this difference was attributed to differences in fixed intelligence. The children of the slums were simply stupid and poorly motivated, and this was considerd to be the nature of the little brutes. Our tests of intelligence tend to bear this out, and when the children from the slums did less well in a standard school environment than the children from the suburbs, they were still doing as well as could be expected—from the tests. From the standpoint of interactionism, underlying the kind of points I have been making, such an interpretation of class difference is no longer sensible. Readiness for any given kind of teaching or encounter with circumstances is not a matter of fixed intelligence, it is a matter of the linguistic and cognitive skills which have been developed in the course of the child's life history. From the standpoint of this 'match' the task of the teacher is to find the kind of circumstances, or the mode of approach, which will *interest* the child and *induce* learning.

It is no easy matter to do this, for the diagnostic instruments that we have are not geared to a natural science of intellectual, linguistic and motivational development. Mental ages are somewhat helpful, but not very. We are, at present, very weak in techniques of assessment. We need techniques or tests which define abilities, techniques that I sometimes like to call 'transitive tests', tests designed to tell us what learning sets and skills a child already has established and what kinds of things to confront him with to induce learning. We have very few tests that tell us how to prepare the circumstances to foster learning. At the present state of our knowledge, I believe that the best cues we have come in those behavioural indications of interest and surprise. When a child shows the behavioural signs of interest, we can feel confident of being on the right track.

I believe it is safer to arrange the circumstances in such a fashion that the child can take them or leave them as his indications dictate. I am not sure of this in the case of culturally deprived children, for it may well be necessary to use some of the reinforcement techniques to change the child's motivation from one already spoiled by his impoverished circumstances before he can begin to learn. On the whole, *I contend that when the child is not interested, when he's bored, then one had better increase the complexity of the circumstances that the child is able to encounter.* When he is frustrated, when he is angered, those circumstances are too complex. When he's interested, and even when he is somewhat surprised, one is on the right track. This holds for both materials and models. What Montessori did, from the motivational standpoint, was to provide graded series of models by using children from three to seven within a given class, and to provide a series of complexity in the various kinds of materials that she prepared for her children to work with. One of the implications of the position I am presenting is that one should arrange the circumstances in a fashion that allows the child to make the choices about the level of complexity which he wishes to encounter. This, I believe, was the trick that Montessori used.

The circumstances should be arranged so that the child can, as it were, walk away from the boring blocks or knock down the too difficult ones with impunity.

To come back to my opening paragraph, teaching is highly important. But what we need to do is to arrange the circumstances so that they will interest children, and to select those environmental circumstances for the prepared environment that will pull children along in the development of those abilities, those motives and those standards which are required for full participation in our highly technological society. Then we need to get out of their way while they go about the business of learning.

16

D. F. *Swift*   Social class and
                     achievement motivation*

The basic facts of social class performance in school are so well known
as hardly to need repeating. As all teachers know, the children who do
the best work, are easiest to control and stimulate, make the best
prefects, stay at school longest, take part in extra-curricular activities,
finish school with the best qualifications and references and get into the
best jobs, tend to come from the middle class. The relationship exists in
the Junior School (Douglas, 1964), manifests itself in the 11+ (Floud
et al., 1956; Fraser, 1959; Swift, 1965) and seriously affects secondary
education (*Early Leaving*, Ministry of Education, 1954).

Swift (1965) found that the children of middle-class parents had six
times as good a chance of selection at 11+ as working-class children.
In this study it became clear that the lack of balance in these 'class
chances' was mainly due to the fact that the sons of middle-class
parents were, to that degree, better able to score on intelligence and
attainment tests. Many psychologists explain this by suggesting that
there is a basic intellectual superiority in the middle class which
is maintained by selective mating and a tendency to inherit innate
intelligence. This explanation begs as may questions as it answers, but
their discussion is irrelevant to the material with which this paper will
deal, since all parties would agree that there is room for some environmental distortion of the basic genetic relationships.

A recent study by a psychologist found that all the factors which are
usually thought to be bad for the intellectual development of the child
(except a working mother) were in fact related to poor performance
in the school. Fraser (1959) found that parental education and reading
habits, income, occupation and living space all related significantly
with IQ and school performance. In the motivational sphere, parental

*Reprinted from *Educational Research*, **8**, 1966, 83–95.

attitudes towards the education and future employment of the child, together with the degree of encouragement which they felt they offered the child towards school work, were all significantly related with IQ and performance. Finally, abnormality in the family was found to be an important correlate of poor performance.

Of the eleven 'aspects' of the environment which Fraser considered, the nine mentioned above can be fairly called important elements of the social class situation. Of the remaining two, one (mother at work) was not significant, whilst the second (abnormal background) is to some extent a social class definition.

Since these 'aspects' are also important elements of the social class system a question immediately arises as to whether they would maintain their significance if the population were separated into groups representing different culture-patterns. Under these circumstances, would the 'aspects' retain their significance for performance, or does it derive from the fact that they are simply dimensions of a certain social class sub-culture? It is unfortunate that social class itself has not received the scientific 'mapping out' necessary to its being treated as a variable which can be strictly controlled, and it is possible to suggest that it never will, but this does not make it permissible to ignore it.

The sociological stream of thought which has provided the most valuable theory concerning the relationship between socio-cultural learning and the development of intellectual and motivational skills is the 'clash of values' approach which began with Allison Davis's (1948) inaugural lecture on social class influences upon learning. (See also Davis, 1949 and 1960.)

It was Davis's contention that there are barriers to understanding *within* societies which are every bit as serious as those which exist *between* societies; barriers which are all the more serious for the fact that the participating members do not realise their existence. Consequently, Davis enjoined educationists to study the social class system to discover those mental problems, solutions and cultural definitions of what is pleasant and desirable which are emphasised within the different social classes. Similarly, Toby (1957) analysed the problems involved in the maladjustment which occurs when the lower-class child brings the attitudes towards education of his culture into the school.

CHILD-REARING TECHNIQUES, MOTIVATION AND SCHOOL ACHIEVEMENT

The Davis critique of objective and subjective intelligence testing in the educational system stimulated research studies which can be grossly separated according to their concern for either child-rearing practices or parental value-systems. These two aspects of the learning process are clearly interdependent and to concentrate in research upon one aspect without the other is to run the risk of discovering irrelevant relationships since important factors in the other perspective are left uncontrolled. This becomes more important the 'nearer' the research approaches the individual. That is, the more detailed the definition of influential factors the greater the danger that its context is ignored. Child-rearing research has suffered greatly from this weakness and despite valiant efforts to take a synoptic view of the many non-comparable and occasionally contradictory findings (Bronfenbrenner, 1958; Clausen and Williams, 1963), headway has been slow. Research has concentrated upon a few of the more obvious mechanisms by which parents attempt to socialise children, and in doing this it has often simplified to a caricature the complex relationship between the environment and the developing personality.

Perhaps the grossest simplification undertaken by these studies is to assume that parental perceptions of what they do to a child are adequate representations of what *is* done to a child by the parent. Human interaction is far more subtle than this. A child is able to 'tune into' the implicit culture of his family life without too much interference from the manifest attitudes of parents towards what he should do in a particular situation. The folk-lore adage, 'do as I say, not as I do', comes nearer to an understanding of this complex relationship than many of the researches.

As an example of the contradictory conclusions which these studies have produced, we can compare Drews and Teaman (1957) with Fraser (1959). Drews discovered the attitudes of mothers of high and low academic achievers of both gifted and average intelligence on scales of permissiveness, protectiveness and domination. Her conclusions were that mothers of high achievers were more authoritarian and restrictive than mothers of low achievers. Parents of high achievers of gifted intelligence also seemed to have more punitive attitudes with respect to child-rearing. In contradiction, Fraser's research implies that the friendliness and spontaneity of a lenient 'democratic' atmosphere provided the 'best' (in terms of school motivation and achievement) family environment. Similarly, Elder (1965) investigated the association between perceived parent–adolescent relations and the likelihood of reaching secondary school in the United States, Great Britain, Western Germany, Italy and Mexico. He found a negative association between parental dominance and access to secondary education in all five countries where the structure of educational opportunity made it feasible.

Despite the contradictions in research findings, Bronfenbrenner, by dint of imaginative understanding and a not altogether persuasive hypothesis[1] perceived a change taking place during the twenty-five year period of research which he reviewed. For Bronfenbrenner, middle-class parents in America have changed from a 'restrictive' to a 'permissive' approach. Fortunately, he avoids the superficially reasonable conclusion that since there has been no change in middle-class ability to out-perform and out-drive the working class, child-rearing methods are of no importance. As Kohn (1963) points out, the researches summarised by Bronfenbrenner were only as good as the questions they used and hence their implied conceptual models. The changes which took place represent faddish alterations in superficial techniques which are not symptomatic of changes in the basic relationships between parents and children. 'Parents have changed techniques in the service of much the same values' (Kohn 1963, p. 473).

A further point of view has been brought to bear on the question by Veroff (1965) who suggests a theoretical background to the problem in motivational research of distinguishing between situational and personality factors in any situation. Veroff's major hypothesis is:

> that there is a critical stage for learning the affective associations attendant to the development of motives and motivational expectancies. If the environment supports learning these associations during the critical period, then strong motivational dispositions will develop; if the environment supports a time earlier than the critical time, anxiety connected with these motivations will develop and if the environment supports learning at a date later than the critical time, very specific motives and expectancies will ensue (p. 17).

This emphasises the specific contribution of the environment. Furthermore, it implies that, in research, we should treat the environment as a whole which has a specific meaning for the developing personality and intellect deriving from the specific configurations of the whole matrix of factors. This is an important point which may help to explain the inconsistencies of research findings. The usual psychological approach has been to isolate particular factors (specific techniques in punishment for example) and relate these to motivation or achievement. It was not understood that this specific research act carried an implicit assumption that the same techniques carried out in this way meant the same thing to the child regardless of the social context. It was thought of as a single 'stimulus' similar to the stimulus which is produced in a

---

[1] that middle class parents are more responsive to mass media child-rearing instruction.

laboratory by manipulation of an independent variable. Unfortunately (or fortunately), family life is not a laboratory and this assumption cannot be made at present.[2] The 'situation' must be seen as a matrix of interrelating factors which is destroyed when a single crude factor is abstracted since the factor derives its meaning from its context. For example, 'but you *must* go to school', does not mean the same in a context of love and mutual respect as it does in a context in which the child fully understands the implicit relief of the parent in being rid of him. Yet the degree of firmness might be exactly the same.

Because of this problem in dealing with the environment,[3] it is to be expected that those studies which looked for a generalised picture of the family environment ('loving', 'supportive', etc.) and those which employed social class analysis, came closest to general agreement.

Before dealing with social class analysis we might mention a fairly elementary relationship which does appear to hold in all situations. Parental encouragement does have an important bearing upon school motivation and performance. Mannino (1962) reported that, with socio-economic status controlled, 'staying on' at school after the minimum leaving age related positively to parental encouragement. Wall (1962) concluded that 'children, particularly boys, do very much better at school if their parents are interested in their progress', and that 'children whose parents are rated as "very interested" improve their test-scores between eight and eleven but those whose parents are "uninterested" show a deterioration in score'. Douglas (1964, p. 61) also suggested that children tend to work well when their parents take an interest in their school progress and to work badly when they are uninterested.

SOCIAL CLASS VALUES AND ACHIEVEMENT MOTIVATION

Many studies have shown a positive association between the level of educational and occupational aspirations on the one hand and various

[2] This is not to say that the logic of research is wrong. The ideal aim is still to discover in the environment all the most important stimuli and to refine the techniques by which they can be measured. It only means that our actual abilities to do this in family life research covering a long period of time are incapable of handling the environment in this way at the present time.

[3] As a sociologist the writer must insist upon including the individual's perception of the social reality as part of 'the environment' since psychologists often do their research studies serious damage by assuming that 'the environment' constituted only the material and geographical aspects of the environment.

measures of social status on the other. Usually it is assumed that this association is a 'real' one which results from the influence of the particular constellations of occupational, educational and action values which are implicit in the culture of the middle class. However, the equally clear relationship between school ability and middle-class status is not usually accepted at face value. At least part of this association is thought to be due to an intervening variable called 'intelligence'. Sewell *et al.* (1957) considered the possibility that the aspiration-social class relationship was also due to the intervention of this factor, intelligence. Tests on a random sample of high school seniors covering the state of Wisconsin confirmed that the relationship between aspiration and social class was not simply due to the common relationship of these variables to intelligence. Social class (whatever that is) makes an independent contribution. This is important because the conclusion was arrived at by controlling for 'intelligence' which itself can be shown to be derived, to some extent, from socio-cultural learning experiences. Thus, the importance of social status showed through even though it was weakened by controlling intelligence.

With Sewell as justification and Davis as inspiration we can now consider the value-systems of the different social classes to be learning environments which participate in the development of motivation and achievement levels. Davis had urged the use of class analysis in investigating the environment for factors in intellectual and personality development because it appears to provide the best means by which the cultural experience of the child may be described. It represents the best shorthand method for summarising the individual's cultural beliefs, his definitions of life problems and possible solutions, the meaning of his language, and his culturally learned conceptions of the teacher, himself and school. As Kohn (1963, p. 471) puts it: 'It is so useful because it captures the reality that the intricate interplay of all these variables creates different basic conditions of life at different levels of the social order.'

Early Leaving was taking a similar, if much cruder, line when, in partial explanation of the fact that working-class children leave grammar school before their middle-class peers, it has the following to say:

One of the man influences must be sought in the outlook and assumptions of parents in various walks of life. Consider first the outlook of parents in professional occupations. Most of them themselves received a grammar school or similar education, and others have made their way into a position in society in which they find such a background taken for granted. They are all engaged on work for which a fairly high level of education is an obvious advantage and many follow professions to which a specified educational standard is a condition of entry. In the circumstances it is not surprising that they assume that their children will not leave school at 15 but will stay as much longer as their ability justifies. This assumption is not due to any conscious sense of the value of education; it may be a mere social convention which has never been questioned. But it is in any case a powerful influence on parents towards keeping their children at school, and on children towards staying (p. 36).

Before *Early Leaving* was published, Kahl (1953) documented a similar phenomenon in the American educational system. During the course of a nationwide mobility study it became plain that 'IQ and family status were useful predictors of the educational and occupational ambitions of high school boys'. However, within the lower-middle range it was found that these relationships were weaker than at the higher and lower reaches of the scale. Kahl, therefore, chose a pair of matched samples of boys from this status group, one representing boys who wished to go to college and another representing boys who did not wish to go. Interviews revealed that, 'although there was a common way of life which identified the common-man class, some members were content with that way of life while others were not'. Discontented parents, seeing that the educational system was a way out for their sons, tended to train them from the earliest years of grammar school to take school seriously. 'Only sons who internalised such values were sufficiently motivated to overcome the obstacles which faced the common-man boys in school; only they saw a good reason for good school performance and college aspirations' (Kahl, 1953, p. 203).

An important finding of the study was that boys, to an extent not previously imagined, took up and held as their own, their parents' perceptions of possible opportunities, the desirability and possibility of status mobility, methods of obtaining mobility, and the goals which they felt appropriate to boys in their position at school. Neither the school nor mass media seemed to have much influence in moulding these ideas. This finding, which has found support in other research, is a very firm invitation to researchers to concentrate upon family environment, and since that time a great deal of research has been carried out on parental values and their effect upon motivation in school.

A further extension of this work within the Harvard Mobility Survey was undertaken by Elizabeth Cohen (1959) who studied fifty matched pairs of boys in the 'common-man' group. Each pair consisted of a 'mobile' and a 'non-mobile' boy matched for IQ, ethnicity, town of origin and parental membership of the common-man group. Attitudes of parents and sons were obtained by Guttman scale testing, and the basic aim was to chart the channels of parental influence upon the motivation of their sons. Cohen's theoretical model included three principal channels of influence; through socio-economic characteristics, through generalised attitudes towards college, and through concrete encouragement. In these ways the parents were expected to influence the decisions of their sons as to whether they wished to go to college or not.

In analysing the influence of socio-economic status, Cohen suggested that a significant difference in motivation is found among children of working-class parents who have close 'on the job' associations with people of higher status. As regards 'pressure' it was found that parents of mobile sons seemed deliberately to encourage them to aim for middle-class occupations and educational qualifications but did not push for higher school performance as such.

A similar sort of study was reported by Reissman (1953), aimed at determining the relationship between class and aspirations. Apart from age, he found that the two important aspects of the individual's value-system were his reference group and certain 'life-orientations'. The reference group is obviously important to the degree of satisfaction the individual has with past mobility and future aims. Thus a low level of aspiration can be based on a feeling of achievement in relation to the normal achievement of his reference group. Orientations other than success and mobility can be dominant for some individuals and thereby lead them to exert their energies in a different direction, or prevent them from aiming for mobility.

In England, Himmelweit (1955) enquired into the relationship between socio-economic background and behaviour on the one hand, and the formation of attitudes and values on the other. It is interesting to note here the use to which a social psychologist has put the Davis hypothesis. For Dr Himmelweit and many American social psychologists, this hypothesis has suggested that 'a kind of adaptive socialised anxiety is generated more rapidly as a result of middle-class methods of upbringing'. The difficulty experienced by working-class children to adapt to the middle-class school culture was also considered. Information was collected on a wide variety of topics with the aim of ascertaining the degree to which Davis's hypothesis could be confirmed in England on representative samples of grammar school and secondary modern school children from middle-middle to lower working class.

The results confirmed some of Davis's and Warner's hypotheses.

Middle-class children were more concerned with how well they do at school, as are their parents. Parents also supervise the leisure of their children more. However—

> despite so many confirmatory results as to the greater pressure to which the middle class child is subjected, both externally by the parents and internally by his more rigid super-ego and more intra-punitive technique of handling frustrations, no evidence of greater overall anxiety or tension was obtained (Himmelweit, 1955, p 34).

A further set of findings was concerned with the transmission of values. One of the hypotheses was that the upwardly mobile working-class boy would try to become like his middle-class co-pupil with the result that his answers might be different from those of the non-mobile members of his class. It was also expected that the two middle-class groups (successful and unsuccessful) would be similar. There were two main results. Firstly, the difference between the school groups of the middle and working classes were so much greater than those between social classes within the same school that differences were thought to reflect, in large measure, differences in educational and intellectual achievement. Secondly, the difference between the working-class groups was most marked. Parents of successful working-class boys had a much more middle-class set of values than even the middle class.

Hyman (1953) saw a system of beliefs and values peculiar to the lower class acting as an 'intervening variable mediating the relationship between low position and lack of upward mobility'. The components of this value-system were:

1. less emphasis on traditional high success goals;
2. increased awareness of lack of opportunity to achieve success;
3. less emphasis on the achievement of goals which in turn would be instrumental for success.

These all add up to a self-imposed barrier to mobility. Thus, apart from the structurally imposed barriers to mobility they have a further set of hindrances in their own ideas about mobility.

Hyman analysed census and other data looking for evidence that motivation to advance to high places and to obtain the right sort of training for doing so was lower in the lower class. Considering first the value placed on formal education, he quoted four studies which supported the idea that the lower class always placed a lower value on education than those above them in the social scale. He found that there were crucial differences in values as regards motivation to advance in the economic structure. For example, when respondents were asked to choose their ideal occupation there was a strong tendency for upper-class people to choose occupations for 'congeniality to person' reasons. On the other hand, the choices of lower-class people indicated much more interest in the economic benefits of the occupation. Only a very few wealthy people chose skilled occupations as being preferable to others, whereas a major proportion of lower-class people chose this form of qualification. In these ways Hyman emphasised that there is reduced striving among the lower classes, an awareness of lack of opportunity, and different ideas as to how social mobility might come about.

The special relevance of values in the family was clarified by Rosen (1956) who expressed dissatisfaction with current psychological and sociological explanations of social mobility. Hitherto, says Rosen, the greater achievement of the middle class has been explained either by a process of social selection—the middle class being more intelligent, healthier and more attractive; or by the differential opportunities open to the two classes—the 'life chances' hypothesis. These explanations, he agreed, were relevant and consistent with each other, but they were not exhaustive:

> since neither explanation takes into account the possibility that there may be psychological and cultural factors which affect social mobility by influencing the individual's willingness to develop and exploit his talent, intelligence and opportunities (Rosen, 1956, p. 203).

Therefore, his thesis was that differential rates of mobility may also be explained as a function of differences in the motives and values of the social classes. Rosen saw that there were two components in the achievement orientations of the different classes. Firstly, a psychological factor—the personality characteristic of 'achievement motivation', which provides an internal impetus to excel. Secondly, there is also a cultural factor consisting of certain value orientations which define and implement achievement motivated behaviour. He suggested that values affect mobility in three ways:

1. they provide a definition of goals;
2. they focus the attention of the individual on achievement;
3. they prepare him to translate motive into action.

Thus, whether or not the individual tries for mobility will be decided by his values. Before the drive for achievement can be expressed in the right, culturally defined terms there must be awareness of, and willingness to undertake, the necessary steps for achievement. These will of necessity involve the ability to plan, to sacrifice, and to strive consistently. Here again, abilities like these will be partly dependent on the values of the individual.

Rosen goes further to make a crucial distinction between widespread values and implementary values. Frequently we can see no difference between classes in the holding of some popular widespread value like the desirability of upward mobility. But a difference is found in the implementary values which facilitate and encourage achievement. He summarised the situation in America in terms of basic or implementary values in this way:

> Middle class children are more likely . . . to embrace the achievement value-system which states that given the willingness to work hard, plan and make proper sacrifices, an individual child should be able to manipulate his environment so as to ensure eventual success (Rosen, 1956, p. 211).

Progress, that is, is not necessarily a question of drive. At least as important is the way in which the individual fits in with the requirements of his present situation. This is obviously so with our education system. Successful mobility can come to those who simply adapt themselves well to each successive stage, the system itself carrying them up as on the crest of a wave. This meshing in with the values, perceptions and behaviours of a culture-pattern constitutes, with the achievement drive, the two basic factors which produce mobility within the framework laid down by the structure of possibilities.

Having established the abundance of theoretical justifications for an analysis of family value-patterns along social class lines, it now remains for us to deal with some of the more recent substantive findings of research studies which have been designed on these lines.

Douvan (1956) sets the stage with an experiment designed to test the hypothesis that 'achievement want' of middle-class children is more generalised than that of working-class children and hence is less likely to vary with changes in the reward offered for achievement. Her conclusion was that the achievement want of the middle-class child was more generalised as well as more dependable.

Douvan and Adelson (1958) also provide us with a useful thumbnail sketch of the upward and downward-aspiring boy. In this survey, the authors classified boys as upward mobile, stable, or downward mobile, depending upon whether their occupational aspirations were higher than, similar to, or lower than their father's occupation. Interviews with the boys revealed the following categorisations. The upward-aspiring boy was described as being unusually lively and energetic. He expressed concern for the intrinsic interest of his future work and has a longer time-perspective when thinking of occupations. A set of pictures was used to discover the degree and form of internalised standards possessed by the two extreme groups. These pictures portrayed an adolescent boy facing conflicting pressures. For example, he might be torn between a promise to parents to be home at a particular hour and a wish to accept pressure from his friends to stay out late. In both groups two-thirds of the respondents decided that the boy would go home. Thus there was no difference in prognosticated *behaviour*. However, there was a difference in perceived motives for the action in that the upward-aspiring boys tended to explain his actions in terms of his promise to his parents, or because his parents had trusted him. The downward-aspirers were more likely to explain his return by fear of punishment. The implications of these findings for the authors was that the upward-oriented have internalised personal controls in contrast to the downward-oriented who showed a tendency to internalise external standards and rebel against them. The upward-aspirer was found to show greater independence from his family whereas the downward-aspirer was at once more dependent on, and rebellious towards, his family. Finally, the upward-aspirer showed high self-acceptance and social confidence in comparison with the downward-aspirer who was more ambivalent towards himself and more unsure in social situations.

These findings fit neatly with those of Kohn (1959) who showed clearly that child-rearing values of middle-class parents stress internalised standards for governing relationships with other people while the working class concentrated upon qualities of honesty and neatness. Apart from demonstrating the importance of social class analysis in this question (as do Kohn and Carroll, 1960) the findings support Duvall's description of working- and lower-middle-class parental values as 'traditional' in comparison with the middle-class 'developmental' emphasis. With the working-class parent it is the actual act that matters. The child must accept externally imposed rules. To the middle-class parent it is the motives of the child which give meaning to the act. Thus we can expect that where the middle-class family is successful in transmitting such a point of view to the child, he will develop a responsibility for his own values and actions which would support his acceptance of the parental views on educational and occupational aspirations. On the other hand, a working-class point of view on education (most social classes feel that education is A GOOD THING) will tend to be imposed upon the child together with other external rules. There is greater likelihood that the child will rebel against this as against other arbitrarily imposed rules. There is then a further factor that even where the working-class child internalises the value it will mean something different to him. Horizons will be lower and understanding of the situation and its requirements less efficient.

Katz (1964) studied the meaning of success among Australian adolescents and found evidence of considerable variation according to socio-economic class of origin. These differences appeared to indicate 'a major difference in the frame of aspirational reference internalised by members of different social classes'. In the case of the middle-class adolescent, the success goal was prestige achievement attained through personal effort and worthiness. Adolescents from the unskilled working class, on the other hand, had little concern for social status. Success is defined in terms of 'possessions which are procured by personal exertion, but limited in possibility of attainment by factors over which the individual has no control'. Between these two extremes, adolescents of skilled worker families showed a great deal of variation, suggesting to Katz that some had internalised middle-class and others, unskilled-class, perceptions.

The importance of chance in the lower working-class perception of the environment is supported by research in Britain and most relevantly by the theories and research of Basil Bernstein (1962). On the basis of his analysis of linguistic forms, Bernstein suggests that middle-class life and language encourage the development of an 'instrumental' attitude to the world around which is distinct from the more intellectually passive perceptions of the working class.

We have seen that the values of working-class life tend to demand adoption of rules which are seen by the child to be external and arbitrary ('because I say so'). We also know that the horizons of social actuality implicit in the specific behavioural imperatives by which working-class parents seek to organise the behaviour of children are 'shorter' and 'narrower' than those of the middle-class families [though none the less 'accurate' for that (Liversidge, 1962)]. Since middle-class children have higher need achievement in relation to education and this clearly is important in actual performance,[4] we can assume that the imposition of arbitrary rules and shorter horizons are both depressive factors in the need for educational achievement. They clearly are when taken together and in certain cultural situations. How-

---

[4] Douglas (1964, p. 60) found that according to teachers, 26 per cent of upper-middle-class children work 'very hard' as opposed to 7 per cent of upper and lower working-class: (p. 64) children who work 'hard' or 'very hard' get 12 per cent more grammar school places than they would be expected on their tests to get, while 'poor' or 'average' workers got 25 per cent fewer places than their tests would lead us to expect.

ever, they need not go together. In line with the earlier theoretical objections to abstraction of a single factor for treatment as a continuously operating variable, we have to consider the possibility that different situations will give very different functions to any single factor.

The lower middle class provides a useful test of this possibility. Duvall (1946) had joined the lower middle class to the working class in categorising their child-rearing ethos as 'traditional'. On the other hand, the work situation, upon which one might expect their achievement values to depend, would be different. They would tend to do work which demanded skills in the manipulation of ideas and persons as opposed to working-class activities with things. Promotion will, superficially at any rate, appear to depend upon the actual performance of the individual. Finally, the lower middle class is likely to be less subject to control than the working class.

With all these points in mind, and in the light of Argyle and Robinson's (1962) suggestion that introjection or projection of parental ambition is important in parent–child relationships, Swift (1964) related the 11+ performance of lower-middle-class children to the mobility pessimism of their fathers. In a ten per cent random sample of a local education authority division it was found that, within the middle class, the father's dissatisfaction with his job and its prospects related significantly to the likelihood of his child's success on the 11+. In addition it was found that mobility-pessimism was very dependent upon lower-middle-class membership. In the sample only one out of nine lower-middle-class fathers of successful children did not have 'high' mobility-pessimism.

On the basis of these very clear but necessarily tentative findings, a second ideal-type of academically successful family was constructed.[5] The principal intention behind this was to emphasise the weakness of the position which tends to see 'the family environment' as a variable which ranges from 'good' to 'bad' in terms of its capacity to produce children who are adaptive to the needs of the educational system. This is a logically reasonable perspective to hold but it carries with it the danger of implicit assumptions about the linearity of relationships between its component elements and educational adaptiveness which are not necessarily valid. In this case, research has emphasised the importance of a supportive, 'democratic' family life which encourages the development of personal confidence and satisfaction with values

[5] An alternative, that is, to the usual ideal-type of 'cultured' upper-middle-class family in which the child is stimulated in a generally tolerant fashion to develop his capabilities in many directions.

which are accepted rather than imposed. The assumption which tends to follow from this is that the 'developmental' environment is best at the top and non-existent at the bottom of the social class hierarchy. In this way it can be seen to be a stimulus which relates in a linear fashion to need for educational achievement and hence educational success.

This second ideal-type of academically successful family was one in which mobility-pessimism was high, and discipline was 'traditional'. Commitment to education was 'high' but of a very different nature to the high commitment expressed in the ideal-type middle-class family where it is valued for its liberating qualities for the individual. Instead (in the light of the 'traditional' discipline ethos) it was seen as a necessary aspect of certificate-collecting which was, in turn, seen to be the major 'external' demand of the social environment. One way in which this family differs from the working-class family lies in the social horizons which the parents hold for their children. Because of similarities in work situation and content, and probably of early educational experience, the lower-middle-class parent will have horizons which are closer to those found in the remainder of the middle class. He is also likely to understand what is involved in school work and will not be burdened by the idea that the people who get into the higher classes represent a different sort of person from himself.[6]

This all adds up to a very different sort of environment to the stereo-typical 'educationally successful' middle-class family. It is also one which cannot logically be placed midway between skilled working and middle class except on a single specific criterion like income. According to the hypothesis, the nearer a family approaches this ideal-type, the more likely is their child to be successful in the school. The whole analytical situation is then made vastly more complicated when we remember that the hypothesis has been framed in terms of two ideal-types, neither of which is likely to exist. Any given family will simultaneously go some way towards both ideal-types. However, social class analysis can help in 'controlling' for certain configurations of variables to the extent that work-situation, income and education tend to encourage their development.

CONCLUSION

An attempt has been made to present a perspective on the relationship between family environment and the need for educational achievement. This is a sociological perspective which employs the concept of values

[6] For the reasons which Hyman (1953) made clear, this has a depressing effect upon aspiration and action.

as the link between the social environment on the one hand and educational motivation on the other. It is suggested that research upon the development of educational potential has tended to oversimplify the subtle relationships between the developing personality and its environment.

However, research and theory which recognised the coherence of the cultural environment have suggested some general propositions. The accuracy of these propositions may not prove to be high, but if British research follows the lead given by American workers, away from descriptive and naïve correlational studies towards socio-cultural analysis, there is real prospect of light.

REFERENCES

ARGYLE, M. and ROBINSON, J. (1962) 'Two origins of achievement motivation', *Brit. Jour. Soc. and Clin. Psych.*, **1**, part 2.

BENE, EVE (1959) 'Some differences between middle class and working class grammar school boys in their attitudes towards education', *Brit. Jour. Sociol.*, **10**.

BERNSTEIN, BASIL (1962) 'Social class linguistic codes and grammatical elements', *Language and Speech*, **5**, 221–40.

BRONFENBRENNER, URIE (1958) 'Socialisation and social class through time and space', in E. E. Maccoby, T. M. Newcomb, and R. L. Hartley, eds., *Readings in Social Psychology*, New York, Henry Holt, pp. 400–25.

CAMPBELL, W. J. (1955) 'The influence of socio-cultural environment on the progress of children at the secondary school level', *Australian J. Psych*, **7**, 140–6.

CENTERS, RICHARD (1948) 'Motivational aspects of occupational stratification', *J. Soc. Psych.*, **28**, 187–214.

CLAUSEN, J. A. and WILLIAMS, J. (1963) 'Sociological correlates of child behaviour', in H. W. Stevenson, J. Kegan, and C. Spiker, eds., Child Psychology section in *Yearbook of National Society for Studies in Education*, **62**, 62–107.

COHEN, E. (1959) 'Parental factors in educational mobility', unpublished Ph.D. thesis, Harvard University.

COHEN, E. (1965) 'Parental factors in educational mobility', *Sociol. of Educ.*, **38**, no. 5, 401–25.

DAVIS, ALLISON (1948) *Social Class Influences Upon Learning*, Harvard University Press.

DAVIS, ALLISON (1949) 'American status systems and the socialisation of the child', in C. Kluckhohn and H. A. Murray, *Personality in Nature, Society and Culture*, Knopf.

DAVIS, ALLISON (1960) *Psychology of the Child in the Middle Class*, University of Pittsburg Press.

DOUGLAS, J. W. B. (1964) *The Home and the School*, MacGibbon & Kee, pp. 60–5 and 159–62.

DOUVAN, ELIZABETH (1956) 'Social status and success strivings', *J. Abnorm. and Soc. Psych.*, **52**, 219–23.

DOUVAN, ELIZABETH and ADELSON, J. (1958) 'The psychodynamics of social mobility in adolescent boys', *J. Abnorm. and Soc. Psych.*, 56, 31–44.

DREWS, ELIZABETH MONROE and TEAMAN, JOHN E. (1957) 'Parental attitudes and academic achievement', *J. Clin. Psych.*, 13, 328–32.

DUVALL, EVELYN M. (1946) 'Conceptions of parenthood', *Amer. J. Sociol.*, 52, 193–203.

ELDER, GLEN H. (1965) 'Family structure and educational attainment; a cross-national analysis', *Amer. Sociol. Rev.*, 30, no. 1, 81–96.

FLOUD, J. E., HALSEY, A. H., and MARTIN, A. M. (1956) *Social Class and Educational Opportunities*, Heinemann.

FRASER, ELIZABETH (1959) *Home Environment and the School*, University of London Press.

HIMMELWEIT, HILDE T. (1955) 'The psychological aspects of social differentiation', *Inter. Soc. Science Bull.*, 7.

HYMAN, HERBERT H. (1953) 'The value systems of different classes', in R. Bendix and S. Lipset, eds., *Class Status and Power*, pp. 426–42.

KAHL, J. A. (1953) 'Educational and occupational aspirations of "common man" boys', *Harvard Educ. Rev.*, 23, 186–203.

KATZ, F. M. (1964) 'The meaning of success: some differences in value systems of social classes', *J. Soc. Psych.*, 62, 141–8.

KOHN, MELVIN (1959) 'Social class and parental values', *Amer. J. Sociol.*, 64, 337–51.

KOHN, MELVIN (1963) 'Social class and parent–child relationships: an interpretation', *Amer. J. Sociol.*, 69, 471–80.

KOHN, MELVIN L., and CARROLL, ELEANOR E. (1960) 'Social class and the allocation of parental responsibilities', *Sociometry*, 23–24, 372–92.

LIVERSIDGE, WILLIAM (1962) 'Life chances', *Sociol. Rev.*, 10, no. 1, 17–34.

MANNINO, FORTUNE V. (1962) 'Family factors related to school persistence', *J. Educ. Sociol.*, 35, no. 5, 103–202.

MINISTRY OF EDUCATION (1954) *Early Leaving*, H.M.S.O.

REISSMAN, L. (1953) 'Levels of aspiration and social class', *Amer. Sociol. Rev.*, 18, June, 233–42.

ROSEN, BERNARD C. (1956) 'The achievement syndrome: a psycho-cultural dimension of social stratification', *Amer. Sociol. Rev.*, 21, April, 203–11.

ROSEN, B. C., and D'ANDRADE, ROY (1959) 'The psycho-social origins of achievement motivation', *Sociometry*, 22, 185–218.

SEWELL, WILLIAM H., HALLER, ARCHIE O., and MURRAY, A. (1957) 'Social status and educational and occupational aspiration', *Amer. Sociol. Rev.*, 22, 67–73.

SWIFT, D. F. (1964) 'Who passes the 11 + ?', *New Society*, 5 Mar., pp. 6–9.

SWIFT, D. F. (1965) 'Meritocratic and social class selection at age eleven', *Educ. Res.*, 8, no. 1, 65–73.

TOBY, JACKSON (1957) 'Orientation to education as a factor in school maladjustment of lower class children', *Social Forces*, 35, 259–66.

VEROFF, JOSEPH (1965) 'Theoretical background for studying the origins of human motivation dispositions', *Merrill-Palmer Quarterly of Behaviour and Development*, 2, no. 1.

WALL, W. D., and MILLER, K. M. (1962) 'Motivation and counter-motivation', in *Child and Education*, proceedings of XIV International Congress of Applied Psychology, vol. iii, 161–75.

17

F. I. Harrison

Relationship between home background, school success, and adolescent attitudes[*]

We know that the majority of the students experiencing success in school come from home backgrounds that can be characterised as advantaged with respect to the expectations which are held by the school. We know also that the vast majority of the students not experiencing success in school are from disadvantaged home backgrounds, again with respect to school expectations. However, there are some students, though they are few in number, whose school performances and home backgrounds are not consistent with the reality just described. Inconsistent with the successful school performance which is associated with advantaged home conditions, there are students from advantaged, or, if preferred, middle-class backgrounds who are not experiencing success in school, and there are also students from disadvantaged lower-class home backgrounds who are successful in school.

The presence of these inconsistent students, as they might be termed, can be detected in the research which has dealt with the nature of the relationship between home background and performance in school. Bloom *et al.* (1965), after an extensive survey of the research literature, stated that the majority of the studies concerned with this relationship resulted in significant (positive) correlations on the order of 0.30 to 0.50 between sociological indices of home background and assorted measures of school achievement. One explanation for the variance which remained unexplained is the presence of the inconsistent students.

Though these students emerged as an aberrant phenomenon in such research, a review of the literature revealed that virtually no effort has

*Reprinted from *Merrill-Palmer Quarterly*, 14, 1968, 331-44.

been expended to try to understand the phenomenon. The research reported here represented such an attempt. Selected for study were the attitudes and views of these students. The reason for focusing on attitudes follows.

In the work by Deutsch (1960), it was stated that, even though psychologists have long recognised the intimate relationship existing between internalised attitudes and individual learning and functioning, attitudes have distinctive characteristics related to environmental conditions and group membership. Two issues arise as a result of this awareness, and they are the ones with which this study dealt. First, what is the specific effect of the home environment on selected attitudes, and, secondly, in what way are these attitudes related to performance in school? A theoretical framework was developed to facilitate the study of these problems.

The theoretical framework of this study was developed out of the model of social behaviour of Getzels (1963, 1966). The components of this model include the values of the culture in which the individuals have been socialised, the values of the culture which serves as the context of an institution, the expectations of that institution, and the internalised motives of the individuals. In operationalising the model for the purposes of this study, the values of the culture in which the students were socialised were the values of the advantaged culture or the disadvantaged culture. These values were represented in the present research by the attitudes of the consistent students, the advantaged-successful students and the disadvantaged-non-successful students. The values of the culture which served as the context for the institution, the school in this instance, are the values of the dominant advantaged middle-class culture, a contention which has been supported by both Getzels (1966) and Charters (1963). The expectations of the schools were assumed to include a successful school performance. Finally, the internalised motives of the individuals were the attitudes of the selected students. Attitude, as the term was used in this study and as it has been used by Charters and Gage (1963, p. 334), is 'an enduring, learned predisposition to behave in a consistent way towards a given class of objects', and attitudes which are internalised operate as motives within the personality of the student.

Within the framework of the model, Getzels (1966) postulated interrelationships among cultural values, institutional expectations, and individual motives for both the majority middle-class child and minority lower-class child, termed, respectively, in this study the advantaged student and the disadvantaged student. Because the postulates of Getzels were used in the development of the hypothesis of this study, a summary statement of these postulates is given here. First, for advantaged students who are successful in school, the expectations of the school and the internalised motives of these students, their attitudes, will tend to be congruent. Furthermore, the attitudes of these students and the values in their advantaged culture will also tend to be congruent. These conditions can, and most often do, provide for preferred behaviour, and this preferred behaviour can, and most often does, result in a successful school performance.

Secondly, for the disadvantaged students who are not experiencing success in school, the expectations of the school and their internalised attitudes will tend to be incongruent. But, the values of the disadvantaged culture and the attitudes of the students will tend to be congruent. The situation for the disadvantaged students, then, is such that the values available during socialisation are not the same as those which are in evidence in the dominant advantaged culture, and, consequently, these values are not the same as those which serve as the context for the expectations of the school. These conditions are such that the disadvantaged student does not, and most often cannot, experience success in school.

Using these propositions, others were derived to make explicit hypothetical interrelationships among cultural values, student motives, and school expectations for the two inconsistent student types.

First, for the advantaged students who are not experiencing success in school, the expectations of the school and the attitudes of the students will tend to be incongruent, and, furthermore, their attitudes and the values of their advantaged culture will also tend to be incongruent. Their lack of success is reflected in the incongruency between their attitudes and the expectations of the school. Because, as previously noted, the values of the advantaged culture are congruent with the expectations of the school, we can expect the attitudes of these students to differ from those attitudes found in the advantaged culture.

Secondly, for the disadvantaged students who are experiencing success in school, their attitudes and the expectations of the school will tend to be congruent, but their attitudes and the values of their disadvantaged culture will tend to be incongruent. Their success in school is mirrored in the congruency between their attitudes and the expectations of the school. Because the values of the disadvantaged are not, for the most part, congruent with the expectations of the school, we can expect to find that the attitudes of these students do differ from the attitudes found in the disadvantaged culture.

To conclude this discussion of the theoretical framework, the proposition basic to the inconsistent student types is given further emphasis. This proposition was, in fact, the major hypothesis of this study. It was hypothesised that the attitudes of the inconsistent students would be incongruent with those of their associated majority group who, for the advantaged-non-successful students, were the advantaged-successful students, and, for the disadvantaged-successful students, were the disadvantaged-non-successful students.

ATTITUDES AND VIEWS

The attitudinal dimensions which were studied were purposely chosen so that attitudes would be included which were thought to be related primarily to (a) home background, (b) home background as well as school performance, or (c) just performance in school. To measure four such attitudinal dimensions, an exploratory opinionnaire with four Likert-type scales was developed explicitly for the purposes of this research. The four scales are presented in the Appendix. These items were randomly distributed in the pupil opinionnaire.

The first three of these scales had twenty items each, with a range of possible scores from a low of 20 to a high of 100, while the fourth scale had ten items with a range of possible scores from a low of 10 to a high of 50. For each item, there were five response categories ranging from strongly agree through cannot decide to strongly disagree. For each item of each scale, the highest weight was assigned to that alternative which was (a) judged to be the response category which would be chosen by the school as the 'preferred' response, and (b) the direction of the tendency expressed by the advantaged-successful students. For all of these items, the advantaged-successful students responded in the direction which had been regarded as 'preferred', thus confirming the judgment. As a result of this scoring scheme, the higher the scale score, the stronger the preference for the 'preferred' attitude and for the attitude towards which the advantaged-successful students tended.

The first of the four dimensions was view of the environment, the continuum of which ranged from the view that man can hope to gain only limited control over his environment to the 'preferred' view that it is possible for man to gain mastery of his environment. An item from this scale illustrating this dimension was: almost every present problem will be solved in the future.

View of the environment is known to be related to home background (Rosen, 1956; Bloom *et al.*, 1965); the advantaged have been found to tend more towards the view that man can gain control of his environment than have the disadvantaged. It was not known with any certainty, at the outset of this study, whether or not this attitude was related to performance in school. In one notable study, however, it was found that successful achievers in mathematics tended to view their environment as being neither threatening nor overwhelming and that these students indicated that they felt they were capable of mastering the problems they encounter (Haggard, 1957).

The second attitudinal dimension was attitude towards education, the continuum of which ranged from the attitude that an education is of little value to the 'preferred' attitude that an education is of real value. A scale item reflecting this dimension was: everybody should get as much education as possible.

Attitude towards education is known to be related to both home background and performance in school. The advantaged have been found to tend more towards the attitude that an education can be of real value than have the disadvantaged (Hieronymus, 1951; Charters, 1953), and successful students have been found to tend more towards this same attitude than have non-successful students (Evans, 1965; Lavin, 1965).

The continuum of the third dimension, attitude towards informal and formal school groups, ranged from the view that associations with school groups are a waste of time to the 'preferred' position that such associations can be of value. An item illustrating this scale was: most of the groups at school don't believe in the same things you do. This dimension and the fourth dimension, which is discussed next, were thought at the outset of this study to be related to performance in school though not necessarily to home background. These two dimensions were developed, the third indirectly and the fourth directly, from the conclusions of Coleman (1959) as to the importance of the student's peer group in influencing his performance in school.

The fourth dimension was peer-group attitude towards education, the continuum of which ranged from the view that the student's peer group did not value an education to the 'preferred' view that his peer group valued an education. A scale item which reflects this continuum was: most of your friends will probably go on to college.

As measures of internal consistency, alpha coefficients (Cronbach, 1951) for each of the scales were calculated on the total sample of the study which numbered 164. Each scale coefficient reflects the degree of reliability in terms of overlapping variance among the items of the scale. The alpha coefficient for scale *1*, view of the environment, was 0·68; for scale *2*, attitude towards education, 0·74; for scale *3*, attitude towards school groups, 0·73; and for scale *4*, peer group attitude towards education, 0·78. The intercorrelations among these four scales, again calculated with the total sample of this study, indicate the relative independence of the four scales and are contained in Table 17.1.

TABLE 17.1. *Intercorrelations among the four attitudinal scales: (1) View of the environment, (2) Attitude towards education, (3) Attitude towards school groups, and (4) Peer group attitude towards education*

Scale	1	2	3
2	0·15		
3	0·22	0·20	
4	0·35	0·22	0·20

SELECTION OF THE SUBJECTS

The four samples of this study were drawn selectively from a pool of 1,156 grade ten students from four high schools in a school district in the Chicago metropolitan area. In selecting the advantaged students and the disadvantaged students, home background was estimated with three socio-economic status characteristics: father's education, mother's education, and status of father's occupation. The work of Warner *et al.* (1960) attests to the significance of these characteristics as estimates of home background. Father's and mother's education were the number of years of education completed, and status of father's occupation was a coded occupational scale with the following codes, given in rank order of status: (1) professional, (2) technical, (3) sub-professional and sub-technical, (4) manual workers, and (5) others. The advantaged students who were selected were those students whose parents had completed twelve years of education or more and whose fathers had occupations which were in the three highest status occupations. The disadvantaged students were those students whose parents had completed only eleven years of education or less and whose fathers had occupations which were in the three lowest status occupations. All three criteria had to be met if a student was to qualify as either an advantaged student or a disadvantaged student. Once the advantaged students and the disadvantaged students had been identified, within each of these two groups, the successful students and the non-successful students were selected.

School success was determined by grade point average and a measure of overall school achievement. Weighted grade point averages were computed for each of the students from their most recent grades in academic subjects. Used as a measure of achievement were battery median grade equivalents on the Stanford Achievement Test Advanced (1953) which had been administered to the students during the second semester of grade nine. The successful students were those students whose weighted grade point averages were 3·6 or better on a five-point scale and whose batttery median grade equivalent on the Stanford Achievement Test was 10·0 or better. The non-successful students were those students whose weighted grade point averages were 3·0 or less and whose battery median grade equivalent was 9·0 or less. To qualify as either a successful or a non-successful student, both criteria had to be satisfied.

With this selection procedure, the original pool of 1,156 grade ten students was reduced to 164, of whom 77 were advantaged-successful, 34 were advantaged-non-successful, 22 were disadvantaged-successful, 31 were disadvantaged-non-successful. The opinionnaire was administered to these 164 students.

STATISTICAL METHODOLOGY

In the non-orthogonal design of the study, home background, either advantaged or disadvantaged, was crossed with school performance, either success or non-success, and a multivariate analysis of variance (Bock, 1963; Finn, 1967) was performed to test these effects. The four attitudinal dimensions were treated first in this analysis as a multivariate set. These four variates were thought of as behavioural samples from the attitude domain of affective behaviours. Hence, the variates needed to be considered simultaneously (Bock, 1966: Bock and Haggard, 1968). The first analysis performed was a two-way four-variate multivariate analysis of variance.

The analysis did not terminate with the omnibus tests of significance when main-class effects were found significant. Additional analyses were needed to determine the source of the differences in terms of the variates which contributed to it (Jones, 1966). In this study, univariate *F*-tests were made with each of the attitudinal dimensions treated as a separate dependent variable. Univariate *F*-tests were chosen for their meaningful and conventional interpretation, rather than other statistical alternatives. However, these separate *F*-tests were not statistically independent because the four variates were obtained from the same subjects (Bock and Haggard, 1968). The estimate of error in the analyses was the pooled within cell variation.

RESULTS

Before presenting the test of the hypothesis of this study, the group means and standard deviations on each of the four attitudinal dimensions are given. These summary statistics are found in Table 17.2. The trends which are evident in these statistics were used in the interpretation of the results of the multivariate and univariate analyses of variance which follow.

TABLE 17.2. *Group means and standard deviations on the four attitudinal scales: (1) View of the environment, (2) Attitude towards education, (3) Attitude towards school groups, and (4) Peer group attitude towards education*

	Group							
Scale	Advantaged successful		Advantaged non-successful		Disadvantaged successful		Disadvantaged non-successful	
	Mean	S.D.	Mean	S.D.	Mean	S.D.	Mean	S.D.
1	72·79	4·96	69·74	6·20	73·91	4·17	68·48	4·96
2	73·94	5·17	72·15	5·03	72·68	5·11	71·61	5·64
3	74·47	5·42	72·12	4·97	72·68	5·59	70·87	5·82
4	39·46	3·74	35·59	4·83	37·46	3·70	33·03	5·51

The test of the effect of school performance, contrasting the attitudes of the advantaged-successful students and the disadvantaged-successful students with those of the advantaged-non-successful students and the disadvantaged-non-successful students, with the effect of home background removed, was considered to be the test of the hypothesis of this study. To reiterate, the hypothesis was that the attitudes of the inconsistent students would differ from those of their associated majority group. In fact, the attitudes of the successful students differed significantly from those of the non-successful students in the omnibus test; the multivariate F was 11·08, $p < 0.01$. The results of this test are shown in Table 17.3. The main effect of school performance was ordered last in this analysis so that an unbiased estimate of this effect could be obtained.

Univariate tests were made to determine those attitudes which distinguished the successful students from the non-successful students (Table 17.3). The view of the environment of the successful students differed significantly from that of the non-successful students. The univariate F was equal to 20·84, $p < 0.01$. The successful students tended more towards the view that man can gain control of his environment than did the non-successful students. The view of the disadvantaged-successful students was even more optimistic than that of the advantaged-successful students. The direction of this tendency can be seen in the statistics of Table 17.2. Next, the attitude towards education of the successful students was congruent with that of the non-successful students. The univariate F was equal to 3·14. Also, the attitude towards school groups of the successful students differed significantly from that of the non-successful students. The univariate F

TABLE 17.3. *Multivariate and univariate analysis of variance with, as dependent variables, the four attitudinal scales*

Source of variation	Scale	Mean square	Multivariate F (4,157)	Univariate F (1,160)
Home background, ignoring school performance	1	44·998	6·36**	1·70
	2	63·529		2·33
	3	162·000		5·49*
	4	415·252		21·92**
School performance, eliminating home background	1	552·445	11·08**	20·84**
	2	85·800		3·14
	3	170·016		5·76*
	4	601·645		31·75**
Home background X school performance, eliminating above effects	1	46·697	0·55	1·76
	2	4·305		0·16
	3	2·419		0·08
	4	2·574		0·14

* $p < 0.05$.   ** $p < 0.01$.

was equal to 5·76, $p < 0.05$. The successful students viewed associations with school groups as more important than did the non-successful students, and the advantaged-successful students agreed more strongly to this importance than did the disadvantaged-successful students (Table 17.2). The attitudes of the successful students' peer groups towards education were significantly different from those of the peer groups of the non-successful students. The univariate F was equal to 31·75, $p < 0.01$. The advantaged-successful students described the attitudes towards education of their peer groups as more positive than did any other group.

Though the effect of school performance was of primary interest, a multivariate test was made of the effect of home background, eliminating the effect of school performance, and the results are presented in Table 17.4.

In the omnibus test, the attitudes of the advantaged students differed significantly from those of the disadvantaged students; in the multivariate analysis of variance, F was 2·90, $p < 0.05$. To determine those attitudes which distinguished the advantaged students from the disadvantaged students, univariate tests were made, and the results of these tests are also given in Table 17.4. The effect of home background was a significant effect because of the differences in peer group attitude towards education between the advantaged students and the disadvantaged students. The univariate F was equal to 9·07, $p < 0.01$.

TABLE 17.4. *Multivariate and univariate analysis of variance with the main effects reordered and with, as dependent variables, the four attitudinal scales*

Source of variation	Scale	Mean square	Multivariate F (4,157)	Univariate F (1,160)
School performance, ignoring home background	1	597·401	14·54**	22·54**
	2	122·132		4·48*
	3	254·670		8·64**
	4	845·091		44·60**
Home background, eliminating school performance	1	0·042	2·90*	0·00
	2	27·197		1·00
	3	77·346		2·62
	4	171·806		9·07**

* $p < 0.05$.   ** $p < 0.01$.

As reported by the students, advantaged students' peer groups valued an education more than the disadvantaged students' peer groups. This trend can be observed in the summary statistics in Table 17.2. With respect to the other attitudes, no other significant differences between the advantaged students and the disadvantaged students were found.

DISCUSSION

The thesis of the study was confirmed. The attitudes of the inconsistent students were found to be incongruent with those of their associated majority groups. The attitudes of all four groups, though, tended towards the 'preferred' direction. Moreover, it can be said that, for the most part, the attitudes of the disadvantaged-successful students were like those of the advantaged-successful students and the attitudes of the advantaged-non-successful students were like those of the disadvantaged-non-successful students. These findings were true for the view of the environment, where the disadvantaged-successful students expressed the most optimistic view of the future, and for the attitude towards school groups, and for the peer group attitude towards education, where the preferred attitudes were agreed to most strongly by the advantaged-successful students followed by the disadvantaged-successful students.

A notable exception to these results was the attitude towards education. In this instance, the attitudes towards education of all four groups were congruent and tended towards the 'preferred' direction, a finding which did not support the hypothesis nor the results of previous research (Hieronymus, 1951; Charters, 1953; Evans, 1965; Lavin, 1965). The conclusion which is suggested by the finding of this study is that the attitude towards education does not distinguish advantaged students from disadvantaged students, nor successful students from non-successful students.

Though the successful students differed from the non-successful students with respect to the attitudes of their peer groups towards education, these attitudes also distinguished the advantaged students from the disadvantaged students, suggesting that this attitude is related to performance in school as well as to home background. This conclusion, it seems, is somewhat incompatible with the conclusion reached as a result of the analysis of the student's own attitude towards education. If we can assume, however, that the students had internalised their own attitudes towards education, then one plausible explanation for the seeming inconsistency is that the student's attitude towards education is not the direct result of the influence of his peers but rather the result of some other, yet undisclosed source.

The major hypothesis of this study was developed as a logical extension of the model of social behaviour of Getzels (1966), and, when this hypothesis was confirmed, the conceptual model was supported. Also, the model was extended to encompass such problems as the one posed in this study and other studies which stem from this one.

In generalising from the results of this study, there are cautions to be acknowledged. Only four attitudes were studied, suggesting a need to replicate this study but to sample other attitudinal dimensions from the affective domain. Consideration should be given while contemplating such a study to estimating home background by means other than socio-economic characteristics as Bloom *et al.* (1965) have suggested. Socio-economic status characteristics are, at best, omnibus estimates of home culture.

At this stage of our knowledge of adolescent attitudinal development and despite the flaws, the conclusion of this study still seems viable: the attitudes of the inconsistent students are incongruent with those of their associated majority groups.

REFERENCES

BLOOM, B. S., DAVIS, A., and HESS, R. (1965) *Compensatory Education for Cultural Deprivation*, Holt, Rinehart & Winston.

BOCK, R. D. (1963) 'Programming univariate and multivariate analysis of variance', *Technometrics*, 5, 94–117.

BOCK, R. D. (1966) 'Contributions of multivariate experimental designs to educational research', in R. B. Cattell, ed., *Handbook of Multivariate Experimental Psychology*, Rand McNally, pp. 820–40.

BOCK, R. D., and HAGGARD, E. A. (1968) 'The use of multivariate analysis of variance in behavioral research', in D. K. Whitla, ed., *Handbook of Measurement and Assessment in Behavioral Sciences*, Addison-Wesley, pp. 100–42.

CHARTERS, W. W., JR. (1953) 'Social class analysis and control of public education', *Harvard educ. Rev.*, 23, 268–82.

CHARTERS, W. W., JR. (1963) 'The social background of teaching', in N. L. Gage, ed., *Handbook of Research on Teaching*. Rand McNally, pp. 715–818.

CHARTERS, W. W., and GAGE, N. L., eds. (1963) *Readings in the Social Psychology of Education*, Allyn & Bacon.

COLEMAN, J. S. (1959) 'Academic achievement and the structure of competition', *Harvard educ. Rev.*, 29, 330–51.

CRONBACH, L. J. (1951) 'Coefficient alpha and the internal structure of tests', *Psychometrika*, 16, 297–334.

DEUTSCH, M. (1960) 'Minority group and class status as related to social and personality factors in scholastic achievement', The Society for Applied Anthropology, Monograph no. 2. Cornell University: New York School of Industrial and Labor Relations.

EVANS, K. M. (1965) *Attitudes and Interests in Education*, Routledge & Kegan Paul.

FINN, J. (1967) *Multivariance—univariate and multivariate analysis of variance and covariance: a Fortran IV program*. State University, New York at Buffalo.

GETZELS, J. W. (1963) 'Conflict and role behavior in the educational setting', in W. W. Charters and N. L. Gage, eds., *Readings in the Social Psychology of Education*. Allyn & Bacon, pp. 309–18.

GETZELS, J. W. (1960) 'A social psychology of education'. University of Chicago (mimeographed).

HAGGARD, E. A. (1957) 'Socialization, personality and academic achievement in gifted children', *Sch. Rev.*, 65, 388–414.

HIERONYMUS, A. N. (1951) 'Study of social class motivation: relationships between anxiety for education and certain socio-economic and intellectual variables', *J. educ. Psychol.*, 42, 193–205.

JONES, L. V. (1966) 'Analysis of variance in its multivariate developments', in R. B. Cattell, ed., *Handbook of Multivariate Experimental Psychology*, Rand McNally, pp. 244–266.

LAVIN, D. E. (1965) *The Prediction of Academic Performance: a theoretical analysis and review of research*, New York, Russell Sage Foundation.

ROSEN, B. C. (1956) 'The achievement syndrome: a psychocultural dimension of social stratification', *Amer. sociol. Rev.*, **21**, 203–11.

WARNER, W. L., MERKER, MARCHIA, and EELLS, K. (1960) *Social Class in America: a manual of procedure for the measurement of social status.* Harper.

APPENDIX: SCALES OF THE PUPIL OPINIONNAIRE

1. View of the environment

People all over the world are pretty much alike in what they believe to be right and wrong.

You should not say unkind things to another person, even if he really makes you mad.

Success depends on luck and fate.

With hard work anyone can succeed.

Someday most of the mysteries of the world will be solved by science.

Almost every present problem will be solved in the future.

You do not need to keep a promise if you had to make it without thinking.

Someday the deserts will be turned into good farming land.

Poverty can be wiped out in the world by improving factory and farming methods.

It should be possible to stop war once and for all.

The most important thing in life is to get along with other people.

The best reason for doing the right thing is that this is how your parents would like you to behave.

Sometimes you know a thing is right or wrong without giving it any thought.

Some things in life are so important that it would be foolish not to cheat a little to gain them.

Some people never feel that urge to do something wrong.

Everybody who lives in Chicago is a little bit responsible for a crime that is committed there.

Anybody might become a criminal if he grew up under extremely poor conditions.

In punishing a person, the important thing is what he did, not why he did it.

For a person who is really good, the right way of behaving comes to him almost automatically.

If you do something wrong, sooner or later you will be caught.

2. Attitude towards education

Education cannot change people in any basic way.

Education can only help people develop their natural abilities.

People who don't have much education enjoy life as much as well educated people.

In school there are more important things than getting good grades.

A man can learn more on a job than he can in school.

Most students have to be made to learn.

The most important thing in school is to learn to get along well with people.

Most school learning has little value for a person.

There are more important things in school than learning to get along well with people.

Anyone can learn if he is willing to study.

Everybody should get as much education as possible.

If you want a good job, then you must go to school.

Getting good grades is the most important thing in school.

You can always learn more in school than you can on a job.

Most students don't have to be made to learn.

There is real value in school learning.

Even though they are willing to study there are some people that just can't learn.

Even if we stopped educating everybody, our country would still prosper.

It is possible to get a good job even if you don't go to school.

Education can change people.

3. *Attitude towards informal and formal school groups*

Students who run around with a school crowd waste too much time.

You should not go around with students who don't believe in the same things you do.

The trouble with school crowds is that they don't really want an education.

Everybody should go around with a group at school.

You should not have to go to the movies alone.

It is important to have at least one close friend in school.

Belonging to a group outside of school is more important than belonging to a group in the school.

Most of the school crowds don't really believe in the right things.

It is very important to have many school friends.

There are some groups of students that won't allow anybody to join them.

School crowds are a waste of time.

Most of the groups at school don't believe in the same things you do.

The only school friends that you should have are those who believe in the same things you do.

You really can't become an adult without having some clashes with your friend at school.

School friends are necessary to the development of your personality.

It is very important to be a leader in a group.

You should only go to a football game with a friend.

It is more important to have one close friend than many friends.
A person who doesn't have many school friends doesn't have a good personality.
Everybody should have at least one close friend.

4. Peer group attitude towards education

Your friends are not the kind of friends your parents would like you to have.
Your parents don't like your friends.
Your friends talk about the books they have read.
Most of your friends think school is a waste of time.
Your friends try to attend most of the school activities.
Most of your friends spend a lot of time studying.
Most of your friends are very different from you.
Most of your friends like school.
Most of your friends want to get good grades.
Most of your friends will probably go on to college.

18

Joan C.
Barker Lunn

The development of scales to measure junior school children's attitudes*

SUMMARY. This paper describes ten attitude scales for use with pupils aged 9 to 11 years. These are: attitude to school; interest in school work; importance of doing well; attitude to class; 'other' image of class; conforming *versus* non-conforming pupil; relationship with teacher; anxiety about school work; social adjustment; self-image.

The scales were derived empirically and each is made up of a number of statements made by children during group discussions and selected after factor analyses and scalogram analyses. For each scale the aim has been to achieve homogeneity of content and where possible a cumulative structure. The internal consistency of each scale is expressed in terms of Cronbach's alpha coefficient. The intercorrelations of the scales with each other and also with external data are given. Information for the latter came from several sources. These were: (*a*) personality and ability ratings of the pupil by the teacher; (*b*) parents' ability ratings and educational aspirations for the child; (*c*) sociometric data; (*d*) achievement test scores; and (*e*) interest scores.

I INTRODUCTION

A large-scale research study was initiated in 1963 by the National Foundation for Educational Research to investigate the effects of streaming and non-streaming in junior schools (Barker Lunn, 1967). Measurement of pupils' attitudes was particularly important and since no measures meeting the requirements of the study were available, attitude scales were developed. The construction and relationship of these scales to other variables are described in this paper. Other research workers may find them of use; for besides meeting the requirements of

* Reprinted from British Journal of Educational Psychology, 39, 1969, 64–71.

the streaming research project, these empirically derived scales offer a means of measuring and describing important attitudinal differences among groups of children in junior schools.

Since little was known about which attitudes were important and relevant for the enquiry, exploratory work in the form of discussions and interviews was carried out. The aim here was to determine what attitudes children actually held and how these feelings were expressed. The exploratory work revealed a number of attitude areas which seemed important for this research. A review of the literature indicated that most of these areas had received little attention. There were scales available for four of them, namely, anxiety (Himmelweit and Petrie, 1951; Sarason *et al.*, 1960; Casteneda *et al.*, 1956), self-image (Bills *et al.*, 1961), attitude to school (Fitt, 1956; Flanders, 1965; Jackson and Getzels, 1959), and attitude to teacher (Tcheschtelin *et al.*, 1940), but none of these scales seemed suitable for the present enquiry. Some of them had been developed for use with older children and most were constructed for a non-British population. Thus a certain amount of item re-writing and adaptation would be required before they could be used in this country. It was considered necessary therefore to develop a total set of new scales for all areas.

The principle in the construction of the scales was to obtain the items from statements actually made by children for whom the scales were intended. To the writer's knowledge this method has not been used before with children, and indeed this might be levelled as a criticism against past work; most researchers in this field have not made clear how they derived their items and one can only assume that they were formulated at the desk out of the researcher's head. Such items are inevitably based on the researcher's own thinking, tend to be written in a language not used by the child, and worse still, cover a biased and artificial viewpoint representing the researcher's ideas about how children think than the way they actually do. Piaget's work has shown conclusively that the language and concepts of children are very different from those of adults. For this reason, discussions were held with children and their language used in the construction of the scales.

II PROCEDURE

The stages involved in the development of the scales were (i) group discussions, (ii) quantitative pilot, (iii) factor analysis and (iv) a second stage of fieldwork to develop the scales further.

Seventeen group discussions were held in five schools and involved approximately 60 third and fourth year junior school children of differing ability levels. The schools were located in London, the Home Counties, the Midlands and the North of England. The group discussions were carried out in a room where no disturbance by other children or members of staff was likely. In most cases the room was a spare classroom. The role of the leader of the group discussion was to steer the conversation to relevant topics, and to encourage development of certain ideas, but at the same time to appear permissive and unobtrusive. A schedule had been prepared beforehand and this was used as a rough guide. It covered the following areas: interests; attitudes to school, teacher, other classes, peers and self; ambitions; wishes. The group discussions were taped and later transcribed.

For the most part, attitudes were coherently formed and the children had no difficulty expressing them in a group situation.

The records of the group discussions yielded a wealth of data about children's values and attitudes and how they viewed school life. Content analysis indicated a number of areas (eight) crucial to a study of this type. One hundred statements were selected from the discussions to represent the range of opinion in each of these attitude areas. A questionnaire was drawn up and items were randomised throughout. After a preliminary screening, the questionnaire containing seventy-three statements, was administered to 355 nine- to eleven-year-old children in twelve schools, six in the North and six in the South of England.

The resulting data were subjected to exploratory factor analysis. The main emphasis here was on the rotated solution. Following the intercorrelation of the items, a principal components factor analysis was obtained; eleven factors were extracted. These were rotated by the Varimax procedure to orthogonal simple structure. Seven interpretable factors were identified. By and large these confirmed the findings of the exploratory research. Although the factor analysis clarified the structure of the attitudes, it did not provide a completely satisfactory set of measuring instruments. Three of the attitude areas consisted of promising sub-sets of items (the average correlation of each set ranging from 0·19 to 0·28) but did not emerge as factors, apparently because the number of suitable items was inadequate. In order to develop instruments in all areas, a revised questionnaire was developed. The transcripts of the exploratory discussions were re-examined and statements which appeared to be related to these 'promising sub-sets' of items were selected. Advantage was also taken of the new questionnaire to improve the other seven areas and items with low loadings were rejected and replaced by other statements. A questionnaire, comprising seventy-nine statements covering ten attitude areas, was developed and used.

The attitude scales were constructed on the basis of the results of a second stage of fieldwork.

Approximately 2,300 third- and fourth-year junior school children, in twenty-eight schools, completed the revised questionnaire. Based on the responses of 400 of the boys and girls, selected at random from the total sample, intercorrelations between the items hypothesised to form an attitude scale were obtained and those items with a low overall level of correlation were rejected. The remaining items for each attitude area were then submitted to scalogram analysis. If the usual Guttman method (Guttman, 1950) was unsatisfactory, the H-technique was tried (Stouffer *et al.*, 1952) and a modified type of Guttman scale was formed. The responses to items in three areas did not form a cumulative pattern and were therefore unsuitable for scalogram analysis; so factor scales were formed. The procedure for this was to carry out a centroid analysis (Harman, 1967) of the inter-item correlations and the first two factors were extracted. And then in order to test whether the correlation matrix could be accounted for by one general factor a comparison of the size of the variance of these two factors was made. Vernon (1950) claims that a ratio of 4 to 1 (i.e., if the amount of variance explained by the first factor is four times as great as that explained by the second) is evidence of unidimensionality.

III RESULTS AND DISCUSSION

Ten attitude scales, as listed in Table 18.1, were successfully constructed. These were found to be positively intercorrelated and their product moment correlations are given in Table 18.1. Thirty-six of the obtained correlations were significant at 0·05 or beyond indicating a degree of overlap.

It will also be noticed that the correlations fall rather neatly into two clusters. The first seven scales (A—G) deal with attitudes towards aspects of school and school work and the other four (G—J) are more concerned with social relations and the personality of the pupil. 'Relationship with teacher' appears to correlate relatively highly with both clusters.

What do the scales mean?

In most cases the titles of the scales are self-explanatory. However, it is proposed to give a short description of each and note its relationship with other variables.

The *attitude to school* scale was made up of items concerned with general rather than specific aspects of school. For example, it included statements such as 'School is fun', 'I would leave school tomorrow if I could' and 'I like school'.

The *interest in school work* scale was composed of items concerned with both school work in general and particular lessons. An example of the former is 'I enjoy most school work' and of the latter 'We spend too much time doing arithmetic'.

TABLE 18.1 *Intercorrelation Coefficients of the Children's Attitude Scales*

Attitude scale		A	B	C	D	E	F	G	H	I	J
Attitude to school	A	—	—	—	—	—	—	—	—	—	—
Interest in school work	B	0·71	—	—	—	—	—	—	—	—	—
Importance of doing well	C	0·44	0·45	—	—	—	—	—	—	—	—
Attitude to class	D	0·40	0·43	0·36	—	—	—	—	—	—	—
'Other' image of class	E	0·21	0·23	0·09	0·25	—	—	—	—	—	—
Conforming *versus* non-conforming pupil	F	0·37	0·38	0·37	0·25	0·14	—	—	—	—	—
Relationship with teacher	G	0·39	0·43	0·36	0·36	0·20	0·36	—	—	—	—
Anxiety (non-anxious *versus* anxious) about school work	H	0·15	0·16	0·02	0·01	0·14	0·09	0·24	—	—	—
Social adjustment	I	0·09	0·13	0·12	0·12	0·10	0·00	0·21	0·23	—	—
Self image	J	0·20	0·25	0·26	0·09	0·09	0·13	0·42	0·40	0·29	—

A correlation of 0·11 is significant at the 0·05 level. $N = 2,087$.

Importance of doing well was made up of items stressing achievement orientation—'I work and try very hard in school,' 'Doing well at school is most important to me.'

These first three scales exhibited a fairly high degree of intercorrelation, particularly 'attitude to school' and 'interest in school work'. It should be pointed out that the latter two scales were 'forced', for during factor analysis only one factor emerged in this area and not two. On inspection of the content, however, it was seen that the items fell into two groups—one dealing with general attitudes and the other with school work. Thus the two groups of items were dealt with separately when forming the two Guttman scales. (For the time being it was felt worthwhile preserving these as two scales, but the results so far show similar construct validity and therefore there is perhaps a case for combining them.)

Of particular interest are the significant positive intercorrelations of all the scales (except 'social adjustment') with 'attitude to school' and 'interest in school work', which would seem to indicate the presence of a general factor. The relationships of the other scales with 'importance of doing well' were also interesting: the child who wanted to do well in school tended to have a favourable attitude to school and school work, tended to be conforming and to have a good relationship with his teacher. There was no consistent tendency for this child to be either anxious or non-anxious.

One would expect some degree of relationship between school performance and attitude. Table 18.2 indicates that this is so, particularly for 'importance of doing well'. This scale correlated positively with the child's English score (0·28) and other achievement test scores and also with the teacher's rating of the child's ability (0·26). However, for 'attitude to school' and 'interest in school work', the highest correlation was with creative interests (0·32) and (0·31) respectively. This is not surprising when one considers the content of the creative interests scale: it includes items such as 'writing stories', 'making up poems', 'acting', 'playing musical instruments', and 'painting',—all activities which may form part of the curriculum. If the child liked doing these things he also tended to like school.

Another noteworthy finding was the relationship between the child's sex and attitude: for the above three scales, girls tended to have more positive attitudes. This finding agrees with those of other workers (Fitt, 1956; Fox, 1964; Sears, 1963).

The scale measuring *attitude to class* contained items referring to the favourableness or otherwise of being a member of a particular school class. For example, 'I'd rather be in my class than the others for my age', and 'I hate being in the class I'm in now'. The emergence of these items as a factor, during the factor analysis, was particularly interesting—for what had actually been hypothesised did not occur. It was thought that the items now forming the 'social adjustment' (or 'getting on well with classmates') scale and items in *this* scale were 'part of the same package'. However, two factors and not one, as expected, were extracted from this set of statements.

It can be seen from the correlation matrix that 'social adjustment' has a low correlation (0·12) with the 'attitude to class' scale. Of all the scales the highest correlation for the 'attitude to class' scale was 'interest in school work' (0·43). It also correlated well with 'attitude to school'

TABLE 18.2. *Product Moment Correlations of Attitude Scales with other Variables*

Attitude scale (Key in Table 1)	A	B	C	D	E	F	G	H	I
Scholastic performance achievement tests:									
English	0·20	0·19	0·28	0·19	0·18	0·17	0·22	0·21	0·25
Problem arithmetic	0·15	0·10	0·20	0·17	0·11	*	0·14	0·20	0·25
Essays	0·17	0·15	0·24	0·18	0·14	0·13	0·21	0·11	0·19
Verbal reasoning	0·17	0·15	0·23	0·16	0·16	0·14	0·16	0·20	0·17
Non-verbal reasoning	0·15	0·15	0·17	0·15	0·09	0·09	0·18	0·17	0·20
Fluency	*	*	0·15	*	*	*	0·10	0·10	0·19
Flexibility	*	0·09	0·17	0·11	*	*	*	0·13	0·17
Originality	*	*	0·12	*	*	*	*	*	0·16
Ratings									
Teacher's rating of ability	0·23	0·19	0·26	0·21	0·12	0·15	0·24	0·20	0·28
Parents' rating of ability	0·19	0·17	0·21	0·14	0·14	*	0·23	0·19	0·21
Arithmetic ability relative to others in class	0·21	0·17	0·23	0·09	*	*	0·23	0·18	0·16
Reading ability relative to others in class	0·13	0·12	0·17	*	*	0·11	0·13	0·20	0·18
Sociometric status	0·13	0·10	0·14	0·11	*	*	0·12	*	0·21
Interests:									
Creative interests	0·32	0·31	0·16	0·16	*	0·15	*	*	*
Logical, analytic interests	*	*	*	*	*	0·11	*	*	0·19
Parents									
Aspirations for child's further education	0·12	0·09	0·15	0·17	*	0·13	0·19	0·15	0·16
Proposed age for child leaving school	0·12	0·12	0·16	0·15	*	0·14	0·18	0·16	0·17
Social class	*	0·10	0·14	0·15	*	*	0·16	0·11	0·11
Behaviour ratings									
Pleasurability	0·13	0·14	0·16	0·17	*	0·20	0·23	0·13	0·10
Fights	*	−0·13	−0·11	−0·15	*	−0·25	−0·19	−0·09	*
Social withdrawal	−0·10	*	*	*	*	*	−0·12	*	−0·11
Teased/picked on	−0·09	*	−0·13	*	*	*	*	*	−0·11
Sex—boys versus girls	0·33	0·25	0·19	0·20	0·15	−0·27	0·15	*	−0·16

Sample = 2,087 nine to eleven-year-old children. All correlations are significant and those greater than 0·11 significant at the 1 per cent level.

* Correlations were not significant.

(0·40), 'importance of doing well' (0·36) and 'relationship with the teacher' (0·36). It was unrelated to 'anxiety' and 'self-image'. Table 18.2 suggests that children who had a favourable attitude to their class also tended to obtain a high rating on ability (0·21). Girls had a more favourable attitude to their class than boys (0·20).

The *'other image'* scale was composed of items concerned with the way children felt that other classes in the school and teachers viewed the child's own class. For example, 'Other children make fun of my class' and 'Other children think we're clever in this class'. The fact that it was given to the pupils in non-streamed as well as streamed schools probably accounts for the lowish correlations in the matrix and Table 18.2. This now needs to be looked at in terms of the streamed children only.

'Relationship with the teacher' items emphasised the teacher's perceived degree of concern for the child rather than the child's liking for the teacher. Some of the items making up this scale were 'Teacher thinks I'm a trouble-maker', 'Teacher is interested in me', 'Teacher is nice to me'. It has already been pointed out that this scale had relatively high correlations with both the school related attitudes and the personality type scales. The highest correlations were with 'interest in school work' and 'self-image'. Table 18.2 also suggests that good school work is an important factor for a satisfactory relationship with the teacher, a finding reported also by Fox (1964) and Rosenfeld (1961): there was a positive correlation with the teacher's rating of the child's ability (0·24), with the parent's rating of the child's ability (0·23), with the child's English achievement (0·22) and essay score (0·21) and with the teacher's judgment of the child's pleasurability (0·23).

As the title might suggest, the items constituting the scale *'conforming versus non-conforming pupil'* covered the range of these two opposing types of behaviour. For example, the scale included items such as 'I dislike children who are noisy in class', 'When the teacher goes out of the room I play about', 'I like people who get me into mischief'. The correlation matrix indicates that the conforming pupil also tended to like school (0·37), school work (0·38) and the teacher (0·36) and believed that it was important to do well in school (0·37). There was no relationship between this scale and social adjustment or anxiety. Table 18.2 indicates that children obtaining high marks on this scale (i.e., conformers) also tended to obtain a high pleasurable rating from the teacher (0·20) and those scoring low marks (non-conformers) to obtain a high fighting rating (−0·25). 'Conformity' was associated with girls and non-conformity with boys (−0·27).

The *'anxiety'* scale (non-anxious *versus* anxious) was composed of items related to anxieties, fears and worries in the classroom. For example, 'I would feel afraid if I got my work wrong', 'Children who can't do their school work feel ashamed', 'I'm scared to ask my teacher for help'. The matrix shows that this scale correlated best with self-image (0·40): children who had a good self-image in terms of school work also tended not to feel anxious in the classroom. This ties in nicely with Table 18.2 where it can be seen that 'non-anxious' children were associated with high test marks (English (0·21), Problem Arithmetic (0·20), Verbal Reasoning (0·20)) and 'anxious' children with low marks. Warburton (1962), summarising work carried out in the United States on relationship between anxiety and attainment, concluded that anxiety is related to poor attainment.) Also the 'non-anxious' pupils tended to receive high ability ratings from their teacher (0·20) and to hold a high position in their class (Reading position (0·20), Arithmetic position (0·18)). Interesting too was the complete lack of relationship of this scale with 'importance of doing well'.

The items making up the *'social adjustment'* scale were concerned with the child's ability to get on well with his classmates. It included such items as 'I have no one to play with at playtime', 'I think the other children in my class like me'. This scale exhibited very low correlations (or no relationship) with the school and school work-related attitudes. It was, however, positively correlated with 'non-anxiety' (0·23), 'relationship with teacher' (0·21) and highest of all with 'self-image' in terms of school work (0·29). Table 18.2 indicates that 'socially well adjusted' was related to high ability ratings from teacher (0·28) and parent (0·21) and to high test scores: English (0·25), Problem (0·25) Children with a high sociometric status score (i.e., highly chosen by other members of the class) also tended to obtain a high socially adjusted score (0·21). Boys obtained higher adjustment scores than girls (−0·16).

The content of the items in the *'self-image'* scale reflected self in terms of school work. For example, 'I'm useless at school work', 'I'm very good at sums', 'My teacher thinks I'm clever'. Self-image seemed to depend somewhat on the child's relationship with the teacher (0·42) and if he had a good 'self-image' he also tended to be a 'non-anxious' pupil (0·40). (Bledsoe (1964) using an adaptation of Bill's Index of Adjustment, found a significant negative correlation between self-concept and anxiety.) Table 18.2 also supports these findings. Those whom the teacher rated as pleasurable tended to be those with a good self-image and similarly also those whom she rated high on ability (0·40). The child's relative ability seemed to be an important factor for self-image, for the highest correlation was with position in the class in arithmetic (0·46), whilst the correlation with reading ability was somewhat lower (0·30). Presumably there was a higher correlation with the arithmetic position than with reading because there are more cues for the child to judge his relative ability in arithmetic through similar ability grouping, marks and tests. Table 18.2 suggests that girls tended to have a poorer self-image than boys. Sears (1963) also found this.

Internal consistency of the scales

The internal consistency of these scales was determined by Cronbach's (1951) Alpha-coefficient. For the Guttman scales, coefficients of reproducibility were also calculated (Guttman, 1950). In all cases, the Guttman scales were replicated satisfactorily on a further two samples of 100 and the reproducibility coefficients given below are based on the average obtained from three separate samples, drawn at random from the total set of pupils.

TABLE 18.3. *Internal Consistency of the Scales*

Attitude scale		Coefficient of reproducibility	Alpha-coefficient
A. Attitude to school	(6 items)	0·95	0·89
B. Interest in school work	(6 items)	0·95**	0·88
C. Importance of doing well	(5 items)	Factor scale*	0·77
D. Attitude to class	(8 items)	Factor scale*	0·91
E. 'Other' image of class	(6 items)	0·92	0·69
F. Conforming *versus* non-conforming pupil	(5 items)	0·95**	0·90
G. Relationship with teacher	(6 items)	0·92**	0·82
H. Anxiety about school work	(7 items)	0·94**	0·80
I. Social adjustment	(4 items)	0·90	0·58
J. Self-image in terms of school work	(9 items)	Factor scale*	0·88

* Guttman scale not obtained.
** Modified Guttman scale constructed by H-technique (Stouffer *et al.* 1952).

IV IMPLICATIONS

Other research workers may find the scales of use; for besides meeting the requirements of the streaming research project, these empirically derived scales offer a means of measuring and describing important attitudinal differences among groups of children in junior school. Some evidence has been given of their validity. But it is hoped to obtain more substantial evidence from further analyses of the sample of 2,000 pupils. The interactions of these attitudes with other factors will also be examined.

ACKNOWLEDGEMENTS. The writer wishes to thank Dr A. McKennell for his constructive criticism of this paper and also Mr J. A. Lunn for his help and advice. Acknowledgement is also due to the heads, teachers and pupils of the schools in which this research was carried out.

V. REFERENCES

BARKER LUNN, J. C. (1967) 'Effects of streaming and non-streaming in junior schools', *New Research in Education*, 1.

BILLS, R. E., VANCE, E. L. and MCLEAN, O. S. (1951) 'An index of adjustment and values', *J. Cons. Psychol.*, 15, 257–61.

BLEDSOE, J. C. (1964) 'Self-concepts of children and their intelligence, achievement, interests, and anxiety', *J. Indiv. Psychol.*, 20, 55–8.

CASTENEDA, A., *et al.* (1956) 'The children's form of the manifest anxiety scale', *Child Development*, 27, 317–26.

CRONBACH, L. J. (1951) 'Coefficient-Alpha and the internal structure of tests', *Psychometrika*, 16, 3.

FITT, A. B. (1956) 'An experimental study of children's attitudes to school in Auckland, New Zealand', *Brit. J. Educ. Psychol.*, 26, 25–30.

FLANDERS, N.A. (1965) 'Teacher influence, pupil attitudes and achievement', *Co-operative Research Monograph*, 12. Washington: U.S. Printing Office.

FOX, R. S., LIPPITT, R. O., SCHMUCK, R. A. (1964) 'Pupil-teacher adjustment and mutual adaptation in creating classroom learning environment', *Co-operative Research Monograph* 1167. Washington: U.S. Department of Health, Education and Welfare.

GUTTMAN, L. (1950) In Stouffer, S. A. (Ed.) *Measurement and Prediction*. Princeton: Univ. Press.

HARMAN, H. H. (1967) *Modern Factor Analysis*. Chicago: Univ. Press (2nd edn.).

HIMMELWEIT, H. T., and PETRIE, A. (1951) 'The measurement of personality in children', *Brit. J. Educ. Psychol.*, 21, 9–29.

JACKSON, P. W., and GETZELS, J. W. (1959) 'Psychological health and classroom functioning; A study of dissatisfaction with school among adolescents', *J. Educ. Psychol.*, 50, 295–300.

ROSENFELD, H., and ZANDER, A. (1961) 'The influence of teachers on aspirations of students'. *J. Educ. Psychol.*, 52, 1–11.

SARASON, S. B., *et al.* (1960) *Anxiety in Elementary School Children*. New York: John Wiley.

SEARS, P. S. (1963) 'The effect of classroom conditions on the strength of achievement motive and work output of elementary school children', *Co-operative Research Project* No. OE 873. Washington.

STOUFFER, S. A., BORGATTA, E. F., HAYES, D. G., and HENRY, A. F. (1952) 'A technique for improving cumulative scales', *Public Opinion Quarterly*, 16, 273–91.

TCHESCHTELIN, M. A., HIPSKIND, M. J., REMMERS, H. H. (1940) 'Measuring the attitudes of elementary school children toward their teacher', *J. Educ. Psychol.*, 31, 195–203.

VERNON, P. E. (1950) 'An application of factorial analysis to the study of test items'. *Brit. J. Psychol. (Stat. Sec.)*, 3, 1–15.

WARBURTON, F. W. (1962) 'The measurement of personality', *Educ. Res.*, 4, 193–205.

19

L. M. *Watson*   Cigarette smoking in
school children*

*A study of the effectiveness of different
health education methods in modifying
behaviour, knowledge and attitudes*

The association between cigarette smoking and lung cancer has
generally been accepted and the evidence concerning this and other
health hazards of smoking has been well summarised in the report of
the Royal College of Physicians (1962). Over the country, anti-smoking
campaigns report varying degrees of success, for it is difficult to modify
people's attitudes to established habits. Experimental anti-smoking
clinics reveal that only a small proportion of people are sincerely interested in stopping smoking, while knowledge and even acceptance
of facts deter very few smokers. The need for research in motivation
and educational methods was indicated by the Joint Committee of the
Central and Scottish Health Services Councils (1964) and the Royal
Society of Medicine (Platt *et al.*, 1964).

THE STUDY

This project was planned to study and compare the effectiveness of
four different health education methods in school children. The
problem of smoking was selected because cigarette smoking is a serious
hazard to health. Most non-smokers and even many smokers are agreed
that action must be taken to prevent young people adopting a habit so
inimical to health, because all surveys prove beyond doubt that the
smoking habit commences at school age, and it is important to evaluate
different methods in controlled groups in comparable situations.

* Reprinted from *Edinburgh Health Bulletin*, 24, 1966, 1–12.

As surveys[1] revealed that the percentage of smokers and the quantity smoked is higher in 'Secondary Modern' schools (i.e. children on three- or four-year courses), pupils of these schools participated in the study. For practical reasons it was decided to collect data from questionnaires with procedure as recommended by Chave (London School of Hygiene, 1959) and Jefferys (1963). In most anti-smoking campaigns the criterion of success has been considered to be the conversion of smokers to non-smokers. In fact, this is not the sole problem whether in a research or practical programme, for, as external stimuli may modify behaviour, knowledge or attitudes separately or in combination, so also do different educational methods vary in their effect upon these three aspects. Hence a questionnaire was designed to measure these aspects and reports are based upon modifications observed in these aspects.

The investigation extended over three school terms. In the first term, information was collected, suitable schools were selected in collaboration with interested headmasters to ensure their all-important enthusiasm, and a preliminary investigation of behaviour, knowledge, emotional motivation and attitudes to smoking was made from the carefully compiled and pre-tested questionnaire. As far as possible, schools were matched in such demographic factors as age, sex, physical health and development, intelligence and socio-economic conditions, to ensure similar samples. The questionnaire was ultimately submitted to about 2,000 pupils of five secondary schools, and this information was analysed and applied where possible in the ensuing programmes.

In the second term the active programmes were presented in five meetings of 45 minute periods in four of these matched secondary schools, the fifth acting as a control. Four separate and clear-cut methods were evaluated. Since all the fieldwork was carried out by the writer, these were presented only to second-year pupils in the second term of the school year. This method ensured a minimum of 100 pupils exposed to each method and no loss of pupils from leaving school in the follow-up study. This report is restricted to these 700 pupils plus 100 in the control school. The programme presented in each method may be briefly summarised:

Didactic approach

The 280 pupils by classes received a course of five meetings, comprising lectures and films on smoking facts, debates and health quiz, and using such visual aids as films, models, flannelgraphs, posters and leaflets.

[1] London School of Hygiene and Tropical Medicine (1959); Cartwright *et al.* (1959, 1960c); Jones (1957); Raven (1957); Morris (1963); Chaike (1964).

Information was as positive as possible, never horrific; emphasis was rather on proven data, and there was always question-and-answer time. The aim was to give all known facts about cigarette smoking, using formal teaching methods to reinforce non-smokers' and to change smokers' aspects of smoking.

Group discussion

Six classes totalling 160 pupils, divided into self-selected groups of about ten pupils, met on five occasions each with a trained group leader. As these children had no previous experience of group discussions nor great knowledge of the subject, and were poor at sustaining discussion and expressing themselves, it was decided to spend five to ten minutes of each period presenting information as a framework for discussion. This included health hazards and lung cancer rates in Edinburgh, tobacco advertising, some facts, rates and rationalisations about smoking as revealed in their own questionnaire answers, *13 Questions and Answers* (a Central Council for Health Education leaflet), and a tape of a role-taking script.[2] 'You die if you smoke' to provoke discussion. Each group drew up seven points for safer smoking and their own posters and slogans were displayed in the school. The aim was, by ensuring personal involvement in group discussion, to come to group decision to reinforce non-smokers' and change smokers' aspects of smoking.

Psychological persuasions

The 101 pupils had five meetings using oblique techniques as, for example 'debunking' advertising; simple psychology of smoking illustrated by their own answers as to why they started and continued to smoke, their 'images' for smoker and smoking and the reasons for these. Teaching aids were questionnaire results, advertising material and posters, thematic projection film, tape of role-taking script 'You die if you smoke', an extract from 'Let's stop smoking' by a psychiatrist, and Bob Newart's amusing record 'Introducing tobacco to civilisation'. The aim was to develop insight into the techniques of persuasion used in promoting cigarette sales; to foster a more critical attitude towards such techniques; and to modify the images and emotional beliefs currently associated with smoking. A minimum of factual knowledge was given, emphasis being on individual choice based on unbiased critical faculty.

[2] The original work of the two Group Leaders from Moray House College of Education.

Total project

The study ranged from no action in the control school to 'all-out' action and project work in this school. The five formal meetings here included lectures, teaching of facts, films, study of the *13 Questions and Answers* leaflet, magazine and television advertising, simple psychology, and participation in a Brains Trust with an exhibition of work done during the term. Teaching aids included flannelgraphs, charts, models, films, leaflets and advertising material. Full staff co-operation ensured repetition in other classes for most subjects, suggestions for the project work being supplied to the head teachers of each subject, while non-smokers extolled the virtues of their state, and smokers regretted their habituation even to the extent of a few ceasing to smoke. Parents of the 170 pupils involved were sent an explanatory letter and invited to an initial meeting to discuss the problem. Pupils were encouraged to tell their parents about sessions. At the end of term each parent was sent a pamphlet and letter summarising the programme and requesting their vital support at home. School health visitor and medical officer gave their sustained interest and support. Following a request to the Chief Constable, police reminded vendors of the byelaws regarding the sale of tobacco to minors. All local youth leaders were requested to reinforce the theme, and finally, a poster competition with prizes was held and the children's own posters placed throughout the school. Thus was composed a programme using a selection of health education methods and reinforced by every opinion leader to ensure sustained impact to strengthen non-smokers' and change smokers' aspects of smoking.

The fifth school supplied the control group of 103 pupils where no special action was taken.

In the third term, that is after the Easter vacation and a full month after the last meetings, the follow-up questionnaire was presented and the effectiveness of the four different methods was evaluated. The questionnaire was presented to all pupils of the five schools to measure change in those pupils directly exposed to each method, and to discover any spread-effect within a school in other pupils not personally exposed to the programme in comparison with the control school pupils. Only those results observed in the 800 second-year pupils are presented in this report.

The immediate aim in all four groups was to improve factual knowledge, to modify emotional attitudes to smoking and to effect change in smoking habits.

The ultimate aim was to compare these aspects of the four different health education approaches in order to obtain information to assist in the selection of future methods, and this was achieved from questionnaire-analysis and fieldwork.

Note. 'Smoking' refers throughout to cigarette smoking.

REPORT ON QUESTIONNAIRE-ANALYSIS AND FIELDWORK OBSERVATIONS

A. Profile

The pupils were mainly on a three-year course, of IQ 70–110, in their second year of secondary school and the majority were aged about thirteen years at the first questionnaire in December 1964. Analysis established general demographic conformity within the five schools of the project and with results of other surveys on smoking as follows:

Demographic factors. With the assistance of school health visitors the children were found to be comparable physically (height, weight, major defects especially vision, taken as indices).

Since all five schools were non-fee-paying local authority schools serving housing schemes on the periphery of the city, education, socio-economic and environmental conditions were very similar. Taking the dividing level frequently used, the children could be graded 'less able' (IQ 70–85) or 'average ability' (IQ 86–110). In four schools the proportion of 'less able' pupils averaged 30 per cent, but in School III there were no 'less able' pupils. As it transpired, this was fortunate in that the psychological persuasion method *as used* would not have been suitable for children of poor intelligence.

Personal habits. It was interesting to note that smokers in all five schools admitted to more hours television-viewing than non-smokers; that they tended to have fewer hobbies and to belong to fewer youth organisations; but that there was no difference in sports activity, where, regardless of smoking habits, 'less able' children, especially girls, played far less sports than 'average ability' children, especially boys.

Smoking habits. The majority of boys (65 per cent) had smoked their first cigarette by twelve years of age and most girls (55 per cent) by thirteen years. Curiosity was given as the main precipitating cause of this first cigarette, with group-pressure reasons ('my friends smoke', 'a dare', 'offered one') a close second for girls. The overall smoking rates were calculated as 30 per cent for boys and 24 per cent for girls. Boys declared they continued to smoke primarily because they enjoyed it and only secondarily because friends smoked; girls' principal reason was that friends smoked and only half as many claimed to smoke for enjoyment in all schools except School III (where 50 per cent girls smoked for enjoyment). These children who did not smoke, or had tried and not persisted, did not because they disliked smoking; girls also declared they were not allowed to smoke, while more boys mentioned cost, health and athletic prowess. Such differences were capitalised in the ensuing health education programmes. More difficult to apply but surely important was the observation made in analysis that the image of Smoking was more positive than the image of the Smoker in smokers and non-smokers alike, although both images were more positive with smokers. The smoker was frequently described as selfish, lazy and a waster of money even while smoking was associated with success, relaxation and friendliness.

It was found that all smokers smoked most often outdoors, but the next favourite place for boys was the anonymity of the cinema, and for girls it was clubs or dances, again revealing sex differences in the *given* reasons for smoking in teenagers.

Most boys bought their cigarettes in shops or from slot machines, while a smaller majority of girls bought in shops, very few used slot machines, and many received them from 'friends'. As may be expected, boys had rather more pocket-money than girls, but smokers had much more than non-smokers. There was also an income increase claimed in the follow-up questionnaire, which was greater in smokers.

More non-smokers (9·6 per cent) were found to have non-smoking parents than had smokers (2·4 per cent) and there were more non-smoking parents of 'average ability' than of 'less able' children. In every school there was a higher rate of smoking in mothers of smokers than in mothers of non-smokers, the overall rates being 71 per cent and 57 per cent respectively. A higher or heavier rate of smoking was not observed in those children who were older than their class norm, as has been reported (Horn, 1963).

The suggestion that smokers are more friendly and extroverted was perhaps supported in that a higher percentage of smokers answered all questions, giving negative or 'wrong' answers rather than no answers.

The importance of this information from questionnaire-analysis lies not in originality but in its consistency within the different schools and with previous surveys, providing a solid basis for comparison.

B. Analysis information

Diagnosis of smokers and non-smokers was made from the question 'how many cigarettes do you smoke weekly?' Those answering 'none' were accepted as non-smokers, but all X's (no answer given) included as smokers. This diagnosis of smoking status was confirmed in a seven-question check in the initial questionnaire and five ways in the follow-up questionnaire, and found to tally reassuringly. It is appreciated that an intelligent liar could still misinform. Smokers of 1–5 cigarettes weekly were arbitrarily graded as light smokers; 6–20 as medium; and over 20 weekly as regular heavy smokers.

With the passing of over four winter months between questionnaires there would normally be an increase in the number of children smoking. This recruitment (Horn, 1960) is in fact observed in the control school. Hence the follow-up smoking rate, when compared with the initial smoking rate, does not reveal its full improvement.

Information from the questionnaires was programmed for full breakdown. It will be appreciated that while some questions provided a simple dichotomy (yes/no answers), others produced multiple-category answers. The collective pattern is important and much time was given to studying processes for measuring sociological variables, especially for this subject where there were differences within each school (before and after the health education programmes) and between the five schools.

Since it was felt that the question of whether or not a child smokes at present was not the only pertinent problem, the questionnaires were designed to measure changes in three aspects, viz.: (*a*) Behaviour, (*b*) Knowledge and (*c*) Attitude to cigarette smoking. Since no one question covers all phases, a set of questions was combined to ensure, as Riley (1954) says, 'that the findings of a single dimension of status is not peculiar to one particular situation'. Each set was composed of the first and major diagnostic parameter and several minor supporting parameters.

On analysis, many changes in themselves were not statistically significant but the trends were consistent enough to be worthy of consideration. To summarise and describe the relative success of each method in affecting an aspect, individual items (or parts of items) have been carefully studied from all angles and ranked from 1 to 5, with top rank 1. Consideration was given to three principal sub-groups (smoking status, sex, and intelligence) and then ranking was based upon 'shifts' observed in rates in before-and-after questionnaires, or if a new parameter was used in the second questionnaire, upon the difference in rates observed in children exposed to the four methods and control. If a higher proportion of children answered the question in the desired direction (e.g. stopped smoking) after the programme, this is recognised as improvement whether or not statistically significant. Changes significant at the 0·05 level were achieved by some method in each major parameter.

Following this nested ranking procedure (Sklaroff, 1965) with parameters, an average rank for each aspect was calculated and then a final evaluation, and this is termed the 'Average ranking' of each method, as summarised in Table 19.2. This crude ranking is used to clarify and present the complex results achieved in order to evaluate and discuss the relative merits of the different methods studied and does not imply statistical reliability to rank order.

C. Evaluation of methods

The general picture is presented in the profile paragraph and here relevant and particular details are given of the effectiveness of each method from each aspect.

Method I. Didactic approach. Evaluation. With the simple nested ranking and scoring technique used, the average rank of the method was first for Behaviour and third for Knowledge and Attitude Aspects, with a final average rank of second. In the behaviour aspect, this authoritative approach was found most effective in converting smokers to non-smokers, which is the most obvious measure of success. In the first questionnaire, 51 (33 per cent) of 153 boys, but only 20 (17 per cent) of 118 girls smoked. So the girl smoker rate was low even before the campaign, and this was maintained in the other six check questions. On further analysis, this was found to be weighted by a low smoking rate (only 13 per cent) in the 91 average ability girls. In other respects, the pupils were comparable with other schools. After the five periods of formal lessons, there was a great improvement, significant at the 0·05 level, in the major behaviour parameter, conversion to non-smokers, where the overall smoking rate decreased from 26 per cent to 17 per cent. This was composed of a reduction of 32 smokers (21·6 per cent) of 148 boys, and 10 smokers (9 per cent) of 112 girls. The number of 'heavy' smokers remained unchanged, so that this method affected only the light smokers who were flirting with smoking. From other questions in the set, the method emerged successful, excepting in minor parameters Cartwright *et al.* (1959), 'Would you join the JNSL?' (Junior League of Non-Smokers) where information was from posters only, and (Jones, 1957) 'How would you stop people smoking?' where in spite of their own high conversion rate there was the greatest pessimism and antagonism to any such action.

The number of pupils associating cardiovascular disease and other health hazards with smoking increased to an extent significant at the

0.05 level, but less than in other schools. There was more 'forgetfulness' among smokers, and altogether too many children declared they remembered nothing of the programme. Although factual information was carefully prepared and presented with a variety of visual aids, it was *not* best retained, so that the method ranked third for improving knowledge.

Nor was the method found very effective in changing children's attitudes to smoking. Results were varied and there was often a rebound effect, reinforcing previous habits rather than changing them.

Fieldwork observations. Such a programme using formal teaching and mass media is simpler to produce and could be used by every teacher. All pupils started off with enthusiasm, but this was markedly lacking by the fifth lesson. Probably three lessons (including films) presenting facts would suffice in a well-balanced programme on this one subject. Only more able classes successfully kept notes or debated. This may be attributable to some inexperience in handling less able children, but is a practical difficulty to be remembered by health educationalists impressed by the obedient behaviour evoked by the voice of authority.

Method 2. Group discussion. Evaluation. The average rank of the method was second in all three aspects and in the final average ranked first.

In the major parameter of the behaviour aspect, there was but poor smoker conversion. In the first questionnaire, 25 (32 per cent) of the 78 boys smoked and 25 (33 per cent) of the 76 girls smoked. After the five group discussion periods there was a decrease of 5 per cent overall, to 21 smokers (26 per cent) in 82 boys and 21 smokers (27 per cent) in 77 girls, still leaving the rate rather high in girls. On further analysis this was found to be due to a whole class of low IQ girl smokers. In the minor parameters the method was successful in changing non-smokers' behaviour, for instance, here were most claims to trying to stop parents smoking and in fact the greatest increase (Horn, 1960) in the number of non-smoking parents; the highest proportion declared they would join the Junior Non-Smokers' League and action was taken to form a branch; many more non-smokers decided to forbid smoking 'everywhere' and 'in all public places'; and there were several recommendations for action to stop smoking with not one voice raised against this. As in all other schools, these suggestions were to increase price or produce fewer cigarettes, while girls also laid stress on shock and fear tactics with one most telling reply from the girl who became active secretary of the JNSL, 'Show people like my uncle who suffered for ages before he died. When he took two pills the noise he made putting them down. I cried when I saw my uncle like this and he was only 39 years of age.'

Knowledge was well improved, again better in the non-smokers. The rate of 'nothing' remembered was pleasingly low in all pupils, and there was quite a good special referral rate to points restricted to this programme.

In none of the attitudes aspect set of questions did group discussion *change* children's emotional attitudes to smoking. Rather were they confirmed in their previous beliefs so that this method was more successful than others in confirming non-smokers' attitudes, but less successful in changing smokers'.

Fieldwork observations. The writer found that children most enjoyed this method. It was not used as first planned because it was found that the children had no previous experience of group discussion and too little factual knowledge to discuss. At least two periods were spent in structuring the groups, and in the first five to ten minutes of each period simple factual information was given to each class before it split into groups. It is felt that the repeated lack of success with smokers was due to the fact that groups were self-selected so that most, if not all, smokers in each class were in one group. Thus their attitudes were perpetuated and feelings of the 'goodness' of smoking, etc. were strengthened without the opposing views of their non-smoking peers. This was most noticeable in one difficult class of low ability resistant and 'heavy' girl smokers where very little progress was made in any aspect. Supporting the theory that smoking in children may be in rebellion, it was observed that nine very impudent and inconsistent follow-up questionnaires were produced by recognised difficult and rejected boys, all smokers.

Method 3. Psychological persuasion. Evaluation. This method ranked first in the Attitude Aspect, third in Behaviour, fourth in Knowledge, and third in final average ranking.

Although these pupils were also on three- or four-year courses, closer analysis revealed none as 'less able' (i.e. below IQ 85), and accordingly rates were comparable to rates of 'average ability' children in other schools. Before the campaign, 9 (18 per cent) of 50 girls smoked, while 14 (31 per cent) of 45 boys smoked. Unfortunately 12 pupils (9 girls and 3 boys) were absent for the follow-up questionnaire, which could bias results in a sample this size. The following changes were observed after the campaign:

In the behaviour aspect major parameter there was a reduction to five smokers (12 per cent) in the 41 girls, but there was no decrease apparent in boys as 13 (31 per cent) of 42 boys smoked and this resistance was borne out in 42 per cent boy-smokers declaring they had not even tried to stop smoking. Other results were mixed; for instance, though there was not a high rate of would-be members of the JNSL, yet in a follow-up three months later, action had been taken and several pupils sported the membership badge; many more smokers were for banning smoking in some public places; and there was little pessimism or antagonism expressed against stopping people smoking. The method ranked only third and was less successful with boys, but on the whole provoked less abreaction than did other methods.

Psychological persuasion was, not surprisingly since the programme gave fewest facts, the least successful method for improving knowledge, but information given was well retained and there were many (in fact 14, or 17 per cent) references to special highlights of the programme, including eight to debunking advertising. The fact that there was significant improvement shows how knowledge can be absorbed without formally announcing facts.

In an aspect where shifts were small and rarely statistically significant overall this method was most successful in modifying attitudes which may be of lasting importance. This it did without stimulating abreaction in smokers.

Fieldwork observations. The writer found it most interesting but most difficult to design a programme purely on these lines and feels that it would be even more exacting to find the language and means of communication for children of lowest ability. A little psychology can go a long way and at times the boys' interest flagged alarmingly. The writer is far from feeling that difficulties encountered indicate that the method be discarded, for there is much promise in this more oblique technique and a good youth leader or health educationalist could make much of it.

Note. Two successful lessons were spent on debunking advertising—advertiser's images were critically assessed for many products, the highly organised and expensive operation of the launching of a new cigarette was revealed, then each pupil analysed cigarette advertisements and composed new captions for the pictures, the best being shown to the class.

Method 4. Total project. Evaluation. This method ranked first in the knowledge aspect, but fourth in behaviour, attitudes, and final average rank. From the behaviour aspect, in the first questionnaire, of the 84 boys, 23 (27·4 per cent) smoked, and of the 80 girls, 22 (27·5 per cent) smoked. These rates were slightly lower for boys, but higher for girls than the overall calculated rates for all schools (30 per cent for boys and 24 per cent for girls). After the term of intensive health education, with assistance from every possible source, there was a 5·5 per cent decrease in girls where 20 (22·5 per cent) of the 89 girls smoked; but a slight increase in the rate of boy smokers, as of 80 boys, 24 (29 per cent) smoked. This could be expressed as a recruitment rate (Horn, 1960) of 6 per cent and tallies with the high rate (45 per cent) of boy smokers who declared they did not wish to stop smoking. There was also abreaction to forbidding smoking and although many agreed to join the JNSL, in fact no action was taken.

In contrast, this method was most successful for imparting knowledge and for this information being remembered by smokers and non-smokers alike. The one exception was the number of children continuing to refuse to accept the cause and effect association between smoking and lung cancer, which was observed in most schools. In explanation it could be argued that this was not new information and those rejecting it reveal a mental block also observed in adults.

In every parameter the Total Project was least successful in changing attitudes and often precipitated an abreaction, especially in smokers.

Fieldwork observations. The project required and received much planning, work, and cooperation from all. General interest and enthusiasm in school appeared well maintained and it is a surprise as well as a disappointment to the writer that the immense effort did *not* pay higher dividends, excepting only in success in teaching facts. It would appear rather that abreaction was provoked, probably from an overdose of the subject since it was administered in many lessons and by many people in school and outside it.

D. General observations

The variety of responses is no less than to be expected since different methods must appeal in different directions and degrees to different individuals. These evaluations and observations summarise the general effects which might be expected of a method.

Absentees. There were 35 absentees for the initial questionnaire from the total registered in the classes and a further 21 absentees for the follow-up questionnaire, and an attempt was made to discover if they could have affected the results. Unfortunately it proved impossible to obtain very definite information although headmasters gave assurance they had no preponderance of chronic school-refusers, problem children or chronic invalids. Nor were they all of lower intelligence since although there were several less able boys, a surprisingly high proportion were average ability girls.

Finally, it should be noted since nine of eleven insolent and contradictory papers were from one school and would have biased results if excluded, all questionnaires were coded, and included in calculating rates. It was also observed that rude answers came solely from smokers and usually from those who were (or claimed to be) in the higher pocket-money income bracket!

Staff attitudes. When considering all the variables, the importance of teachers as opinion leaders was fully appreciated. The possibility of studying the effectiveness of a staff of non- or ex-smokers was regretfully abandoned, but it was deemed valuable to make an early estimate of their own smoking behaviour, knowledge, and attitudes, as well as their feelings about pupils smoking with a 'dipstick' questionnaire offered on a voluntary and anonymous basis. Cooperation was good and analysis revealed no important difference which might have affected the results achieved in any school. The majority were 'for' health education and the few who were against it feared only the precipitation of greater interest in smoking.

The conversion of smokers is a crucial and important effect so these rates were further broken down and studied and are given further consideration with the other major parameters.

Behaviour aspect—conversion to non-smoker status. Smoking rates dropped by at least 5 per cent in all active methods, excepting in the boys exposed to psychological persuasian (no change observed) and total project (where there was actually a recruitment rate of 6 per cent), but only those decreases achieved by didactic teaching were statistically significant. However, it should not be forgotten that the simple decreases observed in the number of smokers does not allow for the normal net recruitment rate (calculated by Horn (1960) as the difference between the proportion of smokers at the beginning and end of the school year expressed as a percentage of the proportion of non-smokers in the primary investigation) which would occur in the intervening months.

A consideration of the net Conversion Rate (where the difference between the proportion of smokers before and after each programme is expressed as a percentage of the proportion of smokers observed before the programme), gives a useful comparison of the effectiveness of each method, as set out in Table 19.1 overleaf.

The didactic method achieved the highest rate of conversion, and this was most obvious in girls, where it approached 50 per cent. Group discussion appeared to be equally effective with girl and boy smokers. Psychological persuasion was quite effective since it converted one-third of the small number of girl smokers and at least prevented recruitment among the boys. The total project had an 18·3 per cent conversion rate in girls, but total failure with boys where a 6 per cent recruitment rate obtained. As was to be expected, there was also a recruitment rate in boys (6 per cent) and girls (4·25 per cent) in the control school.

There are several overall rates of interest. There was a pre-campaign smoking rate of 29·5 per cent in boys compared with only 23·8 per cent in girls, and 38·8 per cent in less able children, as opposed to only 22·4 per cent in average ability children. This corresponds to conversion rates of 16·6 per cent in boys, 21 per cent in girls, 20·6 per cent in less able and 15·2 per cent in average ability pupils.

Thus it appears that health education more readily affects girls than boys, and less able rather than average ability children. Unfortunately, it is also possible that both more malleable groups could as readily be tempted to smoke again.

Deeper analysis showed that it was mainly 'light and medium' smokers (under 20 cigarettes a week) who relinquished the habit, while there was a very slight shift in the 'heavy' smokers (over 20 cigarettes a week) who are already regular smokers and as difficult to convert as adults. Indeed, an increase in the amount smoked was observed in the average ability 'heavy' smokers. Thus while pre-campaign there were 23 less able and 39 average ability, totalling 62 heavy smokers, post campaign there were 18 less able and 42 average ability, totalling 60 heavy smokers.

Knowledge aspect—associated illnesses. Here, two items providing before and after measurements were used as main diagnostic parameters. Firstly there was a great increase in the association between smoking and all illnesses; and the increase was significant in methods I (didactic), II (group) and IV (project). Secondly the association of smoking and cardiovascular disease was chosen as being new and important information and here increases were found to be statistically significant in all but the control school.

TABLE 19.1. Smoker conversion rate

Method	No. at risk. (QI)			Before programme smoking rates (SR1)			After programme smoking rates (SR2)			Conversion rate $\frac{(SR1-SR2)}{(SR1)}$		
	T	B	G	T	B	G	T	B	G	T	B	G
I Didactic	271	153	118	26%	33%	17%	16%	21.6%	9%	38.5%	34.5%	47%
II Group discussion	154	78	76	32%	32%	33%	26%	26%	27%	19%	19%	18.2%
III Psychological	95	45	50	24%	31%	18%	21.6%	31%	12%	14%	0%	33.3%
IV Project	164	84	80	27%	27.4%	27.5%	26%	29%	22.5%	3.7%	*(6%)	18.3%
V Control	93	47	46	20%	15%	26%	24%	20%	29%	*(5%)	*(7%)	*(4.24%)

Code: QI = Questionnaire before programme
      B = Boys   G = Girls
      SR1 = Smoking rate before programme

T = Total number
SR2 = Smoking rate after programme

Note: * Recruitment rate in fact observed.

Attitude aspect—smoking causing ill health. Changes achieved by each method were in positive direction in some children and negative direction in others so that it proved most difficult to assess the success of different methods for this aspect. The main diagnostic question was taken to be 'do you believe smoking causes ill health' and since the answers were in a scale ('always, often, sometimes, never'), the numbers answering 'always' and 'often' were added and tests of significance were carried out. Only two shifts were statistically significant and those were in the non-smokers of methods II (group) and IV (project).

Ranking was the result of nested ranking procedure described, but without a doubt attitudes are more difficult to modify and to gauge.

CONCLUSIONS

Measures of change were based on the analysis of before-and-after questionnaires. Three aspects were measured by a set of some six questions as parameters, with at least one main diagnostic question in each set. The follow-up questionnaire was purposely given after the Easter vacation, and over a month after the last meeting, to avoid claims of evangelistic reform. 'Shifts' obtained were often small and seldom statistically significant, but a trend maintained over separate parts of four or five subsidiary parameters was felt to be of consequence when considered in addition to significant changes observed in the most important parameter. To summarise the relative importance of each method, the changes effected in each parameter (or the several parts of each parameter) were simply scored and ranked in the three aspects studied and summarised in an overall evaluation, giving average ranking as in Table 19.2. Group Discussion thus ranks overall first. It was concluded that each group should contain a minority of smokers, *or*, since the method was found to be so successful with non-smokers, that it should be used at an earlier stage before smoking habits are established.

It is again emphasised that there was a short formal fact-giving session at the beginning of each meeting. The writer strongly supports this procedure wherever the intelligence of the audience is such that it makes improbable any serious study preparation before the group meets.

The Didactic Method ranked second in the final evaluation according to the nested ranking procedure employed. However, there was unquestionable behavioural response to the voice of authority and the smoker conversion rate was significantly high. In any programme where a change in behaviour is the desired end product, this might well be the method of choice, for formal teaching has most trained exponents and has the further advantage of coping with larger numbers than can group work.

TABLE 19.2. *Ranking of methods*

Method	Ranking of methods in 3 aspects			Final average ranking
	Behaviour	Knowledge	Attitude	
Didactic	1	3	3	2
Group Discussion	2	2	2	1
Psychological	3	4	1	3
Total Project	4	1	4	4
Control	5	5	5	5

Psychological persuasion ranked a close third in the final evaluation and holds interesting promise, though it is to be remembered that here it was attempted only with children of average ability. This more oblique technique accomplished changes without provoking abreaction and could be applied within a programme. It may prove to have a valuable long-term effect since behaviour is the active expression of attitudes and beliefs. The debunking of advertising (included more briefly in the total project, and in group discussion) definitely held the pupils' attention and appears well worth repeating in other health education and citizenship programmes.

The Total Project ranked fourth in the final evaluation but was most successful in improving the pupils' factual knowledge of smoking. As a method it *can* teach facts, apparently by sheer repetition and hence could be used with hope of success where this is the sole aim, but this is rarely so in health education.

Even when knowledge is improved, there is no guarantee of improved behaviour, and the writer is convinced that to wait until the second year of senior school is merely to increase the problem. As Jefferys (1963) said, the optimum time to convince children not to smoke is before they start, and before there is the danger of any abreaction from smokers. A programme given at 11–12 years in the last year of primary school would circumvent many difficulties encountered with teenagers. Where smoking is concerned, one might thus avoid the strongly positive image of smoking and the stubborn core of adolescents rejecting the association of smoking and lung cancer. In short, previous attitudes and beliefs would be less firmly held, knowledge could be more readily increased and desired behaviour more certainly ensured.

SUMMARY

In a study extended over a year, an attempt was made to assess the effect of different forms of health education instruction in modifying smoking habits in secondary pupils of five matched schools. The criteria of matching were age, sex, physical development and health, intelligence, socio-economic conditions, parents' and staff smoking habits.

The methods compared were (1) Didactic, (2) Group Discussion, (3) Psychological Persuasion, and (4) Total Project. The fifth school acted as a control. A full programme, carefully restricted to its method, was offered in five meetings to second year pupils. Methods were assessed for their effectiveness in modifying behaviour, knowledge and attitude. It was found that where a method scored best in one aspect it was less successful in others, so that the didactic approach was most effective in converting smokers; the total project was best at improving knowledge but became dangerously wearisome; while attitudes were most affected by the psychological techniques. Group discussion was a close second in effecting changes in all three aspects and holds most promise of success. The study showed that any health education on smoking is better than none at all, while there is promise that, depending upon the end result desired, a programme could be designed predominantly to modify behaviour, knowledge and attitudes in different audiences by a selection or combination of teaching methods.

The views expressed are my own and do not necessarily represent the opinion or policy of my department.

ACKNOWLEDGEMENTS

I wish to acknowledge the assistance received from many colleagues in the preparation of this paper. Particular thanks go to Dr F. Martin for his guidance and advice, and to Mr S. Sklaroff for invaluable assistance with the statistical analysis (both of the Usher Institute of Public Health, Edinburgh). My thanks are also due to the three visiting lecturers, to the two group leaders, to officers of the City Education Department, and to all headmasters, and their staffs and pupils of the schools participating.

The study was initiated by Dr J. H. F. Brotherston, Chief Medical Officer, Scottish Home and Health Department, and sponsored by that department and by the Health Committee of the City of Edinburgh. Finally, I gratefully acknowledge permission from Dr J. L. Gilloran, Medical Officer, Edinburgh, both to carry out the work and to publish this report.

REFERENCES

CARTWRIGHT, A., MARTIN, F. M., and THOMSON, J. G. (1959) *Lancet*, **2**, 725.

CARTWRIGHT, A., MARTIN, F. M., and THOMSON, J. G. (1960*a*) *Lancet*, **1**, 327.

CARTWRIGHT, A., MARTIN, F. M., and THOMSON, J. G. (1960*b*) *Brit. J. prev. soc. Med.* **14**, 160.

CARTWRIGHT, A., THOMSON, J. G. *et al.* (1960*c*) *Brit. J. prev. soc. Med.*, **14**, 28.

CENTRAL HEALTH SERVICES COUNCIL, and SCOTTISH HEALTH SERVICES COUNCIL (1964) *Health education: report of a joint committee*, HMSO.

CHAIKE, H. D. (1964) *Roy. Soc. Health J.*, **84**, 271.

HORN, D. (1960) *Children*, **7**, 63.

HORN, D. (1963) *J. Chron. Dis.*, **16**, 383.

JEFFREYS, M. (1963) *Med. Offr.*, **109**, 91.

JEFFREYS, M. and WESTAWAY, W. R. (1961) *Health Education J.*, **19**, 3.

JONES, A. P. (1957) *Lancet*, **1**, 631.

LONDON SCHOOL OF HYGIENE AND TROPICAL MEDICINE, Study group of the Public Health Department (1959) *Brit. J. prev. soc. Med.*, **13**, 1.

MORRIS S. (1963) *Chest Heart Bull.*, **26**, 135.

PLATT, R., ROBINSON, K., WAKEFIELD, J., and MCKENNEL, A. C. (1964) *Proc. roy. soc. Med.*, **57**, 449.

RAVEN, R. W. (1957) *Lancet*, **1**, 1139.

RILEY, M. *et al.* (1954) *Sociological Studies in Scale Analysis*, Rutgers Universities Press, part 4, p. 272.

ROYAL COLLEGE OF PHYSICIANS OF LONDON (1962) *Smoking and Health: a report on smoking in relation to cancer of the lung and other diseases*. Pitman.

SKLAROFF, S. (1965) Personal communication.

SECTION 5

Learning handicaps

The articles in the preceding sections have been concerned with personality and learning in normal children. They examine cognitive styles in learning and basic questions of motivation and attitudes, as well as social interaction and how this affects learning. We turn now to look at children with acknowledged and often serious handicaps. These fall naturally into two groups—children with adjustment difficulties and those with learning handicaps. The two are, of course, frequently found together, the one being a cause of the other. Attempts to sort out primacy, to decide whether adjustment is at the root of learning difficulties or vice versa, are extremely difficult indeed—this being one of the main messages of Chazan's paper on maladjustment and reading difficulties.

Assigning children formally to classes such as maladjusted or educationally subnormal (ESN) *is a process which reflects the standards set by the society around the child rather than something essential to him. A child is maladjusted if he fails to respond in a way we consider normal, to the social demands of the situations in which he finds himself. Similarly, a child is ESN (or a 'slow learner') if he is unable* to achieve the cognitive (and other) skills which our society expects of children at particular ages.

Four articles have been chosen on the subject of maladjustment and two on the problems of slow learners.

Lunzer's is a specific study, in which an attempt is made to look at different types of children with personality problems, namely the aggressive and the withdrawing, and to compare them on a number of rating-scale measures. His findings provide yet another reminder to the educationalist, that though the problems of the aggressive child are the more noticeable, those of the withdrawing are in most ways of equal significance.

The Mitchell and Shepherd study and the Tizard paper make similar contributions in that they are both concerned with the problem of rating-scale assessment and its reliability. The Tizard paper explores the relative value of different questionnaire measures and comes to the conclusion that skilled use of questionnaires by teachers and parents will result in the 'missing' of few genuine cases of maladjustment. But their value remains as screening devices rather than as precisely sensitive measuring instruments. Mitchell and Shepherd bring out even more firmly the problem of the situational dependence of maladjustment. Children who are rated as well-adjusted at home may be behaviour problems at school; and again, those who are a sore trial to their parents may behave normally at school. There are many reasons for this, not all of them psychometric. Not only do different adults see children differently and children respond in varying ways to the adults they encounter; there is also the possibility that certain kinds of situation are threatening to the child, whereas he copes quite successfully with others.

Chazan supplies a useful review of an intriguing field of study, the question of how far adjustment can be responsible for reading difficulties as well as how far difficulty in learning to read may cause emotional problems. He offers no easy solution, but surveys past research and makes some suggestions for teacher practice.

Considering the importance of the subject and the amount of research which has been carried out into problems of learning handicap, it is surprising how little we know about the personality of the subnormal child. We know indeed that most handicapping conditions correlate positively; that is, the child with learning difficulties is more likely to have emotional difficulties than a normal child and is more likely to have a whole variety of physical complaints. What we are not clear about is how far learning difficulties can be actually caused by personality difficulties, although the work of Bowlby does provide us with some clues here. Nor can we specify the personality types which are likely to occur frequently in the case of children who do persistently badly at school.

The second paper by Chazan brings out some of the problems, both emotional and physical, which are often found in ESN children in the special school. Here again, it is often impossible to separate cause and effect—but clearly, physical problems and poor home conditions can aggravate learning difficulties even in children who are of constitutionally limited ability.

The section concludes with a paper by Hess and Shipman which sets out some of their researches and views in the field of mother–child relations. But unlike most work in this area, they are concerned with the cognitive style of the mother in her relationship with the child—in more ordinary language, with the way in which mother functions as a teacher. For of course, all mothers are their children's first teachers. And what seems to be crucial for the child's later development is not so much what the mother teaches the child, but how she prepares him for the learnings he will later be having to acquire (or struggle with) at school.

Those children whom we describe as slow learners may have intellectual and, at times, physical handicaps. But their main problem may often lie in their seeing the world and the learning opportunities in it in a different way from most of us, so that they respond differently. Here again is a new field, where much study remains to be done.

A. CASHDAN

20

E. A. Lunzer

Aggressive and withdrawing children in the normal school*
Patterns of behaviour

SUMMARY. Forty-two 'aggressive' and forty 'withdrawing' children, selected by teachers out of a total school population of 1,002 children, are compared with each other and with a group of 'exceptionally well-adjusted children'. Comparisons are based on rating scales, Bristol Guides to Social Adjustment, a sociometric test, and a test of social adaptation.

The results indicate that there are probably rather more problems of aggression than withdrawal but that the severity of the two behaviour patterns is comparable. These indicatons are confirmed by a limited one-year follow-up.

I. INTRODUCTION

The work of Wickman (1928) is one of the best-known studies in the field of 'mental hygiene' in school-children. A group of teachers were asked to rank a list of symptoms of maladjustment in what they considered to be their order of severity. A similar list was ranked by a group of psychologists, psychiatrists and psychiatric social workers. Teachers gave a great deal more emphasis to violations of authority and other 'aggressive' forms of behaviour, while those kinds of behaviour which might be held to characterise the shy, recessive personality were relegated to a very low position in their rankings, suggesting that these symptoms were not regarded as serious in their import. The details of Wickman's procedure have been rightly criticised on a number of grounds which need not concern us here. It remains that his investigation has been repeated many times and the results have been substantially the same, even where considerable care was taken to avoid

*Reprinted from *British Journal of Educational Psychology*, **30**, 1960, 1–10.

the procedural errors to be found in the original. The whole of this work has been admirably reviewed in a recent and carefully conducted study by Hollins (1955). This investigation involved a comparison between the rankings of Manchester teachers and those of a group of PSWs. In general, the findings of Wickman were again confirmed.

There is an unstated value judgment implicit in such studies: it is tacitly assumed that the opinions of the clinicians are a correct reflection of the facts, and that if teachers' opinions differ from theirs, it is because teachers are insufficiently aware of the essential principles of child development. Is this something more than an *argumentum ex auctoritate*? The implications of childhood maladjustment for adult mental health are still very largely *terra incognita*. Long-term studies at present being carried out by the London Institute will no doubt go far to remedy this deficiency. At present, the association between persistent delinquent behaviour in childhood and adult criminality is better established than the connection between recessive behaviour in childhood and dysthymic neuroses in later life. This is not to say that because more is known about the relation between aggressive or delinquent behaviour and adult criminality than about the implications of recessive symptoms in children, therefore the latter are necessarily less grave in their prognosis. It may be that they are indeed more serious. Nevertheless, there appears to be a need for more factual knowledge. The present investigation was undertaken as a step in that direction.

II. SAMPLING PROCEDURE

Some twenty advanced students, teachers attending the course in child psychology for the Diploma in Education at Manchester University, were asked to put forward one or two names of children in their class or classes who were most 'aggressive', and one or two, depending on the size of the class, who were most 'withdrawing', together with an equivalent number of 'exceptionally well-adjusted' children. The aim was to obtain two experimental groups who might reasonably be described as deviants at the 5 per cent level—which would correspond in all to 10 per cent of the population from which they were taken. That figure is not disproportionate to the percentages reported in the three pilot surveys carried out for the Committee on Maladjusted Children as requiring some psychiatric attention. Each of these divided the children in a representative cross-section into five categories. Category A were those rated as seriously maladjusted, requiring clinical treatment; category B were those who were probably maladjusted and should be recommended for psychiatric interview, but not necessarily for treatment. The remaining three categories represented freedom from psychiatric symptoms, or relatively minor troubles which could be countered without recourse to the child guidance service. Overall percentages in the first two categories combined were 11·3 in Somerset, 15·8 in Birmingham, and 5·4 in Berkshire.

Teachers were encouraged to nominate more than the minimum for the two 'experimental' categories if they were especially unfortunate in the class that they had, but in point of fact, none of them did so, although there are reasonable indications from a consideration of those children who were included in the sample that some of them might have done so. On the other hand, several teachers put forward fewer names than their statistical allocation, on the ground that they had not enough children in their classes who might be regarded as even remotely 'unsettled', and they may well have been justified.

Since not all the children who were nominated were eventually rated and tested in the course of the subsequent investigation, the final samples were a little smaller than the original, and differed, albeit slightly, from one comparison to another. For most purposes the three samples consisted of forty-five 'well-adjusted' children, forty-two 'aggressive' and forty 'withdrawing'. Only three children in each group were in secondary modern schools, and of the remainder, about ten in each group were infants and the others were of junior age. The total population from which these selections were made consisted of twenty-eight classes drawn from thirteen schools in and around Manchester, i.e. 1,002 children in all.

TABLE 20.1. *Ages of children represented in the three samples* (*W* = Withdrawing. *WA* = Well-adjusted. *A* = Aggressive.)

Age-group	W	WA	A	Total
5 — 7·55	8	9	8	25
7·6— 9·6	12	13	13	38
9·6—11·5	17	20	18	55
11·6 plus	3	3	3	9

Analysis of variance showed the three samples to be strictly comparable in respect of age.

The teachers who made the selection were free to nominate boys or girls, whichever were best fitted to the category for which the selections were made. With a single exception, all of the twenty-eight classes concerned were mixed. In the event the well-adjusted sample consisted of twenty-one boys and twenty-four girls, the withdrawing sample of eighteen boys and twenty-two girls and the aggressive sample of thirty-three boys and only nine girls. Sex differences in the first two groups are not significant, but in the aggressive group, with $\chi^2=6\cdot3$, the difference is significant at the 0·02 level. This fits in with the observation that more boys than girls are referred to child guidance clinics. Since the incidence of recessive behaviour is approximately equal in the two sexes, while aggressive behaviour is considerably more prevalent in boys, and since referrals by parents, teachers and juvenile courts are more likely to be on the grounds of 'difficult' behaviour than excessive shyness, as we know from Wickman, Stogdill (1931) and their followers, it is not surprising that referrals as a whole, that is including those made by LEAs and GPs, should number more boys than girls. It also suggests that aggressive behaviour is more frequent as a whole than recessive—although it tells us nothing as to which is more serious.

Comparisons between the three samples with respect to size of family, position in family and whether the mothers were at home or at work all showed insignificant differences, although the trends (more youngest and only children in the withdrawing sample, more mothers working full-time in the aggressive sample) were in line with expectation.

III. RATINGS

All of the children in each of the three samples were assessed on each of twelve traits. These were selected from a number of available lists[1] to cover a fairly wide range of behaviour with a minimum of overlap. Careful precautions were taken to minimise halo effect. All the children in each class concerned were ranked on separate occasions for each trait, and the ratings themselves were arrived at subsequently by allocating all of these to one of the five categories in approximately a normal distribution. It will be seen that children included in these samples differ very widely from the normal distribution which characterised the population from which they were drawn. The number of children assessed at each of the five points on each of the twelve traits is shown in Table 20.2.

Differences with respect to 'aggression' merely indicate that not all children shared symptoms of aggression or withdrawal to the same degree. The ratings given in respect of concentration, persistence in failure, and maintenance of effort are of particular interest, since these may be held to indicate the effect of maladjustment without being specific as to its direction. It may be said that maladjustment in general

[1] Schonell (1944), NFER (1952) and Fleming (1954).

TABLE 20.2. *Assessments on rating scales:*
trait-ratings on a five-point scale as made by class teachers

	1	2	3	4	5	
1. Aggression Aggressive—Compliant/timid	—	—	6	17	17	W
	—	3	37	5	—	WA
	22	15	5	—	—	A
	Highly significant					
2. Concentration Absorbed—Wandering	1	4	18	12	5	W
	11	18	15	1	—	WA
	2	9	10	10	11	A
	Not significant					
3. Self-Confidence Very confident/cocksure—Over dependent	2	—	5	23	10	W
	8	7	27	3	—	WA
	8	9	16	5	4	A
	Highly significant					
4. Persistence in failure Purposeful—Depressed/resentful	1	3	16	12	8	W
	11	23	9	2	—	WA
	7	9	8	15	3	A
	Significant at 0·01 level					
5. Maintenance of effort Sustained enthusiasm—Listless/ apathetic	—	8	14	10	8	W
	12	20	11	2	—	WA
	2	10	12	17	1	A
	Not significant					
6. Sensitiveness to praise and blame Extremely sensitive—Quite indifferent	10	12	14	4	—	W
	2	6	35	2	—	WA
	1	3	15	19	4	A
	Highly significant					
7. Neat-handedness Skilful—Clumsy	1	4	19	10	6	W
	11	18	13	3	—	WA
	5	5	19	12	1	A
	Not significant					

TABLE 20.2—*contd.*

	1	2	3	4	5	
8. Attitude to adult authority: Highly co-operative—Frequently obstructive/rebellious	1	4	30	5	—	W
	24	14	7	—	—	WA
	1	9	13	11	8	A
	Highly significant					
9. Sociability Only happy with group—Prefers to be alone	—	2	10	22	6	W
	3	13	27	2	—	WA
	2	20	11	8	1	A
	Highly significant					
10. Initiative Marked originality and drive— Very dependent/diffident	—	—	7	19	14	W
	9	23	13	—	—	WA
	4	16	13	8	1	A
	Highly significant					
11. Response in class Exceptionally good talker— Hesitant/difficult to draw out	—	—	5	16	19	W
	10	13	20	2	—	WA
	4	16	17	4	1	A
	Highly significant					
12. Conscientiousness High standard of work/Scrupulous —Irresponsible/no ambition in work	—	9	19	10	2	W
	8	21	15	1	—	WA
	2	6	17	14	3	A
	Not significant					

is a response to stress characterised by anxiety. The nature of the response will vary from one individual to the next and, in particular, it will be greatly different in the recessive children from the aggressive. But whatever the specific response pattern, there will be inhibition of the highest centres of nervous activity, resulting in a loss of concentration, in lack of persistence and in lack of enthusiasm for work tasks.

It appears that more children in the aggressive group show an extreme inability to concentrate, but the difference between this group and the withdrawing is not significant ($\chi^2 = 6 \cdot 9$, d.f. $= 4$). Differences with respect to persistence in failure are significant. Pooling categories $1 + 2$ and $4 + 5$ in a 3×2 table, $\chi^2 = 10 \cdot 0$ which is significant at the $0 \cdot 01$ level (figures for the well-adjusted group are not included in any calculations, since these are clearly significantly different, but reveal no more than the general importance of good adjustment in fostering favourable behaviour traits). Again, the distribution of the two groups when assessed for maintenance of effort favours the aggressive. The disproportion between categories 4 (Only fitful application. Fairly frequent rest) and category 5 (Seems too listless and apathetic to do much) is striking. It is in line with what is known of asthenic neuroses but it accords ill with the characterisation of introverts as readily conditioned or excitatory. Much may depend on the stability of the nervous system and on the level of complexity at which the conditioning is demanded.

Taken as a whole, assessments on the three traits do not warrant more than limited conclusions. There appears to be little difference in the incidence of more or less anxiety in the two groups in so far as concentration on day-to-day tasks is impaired, but the withdrawing group show less determination in the face of failure and a greater tendency to fatigue. However, any inferences as to the quality of work produced by the two groups will be seen to be not warranted by the facts, as is shown in a forthcoming paper (Lunzer, 1960).

The distribution of ratings on the remaining traits point to the marked differences between the two groups of maladjusted children. In several instances the aggressive and withdrawing groups are at opposite extremes, with the well-adjusted control group midway between them. The withdrawing group are significantly more dependent and more sensitive to praise and blame.[2] They show less initiative and less response in class. It would appear that they are also less sociable, although this is not confirmed by the index of popularity as shown in sociometric choices made by their classmates. Differences with respect to conscientiousness and neat-handedness are not significant.

IV. BRISTOL GUIDES

A further indication of the degree of maladjustment present in each of the two experimental groups is provided by an inspection of the Bristol Social Adjustment Guides. These were completed by the class teacher concerned in respect of every child included in the sample. Following on the procedure suggested by Stott (1958) each indicator of maladjustment was given a weighting of two points while the milder symptoms of 'unsettledness' as also the indicators of nervousness and various

[2] It may be of some significance that the ten withdrawing children rated as extremely sensitive, were all among the youngest in the sample. Do these children develop a thicker skin as they grow older?

miscellaneous nervous symptoms were scored as one point. The total number of points awarded to each child thus gives some indication of the degree of disturbance that is present, as measured by the tendency for that child to show more or less considerable deviations from the normal in various aspects of his behaviour. The results are shown in the following table:

TABLE 20.3. *Maladjustment score on Bristol Guides*

	W	*WA*	*A*
Mean	17·56	2·40	20·33
N	39	45	42
S.D.	10·46	3·18	12·34

It will be seen that both experimental groups differ very widely from the control group, but there is little difference between the aggressive and the withdrawing. Here it would appear that the former tend to show more disturbance than the latter, but the differences are not significant. It happens that the Bristol Guides tend to be loaded with items indicative of delinquent tendencies, and if there is anything surprising about these results, it is surely that the differences are so small. Analysis of variance indicated that the degree of disturbance consequent on the predominance of one or other pattern of reaction was not affected by age.

From the qualitative point of view, the Bristol Guides yield a far more telling picture of the type of personality disturbance than can be had from this rough and ready method of scoring and it is of some interest to note the extent to which behaviour deviations fall into distinct patterns for the two groups. Here the hypothesis would be that both groups might be expected to show symptoms of restlessness, nervousness, depression and miscellaneous nervous symptoms, but that the withdrawing group would be characterised by signs of unforthcomingness and withdrawal, while the aggressive group would tend to show combinations of anxiety for affection or approval on the one hand, and, on the other, hostility both in relation to adults and in relation to their own peer group. The dichotomy was fairly clear-cut in thirty-one out of the forty-two aggressive children, and twenty-seven out of the forty withdrawing, while the predominance of one pattern over the other was marked in a further five aggressive and five withdrawing. In four out of the forty-two aggressive, and seven out of the forty withdrawing, the ambiguity of behaviour was more marked. It would be unsafe to accept these tendencies as anything more than a tentative indication of the forms taken by disturbance in childhood, since the method of selection acted in such a way as to reduce the number of children in whom the disturbance took a more ambiguous form. However, it is interesting to note that in a recent paper, Stott (1959) has shown that certain items in the Bristol Guides are better predictors of delinquency than others. These items correspond to those symptomatic of HA (hostility to adults), HC (hostility to children) and K ('knavery' or anti-social tendencies), although not all of the items listed under these heads are equally associated with delinquency. In effect, Stott's study finds the same dichotomy between a withdrawing, non-delinquent group and an aggressive, delinquent or potentially delinquent group as that used in the present investigation.[3]

In view of the comparable scoring of the two groups when assessed by means of these Guides, they afford some indication of the degree of disturbance present in each case. If an arbitrary figure of 16[4] is taken as indicative of more or less serious disturbance, then twenty out of the forty withdrawing cases may be said to be 'maladjusted' and twenty-four out of the forty-two aggressive. Altogether, this would be equivalent to forty-four out of the total population of 1,002 or 4·4 per cent. It would appear that the incidence of disturbance as a whole is approximately equally divided in this sample as between the two behaviour patterns. However, in view of the sex differences already noted, it is probable that more cases might have been brought to our notice in the aggressive sample, although, for the most part, these would have been milder. In addition, there is an unknown but probably limited number of children whose names were deliberately withheld because the disturbance was too ambiguous.

V. SOCIOMETRIC CHOICE-RANKING

An important index of the degree to which the adjustment of a child is impaired by anxiety-induced behavioural patterns may be had from an examination of his capacity to gain the friendship and approval of his peers. Accordingly, a sociometric test was carried out by the teachers of the majority of the classes concerned (over the age of seven). Three

[3] A similar clear-cut dichotomy emerges in a recent study by Peterson *et al.* (1959).

[4] It is probable that the arbitrary figure of 16 represents a somewhat greater degree of disturbance than category B in the three surveys carried out on behalf of the Underwood Committee, though less than category A.

criteria were used, with the first three choices weighted 5, 3 and 2. In addition, to allow for an indication of 'social expansiveness' each child was allowed an unlimited number of choices 'below the line' and these were given unit weightings. The total score obtained by each child was found from the class sociomatrix and all the children in the class were then ranked. Scores of children in the three samples are percentile rankings, and are, therefore, comparable as between classes of different sizes. These are shown in Table 20.4.

TABLE 20.4. *Sociometric percentile rankings*

	W/U	WA	A
Mean	37·26	79·61	37·27
N	27	31	29
S.D.	28·00	19·73	25·89

The differences between the two experimental groups and the control is significant beyond the 0·01 level. The fact that the latter is so high merely indicates the fact that teachers, in choosing children as 'exceptionally well-adjusted', tended on the whole to select children who were popular. What is more revealing is that, here again, there is no difference whatever as between the means for the two experimental groups and the SDs are comparable. The fact that emotional adjustment is a factor in sociometric ranking has been shown by Dahlke (1953). But it is of some interest to note that the relation is so marked that, even within the two experimental groups used in this study, representing approximately only the lower 10 per cent of their population, we found correlations of −0·443 (aggressive), and −0·475 (withdrawing) between sociometric ranking and maladjustment score on the Bristol Guides. Both of these are significant at the 0·02 level. However, although it might be inferred that the two patterns are equally severe in so far as they affect children's relations with one another, it must be admitted that a more detailed study of this aspect of behaviour should be more revealing. Are any of these children actively rejected? How far are their own choices reciprocated? To what extent do they fit in with the 'in-groups' of their respective classes? These are questions which must be left to further investigation.[5]

[5] W. A. L. Blyth (1959) has shown that it is possible to predict choices in approximately 40 per cent of cases, using only ecological data. It seems wholly probable that prediction of such choices could be raised to a very high level indeed by combining temperamental criteria with ecological.

If these findings are compared with the ratings given to these same children on the trait of sociability (see Table 20.2), we see that now there is a marked difference between the two groups, with the aggressive more dependent on company than even the well-adjusted. In some cases this might lead them to feel frustrated by the lack of approval given them by the class as a whole. More often, one may suppose, they tend to form into delinquent or sub-delinquent groups. On the other hand, the tendency to be somewhat unsociable or to prefer being alone which appears in the withdrawing group may be presumed to represent their own response to anxiety—by avoidance.

VI. SOCIAL ADAPTATION

Our final index of difficulty of adjustment was the Vineland-Manchester Scale of Social Adaptation, an experimental unstandardised revision of the Vineland Scale of Social Maturity.[6] Because the scale is unstandardised comparisons are internal to the three groups in this study. Absolute figures have no meaning, but the relation between the three groups is of interest.

TABLE 20.5. *Social adaptation*

	W	*WA*	*A*
Mean	53·19	66·33	61·54
N	36	36	36
S.D.	21·9	19·6	22·5

Previous research has shown that delinquents tend to have low scores on the Doll scale (Dunsden, 1947). It was anticipated that this was largely due to the high weighting of cognitive items in the scale and that the effect would disappear when these items were separated out. This expectation was not borne out, and the relative standing of the three groups remains the same when scores on social perspective items are

[6] The form used was a try-out for the Vineland-Manchester Scale of Social Adaptation which is being standardised for use with British school children. The standardisation is based on individual interview with the child himself acting as informant. The age coverage is less than the Doll-Vineland scale, 6–15, and within this age range the number of items has been increased. The standardisation sample consists of over 400 children in the North-Western area. Unlike the original scale, the Manchester revision will yield separate indices for various aspects of social adaptation, and in particular, for 'Social perspective', which is largely a cognitive attribute, and 'Social responsibility', which is practical or executive.

deducted from the totals. On the other hand the further expectation that the withdrawing group would be particularly low in social independence is fully corroborated. Results on this scale were compared when the three groups were subdivided into three age sub-groups, and tested by analysis of variance. The trends were consistent for all ages and the differences proved significant well beyond the 0·01 level. The conclusion might well be drawn that if some of these children were encouraged to gain greater independence, their adjustment might improve.

VII. ONE-YEAR FOLLOW-UP

The evidence so far adduced suggests that there are probably more cases of maladjustment which take a predominantly aggressive form, but that the severity of the handicap may be comparable for the two groups as a whole, although on some counts at any rate the valuation of Wickman's clinicians is borne out. However, for the most part the results are less decisive, and the problems as a whole seemed to us sufficiently important to warrant a more decisive form of analysis. This can only be done by means of a long-term follow-up study. In the final analysis those forms of behaviour which are overcome in the course of maturation and experience may be regarded as benign, and those which are not merit our more serious attention. As a preliminary to such an investigation, the teachers concerned were asked to complete a second Bristol Guide in respect of the majority of the children rated as severely disturbed (i.e. those who had been awarded a score of 16 or more in our system of scoring the Guides) and at the same time to grade them on a five-point scale as considerably improved, improved, much the same, somewhat deteriorated, or considerably deteriorated, adding any remarks which they thought relevant. On the basis of their returns it was possible to grade eleven of the withdrawing cases and thirteen of the aggressive on a seven-point scale, as shown in Table 20.6.

TABLE 20.6. *Follow-up of results for twenty-four children*

	Marked improve-ment	Improve-ment	Slight improve-ment	No change	Slight deteriora-tion	Deteri-oration	Marked deteriora-tion
W	—	5	1	4	1	—	—
A	3	3	2	4	1	—	—

It is of some interest to note that if the patterns of behaviour shown in these second returns are compared with the patterns shown one year previously, we find some admixture of the anxiety-hostility pattern in two out of the eleven withdrawing cases, although the predominance of items remains unchanged. Similarly, two out of the thirteen aggressive cases now show some signs of withdrawal or 'unforthcomingness'. In all but one of the remaining cases the pattern remains the same even though the number and severity of symptoms may be reduced. In only one case is there a virtual reversal of pattern. These trends tend to confirm the theoretical presupposition underlying the initial selection. First indications would be that spontaneous improvement occurs in something over half of all cases, in both groups, but that the change may be more spectacular in the aggressive, especially those who, though markedly disturbed, are not seriously maladjusted. However, these conclusions are very tentative and it is hoped to focus our attention on this aspect in future investigations.

VIII. REFERENCES

BLYTH, W. A. L. (1959) 'School goups and neighbourhood groups: a study in predictive sociometry', paper read to Section II (1) c (Education), Fourth World Congress of Sociology, Stresa, September 1959.

DAHLKE, H. O. (1953) 'Determinants of social relations among children', *Sociometry*, 16, 327–38.

DOLL, E. A. (1953) *The Measurement of Social Competence*, Vineland, N.J.

DUNSDEN, M. I. (1947) 'Notes on the intellectual and social capacities of a group of young delinquents', *British J. Psychol.*, 38, 62–6.

FLEMING, C. M. (1954) *Cumulative Records, Notes on their Content and Use*, University of London Press.

HOLLINS, T. H. B. (1955) 'Teachers' Attitudes to Children's Behaviour', unpublished M.Ed. Thesis, Manchester University Library.

LUNZER, E. A. (1960) 'Aggression and withdrawal in school children; II—Disparity in attainment'.

MINISTRY OF EDUCATION (1955) *Report of the Committee on Maladjusted Children*, HMSO.

NATIONAL FOUNDATION FOR EDUCATIONAL RESEARCH (1952) *A Survey of Rewards and Punishments in Schools*, NFER Publications No. 3, Newnes.

PETERSON, D. R., BECKER, W. C., HELLMER, L. A., SHOEMAKER, D. J., and QUAY, H. C. (1959) 'Parental attitudes and child adjustment', *Child Development*, 30, 119–30.

SCHONELL, F. J. (1944) *Backwardness in the Basic Subjects*, Oliver and Boyd.

STOGDILL, R. M. (1931) 'Parental attitudes and mental hygiene standards', *Mental Hygiene*, 15, 813.

STOTT, D. H. (1958) *The Social Adjustment of Children*, University of London Press.

STOTT, D. H. (1959) 'The prediction of delinquency from non-delinquent behaviour', paper read to the Annual Conference of the BPS. *Bulletin of the BPS*, **38**, 36A.

WICKMAN, E. K. (1928) *Children's Behaviour and Teachers' Attitudes*. New York, Teachers' College Contributions to Education.

21

S. *Mitchell and*
M. *Shepherd*

A comparative study of children's behaviour at home and at school[*]

SUMMARY. An enquiry carried out among a random sample of children attending local authority schools in Buckinghamshire made it possible to compare information provided by the parents and teachers of over 6,000 children. This revealed that deviant behaviour at home was significantly associated with lack of academic success and also with the manifestation of behavioural disorders in school. There were, however, many children who exhibited disorders of behaviour either only at school or only at home. This suggests that any comprehensive attempt to estimate the distribution of maladjustment in the child population must utilise the information of both teachers and parents.

I. INTRODUCTION

For many years there has been considerable speculation about the extent to which 'behaviour problems', 'maladjustment', or 'emotional disorders' exist among the child population as a whole. Many studies designed to investigate this problem have been carried out in the school situation, including those of Olson (1930), McFie (1934), Rogers (1942), Cummings (1944), Ullman (1952), Bower (1958) and Stott (1958). All these studies imply that the existence of 'maladjusted' or 'problem' behaviour in school is a reflection of a general emotional disturbance which will also be apparent in other aspects of the child's life. Few studies have attempted to estimate the association between the child's behaviour in the two environments though Schonell (1952) has epitomised common knowledge with his remark that 'It must

[*] Reprinted from *British Journal of Educational Psychology*, **36**, 1966, 248–254.

always be borne in mind that some children present a form of dual personality in respect to home and school'. In the main, this deficiency may be due to the greater administrative difficulties involved in obtaining information from a representative group of parents and to the mistaken belief that parents would prove less cooperative than teachers and less reliable in their reports. Most workers who have obtained a great deal of information from a sample of mothers (Mac-Farlane, Allen and Honzik, 1954; Lapouse and Monk, 1958) have not obtained comparative data from schools. Those studies which have attempted to relate adjustment at home and at school show some disagreement in their findings. Douglas (1964), for example, dealing with a national sample of children, found that teachers rated as 'highly strung' a high proportion of eleven-year-old children whose mothers reported them to be suffering from one or more of the following 'symptoms': bedwetting; nightmares; abdominal pain or recurrent vomiting; nailbiting; thumbsucking or other such habits. Children with such behaviour problems were also found to show poor attainment and concentration at school. Glidewell *et al.* (1963) in St Louis, also found in a sample of 830 third-grade children that the number of 'symptoms' reported by the mother showed a positive relationship to the degree of maladjustment reported by the teacher. The pilot investigation carried out in Birmingham for the Underwood Committee (Ministry of Education, 1955) found that psychologists' clinical ratings of the questionnaires completed by parents and teachers agreed in 60–65 per cent of cases. Nevertheless, the same investigation showed that, of sixteen children later seen by a psychiatrist at their parents' request, eleven had been rated free of maladjustment on the basis of their teachers' reports. Similar disagreement is revealed in a small-scale clinical enquiry carried out by Pilzer (1952) who found that fifteen out of forty children selected as well-adjusted by teachers, did not appear so on Rorschach testing and that eight of these were found to show maladjusted behaviour at home.

II. METHODS OF INVESTIGATION

In 1961 questionnaires dealing with behaviour, health and family background were sent to the parents of a one-in-ten random sample of children aged between five and fifteen years, who were attending local authority schools in Buckinghamshire: approximately 6,300 questionnaires (93 per cent) were returned, completed. At the same time, separate questionnaires were also sent to the child's school to be completed by his, or her, class teacher. In this case, approximately 6,600

(97 per cent) were received back. Completed questionnaires from both teachers and parents were available for 6,077 children, comprising 1,870 boys and 1,735 girls, aged five to ten years, and 1,206 boys and 1,266 girls aged eleven to fifteen years.

The information sought from parents about their children's behaviour was of two main types. (1) A series of twenty-two triple choice questions on behaviour traits as measured by the parent's estimate of *intensity* of behaviour (extreme, moderate, absent), e.g. afraid of the dark when in bed at night—a little uneasy without a light—not at all afraid of the dark. Of these items, fourteen were adapted from the fifty-three triple-choice items used by Cattell and Coan (1957) in their study of personality variables. (2) Fifteen items in which the parent had to record an impression of the *frequency* of certain kinds of behaviour (for instance, crying, nailbiting, headaches) on an eight-point scale ranging from 'Never or less than once a year' to 'Every day or nearly every day'.

The items of behaviour included are described in detail elsewhere (Mitchell, 1965). They covered most of the behaviour problems described in the standard works on child psychiatry as occurring in clinic-attending, and therefore, presumably maladjusted, children of school age. The items *excluded* were: (i) the more bizarre forms of abnormal behaviour, e.g., autism, hallucinations, obsessional behaviour; (ii) sexual problems; and (iii) certain kinds of blatantly delinquent behaviour like arson. Such types of behaviour appeared to be rare even in child guidance samples and it was felt that the inclusion of questions about 'wicked' or 'mad' behaviour might worry or antagonise parents and so diminish the response rate. All the items included in the form had previously been piloted for intelligibility and lack of ambiguity by interview with mothers throughout the county.

The teachers' questionnaire covered attendance, attainment and physical disabilities as well as the presence of behaviour 'problems' in school.

In attempting to relate the children's behaviour at home to other aspects of their life, we felt it desirable to obtain some overall index of disturbance. Originally, it was intended to use for this purpose the child's total problem score, obtained by adding together the total number of extreme items underlined by the mother. This crude score would have given each 'problem' the same weight without regard to the frequency with which it occurred. Information gained in the survey about the distribution of each behaviour trait showed clearly, however, that some types of 'problem' behaviour were very much more common than others. For instance, about 20 per cent of girls were described by their mothers as having food fads. Where behaviour was reported as occurring at such a high frequency, it was felt that it was scarcely justifiable to consider it as contributing to an index of abnormality. Furthermore, it was felt necessary to make some adjustment for the changing incidence of various types of behaviour at different ages: for instance, 25 per cent of six-year-old boys were found to cry at least two or three times a week compared with 1 per cent of those aged fourteen years. Clearly, therefore, such crying should be given different weight in the two age groups.

In order to allow for these factors, it was decided to adopt a concept of 'deviant behaviour' framed in terms of a 10 per cent limit. If any type of behaviour was reported to have occurred at an intensity or frequency found in 10 per cent or less of any age (yearly) or sex group, then it was considered as deviant for that age and for that sex. If it occurred in more than 10 per cent of children of that age and sex then it was discounted. Thus, in the example already given, crying two or three times a week would be considered as deviant behaviour in a fourteen-year-old boy, but not in a six-year-old. An overall index of 'deviance' was then constructed by summing the number of deviant items scored for each child. This score, then, indicated the number of types of behaviour shown by any child which were atypical of his age and sex group.

An analysis of the teachers' questionnaires revealed that only one type of behaviour, 'Very quiet or withdrawn' among girls, was recorded as occurring in more than 10 per cent of any age-sex group. The concept of deviance was not, therefore, applied to these items and the overall index of disturbance in school has merely been taken as the number of behavioural items underlined by the teacher in the questionnaire (see Appendix for list of items included).

III. RESULTS

Table 21.1 shows that there was a significant degree of association between the presence of deviant behaviour items at home and the reporting of problems of behaviour in school. Thus, children whose parents reported that they were free of deviant behaviour were also the most problem-free group at school. Similarly, at the other end of the scale, children whose parents reported many deviant items were three times as likely to have multiple (three or more) problems recorded at school as were those who were deviance-free at home. This relationship, however, was by no means comprehensive. Thus, Table 21.1 demonstrates that more than a third of the children who were reported free of deviant behaviour at home, nevertheless, exhibited at least one problem in school and that nearly half of the children whose parents underlined seven or more deviant traits were apparently problem-free at school.

TABLE 21.1 *The relationship between the number of deviant behaviour items underlined by parents and the number of behaviour problems underlined by teachers*

Number of problems underlined by teachers		Number of deviant items underlined by parents							
		Boys				Girls			
		None	1–3	4–6	7–	None	1–3	4–6	7–
None	(No.)	740	846	108	35	817	847	135	47
	(%)	62	55	41	43	65	61	53	45
1	(No.)	259	387	62	20	283	308	68	29
	(%)	22	25	24	24	22	22	27	28
2	(No.)	115	158	43	10	107	127	24	13
	(%)	9	10	16	12	8	9	9	12
3 or	(No.)	85	142	49	17	55	98	27	16
more	(%)	7	9	19	21	4	7	11	15
Total (No.)		1,199	1,533	262	82	1,262	1380	254	105
Significance of association		Chi-squared $=73$: 9 degrees of freedom: p <0.001				Chi-squared $=46$: 9 degrees of freedom: p <0.001			

As for specific types of behaviour at school, there was no overall pattern which distinguished children with many deviant items underlined by their parents from those with few. The school problems of those children who were markedly deviant at home varied with age and sex.

Among the boys at all ages, those with four or more items of deviant behaviour marked by their parents were significantly[1] more likely than the remainder to have been assessed by their teachers as very easily frightened (11 per cent of deviants: 5 per cent of others aged 5 to 10 years; 5 per cent of deviants: 2 per cent of others aged 11 to 15 years), to have been found disinterested in school work (12 per cent: 6 per cent at 5 to 10 years; 17 per cent: 5 per cent at 11 to 15 years) and to have been recorded as having stolen on one or more occasion (4 per cent: 1 per cent for all ages). Among boys in the 5 to 10 years age group, but not among the older boys, those with four or more deviant items

[1] All the differences described were significant at least at the 5 per cent level, using the chi-squared test with Yates's correction for continuity.

marked by their parents were significantly more likely to have been reported as sucking their thumbs (7 per cent: 3 per cent), wetting or soiling themselves at school during the current school year (5 per cent: 1 per cent) and as being quiet and withdrawn (17 per cent: 10 per cent). Among the boys of 11 or older, on the other hand, the deviant group were more likely than their fellows, to have been marked as uncooperative in class (9 per cent: 2 per cent), often telling lies (12 per cent: 1 per cent), very irritable (8 per cent: 3 per cent), aggressive towards other children (8 per cent: 3 per cent) and worrying more than other children (8 per cent: 3 per cent).

Among the girls the only teachers' item which differentiated the deviant group at all ages was 'Often tells lies' (4 per cent: 1 per cent in each age group). Among the older girls, those with four or more deviant items marked by their parents were also more likely to have been described as 'Not interested in school work' (12 per cent: 4 per cent) but this was the only item which distinguished them from the rest of the girls in their age group. Among the younger girls, on the other hand, the deviant children were more likely to be reported as very restless (11 per cent: 4 per cent) very irritable (6 per cent: 3 per cent) and easily frightened (9 per cent: 5 per cent) in school.

Academic success in school was found to be negatively associated with deviant behaviour in the home. Table 21.2 shows that the chance of achieving an above-average rating in general attainment at school

TABLE 21.2. *The relationship between the number of deviant behaviour items under-lined by parents and the child's general attainment level at school*

General attainment level relative to others of the same age at the same type of school	Number of deviant items underlined by parents							
	Boys				Girls			
	None	1–3	4–6	7–	None	1–3	4–6	7–
Above average (No.)	264	279	25	3	335	279	36	7
(%)	23	19	10	4	30	21	15	7
Average (No.)	565	684	110	38	649	715	127	58
(%)	49	46	43	49	58	53	52	58
Below average (No.)	331	522	122	37	132	342	80	35
	28	35	47	47	12	26	33	35
Significance of association	Chi-squared $=40$: 6 degrees of freedom: $p < 0.001$				Chi-squared $=85$: 6 degrees of freedom: $p < 0.001$			

was more than five times as great for boys, and four times as great for girls, who were free of deviant behaviour at home as it was for those who showed seven or more deviant items of behaviour, and about twice as great as for children with four or more items noted by their parents.

A similar pattern emerged with respect to the children's position in their immediate teaching group (see Table 21.3) where the proportion of children with four or more items of deviant behaviour marked by their parents was about twice as great among those in the bottom quarter of the class as among those near the top.

TABLE 21.3. *The relationship between the number of deviant behaviour items underlined by parents and the child's usual position in the immediate teaching group*

Number of deviant behaviour items marked by parent		Position in the teaching group					
		Boys			Girls		
		In top 25%	In middle 50%	In bottom 25%	In top 25%	In middle 50%	In bottom 25%
None	(No.)	352	555	250	441	566	220
	(%)	43	40	32	48	41	37
1–3	(No.)	405	688	400	402	657	276
	(%)	50	49	51	43	47	47
4–6	(No.)	41	123	95	68	116	65
	(%)	5	9	12	7	8	11
7 or more	(No.)	13	23	35	17	56	39
	(%)	2	2	4	2	4	5
Significance of association		Chi-squared =40: 6 degrees of freedom: p <0·001			Chi-squared =42: 6 degrees of freedom: p <0·001		

IV. DISCUSSION

The relationship between poor school attainment and the presence of behavioural disorders in the school setting has been discussed in several previous studies, including Burt (1937) and Stott (1958). The present study indicates that such a relationship also exists between behaviour at home and school conduct and attainment. From the information available, however, it is not possible to postulate any causal relationship. Burt and Howard (1952) found that maladjustment, defined in terms of referral for psychological investigation, was correlated with the child's exposure to too high a standard of work or to contact with an uncongenial teacher among other factors. On the other hand, Pearson (1952) suggested that emotional strains rooted in the home were often the cause of poor performance and lack of concentration at school. It is also possible that some underlying factor in the child, such as slow maturation, slight brain damage or neurological defect, may affect performance both at home and at school without there being any corresponding deficiency in either environment. Unravelling such complex interactions would require more detailed personal investigation than was possible in a large-scale statistical enquiry of the present kind. The types of behaviour which characterised the deviant children in their school setting, however, support the notion of emotional rather than organic causation. Thus, in three out of the four age-sex groups, the children who were most deviant at home were distinguished from the others by a greater tendency to be uninterested in school work, to be easily frightened and to tell lies.

It should also be emphasised that though there is a significant relationship between deviant behaviour at home and the existence of problems of behaviour in school there is still considerable divergence between the two areas of conduct. Thus, the teachers' questionnaire identified 10 per cent of children as exhibiting three or more behaviour problems in the school setting; the same proportion had four or more deviant items recorded on the parents' questionnaire. It might be considered justifiable to pick either of these groups of children as consisting of those who were most likely to be maladjusted. Unfortunately, however, the individuals picked by the two methods are not the same: only about one child in five picked as in the worst 10 per cent by one questionnaire was also picked by the other. This fact is important in any attempt to screen the child population to obtain a general estimate of the incidence of maladjustment. At present it is impossible to say how far the difference lies in the child's actual behaviour and how far in variation in the powers of observation and frames of reference of the persons reporting the behaviour. Clearly, however, it seems very necessary that any comprehensive screening device must study the child in both of his principal environments, the home and the school.

ACKNOWLEDGEMENTS. This study was made possible by the generous financial support of the Nuffield Provincial Hospitals Trust. The authors also wish to acknowledge the great assistance given by the Medical Officer of Health for Buckinghamshire, the Chief Education Officer, Divisional Education and Medical Officers, and Head Teachers and staff of all the schools concerned.

v. REFERENCES

BOWER, E. M. (1958) 'A process for early identification of emotionally disturbed children', *Bulletin of California State Department of Education*, **27**, 1–65.

BURT, C. (1937) *The Backward Child*, University of London Press.

BURT, C. and HOWARD, M. (1952) 'Nature and causes of maladjustment among children of school age', *Brit. J. Psychol. (Statistical Section)*, **5**, 39–59.

CATTELL, R. B. and COAN, R. W. (1957) 'Personality factors in middle childhood as revealed in parents' ratings', *Child Develop.*, **28**, 439–58.

CHAZAN, M. (1963) 'Maladjustment, attainment and sociometric status', *University College of Swansea, Faculty of Education Journal*, pp. 4–7.

CUMMINGS, J. D. (1944) 'Emotional symptoms in school children', *Brit. J. Educ. Psychol.*, **14**, 151–61.

DOUGLAS, J. W. B. (1964) *The Home and the School*, MacGibbon & Kee.

GLIDEWELL, J. C., DOMKE, H. R. and KANTOR, M. B. (1963) 'Screening in schools for behaviour disorders: use of mothers' reports of symptoms', *J. Educ. Res.*, **56**, 508–515.

LAPOUSE, REMA and MONK, MARY (1958) 'An epidemiological study of behaviour characteristics in children', *Amer. J. Publ. Hlth.*, **48**, 1134–44.

MACFARLANE, JEAN W., ALLEN, LUCILLE, and HONZIK, MARJORIE P. (1954) *A Developmental Study of the Behaviour Problems of Normal Children*, University of California Press.

MCFIE, B. S. (1934) 'Behaviour and personality difficulties in school children', *Brit. J. Educ. Psychol.*, **4**, 30–46.

MINISTRY OF EDUCATION (1955) *Report of the Committee on Maladjusted Children*, H.M.S.O.

MITCHELL, SHEILA (1965) 'A Study of the Mental Health of School Children in an English County', unpublished Ph.D. thesis, University of London.

OLSON, W. C. (1930) *Problem Tendencies in Children: a method for measurement and description*, University of Minnesota Press.

PEARSON, G. H. J. (1952) 'A survey of learning difficulties in children', *Psychoanal. Stud. Child.*, **7**, 322–86.

PILZER, E. (1952) 'Disturbed children who make good school adjustment', *Smith Coll. Stud. Soc. Wk.*, **22**, 193–210.

ROGERS, C. R. (1942) 'Mental health findings in three elementary schools', *Educ. Res. Bull.* (Ohio State University), **21**, 69–79.

SCHONELL, F. J. (1952) 'The development of educational research in Great Britain: Part 7. Maladjusted children', *Brit. J. Educ. Psychol.*, **22**, 30–9.

STOTT, D. H. (1958) *The Social Adjustment of Children*, University of London Press.

ULLMAN, C. A. (1952) 'Identification of maladjusted school children', *Publ. Hlth. Monogr.* (U.S.) no. 7.

VI. APPENDIX

Behaviour items included in the teachers' questionnaire

Please underline, in the list below, any items which describe this child as he often is:

(*a*) Very restless, can't sit still for a moment.
(*b*) Cries more than most children.
(*c*) Has a stammer.
(*d*) Has other speech difficulty.
(*e*) Often tells lies.
(*f*) Has stolen things on one or more occasions.
(*g*) Is very easily frightened.
(*h*) Bites finger nails.
(*i*) Sucks thumb or finger.
(*j*) Very irritable, easily becomes cross or annoyed.
(*k*) Has had one or more temper tantrums at school during this year.
(*l*) Is uncooperative in class.
(*m*) Very shy, finds it difficult to mix with other children.
(*n*) Has wet or soiled self at school during last year.
(*o*) Has noticeable twitch of face or body.
(*p*) Worries more than other children.
(*q*) Aggressive towards other children.
(*r*) Very quiet or withdrawn.
(*s*) Very moody—on top of world one minute, down the next.
(*t*) Not interested in school work.
(*u*) Has on one or more occasions during this school year shown fear of school—that is, tears on arrival or refusal to come into the building.

22

J. Tizard   Questionnaire measures of maladjustment[*]

The Underwood Committee (1955) and the Scottish Education Department's Committee on the Ascertainment of Maladjusted Children (1964) found it impossible to estimate either the prevalence of maladjustment in school children or the unmet needs for services. But without guidelines as to numbers, any rational planning of services is impossible (Tizard, 1966). It is good, therefore, that psychologists and psychiatrists are again taking up the study of epidemiological problems of mental ill-health in children—problems first explored in this country by Sir Cyril Burt (1933).

Among the questions raised in the discussion of the papers presented to the Cambridge Symposium,[1] three have been singled out for comment:

1. How should we classify the psychiatric disorders of childhood? Stott's classification appeared to most of the participants in the Symposium to have no advantages over the more widely used Child Guidance classification (Underwood, 1955) or the empirically based classification outlined by Rutter (1965). The introduction of terms such as 'unsettled', 'inconsequential', 'restless' etc., implies that certain reported symptoms constitute a syndrome which is in some way different from or more precisely defined than the types of behaviour described under such terms as 'sthenic neurosis' (Burt, 1933), 'con-

[*] Reprinted from British Journal of Educational Psychology, 38, 1968, 9–13.
[1] Annual Conference of the Education Section of the British Psychological Society, Sept. 1967, Cambridge. Chaired by J. Tizard.

duct disturbance' (Beller, 1962; Cameron, 1955), 'acting out behaviour' (US literature, *passim*), or 'behaviour disorder' (usual Child Guidance classification). This has not been established and the mere proliferation of terms has nothing to recommend it. (Incidentally, a WHO Working Party is at present discussing classification in child psychiatry, and their report, which is likely to be produced in 1975,[2] should do something to bring order and standardisation into the terminology.)

2. Does the *Bristol Social Adjustment Guide* offer advantages over other inventories? The Guide is widely used, and is said to be liked by teachers. On the other hand, it is expensive to buy and tedious to score in large numbers. Vernon (1964) has given a balanced appraisal of its usefulness and limitations: 'To the psychometrist, Stott's instruments are likely to seem distressingly amateurish; but their virtue lies in their simplicity—that they use terms to describe deviant patterns which lay observers can readily apply, and that the psychologist or psychiatrist is presented with an overview, only roughly categorised, so that he can further explore particular symptoms. No doubt the categories overlap a good deal, and might be purified by more thorough statistical analysis. Doubtless also, despite Stott's claim for high inter-rater agreement, there is still a good deal of subjectivity and halo in a typical record as filled in by, say, a teacher.'

As there is virtually no information about the comparative advantages of any one of the currently used questionnaires and inventories over any other, psychologists looking for a screening measure might do well to consider whether their needs might not be equally well served by inventories which have not been copyrighted. Among these are Bowlby's (1956), Mulligan's (1964) and Rutter's (1966).

3. How valid are inventories anyway as screening devices? This is the central question. It has been little studied. However, both Mulligan and Douglas (1963) and Rutter and his colleagues (e.g. Rutter and Graham, 1966; Graham and Rutter, personal communication) have provided data bearing on this question, and for the record, their findings are summarised below.

Mulligan and his colleagues had teachers' complete questionnaires in respect of thirteen-year-old children who were attending Child Guidance Clinics, and who had been diagnosed by psychiatrists as suffering from an aggressive and troublesome disorder, or a nervous or neurotic disorder. They compared the findings obtained on these children with those obtained when the same teachers were asked to report on matched controls. The findings are summarised in Table 22.1.

[2] An interim report has been published, see *Journal of Child Psychol. Psychiat.*, **10**, 1969, 41–61.

About a quarter (24 per cent) of the maladjusted children were wrongly classified as normal on the basis of the inventory data, while 29 per cent of normal children were wrongly classified as maladjusted. As maladjusted children constitute only 5–10 per cent of the general population, the screening power of this inventory still leaves a good deal to be desired. Let us, for example, assume (*a*) that 6·6 per cent of children are maladjusted; (*b*) that 75 per cent of these will be correctly identified on the basis of information obtained from Mulligan's in-

TABLE 22.1. *Maladjustment classification—based on teacher ratings—of male child guidance children and their controls. Results in percentages*

Classification based on teacher ratings	Child guidance children			Controls
	Nervous N=50 %	Aggressive N=40 %	Total N=96 %	N=96 %
Nervous	56	6	32	18
Aggressive	4	63	32	9
Mixed	14	9	12	2
Normal	26	22	24	71

ventory; (*c*) that 30 per cent of normal children are misclassified as maladjusted on the basis of inventory scores. The results which would be obtained, if 1,000 children were screened with the help of this inventory, are as in Table 22.2.

TABLE 22.2

Inventory diagnosis		Final diagnosis	
		Normal	Maladjusted
Normal	670	654	16
Maladjusted	330	280	50
Total	1000	934	66

In correctly identifying fifty maladjusted children (and missing sixteen) one would also classify as maladjusted 280 normal children.

The Isle of Wight findings, if only because they are epidemiologically based and because they do not rely on clinic cases for the validation data, give information which bears more directly on our question. Of

2,193 children screened by both parent questionnaire and teacher questionnaire, both of which had been previously piloted extensively (Rutter, 1966), 157 were selected as 'maladjusted' on the basis of the teacher questionnaire, and 133 were selected as 'maladjusted' on the basis of the parent questionnaire. Only nineteen children were selected on the basis of both teacher and parent questionnaires. Virtually all of these selected children were seen individually by a child psychiatrist, and much additional information about them and their families was obtained through records and home interviews with parents (Rutter and Graham, 1966; Yule and Rutter, 1968). On the basis of all the available information, a *final diagnosis* was arrived at in respect of each child.

Of the 157 children selected on the basis of the teacher questionnaire, sixty-four were finally diagnosed as maladjusted. The corresponding figures for the other groups were: parent questionnaire, 133 selected, sixty-six finally diagnosed; both questionnaires, nineteen and fourteen.

Assuming the final diagnosis to be valid, these data give us both the numbers of maladjusted children who were correctly identified as such by each questionnaire ('true positives'), and the numbers of children finally diagnosed as normal who were *incorrectly* judged to be maladjusted on the questionnaires ('false positives').

An estimate was also made of the number of 'false negatives'—that is, the numbers of maladjusted children in the population who were not identified as such on either questionnaire. A group of 108 physically handicapped children in the same age group served as the validation group for this purpose. These children were selected for special study on physical grounds (through school medical records, hospital records, etc.), and were also studied by questionnaire and by psychiatric examination in virtually the same way as were the other selected children. There were twenty-four who were finally diagnosed as maladjusted, and for twenty of these twenty-four there was questionnaire information available on both teacher and parent inventories. In sixteen cases (80 per cent) the inventory scores were above the maladjustment cut-off point on one or other of the questionnaires. Thus, the proportion of false negatives was 20 per cent, or to put it another way, for every sixteen children correctly identified by inventory, four children were missed.

In Table 22.3 the data are expressed as rates per thousand, as was done in Table 22.2. The prevalence of maladjustment is once again presumed to be 6·6 per cent.

Assuming the 'final diagnosis' to be valid, Table 22.3 shows (*a*) that both the teacher inventory and the parent inventory select about equal numbers of maladjusted children (true positives). The teacher inventory selects forty-two false positive for every twenty-nine true positives, and the parent inventory selects thirty-one false positives for every thirty true positives; (*b*) that each questionnaire taken by itself selects under half the total number of maladjusted children in the community: (*c*) since, however, each questionnaire picks out different children (the overlap is surprisingly small), when used in combination they pick out four-fifths of the true positives (fifty-three out of an estimated sixty-six) together with one-and-a-third times as many false positives (seventy-one in the present instance compared with fifty-three true positives).

TABLE 22.3

Inventory diagnosis		Final diagnosis	
		Normal	Maladjusted
Normal	876	863	13
Maladjusted:			
(i) on Teacher inventory	71	42	29
(ii) on Parent inventory	61	31	30
(iii) on *both* inventories	8	2	6
(iv) on *either* inventory	124	71	53
Totals (Normal + those selected on either inventory)	1000	934	66

CONCLUSION

It has yet to be established that any other screening devices will be more efficient than these, and the data from the Isle of Wight Study and from Mulligan's both indicate that teacher questionnaires alone cannot be regarded as valid indices of maladjustment. However, teacher questionnaires and parent questionnaires, used in combination to select children for special examination, can cut down very markedly the numbers requiring to be seen. If such questionnaires have been carefully piloted, *and if correct cut-off points are used* (Meehl, 1955) rather few 'cases' need be missed, though large numbers of false positives will be obtained. The evidence thus indicates that inventories can be used very effectively as screening devices but that they are not in themselves sufficient for epidemiological or clinical work.

REFERENCES

BELLER, E. K. (1962) *Clinical Process: a new approach to the organisation and assessment of clinical data*, New York, Free Press.

BOWLEY, J. (1956) 'The effects of mother-child separation: a follow-up study', *Brit. J. Med. Psychol.*, 29, 211.

BURT, C. E. (1933) *The Subnormal Mind*, Oxford University Press.

CAMERON, K. (1955) 'Diagnostic categories in child psychiatry', *Brit. J. Med. Psychol.*, 28, 67–71.

MEEHL, P. E. and ROSEN, A. (1955) 'Antecedent probability of the efficiency of psychometric signs, patterns or cutting scores', *Psych. Bull.*, 52, 194–216.

MULLIGAN, G. (1964) Unpublished Ph.D. thesis, University of London.

MULLIGAN, G., DOUGLAS, J. W. B., HAMMOND, W. A. and TIZARD, J. (1963) 'Delinquency and symptoms of maladjustment: the findings of a longitudinal study', *Proc. R.S.M.*, 56, 12, 1083–6.

RUTTER, M. (1965) 'Classification and categorisation in child psychiatry', *J. Child Psychol. Psychiat.*, 6, 71–83.

RUTTER, M. (1966) 'A children's behaviour questionnaire for completion by teacher: preliminary findings', *J. Child Psychol. Psychiat.*, 8, 1–11.

RUTTER, M. and GRAHAM, P. (1966) 'Psychiatric disorder in 10 and 11-year-old children', *Proc. R.S.M.*, 59, 382–7.

RUTTER, M., LEBOVICI, S., EISENBERG, L., SNEZNEVSKIJ, A. V., SADOUN, R., BROOKE, E. and TSUNG-YI, L. (1969) 'A tri-axial classification of mental disorders in childhood. An international study', *J. Child Psychol. Psychiat.*, 10, 41–61.

SCOTTISH EDUCATION DEPARTMENT (1964) *Ascertainment of Maladjusted Children: Report of the Working Party appointed by the Secretary of State for Scotland*, Edinburgh, HMSO.

TIZARD, J. (1966) 'Mental subnormality and child psychiatry', *J. Child Psychol. Psychiat.*, 7, 1–15.

UNDERWOOD COMMITTEE (1955) *Report of the Committee on Maladjusted Children*, London, HMSO.

VERNON, P. E. (1964) *Personality Assessment: a critical survey*, Methuen.

YULE, W. and RUTTER, M. (1968) 'Educational Aspects of Childhood Maladjustment: Some Epidemiological Findings', *Br. J. Educ. Psychol.*, 38, 7–9.

23

M. *Chazan*

Maladjustment and reading difficulties[*]
Recent research and experiment

The complex problem of the relationship between maladjustment and reading difficulties has already received a considerable amount of attention from writers both in this country and elsewhere, and there is no need to go over ground covered by Vernon (1957) and Sampson (1966), among others, in reviews of the literature on this topic. It may, however, be useful to introduce this symposium on maladjustment and reading difficulties with a brief reference to current views on the main questions which research workers, clinicians and remedial teachers have raised. These questions are:

1. How closely are maladjustment and reading difficulties linked?
2. To what extent is maladjustment the cause, and to what extent is it the effect of reading difficulties?
3. Are there specific forms of maladjustment which are particularly associated with reading difficulties?
4. How can we best treat maladjusted children with reading difficulties?

It can be stated at this point that these questions have not yet received adequate or consistent answers. The research literature is still, to use Sampson's (1966) apt words, 'beset by semantic uncertainties'. The term 'maladjustment' continues to be used in many varied senses, adding to the confusion caused because different studies use widely differing measures of reading attainment: and important variables such as that of chronological age are not always fully considered. Nevertheless, we are gradually gaining a better understanding of the variables involved in research work on this subject, and some of the recent enquiries and experiments point the way to further developments. It is

[*] Reprinted from *Remedial Education*, 4, 1969, 119–23.

with a selection of such studies and experiments that this paper will be concerned.

This problem has been looked at from two main angles. The incidence of maladjustment has been ascertained in groups of retarded readers, and also the extent of reading difficulties has been studied in samples of maladjusted children. In particular, comparisons of extreme groups of 'poor' and 'good' readers highlight the difference in adjustment of these groups. Joyce Morris (1966), for example, in her investigation of standards and progress in reading in Kent primary schools, compared the social adjustment of 101 'poor' readers (having a Reading Quotient of 85 or below on Watts Sentence Reading Test I) with that of 98 'good' readers (RQ of 119 or above on the same test), selected at 8+ years in their second year in the junior school, and looked at again in their third and fourth years. On the whole, the good readers adapted themselves to the school situation significantly better than the poor readers, who, on the basis of the Bristol Social Adjustment Guide, showed many more signs of maladjustment in their last two years of the primary school. It is of interest to note that there seemed to be some improvement in the behaviour of the 'poor readers' in the fourth year of the junior school.

The relatively high incidence of symptoms of maladjustment found by Morris in very poor readers is confirmed by the Isle of Wight studies described in Yule (1969), who also points to the extent of reading problems found in populations of markedly maladjusted children. Marie Roe (1965), too, stresses the scholastic difficulties of children receiving special educational treatment predominantly because of their emotional maladjustment. In her survey of 142 pupils, aged five to fifteen, in ILEA boarding and day school and tutorial classes for maladjusted children, she found that, although most of the sample were of average or superior intelligence.

1. only 8 (5.6 per cent) out of the 142 children could read at a level equal to or above their chronological ages;
2. 27 per cent had reading quotients (on Neale's Analysis of Reading Ability) of less than 70;
3. over 50 per cent had reading quotients below 80; in the special 'tutorial' classes as many as 79 per cent had reading quotients below 80.

Although the general association between maladjustment and read-

ing difficulties is most clearly shown when extreme groups are compared. Douglas and Ross (1968) consider that it is not only the grossly
disturbed pupils whose scholastic progress (including progress in reading) is adversely affected by their maladjustment.

They studied approximately 4,000 boys and girls through their
primary and secondary school careers, classifying them on the basis
of teachers' opinions, symptoms reported by mothers and a self-rating
inventory into six groups ranging from 'well adjusted non-neurotic'
to 'least well adjusted neurotic'. The school progress of these six
groups was very different at each age studied (8, 11 and 15 years); the
greater the evidence of maladjustment, the lower, on the whole, was
school performance. Douglas and Ross suggest that the basis of the
children's educational difficulties lies in their early years, thus sup-
porting the plea made by many nowadays for avoiding undue delay
in identifying and helping children who are educationally at risk for
any reason.

MALADJUSTMENT: CAUSE OR EFFECT OF READING DIFFICULTIES?

It is extremely difficult to assess to what extent maladjustment is the
cause, and to what extent it is the effect, of reading difficulties. Broad
surveys shed little light on this question, and there have been very
few research enquiries using a comprehensive clinical approach, thus
investigating the problem in depth. Even when an individual child is
carefully examined, it is rarely easy to decide whether emotional maladjustment has *caused* reading retardation or whether it has *followed*
failure to make progress in reading.

Those studies which have attempted to answer this question reveal
marked differences in emphasis. Mangus (1950), on the basis of a study
of 1,232 children in Western Ohio, suggests that it is experience of
failure in the basic subjects which often damages a child's self-
confidence and self-respect, leads to his rejection by his teachers and by
his more successful age mates, produces symptoms of maladjustment
and makes him vulnerable to neurotic or delinquent behaviour. Inability to learn at a normal rate, he states, may be one of the basic
causes of maladjustment, and this seems especially true when the inability to learn is allowed by the school to involve the child in a
prolonged series of failures. However, there are also many cases where
failure to learn to read is a direct result of emotional blockage or disturbance which arises from other sources. A survey in this country,
for example, involving 220 retarded readers of average intelligence,
aged seven to seventeen, reported that, in as many as 92 out of 116

cases where emotional factors were considered to be associated with the reading difficulties, the emotional disturbance was *primary* (Ministry of Education, 1962).

READING DIFFICULTIES AND SPECIFIC TYPES OF MALADJUSTMENT

Vernon (1957) found no real evidence, in a review of the literature, that backwardness in reading was associated with any *particular type* of personality defect or emotional disturbance. However, recent studies suggest that we need to examine this question more closely. Gregory (1965), studying fifty-three children, aged six to ten years, in a small village school, found a significant connection between *reading failure* and *restlessness* throughout the school. In the group of thirty-five children who were aged eight to ten years, he found symptoms of withdrawal, anxiety and restlessness to be more prevalent among the fourteen severely retarded readers or non-readers than among the other twenty-one children, and he suggests that the further study of the sequence restlessness→reading failure→anxiety would be justified. As Yule (1969) shows, the Isle of Wight survey revealed an important association between *antisocial* disorders and reading retardation. Stott (1966), however, presents evidence which suggests that *high anxiety* is detrimental to school attainment, including reading. Morris (1966) found that boys and girls suffering from reading disability in the junior school exhibited rather different patterns of behaviour reaction. The boys tended to focus greater attention upon themselves than the girls, by showing more irritability, anxiety and restlessness.

The picture is thus still far from clear, but the studies mentioned above do provide leads for further investigation of this question.

METHODS OF TREATMENT

When one is faced with the problem of dealing with children who are handicapped by both reading difficulties and maladjustment, it is desirable that methods of treatment should be decided upon only after a full investigation of the case by a child guidance team. The way in which such a problem may be tackled by a child guidance service is discussed by Williams in his contribution to this symposium.

In addition to the therapeutic approaches outlined in Williams's paper, there have been limited experiments using the 'behaviour therapy' approach. As Rachman (1962) points out, behaviour therapy has been used chiefly with adults, and has not been systematically applied to symptoms of disturbance, other than enuresis, in children. He considers, however, that *operant conditioning* seems to provide a tool for building up deficient responses in children, and is applicable to remedial reading cases. In simplified terms, the use of operant conditioning is based on the hypothesis that a response followed by reinforcement (satisfaction or reward in a variety of forms) will in the future occur more frequently, i.e. the response will be strengthened. In the case of younger children, very tangible rewards are most efficacious in strengthening responses; older children will respond to less concrete forms of reinforcement.

This approach is illustrated in a paper by McKerracher (1967), who reports on his attempt to treat a highly anxious enuretic boy of eleven, of average intelligence but with a reading age of only eight years, by an operant conditioning technique employing both reward conditioning and avoidance conditioning. In the first three months of treatment conventional methods were used. The boy was given half-an-hour's weekly reading practice by the psychologist, this practice being initiated by ten minutes of supportive therapy, during which time the boy was encouraged to discuss the difficulties that he had encountered in school or at home during the preceding week. A fairly good relationship was formed, but the boy remained unforthcoming and continued to stammer badly both when reading and when talking about his various experiences. During the second period of three months, dual operant conditioning techniques were used; within two weeks the boy spontaneously said that he felt much more relaxed. In the final treatment period, also of three months, avoidance conditioning was dropped and reward only was used; the boy became more interested in what he was doing. For a description of the apparatus used, which is very easily constructed, the reader is referred to the original article by McKerracher.

During the first period the boy made 1 month of reading gain, during the second 4 months, and in the final period 9 months, i.e. 1 year 2 months gain over the nine-month period of treatment. There was less improvement in the boy's emotional condition than in his reading.

Results on the basis of a single case do not prove anything and McKerracher is at pains to state that operant conditioning methods may not work with some children and may have only limited usefulness with others. However, as he says, such procedures ought to be standard skills in every clinician's repertoire. A further contribution to the experimental approach is one by Brown (1965), whose paper illustrated a controlled attempt to minimise extraneous stimuli in order to facilitate the learning of reading on the part of a highly distractible youth.

Remedial teachers working closely with educational psychologists should find the experimental approach useful to them in their very difficult task of dealing with emotionally disturbed children with reading difficulties. Experimental techniques may help them to reconcile their conflicting roles, those of the teacher and the therapist. For although the professional role and functions of a remedial teacher is not the same as a therapist's, when dealing with maladjusted pupils he must look at his work from the point of view of the therapist as much as that of the teacher. As a teacher, he is anxious to get the children to learn, to make measurable progress; he feels unhappy if he has little to show for his efforts, and he is often under some pressure to show results to parents and school. Furthermore, as he has a long waiting list, he wants quick results. However, he also wants the child to feel relaxed, to talk freely to him, and perhaps to indulge in creative activities which may seem to lead nowhere but satisfy and soothe the child. The remedial teacher tries to combine these two approaches, but those who work in remedial centres or units for the maladjusted know how difficult it is in practice to combine 'therapy' with an attack on the child's specific learning problems.

Generalisation about treatment is profitable only to a limited extent. In some cases, a direct approach to teaching the child to read will prove successful and the child will gain confidence and stability from his very success; in some, the emphasis will need to be put on play, talk, or creative work; in other cases, experimental techniques may be most rewarding. Considerable skill is needed in selecting the most appropriate method of treatment, as Williams (1969) stresses.

CONCLUSION

We still know far too little about the success of methods used by remedial teachers in helping maladjusted retarded children both to readjust and to read adequately. In the case of remedial reading in general, short-term results are much more rewarding than long-term results (Chazan, 1967; Shearer, 1967); in the case of the treatment of retarded and maladjusted children, the literature is too thin to be very informative. Child guidance services, remedial teaching centres and schools for the maladjusted now have a considerable expertise in dealing with the problems discussed in this paper, but they have not told us much about either their methods or their results. There is a need for many more reports on the treatment of specific problems as well as for more systematic studies of methods of treatment. *Remedial teachers are often in a good position to provide reports and to carry out studies along the lines suggested.*

We also need much more comprehensive facilities in order to cope with the problems which are, these days, being more readily referred for specialist help. Yule (1969) states that, of the eighty-six children on the Isle of Wight who were at least twenty-eight months retarded in reading, at the time of the survey only one quarter were receiving special help; this is probably not a typical situation.

Marie Roe (1965) suggests that, within the special unit or school for maladjusted children there is a need for remedial teaching on an individual basis or in groups of two or three away from the distractions even of the relatively small class which may be expressing itself freely. An extra or part-time remedial teacher may be useful here, as regular short sessions in optimal conditions should be much more effective than longer periods of haphazard casual work. But, as Roe adds, this approach may not be appropriate for children who are going through a particularly disturbed period. In her survey of the progress of 142 maladjusted pupils mentioned above, the *average* gains in reading over 12 months (not, of course, a long period for very maladjusted children) ranged from 7 to 20 months in accuracy, and from 12 to 16 months in comprehension. This is generally satisfactory, but 26 children gained less than 5 months. Some of these had specific difficulties such as in visual perception, and some had a continuing high level of emotional disturbance related to unresolved home problems; but others were possibly understimulated in the classroom.

The papers in this symposium[1] will not provide readers with easy solutions for the problems they may have in dealing with combinations of emotional and reading difficulties, but it is hoped that they will stimulate further thought and reading on the topics discussed and encourage further contributions on the subject from those actively engaged in remedial education.

[1] See *Remedial Education*, 4, (1969) pp. 124 ff.

REFERENCES

BROWN, R. I. (1965) 'Distractibility and some scholastic skills', *J. Ch. Psychol. Psychiat.*, 6, 55–62.

CHAZAN, M. (1967) 'The effects of remedial teaching in reading: a review of research', *Remed. Educ.*, 2, no. 1, 4–12.

DOUGLAS, J. W. B. and ROSS, J. M. (1968) 'Adjustment and educational progress', *Brit. J. Educ. Psychol.*, 38, 2–4.

GREGORY, R. E. (1965) 'Unsettledness, maladjustment and reading failure: a village study', *Brit. J. Educ. Psychol.*, 35, 63–8.

MCKERRACHER, D. W. (1967) 'Alleviation of reading difficulties by a simple operant conditioning technique', *J. Ch. Psychol. Psychiat.*, 8, 51–7.

MANGUS, A. R. (1950) 'Effect of mental and educational retardation on the personality development of children', *Amer. J. Ment. Defic.*, 55, 208–12.

MINISTRY OF EDUCATION (1962) *The Health of the School Child. 1960 and 1961*, HMSO.

MORRIS, JOYCE M. (1966) *Standards and Progress in Reading*, London, NFER.

RACHMAN, S. (1962) 'Learning theory and child psychology: therapeutic possibilities', *J. Ch. Psychol. Psychiat.*, 3, 149–63.

ROE, MARIE (1965) *Survey into Progress of Maladjusted Pupils*, Inner London Education Authority.

SAMPSON, OLIVE C. (1966) 'Reading and adjustment: a review of the literature', *Educ. Res.*, 8, 184–90.

SHEARER, E. (1967) 'The long-term effects of remedial education', *Educ. Res.*, 9, 219–22.

STOTT, D. H. (1966) *The Social Adjustment of Children*, 3rd edn., University of London Press.

VERNON, M. D. (1957) *Backwardness in Reading*, Cambridge University Press.

WILLIAMS, D. J. (1969) 'Maladjustment and reading difficulties: remedial treatment', *Remed. Educ.*, 4, 129–33.

YULE, W. (1969) 'Maladjustment and reading difficulties: the findings of the Isle of Wight studies', *Remed. Educ.*, 4, 124–8.

24

M. Chazan

Factors associated with maladjustment in educationally subnormal children*

SUMMARY. This article discusses the findings of the second stage of an enquiry into the incidence, nature and aetiology of maladjustment among children in special schools for the educationally subnormal in South Wales. An intensive study was made of the thirty 'most maladjusted' ESN children in the larger sample studied in the first stage, as well as of a control group of the thirty 'best adjusted' ESN children, matched with the maladjusted children for age, sex and school.

Significantly more of the maladjusted children (i) showed some physical weakness or defect, (ii) were subjected to adverse psychological pressures and unsatisfactory discipline at home, related to parental instability, and (iii) had had interrupted or incomplete relationships with their parents. There was little difference between the two groups in respect of the incidence of adverse congenital factors, difficulties in early development and poor material conditions at home. Significantly fewer of the maladjusted children had a positive relationship with their father. Maladjustment was, in many cases, associated with a lack of progress in the basic subjects at the special school.

Maladjustment of the 'withdrawn' type tended to be associated with physical deficiency in the child and positive but weak parental discipline; aggressive behaviour was often linked with insecurity at home and hostile parental attitudes.

These findings emphasise the need for comprehensive guidance services for the parents of educationally subnormal children.

* Reprinted from *British Journal of Educational Psychology*, 35, 1965, 277–85.

I. INTRODUCTION

In a previous article (Chazan, 1964) the findings of the first stage of an enquiry into the incidence, nature and aetiology of maladjustment in special schools for ESN children in South Wales were discussed. This article describes the second stage of the investigation, in which an intensive study was made of the thirty 'most maladjusted' children in the larger sample, together with a control group of the thirty 'least maladjusted' children, in order to examine the factors associated with maladjustment in ESN children. The small sample of children studied permitted an approach in some depth, but it is realised that the results of the enquiry must be interpreted cautiously and need to be confirmed by means of larger-scale and longer-term studies.

Although there is a considerable literature on causative factors associated with maladjustment in childhood, relatively little has been written about factors associated with maladjustment in the ESN child. Stott (1957, 1959) has suggested that congenital factors, especially stress during pregnancy, are particularly important as they are likely to result in the multiple impairment of mental retardation, a tendency to physical weakness and proneness to emotional maladjustment. Walker (1950) emphasises the effects of attitudes *towards* subnormality, considering that parental rejection always exists to some degree even through unexpressed or camouflaged by over-concern and protectiveness. McLachlan (1955) and Evans (1956), however, put more stress on other aspects of the parent–child relationship as sources of difficulties, considering that broken homes, constant discord, illegitimacy, and unrealistic parental ambition have particularly adverse effects on the ESN child. The effects of failure to meet the subnormal child's needs in school are stressed by Mangus (1950) and Tansley and Gulliford (1960), who consider that the emotional problems of ESN children are often related to the educational and social consequences of low intelligence.

II. METHODS OF ENQUIRY

In this stage of the enquiry, the most maladjusted children in each of the nine special schools involved (some of the children in the original sample had been transferred to a new special school for junior ESN children) were selected for further intensive study, on the basis of the Bristol Social Adjustment Guide rating and discussion with the head teachers concerned. In all, thirty children in the 'maladjusted' category were studied, and the thirty 'best adjusted' children, matched with the maladjusted pupils in respect of age, sex and school, comprised the control group.

An experienced social worker, appointed specifically to the project, visited the homes of the sixty children to obtain data on the personal and family background of each child. The interviews were conducted in an informal way, which varied according to the circumstances, but the information obtained was recorded in standard and structured form. Whenever possible, information was obtained from both parents, and two or more visits were made to the home when this was considered necessary. All the mothers who had care of their children were seen, as well as 73 per cent of the fathers, a number of whom stayed at home because they thought that the project might in some way prove helpful to their children. Judgments about parental discipline and attitudes as well as about the personality of the parents were necessarily subjective, though the opinions and experiences of the head teachers, teachers and other professional workers concerned with the families were taken into account in arriving at the final ratings. Apart from the data obtained on each child in the first stage of the investigation, both the writer and the social worker visited the schools to discuss the children with the head teacher.

The sixty children themselves were seen individually at their own schools by the writer on two occasions. Two specifically devised standard oral interview schedules were used, as well as the Bene–Anthony *Family Relations Test* (1957). The schedules aimed at eliciting the children's main worries, fears and sources of frustration and their attitudes to home, school and self. The questions were framed in simple terms, and mostly required a choice of brief answers in standard form, though a few questions were included which gave scope for freer response.

III. THE RESEARCH SAMPLE

As allowance must be made for a certain amount of overlapping between the 'stable', 'unsettled' and 'maladjusted' categories as defined by arbitrary scores on the Bristol Social Adjustment Guide, the 'most maladjusted' children and the 'best adjusted' children were selected for comparison. In each of these groups of thirty children there were eight junior and twelve senior boys, five junior and five senior girls. The mean score on the Bristol Social Adjustment Guide was 30.20 in the case of the maladjusted group, 6.37 for the control group.

Evidence from other sources confirms this difference in adjustment between the two groups. There was a significant difference in their adjustment in the home situation: seventeen of the maladjusted children, three of the control group presented problems to their parents (χ^2 14.7, df.1, significant at the 0·1 per cent level). Seventeen of the maladjusted group, and again only three of the control group had speech defects, evidence about which was obtained from the interviews with the children and their parents, as well as from the Bristol Social Adjustment Guides; and sixteen of the maladjusted children, six of the controls, had a history of enuresis or soiling (χ^2 7.18, df.1, significant at the 1 per cent level).

TABLE 24.1. *Sociometric status of children in maladjusted and control groups*

Sociometric status	No. of choices received (3×3 criteria)	Number of children	
		Maladjusted ($N=30$)	Control ($N=30$)
Star	15+	4	8
Above average	10—14	—	10
Average	9	2	1
Below average	4—8	14	8
Neglectee	3	2	1
Isolate	0—2	8	1
Not rated (recently joined class)	—	—	1

Table 24.1 shows that there was also a considerable difference in the sociometric status of the children in the two groups. Whereas twenty-four of the maladjusted children were below average in sociometric status (including eight 'isolates' and two 'neglectees'), only ten of the control group were below average, with no more than one 'isolate' and one 'neglectee'.

Eighteen of the maladjusted children showed a predominantly aggressive pattern of symptoms, eight were withdrawn, and in the case of the remaining four there was a mixed pattern of behaviour.

IV. MAIN FACTORS ASSOCIATED WITH MALADJUSTMENT

Table 24.2 shows to what extent various factors were associated with maladjustment in the research sample. While the factors were investigated from the point of view of their aetiological significance, it is realised that a statistically significant association between maladjustment and a particular factor does not necessarily mean that there is a direct causal relationship. It is usually found, too, that a number of factors combine to produce maladjustment in any one case: in twenty-four out of the thirty cases of maladjustment, five or more of the eight groups of factors listed in Table 24.2 were found in combination.

It will be seen from the table that there were no significant differences between the two groups of children in respect of congenital factors or early developmental difficulties, though in the light of Stott's hypothesis quoted above, it is worthy of note that fourteen of the maladjusted children showed a combination of adverse congenital factors and physical weakness or defect, as compared with eight of the control group. Significant differences between the groups were found in respect of certain physical factors, intellectual and scholastic factors, and factors connected with the home and especially with the parent–child relationship; these factors are discussed below.

Physical factors.—On the basis of information obtained from the Bristol Social Adjustment Guide, Form 2 H.P., and the mothers of the children, significantly more of the maladjusted children were found to have a record of poor health. Although the difference between the two groups with regard to the incidence of physical defect did not quite reach the 5 per cent level of significance (χ^2 3.78, df.1), in the maladjusted group there were seven children with a history of epilepsy, two spastics, two cases of asthma and one child who had suffered from tuberculosis, whereas none of the children in the control group had had serious defects or illnesses.

All the eight children showing a 'withdrawn' pattern of behaviour disturbance had an unsatisfactory physical history, as compared with two-thirds of the aggressive children. An association between a 'physical deficiency' cluster and over-inhibited behaviour is reported by Hewitt and Jenkins (1946).

As physical appearance was considered likely to affect the child's acceptance by his parents, relatives, peers and teachers, on the grounds that the child who obviously looks subnormal is more apt to arouse feelings of rejection in others, a rating of each child's appearance was made by the writer. The figures given in Table 24.2 lend some support to this hypothesis.

Intellectual and scholastic factors

Although the mean IQs of the two groups, as assessed by individual scales, were almost identical (mean IQ of maladjusted children 66.93, σ 8.5; of control group 67.97, σ 6.4), fewer of the maladjusted children were making satisfactory progress in school. It is, of course, difficult to discover whether unsatisfactory progress in the basic subjects is a causative factor in maladjustment or an effect of maladjustment, but whichever it may be, continued failure to make satisfactory progress in school is likely to cause feelings of frustration in the child and to aggravate any primary disturbance which is present. Overtly, however,

TABLE 24.2. *Incidence of main factors investigated*

Factors	No. of children affected		χ^2 (df.1) where significant
	Mal-adjusted group (N=30)	Control group (N=30)	
(a) *Congenital factors*			
(i) Difficulties during pregnancy	11	9	
(ii) Difficulties at birth	8	7	
(iii) Prematurity (5½ lb. or less at birth)	4	8	
History of at least one adverse congenital factor	18	18	
(b) *Early developmental difficulties*			
(i) Disturbed feeding in infancy	5	5	
(ii) Hospitalisation or institutionalisation before 5 years of age	16	16	
History of difficulties in first five years	17	17	
(c) *Physical Factors*			
(i) Unsatisfactory physical condition	20	8	9·82*
(ii) Physical defect	13	6	
(iii) Appearance arousing negative re-action	12	2	9·32*
At least one adverse physical factor	25	12	11·9*
(d) *Intellectual and scholastic factors*			
(i) I.Q. below 60	5	3	
(ii) Unsatisfactory progress in reading at special school	14	8	
(iii) Unsatisfactory progress in number at special school	18	5	11·33*
(iv) Irregular attendance at school	8	7	
(v) History of frequent changes of school	4	5	
At least one intellectual or scholastic factor	24	16	4·8†

TABLE 24.2—*cont.*

Factors	No. of children affected		χ^2 (*df.1*) where significant
	Mal-adjusted group (*N=30*)	Control group (*N=30*)	
(e) *Material home conditions and family circumstances*			
(i) Overcrowding	8	3	
(ii) Very low material standards	6	4	
(iii) Father unemployed or in irregular employment	7	7	
(iv) Problem family	2	1	
(v) Financial hardship	5	4	
Adverse material conditions at home	14	12	
(f) *Psychological factors in the home*			
(i) Parental instability or unreliability	17	6	8·53*
(ii) Unsatisfactory discipline and attitudes to child	17	6	8·53*
(iii) Lack of appreciation of child's handicap	7	1	
(iv) Lack of harmony between parents	7	2	
(v) Rejection of child by mother or father	4	1	
(vi) Family unhappy in present home	3	3	
(vii) Intellectual standards of family too high for child	2	—	
At least one adverse psychological factor in home	27	12	16·48*
(g) *Interrupted or incomplete relationships with parents*			
(i) Broken or incomplete home	3	4	
(ii) Child illegitimate	4	—	
(iii) Child adopted	1	—	
(iv) Period in care	4	1	
(v) Substantial period with relatives	3	1	
(vi) Period in residential school or nursery (excluding current residential school)	1	1	
(vii) In hospital for 1 month or longer	11	9	
(viii) Frequent periods in hospital	2	—	
Interrupted or incomplete relationships with parents	20	12	4·29†

TABLE 24.2—*cont.*

Factors	No. of children affected		χ^2 $(df.1)$ where significant
	Mal-adjusted group $(N=30)$	Control group $(N=30)$	
(*b*) *Illness of parents*			
1. Mother:			
(i) In poor health	6	3	
(ii) Minor complaints about health	7	6	
(iii) Disabled	1	1	
2. Father:			
(i) In poor health	2	2	
(ii) Minor complaints about health	2	3	
(iii) Disabled	1	—	
Mother unwell or disabled	14	10	
Father unwell or disabled	5	5	

* Significant at 1 per cent level or beyond.
† Significant at 5 per cent level or beyond.

the children in both groups expressed little worry, fear or dissatisfaction concerning school, their teachers or school work.

Material and psychological factors in the home

Psychological factors in the home were much more closely linked with maladjustment in the research sample than were material home conditions. There was, as Table 24.2 shows, very little difference between the two groups in respect of adverse material conditions at home. Although approximately 23 per cent of the fathers in both groups were in irregular employment and one-half of the families in the total sample were just managing financially or were in difficulties, few of the mothers were in full-time work and the care of the home was generally satisfactory; over one-half of the sixty families lived in modern homes. The most important factors in the home were the instability or unreliability of the parents and the kind of discipline which they exercised over the child. Inconsistency of discipline and handling was a particularly marked feature in the homes of the maladjusted children. Overprotective and unrealistic attitudes on the part of the parents were also prominent in the sample, but there was relatively little outright rejection of the children.

Table 24.3, in which the main family relations of the sample, on the basis of the Bene–Anthony Family Relations Test are shown, demonstrates that the attitudes of the children in the maladjusted group towards their fathers, and the attitudes of the fathers towards the children (as seen by the children themselves) were significantly less positive than in the case of the control group. In both groups, positive attitudes of and towards siblings were outweighed by negative and ambivalent attitudes.

Significantly more of the maladjusted children had had interrupted or incomplete relationships with their parents. There were four illegitimate children in the maladjusted group, none in the control group; and four of the maladjusted children, one of the control group, had spent a period in the care of the local authority.

There were thirteen eldest children in the maladjusted group, as compared with six in the control group; there was some evidence that children in this position are given an extra burden of responsibility in the family, particularly as nearly a third of the research sample were members of large families with five or more children.

The attitudes of the parents of the withdrawn children tended to be positive, but discipline was usually weak. In two cases, withdrawal seemed to be the reaction to having siblings or other members of the family who were much brighter. Thirteen of the eighteen aggressive children had a background of insecurity, deprivation, or impatient and intolerant parental attitudes.

Although there had been little difference between the groups in the parents' attitude to their child's transfer to the special school at the time when this was first suggested, about half of each group being hostile towards the idea or very doubtful about it, the parents of the maladjusted children tended to remain fixed in their negative attitude, while some of the parents of the controls became more positive in their attitude towards the special school as the children settled down there.

V. DISCUSSION

The above findings, which are supported by a number of other studies which stress the effects of unsatisfactory parental attitudes on the child's emotional development (Kanner, 1953; Beck, 1958; Andry, 1960), underline the need for comprehensive guidance services for the families of educationally subnormal children. The basic financial needs of the families and the physical needs of the children were met in most cases, and the social welfare services were used by a considerable number of parents. Few of the parents, however, were fully aware of the implica-

TABLE 24.3. *Family relations of the research sample as shown by the Bene–Anthony Family Relations Test*

Attitudes of child towards	Father			Mother			Siblings		
	Mal. children	Controls	χ^2 df.1	Mal. children	Controls	χ^2 df.1	Mal. children	Controls	χ^2 df.1
N	25	25		27	28		27	28	
Positive	9	17	5.13†	18	23	n.s.	29	35	n.s.
Negative or ambivalent	16	8		9	5		53	57	
Attitudes towards child of	**Father**			**Mother**			**Siblings**		
Positive	5	14	6.88*	17	19	n.s.	28	28	n.s.
Negative or ambivalent	20	11		10	9		54	64	

* Significant at 1 per cent level or beyond.
† Significant at 5 per cent level or beyond.

tions for them of having a subnormal child in the family or had received advice about dealing with the situation. The labelling of their child as 'educationally subnormal' and the subsequent transfer to a special school had been interpreted by most of them as a negative act by 'the authorities'. Only four of the maladjusted children had attended a child guidance clinic.

Although many of the parents will not take the initiative in seeking advice about their child, most of them welcomed the opportunity to discuss the child with the social investigator who called at their homes. It was clear from the interviews that the unsatisfactory attitudes of the parents could be modified to some extent and it seems desirable, therefore, that guidance to parents should be given by a professional worker visiting the homes of pupils in special schools. This work could, perhaps, be best carried out by social workers appointed to the staffs of special schools, having close links with the school psychological service and other agencies concerned in the welfare of the child.

In addition to guidance services for parents, there is a need for experiments with therapy both within special schools and in a clinical setting. As the interviews showed, ESN children can rarely verbalise their difficulties and in many cases are not fully aware of them. Direct interview therapy with the children, therefore, is unlikely to be successful in the majority of cases, though experimental individual and group therapy of this kind with the older and less dull pupils would be of interest. Activity group therapy (Slavson, 1952), modified to suit children of limited intelligence, seems a more suitable form of treatment for many maladjusted ESN children, as Evans (1956) demonstrated. Mundy (1957) suggests that even severely subnormal children who are not psychotic or organically impaired can be helped by psychotherapy.

Smaller classes in special schools for the ESN would help teachers both to cope with behaviour problems and to give more individual attention to pupils. The close link between maladjustment and low attainment shows that a number of children continue, even at the special school, to fail to derive satisfaction from a sense of progress and achievement. The 1964 Report of the Department of Education and Science records that in January 1963, 13·6 per cent of the pupils in special schools for the ESN were in 'oversize' classes, that is, in classes of over twenty children, and three-quarters of the classes contained sixteen or more children. In schools which have a high proportion of maladjusted children, twelve children in a class would be a more desirable maximum number, especially in the light of the Underwood Report (Ministry of Education, 1955) which, discussing the educational needs of maladjusted children, concluded that ordinarily a teacher cannot satisfactorily meet the needs of more than ten maladjusted children.

The prevention of situations conducive to maladjustment might be helped by the establishment of special centres as in the United States (Giannini, 1957; Kanner, 1961), where parents of subnormal children can obtain expert advice at an early stage. Such centres might also encourage systematic research into the many problems connected with educationally subnormal children which are still awaiting attention.

ACKNOWLEDGEMENTS. The writer is particularly indebted to Miss Elisabeth Gruber, Research Officer to the project, who was responsible for carrying out the home visits and who contributed much to the analysis and interpretation of the data. He would also like to thank the following for their help and co-operation: the Directors of Education and Medical Officers for Cardiff, Carmarthenshire, Cardiganshire, Monmouthshire, Newport and Swansea; the Children's Officer for Cardiff; the head teachers and staff of the special schools concerned; Dr D. H. Stott, for helpful comments on this paper; Miss Margaret Lewis, secretary to the project; and the Department of Education and Science, for their interest and financial support.

VI. REFERENCES

ANDRY, R. E. (1960) *Delinquency and Parental Pathology*, Methuen.

BECK, MARIGOLD A. (1958) '*Some Environmental Factors in Mental Retardation*'. Ph.D. Thesis, University of Cambridge.

BENE, EVA, and ANTHONY, J. (1957) *Family Relations Test*, NFER.

CHAZAN, M. (1964) 'The incidence and nature of maladjustment among children in schools for the educationally subnormal', *Brit. J. Educ. Psychol.*, 34, 292–304.

DEPARTMENT OF EDUCATION AND SCIENCE (1964) *Statistics of Education*, Part I, 1963, HMSO.

EVANS, D. (1956) 'An Experimental Study of a Group of Seriously Maladjusted Educationally Subnormal Children', M.A. (Education) Thesis, University of Birmingham.

GIANNINI, MARGARET J. (1957) 'Diagnostic approach in mental retardation', *Public Health News*, 38, 10, 322–32.

HEWITT, L. E., and JENKINS, R. L. (1946) *Fundamental Patterns of Maladjustment: the Dynamics of their Origin*, Illinois, Green.

KANNER, L. F. (1953) 'Parents' feelings about retarded children', *Amer. J. Ment. Defic.*, 57, 375–83.

KANNER, L. F. (1961) 'Parent counseling', in *Mental Retardation*, ed J. H. Rothstein, Holt, Rinehart & Winston.

MCLACHAN, D. G. (1955) 'Emotional aspects of the backward child', *Amer. J. Ment. Defic.* 60, 323–30.

MANGUS, A. R. (1950) 'Effect of mental and educational retardation on personality development of children', *Amer. J. Ment. Defic.*, 55, 208–12.

MINISTRY OF EDUCATION (1955) *Report of the Committee on Maladjusted Children*, HMSO.

MUNDY, LYDIA (1957) 'Therapy with physically and mentally handicapped children in a mental deficiency hospital', *J. Clin. Psychol.*, 13, 3–9.

SLAVSON, S. R. (1952) *Child Psychotherapy*, Columbia University Press.

STOTT, D. H. (1957) 'Physical and mental handicaps following a disturbed pregnancy. *Lancet*, i, 1006–12.

STOTT, D. H. (1959) 'Evidence for pre-natal impairment of temperament in mentally retarded children', *Vita Humana*, 2, 125–48.

TANSLEY, A. E., and GULLIFORD, R. (1960) *The Education of Slow Learning Children*, Routledge & Kegan Paul.

WALKER, G. H. (1950) 'Social and emotional problems of the mentally retarded child', *Amer. J. Ment. Defic.*, 55, 132–8.

25

R. D. Hess and
V. C. Shipman

Maternal influences upon early learning*

The cognitive environments of urban pre-school children

CONCEPTUAL ORIENTATION

Several studies now under way at the Urban Child Center of the University of Chicago are designed to describe the maternal influences that shape, or socialise, the cognitive behaviour of children. The major study, now nearing completion, is an examination of the effect of maternal behaviour upon the growth and structure of the child's thinking and upon his orientation (including achievement motivation) towards the school and formal classroom learning. While we do not discount the significance of genetically or congenitally determined mental resources which the indivdual child has at his disposal or the developmental sequences through which he may, or perhaps must, proceed, our concern is with the input processes—the features of the external world and the child's interactions with them which are particularly relevant in determining the form his ability will take and the patterns of interaction with adults which will elicit various responses and response sequences.

In line with this orientation, we are studying groups of mothers and children from different social-class levels in an attempt to understand the variations in cognitive experience that children from privileged and underprivileged homes encounter. From this perspective, this is a study of the specific cognitive components of mother–child interaction in different social classes. An examination of the details of cognitive exchange makes it possible to exploit two lines of analysis—the cognitive features of maternal behaviour (which have received little

*Reprinted from R. D. Hess, R. M. Bear, eds., *Early Education*, Chicago, Aldine Publishing Co., 1968, pp. 91–103.

research attention in the past) and the description of social-class experience and impact in terms of specific points of exchange between the young child and his environment. Social class is a useful but gross variable—a statement of probability that the child will encounter certain types of experiences. More precise and detailed information is needed in order to understand the effect of social class and of cultural or educational deprivation upon cognitive behaviour.

Our project, which began in 1962, is based on the notion that the mother can be viewed as a teacher, as a programmer of input, during the pre-school years and that mothers from different social-class levels will programme or socialise the cognitive behaviour of their children in different ways. This is not primarily an enquiry about differences in *level* of mental performance by child and mother from different social classes but an investigation of the different *styles* or *strategies* of information processing that the young child develops in interaction with his mother.

The feature of this interactive system which we regard as particularly important is the extent to which the mother and other instruments of the environment provide an array of alternatives for thought and action which permit the development of the child's ability to discriminate and select the relevant stimuli in the environment and to make rational choices among the possibilities that the environment makes available to him. The significance of the mediating functions of maternal and other important figures in the young child's experience, so far as early education and cultural disadvantage are concerned, derives from the fact that the mother–child dyad is part of a larger social system: the nature of the interaction between mother and child reflects the position and circumstances of the family in the community. In short, we argue that the development of thought—that is, strategies for dealing with information and with one's own inclination to act—is most usefully considered in terms of its relationship to the social and cultural structures in which it occurs.

These considerations lead to four related arguments which constitute the conceptual context of the study: first, that strategies for processing information and for dealing with the environment, whether they lead to cultural deprivation or poverty or to affluence, are learned; second, that a significant part of this learning (and teaching) typically takes place in the early (pre-school) interaction between mother and child; third, that the growth of cognitive processes conducive to success in formal educational settings is fostered in family control systems which offer a wide range of alternatives of action and thought, and it is constricted by systems of control which offer predetermined solutions and few alternatives for consideration and choice; and fourth, that the nature of the dyadic exchange between mother and child is related to the social structure in which the exchange takes place.

RESEARCH PLAN AND VARIABLES

In attempting to delineate the input features of the socialising process, the research focused on three characteristics of the mother–child interaction. The first is the nature of the control or regulatory system employed by the mother in her interaction with the child. We define three types of maternal control.[1] The first of these, *imperative-normative*, is based on appeals to social norms, to what is generally regarded as right and proper, and to the power and authority of the participants; for example: 'Girls don't act like that', or, 'You'll do that because I told you to', or other arguments based on norms or on the arbitrarily vested power or authority of the rule-enforcing figure. This approach asks the child for a minimum of thought; indeed, it often cuts off thought, giving regulations without rationale or with a rationale based only on tradition or status. The information provided the child is limited. The child is offered no alternative to consider, to compare, to evaluate, to select. It is a system of control based on non-rational appeals, and it does not require complex linguistic communication (Bernstein, 1961).

In the second type of regulatory manoeuvres, *personal-subjective* authoritarian demands and norms are modified by personal considerations, feelings, and preferences. Where the imperative-normative system imposes the rules of the group, the personal-subjective attends to the motivations, the intent, the inner states of the individual. Control statements such as, 'You shouldn't say things like that—they hurt your sister's feelings', or, 'How do you think you will feel if the other kids get better grades than you do?', or, 'Do your homework now, you'll feel better when it's done', are examples. The basis of appeal is interpersonal or intrapersonal comfort. This type of regulatory procedure encourages a more specific and complex mode of communication with which to describe the motives and other inner states of the participants. It obviously orients the child to be aware of a somewhat different type of stimulus or cue in his environment than does an appeal to norms.

---

[1] This formulation of family control is related to the research and conceptualisation of several other researchers, particularly unpublished papers and personal communication with Basil Bernstein, but also of Baldwin (1949), Kohn (1959), and Hess and Handel (1959), as well as our current work.

In the third control manoeuvre, *cognitive-rational*, appeal is to the results of a sequence of events, a long-term payoff, or a principle which states the rationale behind a rule or demand. Examples are: 'If you eat cookies now, you won't want your dinner', or, 'You should keep quiet in school because the teacher can't teach when kids talk, and then you won't learn your lessons', or, 'Wear your rubbers today so you won't get your feet wet and catch cold and have to stay in bed'. These explanations are obviously much more complicated than the imperative appeals. They call for a more complex response on the part of the child, for he must attend to a sequence of ideas and observe the relationships of events which, though separated in time, are brought together in anticipation of alternative consequences which may be expected to follow different immediate actions. They offer more information, they call for more cognitive activity, language, and attention, and they give the child a means of applying a logic of long-range consequences as a basis for behaviour. Unlike the normative appeal, this technique orients the child to the future and towards symbolic manipulation of his world.

The relevance of complex language in contrast to simple restricted codes in the process of cognitive development and educability we take as given, although there is still a great deal to be learned about the nature of the relationship between language and the development of thought. Thus the second important concept of the study is that the communication modes of the mother may usefully be described as *elaborated* or *restricted*. This view of communication is taken from the work of Bernstein of the University of London (1961). In his definition, *restricted* codes are stereotyped, limited, and condensed, lacking in specificity and the exactness needed for precise conceptualisation and differentiation. Sentences are short, simple, often unfinished; there is little use of subordinate clauses for elaborating the content of the sentence; it is a language of implicit meaning, easily understood and commonly shared. The basic quality of this mode is to limit the range and detail of concept and information involved.

Elaborated codes are those in which communication is individualised and the message is specific to a particular situation, topic, and person. They are more particular, more differentiated, and more precise. They permit expression of a wider and more complex range of thought, tending towards discrimination among cognitive and affective content.

The third cluster of variables and ideas we have used is related to the development of educability in the child, particularly the mother's influence upon the child's understanding of what it means to be a pupil in the public (or private) school. Educability is defined for our purposes as a composite of three attributes: cognitive skills specific to the classroom, motivation to achieve within a formal learning situation, and learning the role of pupil in relation to the class, the teacher, and the authority system of the school. The transition between the methods of control and cognitive exchange in the home and those in the school is especially difficult and important for the child from an under-privileged background. The teacher has less to build on that is familiar and consistent with her own background and frequently, perhaps typically, she has little accurate conception of the experiences with school-type tasks and images of school that the child brings to the classroom. In this connection, we are especially concerned with the images and beliefs the mothers hold about the school and about the role of a parent in relation to the efforts of teachers and the task of the school. This early maternal orientation has consequences for the emergence of the motivation to succeed which the child develops in his initial experiences in the classroom.

This general set of ideas attempts to relate the linguistic and regulatory behaviour of the mother to the information-processing strategies and styles induced in her child. By this we mean such things as the child's tendency to adopt an *initiatory, assertive* approach to the world of information around him or a *passive, compliant* stance to new experience, including the teacher and the stimuli of the classroom. Other strategies or styles are expressed in problem-solving behaviour, which may be *reflective* or *impulsive*, borrowing the concepts of Kagan and his associates (1963, 1964). Our hypothesis is that the mothers who exercise control through appeals to norms or to status tend to induce styles in their children which are passive, that is, waiting to be told, and impulsive, that is, moving to a solution without reflective thought and comparison of a range of possibilities.

These teaching styles also have implications for the child's *self* concept and for the motivational components of his learning style. This can be clarified by describing briefly some results of the project in which we and our colleagues, Dr Ellis Olim, Mrs Roberta Meyer Bear, and Mr Jere Brophy have been engaged for the past three years. This project includes four groups of Negro mothers and their four-year-old children— Group A from upper middle-class, professional, and managerial family backgrounds; Group B from skilled-work occupational levels, Group C from unskilled occupational origins. Each group had approximately forty mother–child pairs; all subjects came from intact homes, were economically self-supporting, with equal numbers of boys and girls within each subgroup. A fourth group (D) of similar size was composed of mothers on public assistance who were not living with their husbands or other adult males. The three working-class groups were evenly divided between those from public and those from private housing.

We have studied various aspects of the mothers' behaviour—language, concept formation, resources of the home and community, aspirations, and other variables relevant to the cognitive stimulation of the child. Mothers were interviewed in their homes, then brought with their children to the University of Chicago for testing and additional interviewing. This was necessary in order to obtain sessions between mothers and children uninterrupted by noise and by other members of the household, telephone, neighbours, etc. The interview included a number of semi-structured techniques designed to elicit attitudes towards methods of family control and the mothers' orientation towards the school and the teacher. The most useful technique on this point was the question: 'Let's just imagine that (*child*) is old enough to go to school for the first time. How do you think you would prepare him? What would you do or tell him?' Two typical responses of the mothers were these:

1. 'First of all, I would take him to see his new school, we would talk about the building, and after seeing the school I would tell him that he would meet new children who would be his friends; he would work and play with them. I would explain to him that the teacher would be his friend, would help him and guide him in school, and that he should do as she tells him to. That she will be his mother while he is away from home.'

2. 'Well, I would tell him he going to school and he have to sit down and mind the teacher and be a good boy, and I show him how when they give him milk, you know, how he's supposed to take his straw and do, and not put nothing on the floor when he get through?'

These replies were grouped along the general lines described above; using categories such as *imperatives*—an unqualified injunction or command, such as, 'Mind the teacher and do what she tells you to do', or, 'Be nice and do not fight', and *instructives*—information or commands which carry a rationale or justification for the rule to be observed, such as, 'I would tell him that it is important to mind the teacher. If he doesn't obey the teacher won't be able to teach the lesson.' Other data were coded and grouped in various ways in keeping with the orientation of the study.

The conclusion of the testing and interview sessions for each mother–child pair was an observation of the mother's teaching behaviour in a semi-structured situation. We brought mother and child to the nursery school, taught the mother three simple tasks involving cognitive and motor performance (sorting objects and copying designs) and asked her to teach these tasks to her child. Her verbal behaviour and that of the child were recorded on tape; the non-verbal interaction was described by an observer and recorded on a parallel tape. Here is an illustration from one interaction session in which the mother is attempting to teach the child to sort objects by colour:

Mother: Do you want a cracker? Now ... do you want one? ... You want to sit there? ... Okay.... Mommy will show you something, sit down, here, now you watch, okay? You see these three different sections on the board, hmm? ... I'm going to put these things together, in three sections, and I'm going to tell you why I'm doing it that way, and then I want you to be able, you have to listen to Mommy and then you tell me why I did it, okay? ... (extended pause) Okay

Child: What is that for, Mom?

Mother: Wait, you're going to tell me. Now what are these?

Child: Trucks.

Mother: Trucks, yes. Why did Mommy put these things here? In this section, what is there ... why did I put all those together? ... First, I'll tell you, see I'm putting them off, I, I'm ... making groups, here, and we have three different things to work on, and I put all these in groups because they're all trucks ... All right? And I put all these together, because they're chairs ... and I put these things, articles, together because they're all spoons, right? ... And—okay, now. You see the colour of this truck? It's red.... And this colour is yellow ... right? And this colour is green, just like your.... Okay.... Now I'm going to group all the red things together, I've got a red truck, a red chair, and a red spoon. I've got a green truck, a green chair, a green spoon. Have a yellow, no, I've got a yellow truck— wait, let me do it first—a yellow chair, and the yellow spoon. Now I put this group together 'cause it's all red.... I put this group together because they're all green ... and I put this group together because they're all yellow, right? Okay. Mommy going to do all this over again and you tell me why I put these things together....

Child: Mommy, can I have a turn?

Mother: Wait you can have a turn, if you tell me this time, then you can have a turn, okay now wait ... then you supposed to do what I do, you supposed to learn this now.... Now why did Mommy put these things in this section? ...

Child: [?] right there.

Mother: Why? ... You weren't listening were you?

In line with the theoretical context of the study we have concentrated upon these aspects of maternal behaviour:

1. the mother's use of various control techniques in dealing with her child;
2. the mother's teaching style in the laboratory teaching situations;
3. orientation towards the school, particularly the mother's feelings of efficacy in relation to the power of the teacher or principal;
4. language from protocols of the interview session;
5. measures of preference in sorting tasks.

The age of the children limited the amount and complexity of information we could obtain, but these measures indicate the cognitive performance of the children:

1. scores on Stanford-Binet IQ test (Form LM);
2. performance in the maternal teaching sessions;
3. concept attainment on the Sigel Sorting Task, which requires the child to group objects and verbalise the basis for his grouping;
4. behaviour in the test-taking situation as rated on the face sheet of the Binet.

Additional measures of the children's scholastic and cognitive performance are being obtained in a follow-up study. The association between maternal behaviour and these subsequent behavioural data will be reported when the analysis is complete. Evidence that these relationships exist is available in the research of Stodolsky (1965) who did a short-term follow-up on a part of the research group.

RESULTS AND CONCLUSIONS

Consistent with the familiar social class differences in mental performance, there are marked discrepancies between the upper middle-class and the three working-class groups on all cognitive tasks. Mean intelligence test scores for the mothers (WAIS Verbal IQs) ranged from 109·4 for high-status mothers to 82·4 for mothers from Group D. The range for children was not great—109·4 to 94·5 (Stanford-Binet, Form LM).

One of the most striking differences among the social-status groups was in their verbal behaviour. This is reported in detail in papers by Olim (1965) and Olim, Hess, and Shipman (1965). However, Table 25.1 gives a very gross picture of differences in *verbal output* on open-ended responses to a number of questions asked of all the mothers. (Table 25.1

shows the total number of lines of type used to transcribe these verbatim protocols.)

TABLE 25.1. *Mean number of typed lines in three data-gathering situations*

	Upper middle N=40	Upper lower N=40	Lower lower N=36	ADC N=36
School situations	34·68	22·80	18·86	18·64
Mastery situations	28·45	18·70	15·94	17·75
CAT card	18·72	9·62	12·39	12·24
Total	81·85	51·12	47·19	48·63

Similar differences existed in the *control strategies* of the mothers as indicated in the content of the responses to open-ended questions. Figure 25.1 shows the proportion of comments made in response to the

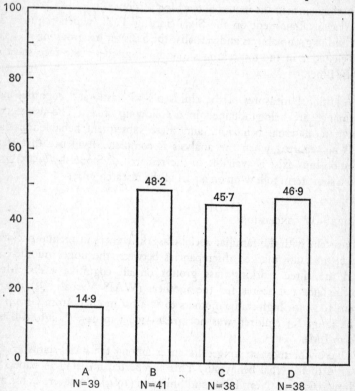

Fig. 25.1. Percentage use of imperative responses on first day protocols (means)

first-day question which were categorised as *imperative*. In passing, it should be mentioned that the tendency to use imperative statements is negatively related to the child's cognitive performance for both the total group and within the three working-class groups (see Fig. 25.2).

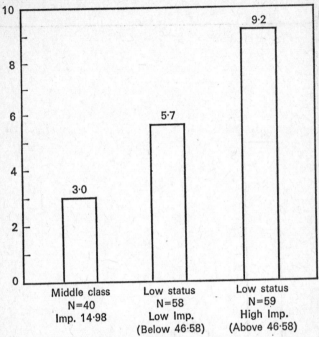

Fig. 25.2. Number of non-verbal responses on Sigel Sorting Test by children whose mothers are high and low on imperative responses (mean scores)

There were also differences among the social-status groups in their behaviour in the teaching sessions that appear to be related to style rather than to intelligence. In the third teaching session, we use an Etch-a-Sketch, a commercially available toy. This is a flat, small box with a screen on which lines can be drawn by a device inside the box controlled by two knobs: one for horizontal movement, one for vertical. The mother is assigned one knob, the child the other, and the mother is given five designs which are to be copied, or reproduced, on the screen of the Etch-a-Sketch through cooperative effort. It is the mother's task to instruct and guide the child through the necessary manoeuvres. One helpful technique is to show the child the design which is to be copied. Usually this was placed on the table where the mother and child were working, but a considerable number of mothers did not utilise the design in working with the child on this task.

Fig. 25.3 shows the percentage of mothers in each status group who showed their children at least four of the five designs they were asked to help reproduce. It is in the use of simple, orienting techniques such as these, as well as in the more difficult problems, that social-class differences appear.

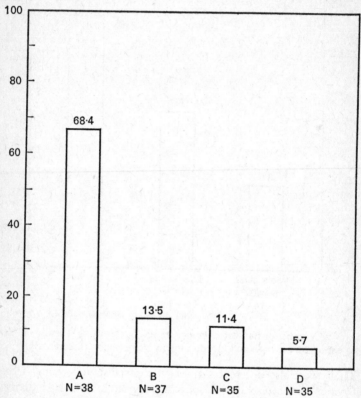

Fig. 25.3. Percentage of mothers using model for at least four designs during Etch-a-Sketch teaching session

The performance of the children showed similar social-class differences, as indicated in Table 25.2 which shows the relative success of children in each social-status group in attaining the two concepts involved in the first maternal teaching session. Similar differences appear on other measures, although there is considerable variability in the magnitude of these social-class discrepancies from one task to another.

The study was designed to examine these social-class differences in specific terms of maternal behaviour and mother–child interaction.

Reporting an obtained correlation of −0·41 between social-status level and Binet IQ, or 0·49 between mother's WAIS Verbal IQ and her child's Binet IQ, does not sufficiently explain such differences. We wish to determine the predictive power of certain maternal behaviours, and to be more specific about the behaviours encompassed in a global

TABLE 25.2. *Differences among status groups in children's performance in teaching situations (8-block task)*

| Social status | Percentage distribution | | | | | N |
	Placed correctly	One-dimension verbalised		Both verbalised		
A. *Short O*						
Upper-middle	75·0	52·5	70·0*	25·0	33·3*	40
Upper-lower	51·2	29·3	57·1	2·4	4·8	41
Lower-lower	50·0	27·5	55·0	15·0	30·0	40
ADC	41·5	19·5	47·1	2·4	5·9	41
B. *Tall X*						
Upper-middle	60·0	47·5	79·2*	27·5	45·8*	40
Upper-lower	48·8	31·7	65·0	17·1	35·0	41
Lower-lower	35·0	17·5	50·0	7·5	21·4	40
ADC	26·8	9·8	36·4	0·0	0·0	41

* Percentage of those who placed object correctly.

measure like IQ. To do this, we computed multiple *r*'s and found that maternal behaviours are as useful or better than IQ or social class in predicting the child's cognitive behaviour. The performance of children in our teaching situations can similarly be predicted with considerable efficiency; for example, using three such teaching variables, the multiple *r* with performance was 0·64; the multiple *r* using the mother's IQ, the child's IQ, and social-class level as predictors was 0·47. When all measures were combined, the multiple *r* was 0·67, or only slightly higher than that obtained by using material teaching variables alone.

This general pattern is repeated in other sectors of the data. The child's performance on cognitive tasks is associated with specific maternal behavioural variables at a level comparable to or higher than that obtained by the more traditional measures of maternal IQ and social class. We regard this finding as progress towards identifying the specific maternal behaviour in the mother–child interactional system which codes and translates social class and maternal intelligence into modes of interaction that affect the child's cognitive processes.

It appears that the learning styles and information-processing strategies that the child obtains in these early encounters with his cognitive and regulatory environment may set limits upon the potential mental growth of the child unless an intervention programme is instituted which *resocialises* or *re-educates* the child towards more effective cognitive strategies.

The cognitive environment of the culturally disadvantaged child is one in which behaviour is controlled by imperatives rather than by attention to the individual characteristics of a specific situation, and one in which behaviour is neither mediated by verbal cues which offer opportunities for using language as a tool for labelling, ordering, and manipulating stimuli in the environment, nor mediated by teaching that relates events to one another and the present to the future. The meaning of deprivation would thus seem to be a deprivation of meaning in the early cognitive relationships between mother and child. This environment produces a child who relates to authority rather than to rationale, who may often be compliant but is not reflective in his behaviour, and for whom the consequences of an act are largely considered in terms of immediate punishment or reward rather than future effects and long-range goals. If this general picture is valid, it would seem that the goal of early education is to promote the development of strategies or structures for dealing with information, rather than merely transmitting a supply of concepts, information, and mental skills.

REFERENCES

BALDWIN, A. L. (1949) 'The Effect of Home Environment on Nursery School Behaviour', *Child Development*, 20, 49–62.

BERNSTEIN, B. (1961) 'Social class and linguistic development: a theory of social learning', in A. H. Halsey, Jean Froud and C. C. Anderson, eds., *Education, Economy and Society*, New York, Free Press.

HESS, R. D. and HANDEL, G. (1959) *Family Worlds: A Psychosocial Approach to Family Life.* University of Chicago.

KAGAN, J., MOSS, H. A. and SIGEL, I. E. (1963) 'Psychological significance of styles of conceptualization', in J. C. Wright and J. Kagan, eds., 'Basic cognitive processes in children', *Monogr. Soc. Res. Child Develpm.*, 28. no. 2 (whole no. 86).

KAGAN, J., ROSMAN, B. L., DAY, D. A. J. and PHILLIPS, W. (1964) 'Information processing in the child: significance of analytic and reflective attitudes', *Psychol. Monogr.*, 78, no. 1 (whole no. 578).

KOHN, M. L. (1959) 'Social Class and the Exercise of Parental Authority', *Am. Sociol. Rev.*, 24, 252–366.

OLIM, E. G. (1965) 'Mothers' Language and Children's Cognitive Styles', unpublished doctoral dissertation, University of Chicago.

OLIM, E. G., HESS, R. D. and SHIPMAN, V. C. (1965) 'Maternal language styles and their implications for children's cognitive development', paper read at Amer. Psychol. Assn., Chicago, September.

STODOLSKY, S. S. (1965) 'Maternal behaviour and language and concept formation in Negro pre-school children: an inquiry into process', unpublished doctoral dissertation, University of Chicago.

SECTION 6

Intervention

This section consists of four articles, all of which relate to the way in which the teacher can affect the personality and learning relationship by intervening in the classroom situation. The first two articles are concerned specifically with the role of the teacher herself and the points to which she can pay attention in deciding how best to try to modify children's behaviour in the classroom. The next two are concerned with illustrating the operation of services on which teachers can call to extend their resources for modifying behaviour.

When teachers analyse their classroom activity in order to see which behaviour they reward by praise or high marks and which behaviour they punish by criticism or ignoring, the results are often surprising. The Bijou article (26) argues for reconsidering the teaching process by first making a careful analysis of behaviour in order to see which kinds of behaviour help and which hinder learning. From this analysis the teacher can decide which behaviour to reinforce and which behaviour not to reinforce.

Bijou illustrates his theme with five examples, four of which are taken from the field of children with learning and personality handicaps, largely because most of the applications of this approach to classroom activity have started in those areas where learning difficulties are most obvious. But Bijou does discuss projects which have devised programmes for helping children with marked reading and arithmetic problems in the ordinary schools.

In the second article in this section Leith and Trown (27) describe an experiment which explores two areas of enquiry, employing analysis of variance to handle their data. In the first of these areas the authors examine the relative value of placing summaries before or after a learning task. The second area is much more important for this source-book and in it Leith and Trown consider how the relationship between children's personality and learning can be affected by the way the teacher structures the material to be learnt. In this part of the article the authors make the interesting suggestion that when learning material is gently graded the relationships between personality factors and achievement, such as were discussed in the article in Section 2, may not emerge. The article is also of relevance to Section 1, since it sheds light on the issue of learning styles and their implications for teaching.

The enquiries reported in this article all took place under normal school conditions and illustrate ways in which teacher intervention through careful planning or programming of learning activities can affect the influence which personality has on classroom learning.

The third article, by Woody (28), discusses the ways in which the school counsellor might handle problems which have been referred to him. The illustration which Woody gives refers to a vocational problem, a boy about to leave school and seeking advice on finding a job. Later, in Table 28.1, Woody gives examples of learning and personality situations which counsellors could treat in three different ways. In discussing these three different approaches to counselling children Woody argues for a learning theory approach, which he calls 'behavioural counselling'.

Several questions may spring to mind on reading this article. One is the link between Woody's 'learning theory' approach to counselling and Bijou's approach to teaching. Another question is whether counselling children's problems should be limited to the secondary school situation, or whether this is an approach which, with modifications, could well be adopted throughout the whole of our educational system.

The final article in this section (29) deals with an older service, the school psychological service. This differs from the counselling service in that it is based not on the school itself but outside it, and is thus *responsible directly to the Chief Education Officer. It therefore has access to different resources.*

The operations of a school psychological service have changed since this article[29] appeared. For example, with the disappearance of selective secondary education, the advisory role which a minority of educational psychologists played in the 11 + procedure has vanished. On the other hand, some of the points mentioned in Section IV of the article, have now become standard practice in some areas. New psychological knowledge has led to new emphasis in the work.

A much fuller and more detailed account of the school psychological service is given in 'Psychologists in Education Services', the report of the Summerfield Working Party, which was published by HMSO in 1968. But this short reader article describes a framework of activity which is still basic to the operations of many school psychological services.'

The personnel of a school psychological service are different in background and training from counsellors. They bring different skills to bear on their work. The personality and learning problems with which a counselling service can deal are therefore different from those with which a school psychological service can deal. The way in which these problems differ is an interesting point of discussion and an important question for the teacher.

P. WILLIAMS

26

S. W. Bijou

Promoting optimum learning in children*

From at least as far back as the early nineteenth century and the teachings of Pestalozzi, educators and psychologists have been 'promoting optimum learning' in children. But somehow we are not convinced that we have succeeded. There is too much evidence to the contrary. Despite the fact that we now have more elaborate school buildings, more complicated teaching aids, and more teachers with advanced degrees, we still find too many children, especially in the low and middle socioeconomic classes, who have failed to learn to read, write, and do arithmetic well enough to cope with the demands of modern living; we still find too many children, especially bright children, who are indifferent or hostile towards school; and we see too many retarded and otherwise handicapped children who are merely custodialised or 'made comfortable' in special classes (Johnson, 1962).

Undoubtedly our failure to promote optimum learning in children stems from many causes, some fairly obscure. However, there are at least two that can be identified and eliminated. One of these is inherent in our current psychodiagnostic practices, i.e. in the way psychological problems are diagnosed. Conventional diagnostic practices tend to attribute learning failures to 'hypothetical causes that reside in the child'. We hear, 'Johnny can't read because he has dyslexia', 'Mary can't concentrate on reading or arithmetic much because she has minimal brain damage', 'Henry is handicapped because of a perceptual

* Reprinted from P. Wolff and R. MacKeith, eds., *Planning for Better Learning* (Clinics in Developmental Medicine, 33), Spastics/Heinemann, 1969, pp. 58–67.

disability', 'Jimmy can't make progress because of his emotional disturbance, and Aggie because of her mental retardation'.

The second cause for less than optimum learning in children is inherent in the traditional concept of teaching. The great majority, educators and laymen, alike, consider teaching an *intuitive art*. They hold that a good teacher is one with a certain unanalysable, creative power, and so we hear that 'she's a born teacher', by which is meant that she is patient, energetic, enthusiastic, optimistic, dedicated, inspirational, understanding, and resourceful.

The thesis of this paper is that we can promote optimum learning in children by revising our notions of psychodiagnosis and teaching and by taking cognisance of recent advances in experimental psychology. More specifically, we contend (*a*) that psychodiagnosis should be oriented towards identifying *observable, manipulable, causal conditions* and towards prescribing, in specific and concrete terms, remedial procedures, and (*b*) that teaching should be conceived of as a skilful *art* analysable in terms of the principles of modern behavioural theory.

PSYCHODIAGNOSIS: A SEARCH FOR OBSERVABLE CAUSES

Psychodiagnostic procedures which attribute learning failures to hypothetical internal causes (e.g. word blindness, perceptual disability, or insufficient intelligence), require radical revision because they ignore the role of objectively defined causal conditions which have been brought to light by recent advances in psychology.

A psychodiagnosis which concludes that a learning failure results from some assumed internal condition contributes no information as to the cause and treatment of the problem. The reasoning involved is circular. For example, a child is referred to a doctor because he has not learned to read despite the diligent efforts of his mother, his teacher, and a remedial specialist. After reviewing the child's background, medical reports, and psychological test results, the psychodiagnostician concludes, let us say, that the child's failure to read is caused by dyslexia. Hence, information about the child's recalcitrance in learning to read is taken as evidence for the existence of some condition of the brain which prevents learning. Inferring an internal cause on this basis merely stamps a label on a pattern of behaviour. Sometimes the label suggests pathological anatomical structure (e.g. hyperactive behaviour may be taken as the sign of minimal brain damage); sometimes the name denotes pathological physiological functioning (e.g. high frequency of making letter reversals may be taken to indicate right-hemisphere brain dominance); and sometimes the nomenclature refers to mental capacities or states (e.g. low academic achievement may be considered the prime indicator of defective intelligence; or limited progress in social learning may indicate infantile neurosis or a schizoid personality). It might be pointed out in passing that a valid diagnosis involving pathological biological structure or functioning requires both independent physiological evidence and research data which demonstrate a functional relationship between similar physiological findings (e.g. gross lesion in the parietal lobe) and the behaviour at issue (e.g. lack of progress in reading).

It may even be said that conventional psychodiagnostic practices hamper *our* learning of the observable conditions which hamper children's learning! This is certainly true to the degree that conventional practices give professional workers a false security by leading them to believe that their procedures are adequate. As long as clinicians believe that improvements in psychodiagnostics depend solely on advances in neurophysiology and biochemistry, they will not be sensitive to research findings which suggest that powerful relationships exist between learning difficulties and observable, manipulative conditions. Such findings are now available and deserve attention.

Based on the assumptions of natural science and founded on concepts derived entirely from experimental investigations, an objective approach to an analysis of behaviour has been evolving over the past sixty years (Kantor, 1959; Skinner, 1953, 1961). From this point of view, learning refers to *changes in observable behaviour generated by objective conditions*. A performance, act, or a response sequence of a person (e.g. turning on a radio switch, testing the acidity of a chemical solution, reciting a poem) is analysed in terms of the situation in which it occurs (e.g. the radio is switched on because the housewife wishes to hear the news; the acidity of a chemical solution is tested because the student must fulfil a course requirement; and a poem is recited because Jennifer's mother asked her to recite for the guests). The response sequence is also analysed in terms of the effect it has on the immediate environment (e.g. the radio gives forth the news broadcast; the litmus paper dipped in the chemical solution turns red; and the mother's guests lavish praise upon Jennifer) and on the future behaviour of the person performing the act. In the examples given, it is highly probable that all of the environmental changes described would strengthen the behaviour which produced them. The housewife is more inclined to turn on her radio when she wishes to hear the news, the student is more likely to approach the next laboratory assignment in his chemistry course, and Jennifer is more prone to 'entertain' her mother's guests on request. This interactional analysis of learning (the antecedent setting, the individual's response, and the consequences) may be used to account for the acquisition and maintenance of all the varieties of cognitive behaviour as well as for the development of social, recreational, and vocational skills.

Learning may fail to occur or may occur very slowly and inefficiently when any of the components described above are absent or are ineffectively arranged. For example, a child's learning rate in school will be slow if the curriculum is poorly sequenced in relation to the behaviour repertory he has at that time, if the teacher does not reinforce him for paying attention to the details in his assignments, and if his responses are not followed by effectively arranged, meaningful feedbacks. Continual exposure to a poorly arranged learning environment (and this includes materials) not only reduces the child's learning rate but creates escape and avoidance behaviour. The last thing in the world a school failure wants to do is to get into a learning situation that resembles school.

It is thought that a behaviourally oriented diagnosis of learning problems would include detailed information regarding (*a*) the child's repertory of behaviour with respect to the learning problem at hand; (*b*) the specific kinds of programmes needed; (*c*) the kinds of objects and events that would be likely to serve as reinforcers for the child, at least at the beginning of treatment; and (*d*) the probable support for such treatment from the parents, teachers, and others responsible for the child.

TEACHING: AN ANALYSABLE ART

A behaviourally oriented diagnosis calls for psychological treatment, and a behavioural analysis of treatment inevitably points to an examination of the teaching process. Before scrutinising the nature of teaching, however, it would be helpful to describe the range of activities that are included under the term. Teaching here refers not only to actual instruction in the normal classroom, in the classroom for the retarded, emotionally disturbed or otherwise handicapped child, and in the remedial reading and speech situation, but also to the interchanges between the tutor and the child, the psychotherapist and the patient, the rehabilitation worker and the client and the mother and her child, when the former assumes the role of teacher.

Teaching may be viewed as an art and still not be defined as an activity that is performed by a person with unanalysable creative power. It may be conceived of as an art in the sense that it is an activity carried on by a person who, through experience and study, has acquired the skill to enable a child, alone or in a group, to learn a task and to utilise it under proper future circumstances. In other words, teaching as a skilful art is an activity conducted by a teacher, who, while not necessarily blessed with inherent personality traits, is capable of making rapid evaluations of learning difficulties, preventing and eliminating behaviour which interferes with learning and using available circumstances (school materials, procedures, privileges, etc.) to strengthen learning and to generalise it.

With this view of teaching and the teacher, the concepts and principles of modern learning theory can be applied to enhance our understanding of what occurs in an instructional situation and to open the way to make learning more effective. The question is: which learning theory should be applied? Should one analyse the teaching situation in terms of the principles of Pavlov, Hull, or Skinner? One's choice of a system will, of course, depend on many factors, and especially on the personal appeal of the assumptions of each approach to psychology as a science. For example, one systematist may assume that the purpose of psychology is to understand the nature of the mind; another may postulate that the goal is to understand the intricate functioning of the brain; and still another, to predict and control behaviour. Be that as it may, it will be worthwhile to comment briefly on the suitability of those three learning theories for analysing teaching.

First, Pavlovian conditioning principles cannot be applied to the teaching situation with any degree of efficiency. Several attempts to do so have been found wanting (e.g. Goodenough, 1945). The main difficulty is that Pavlovian conditioning principles pertain to behaviour controlled by *antecedent stimulation*—unconditioned and conditioned stimuli, whereas the behaviour involved in cognitive, social, and motor learning is modified by *contingent stimulation*, that is, by stimulus events which come *after* the behaviour. Pavlovian conditioning principles are best reserved for an analysis of some of the components of emotional behaviour, and to aversive reactions.

Second, the learning principles of Hull (frequently called instrumental conditioning or social learning theory, and associated with Bandura and Walters, 1963; Dollard and Miller, 1950; Sears, 1951) have also been applied to the teaching situation and are appropriate in so far as they are concerned with behaviour which is sensitive to consequential stimulation. However, as Baldwin (1967) states, attempts at practical application of Hullian principles have been highly speculative, and subjective elements have crept into the concepts without being explicitly recognised.

Third, the operant conditioning principles, advanced by Skinner and his colleagues, have been applied to teaching dating roughly from the time of Skinner's (1954) paper on 'The science of learning and the art of teaching'. The fact that these concepts and principles are all empirically derived and that they are all *directly* applicable to practical situations has had wide appeal (Skinner, 1963). It should be noted that operant conditioning principles are similar to instrumental conditioning principles in that both centre on behaviour controlled by events which come after the behaviour—reinforcement contingencies. However, operant principles differ from instrumental principles in two major respects: (1) operant principles are restricted exclusively to observable, objective concepts derived solely from experimental studies, while instrumental principles deal with both observable and non-observable concepts (drive, habit strength, and excitatory potential); (2) operant conditioning principles are assumed to be different from classical (Pavlovian) conditioning principles; instrumental conditioning principles, on the other hand, are assumed to be the same as classical conditioning principles. Both instrumental and classical responses, for example, are strengthened by drive reduction.

Teaching, from the point of view of operant analysis, is the *management of contingencies to expedite learning* (Skinner, 1968). The teacher, with or without awareness, arranges all the 'things' at her disposal to expedite learning by a child, whether he is in a tutorial situation, a small group, or a large class. This means that she manages the circumstances so as to eliminate behaviour that competes with academic and social learning, e.g. she may ignore or reprimand a child's disruptive behaviour or emotional outbursts depending on her evaluation of their significance. She arranges contingencies to strengthen better study behaviour and hopefully she arranges them so that this behaviour becomes part of a child's way of dealing with future assignments (Mager, 1968). Finally, she arranges appropriate contingencies by programming the subject matter of both the visible (academic subjects) and the invisible (manners and moral behaviour) curricula so as to facilitate learning.

Teaching, seen as the management of contingencies, suggests that a teacher is effective in proportion to her skill in using consequences that are meaningful (functional) for each child; in sequencing the school programmes so that a child can start at the level of his behaviour repertory and make progress in the subject matter at a reasonable rate; in using teaching procedures which attenuate incorrect answers and disruptive social behaviours; and in building desirable attending and work responses in the child.

Keeping daily records (e.g. units of work completed, number of errors) is also crucial because it provides the teacher with a guide for revising the programmes. This stipulation deserves emphasis for it is not generally recognised as one of the essential tools for dealing with learning failures. In an operant learning approach, a cardinal assumption is that changes in the child's behaviour result from changes in the learning situation. Conversely, a lack of change in behaviour indicates that the circumstances are constant or non-functional for the child. The importance of this assumption for teaching is this: when learning does not occur, it means that the materials and procedures should be changed, and if necessary, changed again and again until learning does begin to take place.

EXAMPLES OF PROMOTING OPTIMUM LEARNING IN CHILDREN BY THE
APPLICATION OF OPERANT PRINCIPLES

I shall elaborate on my thesis that one can promote optimum learning in children by revising one's concepts of psychodiagnosis and teaching along the lines of modern behaviour therapy, by presenting some examples of the application of operant principles. This brief survey of research will touch upon the kinds of learning problems that have been diagnosed and treated, and the situations in which the treatment was carried out.

The Arizona State University study

Meyerson *et al.* (1967) reporting on their work at Arizona State University on the rehabilitation of the retarded and physically handicapped, describe the diagnosis and treatment of four cases in a residential institution; an adolescent boy with traumatic quadriplegia who lacked motivation to learn; a cerebral-palsied boy who was afraid of falling; a retarded girl who was not able to walk; and a preschool autistic boy with self-destructive behaviour. The procedures used in treating the non-ambulatory retarded girl are typical and are summarised here. This nine-year-old youngster Mary, classified as congenitally retarded, crawled when she was two years old and remained at the stage of locomotion until the time of the study. The authors wrote:

> She was somewhat bow-legged, as if she had rickets at the age when most children begin to walk, but there were no physical abnormalities now that would tend to interfere with walking or standing unsupported.
>
> Mary, except for her very thin legs, and lack of muscular development in the calf, seemed physically capable of walking. Her primary mode of locomotion, however, was scooting across the floor on the

buttocks by pushing with her feet and hands. She could be pulled to a standing position if the experimenter supported most of her weight, but she could not be induced to move her legs, and she would drop to the floor as soon as support was removed or relaxed (pp. 224-5).

The objective of the study was to devise procedures based on the application of operant principles that would enable Mary to stand unsupported and walk independently. Since she enjoyed popcorn, raisins, crackers, nuts, and ice cream, these foods were used to initiate walking. The consequences of walking, i.e. approval by peers and adults, being able to get from place to place, and so on, were used to maintain walking behaviour on the ward. Biweekly sessions lasted from 20 to 45 minutes, with long rest periods in the early stages of the training.

Training was conducted in three phases. In Phase I, which consisted of only one session, Mary was lifted to her feet and given a sweet while standing. At the end of that session, she could stand from 5 to 15 seconds without support. In Phase 2, she was placed on the floor between two chairs standing back to back, 30 inches apart. The experimenter stood behind one chair and encouraged Mary to pull herself to her feet by grasping the back of one chair, turn around, and grasp the back of the other chair, first with one hand, and then with both hands. When Mary attained an upright position, the experimenter would say, 'Mary, come over here'. If she complied, she was given a treat. Over the seven sessions of Phase 2, the distance between chairs was increased to 45 inches, requiring the girl to take more steps. In Phase 3, the chairs were removed. One experimenter held Mary's hands while another experimenter, several feet away, held out a 'goodie'. The first experimenter withdrew his hands after Mary had taken a few steps and the second experimenter backed slowly away. Initially she was given a reinforcer for every three or four steps taken, but this requirement was gradually increased in each session. By session 12, at least 25 steps were required to obtain a reinforcer. In the last three sessions—sessions 13, 14, and 15—the two experimenters stood at opposite sides of the room, and Mary walked from one to the other. During the training period, she took a total of 4,600 steps, with and without support. A progress report six months after the termination of training showed that Mary was walking freely and frequently throughout the institution.

The Rainier School study

A second example of the application of operant principles to facilitate learning is a study carried out at the Ranier School, Buckley, Washington, on teaching reading, writing, and arithmetic to institutionalised, retarded children (Bijou *et al.*, 1966). The children, classified as ineducable by the schools system, had IQs as low as 44 and represented almost all the clinical categories including brain-damaged, mongoloid, cultural-familial, unknown, and undifferentiated. In addition, many of the children had conduct problems and most had made no progress in regular schools prior to admission to the institution.

No attempt was made to devise academic programmes for these children according to their diagnostic category (e.g. one programme for the brain-injured, one for the cultural-familial, etc.); rather, an all-out effort was made to develop a motivational system that would be effective for each child in the class, and a programmed curriculum in reading, writing, and arithmetic that would be suitable for all the children regardless of the level of each child's current behaviour repertory (achievement). A further requirement was that the programmes were to be constructed in such a way that they could be used by the child, first with assistance from the teacher, and later, quite independently.

It was necessary to invent a contrived motivational system (Birnbrauer *et al.*, 1965) because these children were not responsive to the motivators ordinarily used by teachers (giving a compliment for correct answers to an arithmetic problem, marking an 'A' on a paper with all the words correctly spelled, etc.). After considerable experimentation, a system was finally developed that consisted of tokens (marks) which were given contingent upon the child's desirable behaviour. These marks were exchangeable for candy, toys, school supplies, personal items for the child's room, privileges, social outings, and the like. Desirable behaviour was defined as (1) correct responses to the academic exercises; (2) progressive improvement in attending to school work; and (3) appropriate social behaviour.

The curricula consisted of reading, writing, and arithmetic sequences which began at the most primitive level (discriminating forms, colours, and pictures) and extended to the performance of the most advanced child. The exact sequential arrangements of the materials were dictated by a study of the children's actual performances (Greene, 1966). This special feature of the study deserves emphasis because it exemplifies a method of curriculum construction that is based not on the dictates of 'authorities' in special education, but rather on the responses of children for whom the curriculum is intended. To put it differently, the materials designed for these children were based on the successes and failures of children with similar educational histories.

The Rainier study has been in operation for over seven years. During that time most of the children have made substantial advances in academic learning. Many have been motivated to work several hours on schools subjects to obtain the reinforcers that come naturally from that activity. Many have also become adept at tutoring other children in reading and arithmetic.

Other methods

Research and demonstration studies in regular community schools constitute still another example of the ways in which operant principles have been applied to learning. These studies fall into two categories: those concerned with devising reading, writing, and arithmetic programmes for the normal elementary school child, and those concerned with improving the management of children in the classroom. An example of the former is the work of Glaser and his associates (1967) at the University of Pittsburg. Currently the materials developed by this group are being evaluated in elementary schools in many States, including Pennsylvania and Illinois. An example improving the management of children in the classroom is the work of Becker *et al.* (1967). By using direct observational methods, these investigators have shown that the classroom is better managed and the teacher is more effective when she attends to and praises a child's desirable academic and social behaviour, than when she pays attention to remarks on a child's disruptive behaviour. Similar results have been obtained in a junior high school special education class (Broden and Hall, in press).

A fourth example is the work being done in remedial language and speech. Programmes applying operant principles to the improvement of communication skills have been used in nursery schools, hospitals, and clinics. The objectives of this work include initiating speech in severely impaired children, eliminating echolalic speech, reinstating speech in mute children and adults and remediating articulary difficulties and stuttering (Sloane and MacAuley, 1968). For instance, in treating echolalic speech, training techniques using differential reinforcement were prepared in which echolalic behaviour was gradually weakened while normal speech was gradually strengthened. At the same time, longer and longer units of conversation were instituted by systematic differential reinforcement procedures (Risley and Wolf, 1967). In treating the child who is completely devoid of verbal behaviour, the emphasis has been on procedures which strengthen the relationships between phonemes in the repertory of the child and the names of things which approximate them (e.g. 'wah-wah' and water), facilitate progressive refinements in pronunciation (e.g. from 'wah-wah' to 'water'), and extend verbal chains to make simple phrases and sentences) e.g. from 'water' to 'glass of water') (Lovaas, 1968).

A fifth and final example of the application of operant principles to enhance learning is the entire field of behaviour modification with children. Here we include psychotherapy with children classified as retarded, schizophrenic, autistic, neurotic, and emotionally disturbed. Here the diagnostic procedures are characterised by the assessment of the current relevant repertory of the child and the establishment of reinforcers functional for him. The treatment procedures consist of: the development of a programme with a behaviourally defined terminal objective, having a starting point commensurate with the child's behavioural repertory; units of training designed to move the child ahead at his own pace; and a recording method which permits the therapist to monitor changes on a session-to-session basis. Therapy is conducted in the natural settings of the home, school, institution or clinic, and the actual treatment is carried on by a childcare worker (Lovaas *et al.*, 1965; Wolf *et al.*, 1964), a teacher (Sloane *et al.*, 1967), a nurse (Peterson and Peterson, 1968), or the mother (Hawkins *et al.*, 1966).

SUMMARY

The view presented here is that optimum learning in children can be promoted by revising our current concepts of psychological diagnosis and treatment (teaching) to incorporate recent advances in experimental psychology. The consequences of this proposal are straightforward: the goal of diagnosing a learning problem would be to identify the observable, manipulable, causal conditions rather than to infer pathology in some hypothetical, internal, causal condition and teaching (including remedial teaching) would be viewed as an analysable activity rather than an intuitive art.

A behaviourally oriented diagnosis of learning problems would provide, in addition to a delineation of probable antecedent conditions and prevailing circumstances, information on the child's repertory of behaviour with respect to the problem, the specific kind of programme needed, and the kinds of things and activities that would probably serve as reinforcers, at least at the beginning of treatment.

Teaching, which includes academic instruction, psychotherapy, rehabilitation, remedial speech and remedial reading, is viewed as a situation in which the teacher manages the learning environment to expedite learning. Specifically, she programmes contingencies of reinforcement and the subject matter so that the learner starts at the level of his current behavioural repertory (determined by informal evaluation) and progresses to a rate reasonable for him. In order to promote a positive attitude towards the material to be learned and to increase the likelihood that it will be utilised and generalised, the teacher strengthens learned responses with positive reinforcement contingencies.

ACKNOWLEDGEMENT. This analysis has generated in large measure from the research supported by the US Office of Education, Division of Research, Bureau of Education for the Handicapped, Project no. 5-0961, Grant no. OEG 32-23-6002.

REFERENCES

BALDWIN, A. L. (1967) *Theories of Child Development*, Wiley.

BANDURA, A. and WALTERS, R. H. (1963) *Social Learning and Personality Development*, Holt, Rinehart & Winston.

BECKER, W. C., MADSEN, C. H., ARNOLD, C. R. and THOMAS, D. R. (1967) 'The contingent use of teacher attention and praise in reducing classroom behavior problems', *J. Spec. Educ.*, 1, 287.

BIJOU, S. W., BIRNBRAUER, J. S., KIDDER, J. D. and TAGUE, C. (1966) 'Programmed instruction as an approach to the teaching of reading, writing, and arithmetic to retarded children', *Psychol. Record*, 16, 505.

BIRNBRAUER, J. S., WOLF, M. M., KIDDER, J. D. and TAGUE, C. (1965) 'Classroom behavior of retarded pupils with token reinforcement', *J. Exper. Child Psychol.*, 2, 219.

BRODEN, M. and HALL, V. R. (in press) 'Effects of teacher attention and a token reinforcement system in a junior high school special education class', *Except. Child.*

DOLLARD, J. and MILLER, N. E. (1950) *Personality and Psychotherapy*, McGraw-Hill.

GLASER, R. (1967) *Adapting the Elementary School Curriculum to Individual Performance*, University of Pittsburg Press.

GOODENOUGH, F. L. (1945) *Developmental Psychology*, 2nd edn., Appleton-Century-Crofts.

GREENE, F. M. (1966) 'Programmed instruction techniques for the mentally retarded', in N. R. Ellis, ed., *International Review of Research in Mental Retardation*, 2, 210.

HAWKINS, R. P., PETERSON, R. F., SCHWEID, E. and BIJOU, S. W. (1966) 'Behavior therapy in the home amelioration of problem parent-child relations with the parent in a therapeutic role', *J. Exper. Child Psychol.*, 4, 99.

JOHNSON, G. O. (1962) 'Special education for the mentally handicapped—a paradox', *Except. Child*, 29, 62.

KANTOR, J. R. (1959) *Interbehavioral Psychology*, 2nd rev. edn., Bloomington, Ind., Principia Press.

LOVAAS, O. I. (1968) 'A program for the establishment of speech in psychotic children', in H. N. Sloane, and B. D. MacAuley, eds., *Operant Procedures in Remedial Speech and Language Training*, Houghton Mifflin.

LOVAAS, O. I., FRIETAG, G., GOLD, J. and KASSORLA, I. C. (1965) 'Experimental studies in childhood schizophrenia. I. Analysis of self-destructive behavior', *J. Exper. Child Psychol.*, 2, 67.

MAGER, B. F. (1968) *Developing Attitude Toward Learning*. Palo Alto, Calif.: Fearson.

MEYERSON, L., KERR, N., MICHAEL, J. L. (1967) 'Behavior modification in rehabilitation', in S. W. Bijou and D. M. Baer, eds., *Child Development: Readings in Experimental Analysis*. Appleton-Century-Crofts, 214.

PETERSON, R. F. and PETERSON, L. W. (1968) 'The use of positive reinforcement in the control of self destructive behavior in a retarded boy', *J. Exper. Child Psychol.*, 6, 351.

RISLEY, T. R. and WOLF, M. M. (1967) 'Experimental manipulation of autistic behaviors and generalisation into the home', in S. W. Bijou and D. M. Baer, eds., *Child Development: Readings in Experimental Analysis*. Appleton-Century-Crofts.

SEARS, R. R. (1951) 'A theoretical framework for personality and social behavior', *Amer. Psychol.*, 6, 476.

SKINNER, B. F. (1953) *Science and Human Behavior*, New York, Macmillan.

SKINNER, B. F. (1954) 'The science of learning and the art of teaching', *Harvard Educ. Rev.*, 24, 86.

SKINNER, B. F. (1961) *Cumulative Record*, enlarged ed., Appleton-Century-Crofts.

SKINNER, B. F. (1963) 'Reflections on a decade of teaching machines', *Teachers College Record*, 65, 168.

SKINNER, B. F. (1968) *The Technology of Teaching*, Appleton-Century-Crofts.

SLOANE, H. N., JOHNSTON, M. K. and BIJOU, S. W. (1967) 'Successive modification of aggressive behavior and aggressive fantasy play by management of contingencies', *J. Child Psychol. Psychiat.*, 8, 217.

SLOANE, H. N. and MACAULEY, B. D., eds. (1968) *Operant Procedures in Remedial Speech and Language Training*, Houghton Mifflin.

WOLF, M. M., RISLEY, T. R., MEES, H. L. (1964) 'Applications of operant conditioning procedures to the behavior problems of an autistic child', *Behaviour Research and Therapy*, 1, 305.

27

G. O. M. Leith
and
E. A. Trown

The influence of personality and task conditions on learning and transfer*

ABSTRACT. To test hypotheses about the optimal place of rules in school learning tasks 124 twelve-year-old children from a single campus were categorised by ability, sex and two personality traits—extraversion/introversion and general anxiety. The learning task was a programme on vectors from which rules were abstracted and given either before or after sections of the programme containing practice examples.

Further evidence for the superiority of rules following practice was obtained. Significant interactions of treatments and extraversion on post- and transfer-tests showed, however, that this occurred because the 'rules before' was significantly poorer than the 'rules after' condition for extraverts of both above and below average ability. There was no significant difference between the treatments for introverts. Anxiety level differences were not significant, but anxious children were slightly better than non-anxious.

INTRODUCTION

This experiment was undertaken as a further exploration of two areas of study. One of these is a series of investigations of the role of reviews and previews in overcoming conflict and interference between successive parts of a learning task. The other concerns the influence of two personality variables—anxiety and introversion/extraversion—on learning.

One of the authors has found that losses in recall and transfer from meaningful learning tasks may be accounted for by the occurrence of large amounts of inter-section interference between parts of a task,

* Reprinted from *Programmed Learning*, **7**, 1970, 181–88.

but that such conflict can be overcome by including summaries at the end of each section. Also effective is the provision of an overall final summary, though previews, whether given as a whole or distributed throughout the learning material, are ineffective (Leith and McHugh, 1967; Leith and Blake, 1967; Leith and Webb, 1968; Leith *et al.*, 1969). The present report takes up the same theme, while varying the breadth of summaries and the subject-matter. Single or double rules were employed rather than the much more extended summary passages of three of the experiments (e.g. ten propositions, a half-hour lesson, 1,000 words) though one other study used relatively short abstractions. Previous work was concerned with Social Anthropology, English, Geography and Physics. Modern Mathematics was chosen to extend the scope of the experiments.

The other aspect of the research is an enquiry into the extent to which anxiety and extraversion are influential in determining achievement. In refining our knowledge of psychology, there is a growing rapprochement between the psychology of individual differences and the psychology of learning. Not merely are questions being asked about the ways in which children and adults may differ from each other in abilities, attainments and personality or about the general principles of learning which apply to all organisms. There is a growing tendency to ask: 'What significance have individual differences for *how* particular people learn and *what* they achieve?' *The implication is that* individuals may well differ in their manner of approaching learning tasks, that some methods of instruction may be suitable for a proportion but not for *all* pupils and that ideally we should match methods, media and order of presentation, in teaching, to particular students' strategies and modes of learning, their previously acquired knowledge, skills and aptitudes and their experience of success and failure.

This is the eventual aim of those teachers and psychologists who are endeavouring to establish principles for genuinely individual instruction and is a prime motive for research into computer-aided instruction. There has, however, been little success, as yet, in arriving at settled conclusions—indeed most of the work has been carried out in the tradition of individual differences only. Thus research has largely been directed at questions like: 'Is anxiety correlated with achievement in school?'; 'Which personality type is most or least successful in school and university?' Again, there have been inquiries into the validity of theoretical points of view, e.g. that anxiety hinders complex learning at extremes of the scale (too much, too little), though moderate amounts may be helpful.

Research on these points tends to be conflicting (Warburton, 1962;

Lavin, 1967; Rushton, 1966). Several reasons may be put forward for the conflicts. Thus, there may be changes with age in the personality structures which most readily meet with success. The different conditions of primary, secondary and university education give prima facie grounds for expecting that independence and submissiveness may find fulfilment at different times or in different places. Another reason may be a fundamental instability in personality assessments in contrast with the *relative* consistency of cognitive measures. A third reason might be that conditions of learning, teaching and testing have different effects on different people so that, if these differences are neglected in a study, they will tend to cancel each other out or become revealed, now in one direction, now in another, depending on the predominance of unreported features of the situation or the sample.

That personality assessment is less consistent than attainment or intelligence measurement need not be argued. Evidence for the first and third of the above points is beginning to accumulate. Some of this evidence has been summarised elsewhere (Leith, 1969; Amaria and Leith, 1969). A brief outline is given below.

Ten-year-old children in an experiment on the influence of several degrees of guidance on learning and applying concepts showed that, though there were no overall differences, this was because absence of structure and guidance favoured non-anxious but not anxious children, while a great amount of structuring and prompting was helpful to anxious but not to non-anxious children (Leith and Bosett, 1967). In comparing children of different personality types, the most successful were anxious introverts—a finding which was repeated with twelve-year-olds in a study of social reinforcement and achievement (Leith and Davis, 1969). The learning materials of the first study were used again with students in a further education college where the finding was, once more, that the methods of guidance made no overall difference but that, within methods, opposite types benefited or were unsuccessful. This time, however, the maximum amount of prompting and guidance led to poor performance on the part of the extraverts and good performance by introverts. There was also a very great difference between anxious and non-anxious halves of the sample—the latter having the clear advantage.

A further study employed two carefully validated forms of a programmed text which were prepared and tested so as to give equivalent results. One form was highly structured, the other required a much greater tolerance of uncertainty in searching for explanatory principles. Over 200 college of education students worked through the programmes and were given transfer tests which required application and reorganisation of principles. Extraverts were more successful than introverts with the discovery type of programme. Introverts were good with the clearly structured well-guided one though extraverts were significantly poorer with this type of learning. Overall, and cutting across this finding, non-anxious (below the median) subjects were better than anxious ones (Shadbolt and Leith, 1967).

One further study may be cited which brings in another dimension. Adults (aged around forty) were given training in the new decimal currency system and exchange, and conversion from the present coinage. One method was a succinct set of rules followed by a self-correctional test (together with a set of simulated coins). This may be considered to involve less structuring and guidance than the other methods which were: a linear programmed text with explicit practice in conversion, etc. and with directed coin handling; and the same material presented simultaneously (i.e. group paced) on sound tape. The unstructured method showed a significant positive relationship with extraversion (i.e. extraverts got higher scores than introverts) and a significant negative relationship with neuroticism (general anxiety)—in other words the greater the degree of anxiety, the lower the test score. On the other hand, the linear programmed text group showed zero relationships between personality and scores and the tape group larger but also non-significant correlations (Leith *et al.*, 1968). A small-step linear programme on spelling given to secondary school children also showed no relationships between personality and achievement. The possibility thus arises that when the stress of difficulty is avoided, as in small-step programmes, personality differences do not emerge but, when the mental effort is great, as in the studies cited earlier, personality factors have some influence on achievement.

THE EXPERIMENT

The entire project, of which this is one part, was carried out in two Leicestershire junior high schools which are situated on the same campus, children being allocated to one school or the other alphabetically. From a pool of 371 boys and girls aged between 11 years 8 months and 13 years 4 months in the second-year classes, 160 children of each sex were randomly chosen. After being dichotomised within schools and sexes at the median scores for general ability (Raven's Matrices) anxiety and extraversion/introversion (H.B. Personality Inventory, Hallworth, 1962), they were assigned randomly to one of ten groups. Thus each group contained thirty-two children, a boy and a girl from each school above the median intelligence, of more than average anxiety and of greater than average extraversion and so on, completing all combinations of ability, anxiety and extraversion. Four of these groups were assigned to treatment conditions in which, in addition to working through a programmed text on modern mathematics, children were given verbally formulated rules either one at a time or two at a time and either before the section(s) they applied to or after them. In other words, a learner would read a rule, and a short section of programme, then a second rule and another section of programme, or he would be given the two rules together followed by the two sections. Alternatively, he got the rules after sections.

The programmed texts were based on the approach of the Midlands Mathematics Experiment, chapter 12, Book I. This was considered particularly suitable since it was completely new work and yet required no particular background in order to enter it. They were validated in four schools different from the experimental schools.

Sixteen rules were identified, each of which was given expression in a sequence of frames containing exemplification in exercises and problems. Each of the frames in sequences embodying the rules required a response by the pupil, upon completion of which he was given immediate feedback in the form of knowledge of correct result. The total number of frames was 246.

In one of the schools the programme was administered twice a week in lessons of forty-five minutes duration for four weeks. The other school had some lessons of thirty-five minutes only. It was intended that two sections should be completed in each lesson but since lesson time was too short in one of the schools, these pupils were not strictly scheduled but nevertheless completed the task within the same total period. The tests were given immediately after completion of the programme (i.e. in the fifth week). One of these assessed knowledge of the material of the programme by means of test items on addition of vectors. The transfer test was made up of items not taught, viz. subtraction of vectors.

For the purpose of this analysis the groups reading rules one or two at a time were pooled. The treatments compared are thus reading rules before or after practice examples. This design gives a total of 128 children with eight in each sub-group (categorised by treatments, ability, anxiety and extraversion). Four subjects were 'lost' during the course of the experiment, two from one cell and one each from two of the others. To compensate for this, the missing scores were filled in by inserting the mean score of the original cell (i.e. group of four subjects) and four degrees of freedom were subtracted from the total number. This is essentially equivalent to carrying out an analysis on the means of the subgroups and makes computation easier.

It was expected that the children reading rules after practice would achieve higher mean scores than those receiving rules first. The more anxious children were expected, at this stage, to score higher than the non-anxious. The most difficult prediction to make was that of the interaction of personality and attainment. Learning from the rules-first condition was expecting to benefit pupils who welcome clear guidance and precisely outlined structure but to handicap those who react against the imposition of structure. From previous evidence and from observation there seems to be a class of individuals whose pre-ferred method of learning is to plunge into an initially confused situation, manipulate and test correspondences and connections, and try hypotheses until a structure emerges. They are perhaps those people who resist being told how to get to places in a locality but prefer to keep trying alternative routes until they can get from any-where to any other place without always knowing how they did so or being able to explain. This class of pupils was thought likely to get lower scores when reading rules before practising, even though the opportunity for engaging in a search strategy was limited, since they are probably impatient of initial attempts to define structure. Which categories of personality fit pupils with these different strategies or styles are less certain. In older subjects the strategies go along with extraversion and introversion, whereas there is some evidence for expecting anxious and non-anxious junior school age children to react in these ways. The possibility is open, too, that twelve-year-olds are at a transition point in development.

RESULTS

The post-test and transfer test scores were each given a $2 \times 2 \times 2 \times 2$ factorial analysis of variance. The post-test data showed two significant effects. An ability levels difference accounted for more than a third of the total variance, the more intelligent children having very signifi-cantly higher scores than those below average in IQ. The second find-ing was a significant treatments $\times$ extraversion interaction ($p < 0.05$) which is shown in Table 27.1.

Follow-up tests were made at each level of personality. There was no difference between the two groups of introverts, but the Rules After condition was superior to the Rules Before in the case of extra-verts $t = 2.46$; $p < 0.02$, two-tailed). In fact, the rules before practice debilitated extraverts whose performance under this condition was clearly different from that of the other three groups.

Analysis of the transfer test scores revealed a similar pattern. Over one-third of the total variance was taken up by the difference between ability levels. There was also a treatments × extraversion interaction which was significant at less than the 0·05 level. Table 27.2 summarises the results.

TABLE 27.1. *Mean post-test scores of introverts and extraverts under two conditions of learning*

Personality	Position of rules		
	Before practice	After practice	Overall
Introverts	54·75	52·56	53·66
Extraverts	42·72	55·06	48·88
Overall	48·74	53·81	51·27
	$\sigma_{x_1 - x_2} = 5\cdot02$;	df 108	

TABLE 27.2. *Mean transfer test scores of introverts and extraverts under two conditions of learning*

Personality	Position of rules		
	Before practice	After practice	Overall
Introverts	39·75	36·88	38·31
Extraverts	25·16	42·88	34·02
Overall	32·45	39·88	36·17
	$\sigma_{x_1 - x_2} = 6\cdot33$;	df 108	

Introverts, though again better if they were given their rules before practice, were not significantly so. Extraverts, however, were much lower in transfer when given rules first. A t-test (two-tailed) showed that the difference was significant at less than the 0·01 level (t=2·80).

Two further points were of interest in the analysis. The non-significant anxiety levels effect appeared both in the post-test and transfer test data and all interactions of anxiety with the other factors had F ratios of less than 2·00. Subjects above the median anxiety level were, in fact, slightly higher in post-test and in transfer test scores.

The other question under investigation was whether the provision of rules before or after practice gives better achievement—in conformity with four previous investigations.

In the present case this has been established for extraverts, though not for introverts. Since, however, the rules-after condition was expected to give better results, one-tailed t-tests were carried out to compare the means of those receiving rules before and rules after practice. The results are tabulated below in Table 27.3. Though results were in the expected direction, they achieved significance overall between the two conditions of learning only in the test of transfer.

TABLE 27.3. *One-tailed comparisons of groups learning rules before and rules after practice*

	Rules before	*Rules after*	*Difference*	*t*	*p*
Post-test	48·74	53·81	5·07	1·43	N.S.
Transfer test	32·45	39·88	7·43	1·66	0·05

A further aspect of the results should be noted. The pattern in which rules after was better than rules before, for extraverts (but not for introverts) was repeated at both levels of ability.

DISCUSSION

Many previous studies have discussed relationships between personality and achievement. Almost all of them, however, have failed both to enquire into the nature of the teaching given and to consider the possibility that individuals of different temperaments may be helped or hindered in their learning by differences in teaching method. The present research is based on findings in two series of experiments. In one it has been shown that interference between the sections of verbal learning tasks may be overcome by means of reviews or summaries given at the end of sections, though the same material given in advance is of no value in enhancing learning. One question which arises is how small or large each section should be for optimum effectiveness. The sections in this experiment were short and the rules were somewhat difficult and abstract.

The second series of experiments which suggested the hypotheses tested, obtained results in which children of ten to eleven years and students of over sixteen years learned to solve problems under varying conditions of ambiguity and structure. Thus one condition contained sets of problems which had been given a random sequence, whereas another arranged them in sets and gave structuring prompts such as statements of rule and correct answers. With younger children, an interaction of anxiety with method was found, whereas the older students showed an interaction of extraversion and learning condition, anxious subjects being poorer than non-anxious.

This gave rise to the hypothesis that teaching materials constructed so as to induce errors and to arouse ambiguity and uncertainty would favour extraverts, while carefully structured, clearly defined sequences of teaching material would give better results with introverts, the anxious having lower scores than non-anxious subjects. These predictions were confirmed with college of education students who were given carefully prepared self-instructional programmes on genetics which were constructed to implement these conditions.

Further work was clearly demanded which sought to find if the effects of anxiety, and extraversion, could be replicated with children of twelve to thirteen years and if the proposed explanation of the interaction in terms of tolerance for structure could be confirmed. It was considered that giving rules which explain or cover the logic of practice examples would be likely to impose a greater degree of structuring than giving the same rules after practice examples. Thus, some learners would react unfavourably to the rules-first condition, and hence, achieve a poorer performance than when the results of their mode of attack are confirmed by means of a formulated rule. On the other hand, other pupils—those having a greater tolerance for formal guidance—would not be put off by the initial position of the rules though their status with rules after practice in a programmed learning sequence might not be seriously lowered.

The results of the experiment support the notion that individuals have different approaches to these learning tasks. Furthermore, at the age of twelve to thirteen years, these differences in methods of learning can be categorised as belonging to children who are more or less introverted or extraverted (above and below the median score on a personality inventory).

The writer's previous work with children of about this age has indicated that, if anything, greater anxiety (scores above the median) results in higher achievement. In the present case this is in fact so, though no significant differences were revealed.

It may be stressed that the findings were obtained under regular school conditions (save that self-instructional programmes were used to avoid teacher variance). Children from two different schools and both sexes were equally distributed across the experimental conditions but no attempt was made to reduce these sources of variance in the analysis. These measures were taken in order to overcome the objection that experimental results obtained in controlled conditions are unlikely to show up in the 'noisy' conditions of the school situation.

REFERENCES

AMARIA, RODA P. and LEITH, G. O. M. (1969) 'Individual versus co-operative learning II: the influence of personality', *Educational Research*, 11, 193–9.

HALLWORTH, H. J. (1962) 'The H.B. Personality Inventory', unpublished, University of Birmingham.

LAVIN, D. E. (1967) *The Prediction of Academic Performance*, Wiley.

LEITH, G. O. M. (1969) 'Learning and personality', in W. R. Dunn and C. Holroyd, eds., *Aspects of Educational Technology II*, Methuen.

LEITH, G. O. M. and BLAKE, I. H. (1967) *Teaching the Formulation of Definitions; a further study of the place of integrating rules*, Research Reports on Programmed Learning no. 16, University of Birmingham.

LEITH, G. O. M. and BOSETT, R. (1967) *Mode of Learning and Personality*, Research Reports on Programmed Learning no. 14, University of Birmingham.

LEITH, G. O. M. and DAVIS, T. N. (1969) 'The influence of social reinforcement on achievement', *Educational Research*, 11, 132–7.

LEITH, G., LISTER, A., TEALL, C. and BELLINGHAM, J. (1968) 'Teaching the new decimal currency by programmed instruction', *Industrial Training International*, 3, 424–7.

LEITH, G. O. M. and MCHUGH, G. A. R. (1967) 'The place of theory in learning consecutive conceptual tasks', *Educational Review*, 19, 110–17.

LEITH, G. O. M. and WEBB, C. C. (1968) 'A comparison of four methods of programmed instruction with and without teacher intervention', *Education Review*, 21, 25–31.

LEITH, G. O. M. and WISDOM, B. (1969) 'An Investigation of the Effects of Error-making and Personality on Learning', unpublished report, University of Birmingham.

LEITH, G. O. M., BIRAN, L. A. and OPOLLOT, J. A. (1969) 'The place of review in meaningful verbal learning sequences', *Canadian Journal of Behavioural Science*, 1, 113–18.

RUSHTON, J. (1966) 'The relationships between personality characteristics and scholastic success in eleven-year-old children', *British Journal of Educational Psychology*, 36, 178–84.

SHADBOLT, D. R. and LEITH, G. O. M. (1967) *Mode of Learning and Personality II*, University of Birmingham.

WARBURTON, F. W. (1962) 'The measurement of personality III', *Educational Research*, 4, 193–206.

28

R. H. *Woody*   Britsh behavioural counselling*

Educational counselling is still in its infancy in Britain. But despite a
few frustrating initial experiences, counsellor education programmes
are now flourishing and experienced staff with specialised training in
counselling and guidance are becoming more common in schools.

In this initial stage of counselling and guidance services, it is necessary to specify what functions belong to the professional role, and to
sort out existing psychological and educational theories and principles
for the derivation of a theoretical rationale. Daws (1967) has provided
an overview of the counsellor's role and specified how the factors
intrinsic to the American guidance and counselling movement can
be interpreted and applied in British schools. Further clarification
of counselling functions is available in the writings of Fuller (1967),
Fuller and Juniper (1967), and Raynor and Atcherley (1967). There
seems to be, however, a distinct lack of attention to the question of
which theoretical approaches to counselling are the most suitable for
use in British education.

THEORIES OF COUNSELLING

Theories of counselling tend to be concerned with insight or action
(London, 1964). Freud's psychoanalysis and Rogers's client-centred
counselling illustrate insight approaches. Insight theories imply that
the primary objective of counselling is to help the pupil to gain understanding or of insight into his thoughts, feelings, and behaviour. The
responsibility for the counselling processes rests with the pupil, with the

* Reprinted from *Educational Research*, 10, 1968, 207–12.

counsellor facilitating rather than directing his efforts at insight, and the efforts and decisions regarding behavioural change, after counselling, also remain the responsibility of the pupil. The criterion of success, according to the insight theory, is not the elimination or alleviation of the pupil's problems but the development of greater insight by the pupil into 'why he is what he is' as a person.

Action theorists, on the other hand, do not strive primarily for insight or understanding, but hold that the criterion of success is the elimination of the pupil's problems or symptoms. They maintain that behavioural problems represent maladjusted habits which can be modified or eliminated by conditioning techniques, and this modification of behaviour can alleviate the problem.

At the present time, it seems safe to say that most counsellors are insight-orientated and place the responsibility on the pupil. But recently a system has been initiated in the field of counselling: *behavioural counselling*, which is action orientated. It rests on the assumption that the counsellor's responsibility is to help the pupil to alleviate his problems, and that the counsellor must therefore actively plan towards this goal. The counsellor both facilitates and directs.

BEHAVIOURAL COUNSELLING TECHNIQUES

The techniques of behavioural counselling are based on positive reinforcement: that is, when the pupil behaves in an appropriate way the counsellor reinforces his behaviour. According to the principles of learning theory, reinforced behaviour will tend to become established, but unreinforced behaviour will tend to occur less frequently. Generally the counsellor uses verbal and non-verbal reinforcements to promote or condition certain verbal responses in the pupil. Having assessed the pupil's reasons for needing counselling, he determines which classes or types of verbal responses he will reinforce; subsequently, each time the pupil makes a comment which falls into the previously determined classes or types, the counsellor gives a non-verbal reinforcing stimulus (such as a smile, or approving nod of his head) or a verbal reinforcing stimulus (such as saying 'good', or 'fine idea', or 'I agree'). But the counsellor does not respond positively to other types of responses which are not directly relevant to the established counselling objectives; in fact, he does not respond at all, not even negatively in most cases, to responses that are not to be reinforced: any response, even if negative, could potentially have reinforcing power.

These behavioural counselling procedures have been effective with adults, college and university students, adolescents, and children. Ryan and Krumboltz (1964) found that *deliberation-type* responses made by college students occurred more frequently when counsellors selectively reinforced them. It should be pointed out that in counselling in general, and personal-social and educational-vocational counselling in particular, the pupil has to think positively; so that this reinforcing procedure could be used to facilitate any form of counselling, including insight-orientated. Similarly, Krumboltz and Thoreson (1964) successfully reinforced verbal *information-seeking* behaviour with teenage students. It was found that those students who received behavioural counselling (that is, reinforcement for their information-seeking responses) engaged in more information-seeking activities outside the counselling sessions than those who received regular (non-reinforcing) counselling. This study suggests that students who want educational and/or vocational counselling might seek information on occupations, careers, or higher education if their information-seeking responses were reinforced during counselling. These are but a few examples of possible uses for behavioural counselling in educational settings. Other relevant studies provide further support for its use: Krumboltz (1965) has discussed the rationale for behavioural counselling, Krumboltz and Schroeder (1965) reveal data to support its efficacy in promoting career planning, Thoreson (1966) provides a step-by-step practical example of how to use behavioural counselling with a student, and Woody (1966) presents a critical survey and analysis of relevant research.

In order to clarify the procedure and illustrate theoretical-technical comparisons, let us consider a hypothetical case in which a teenage boy wants vocational counselling and guidance. If a non-direct or client-centred counsellor were involved, the dialogue might go something like this:

Boy. What I wanted to talk to you about was getting a job. I'll be leaving school in a few months and I really don't know what I would like to do.
Counsellor. You are pretty uncertain about your goals.
Boy. Yes, I've thought about it, but I just don't know. (long silence)
Counsellor. Mmm.
Boy. The other day I started to ask my mum what she thought, but she had to go off to the hospital for a checkup. She's been sick, you know.
Counsellor. No, I didn't know.
Boy. Yes, she caught some virus last winter and has never got over it.
Counsellor. This must worry you.

Boy. Well I suppose, but it really is an inconvenience more than anything else. I have to take care of my brother when she isn't able to.

Counsellor. You resent this.

Boy. Yes, but I suppose I have to do it, don't I? I mean there's nobody else when my dad has gone to work.

This example illustrates how the non-directive or client-centred counsellor, who is usually associated with the insight-orientated theory of Dr Carl R. Rogers, allows the pupil to establish the form and/or direction of the interview; the counsellor's job is to provide the pupil with a warm, non-evaluative, understanding relationship and to facilitate self-understanding or insight regardless of where the dialogue might lead. In this interview, the boy was allowed to leave the topic of vocational-choice which had brought him into contact with the counsellor.

In contrast, a dialogue in a behavioural counselling context might proceed as follows:

Boy. What I wanted to talk to you about was getting a job. I'll be leaving school in a few months and I really don't know what I would like to do.

Counsellor. You are pretty uncertain about your goals for work and you would like to make a logical decision soon. [Note the counsellor's response adds a bit more emphasis to making a vocational choice, but is still reflective of what the boy said.]

Boy. Yes, I've thought about it, but I just don't know. (long silence)

Counsellor. What have you done to help you to make a decision? For example, have you read about various careers, or talked to people who are actually working in the jobs you're interested in? [Note the counsellor, following the silence, assumed the initiative and structured the discussion back to vocational choice, and his questions are really suggestions.]

Boy. Well I haven't done much. I started to ask my mum what she thought, but she had to go off to the hospital for a checkup. She's been sick you know.

Counsellor (remains silent). [By remaining silent, he does not reinforce responses unrelated to the matter of vocational choice.]

Boy. Yes, she caught some virus last winter and has never got over it. (long silence)

Counsellor. You thought it would be good if your mum discussed it with you? Perhaps your dad could help too. I suppose they both have ideas about the kind of job they would like you to have. [Note the counsellor refused to reinforce talk about the mother's illness since it presumably was not related to the counselling goal; then he reverted to vocational choice.]

Boy. Well, my mum has never really said much, and my dad has always said he hoped I could do better than he has done.

Counsellor. But you have never really come right out and asked them their opinions.

Boy. No I haven't, but I probably should.

Counsellor. Yes, that seems a good idea. [A positive verbal reinforcement.]

This brief example illustrates how the counsellor remains silent and does not reinforce the pupil's statements which are unrelated to the primary counselling objective, such as the boy's talk about his mother's illness. Instead, the counsellor brings the verbal responses back to the problem area and gives positive reinforcement when the boy offers a pertinent response, such as his statement that he should probably talk to his parents about their opinions on his career.

Another means of clarifying the composition of behavioural counselling is to compare the responses that would possibly be made by counsellors of differing theoretical orientations to the same response from a pupil. In Table 28.1, several examples of various response classes are presented; the pupil's response, in each case, is followed by feasible responses based on three counselling theories: psychoanalytical, client-centred and behavioural.

It is readily apparent that behavioural counselling is quite different in many ways from insight-orientated approaches to counselling. But the main point is that there are several reasons why educational counsellors should consider learning theory procedures (Woody, in press (c)). For example, behavioural counselling seems to be more strongly supported by research and to be more efficacious than some forms of insight-orientated counselling. It is also interesting to note that in an analysis of client-centred counselling conducted by Dr Carl R. Rogers, Truax (1966a, 1966b) found that even Rogers reinforced certain types of client behaviour, although his reinforcements were not systematically planned as in behavioural counselling.

APPROPRIATENESS OF BEHAVIOURAL COUNSELLING FOR BRITAIN

There are three reasons why behavioural counselling seems especially appropriate for use in the British setting.

First, much of the research that serves as a basis for behavioural counselling comes from British psychology and psychiatry. Most notable

TABLE 28.1. *Comparison of counsellor responses*

Response class	Client	Psycho-analytically-orientated counsellor	Client-centred counsellor	Behavioural counsellor
Decision-making	It's one of those things. I would like to decide on what job to take, but there are so many considerations. And I have to respect my parents' ideas.	You have a real need to depend upon your parents for a decision, just like when you were a child. Is that what you mean perhaps?	You feel quite frustrated, wanting to make a decision, yet unable to sort out all the factors that would influence such a case.	But despite the ambivalence, you realise that you are the one who has to make the decision.
Self-understanding	Sometimes I just want to scream out to the whole world: 'Leave me alone; just let me be the way I am.'	You view the world as a threatening, constricting entity, and you would like to fight back, to aggressively retaliate.	Mmm (pause), sometimes you just want to let loose.	Down in your guts you're feeling that you want to know and be what you really are. Just what are you anyway, in your own eyes?
Educational Planning	I would like to do better in school, get involved—you know, really committed to	Your aspirations and current behaviours are quite incompatible, aren't they? Perhaps	It would be very satisfying to you if you could succeed	The one thing that is apparent is that before you can make a really intelligent decision, you

Planning **Personal-social Involvement**	studying, and eventually try to get in some kind of college programme. What do you think I should do?	this suggests a denial of what your capabilities are. Perhaps you're talking about college is unrealistic, but perhaps not. You certainly are unfocused; for example, most people of your age have already decided where they're going,	in school and go on to college. (Ignores client's question).	will have to begin some serious systematic planning. This may mean taking some aptitude and vocational interest tests, seeking out some information about what is required in various areas of college studies, and eventually deriving some distinct plans for the future.
	On Sunday, I went for a ride to Brighton with some of my mates. It really wasn't much. Oh, we tried chatting up some birds and things, but in the end it was probably just a waste of petrol.	Such activities don't satisfy any recognisable need of yours.	You didn't find it very enjoyable.	Despite the fact that you didn't enjoy it very much, it did provide you with an opportunity to be with others. That's something you said once before was important to you, didn't you? I think that it was good for you to get out like that. It's certainly a contrast to last year when you stayed at home alone all the time, isn't it?

perhaps is the work of Professor Hans J. Eysenck and his colleagues at the Institute of Psychiatry, University of London (Eysenck, 1960; Eysenck and Rachman, 1965). Consequently, the use of learning theory techniques, inherent in behavioural counselling, has already received some enthusiastic acceptance and support from professional and lay sources in Britain. The fact that both educational and clinical psychologists in Britain have been using these conditioning procedures for behaviour problems in other settings should facilitate a smooth transition to the educational context for behavioural counselling.

Secondly, despite the claims of some behaviour therapists, there is theoretical and clinical evidence to support the belief that insight and action approaches are much more compatible than might at first appear (Marks and Gelder, 1966). For example, it appears that the relationship between the counsellor and the pupil is indeed valuable in behavioural counselling, and it is preferable, therefore, that the usual guidelines for counselling (such as an understanding, supportive, warm relationship between the counsellor and the client) should be maintained in addition to using the reinforcing techniques. Moreover, these theories have been studied in practical situations, and there is evidence that insight-counselling and behavioural counselling can be integrated to give more successful results (Woody, 1968 and 1969).

Thirdly, the goals and techniques used in behavioural counselling are clearcut. During this period of beginning counselling and guidance services in Britain, it would be advantageous to use an approach with objectives which are readily recognisable by heads and senior teachers. That is, if a lesson can be learned from American school counselling, it is that professionals who are not trained in guidance and counselling are unsure and dubious about what the educational guidance counsellor is supposed to be doing. If the counsellor states that he is trying to help the students who come for counselling to achieve greater self-understanding, it is likely that there will be more scepticism and perhaps more open resistance from other relevant professionals, such as educational administrators, than if he can state concretely that he hopes to help the students to diminish the seriousness of the overt problems that are bothering them.

CONCLUSIONS

It is essential that counsellors should be cautioned against limiting their counselling solely to behavioural techniques. There should not be such a person as a 'behavioural counsellor'; rather there should be counsellors who are well-trained generically and who can use behavioural techniques appropriately as part of their array of professional skills. As has been suggested, behavioural counselling can be integrated with more conventional forms of guidance and counselling, and if comprehensive application and acceptance of guidance and counselling is to be achieved in British schools, the counsellor must conscientiously attempt to provide the complete continuum of guidance and counselling services.

The inclusion of behavioural counselling in the counsellor's professional repertoire of techniques has definite implications for counsellor education training programmes. Counsellor trainees must be academically prepared to understand behaviour; this involves knowledge of abnormal psychology as well as of mental hygiene, and an understanding of personality development, the psychology of exceptional children, and the basic principles of experimental psychology. The counsellor trainee should also learn to determine what classes or types of responses should be reinforced in dealing with a particular problem presented by the pupil, to make immediate and accurate classifications of responses during counselling, to formulate strong reinforcing counsellor responses, and how and when properly to withhold reinforcements for responses that are not germane to the counselling goals. As has been elaborated elsewhere (Woody, in press (d)), the additional academic material can easily be included in existing lecture programmes, with only slight modifications of the curriculum, and the trainee's technical skills in behavioural counselling can best be cultivated under practical supervision. The first priority is that university instructors should themselves receive specialised training in and supervised experience with behavioural procedures.

It should be acknowledged that the scope of behavioural counselling, at present limited to verbal conditioning, is likely to, and indeed probably should, expand. That is, it will probably move towards the behaviour therapy model, employing numerous other conditioning techniques and dealing with a wider variety of problem behaviours. This expansion will, of course, lead to changes in training, but in view of the high status of behaviour therapy in Britain, both the training needs and the practical role functions should be readily accommodated.

Behavioural counselling, based on principles of learning theory, provides an effective means of helping students with their problems. Because it is derived, to a large degree, from behaviour therapy research conducted in Britain and because behaviour therapy is currently practised by British psychologists, it seems undeniable that there is a ready-made place for it in British educational counselling.

REFERENCES

DAWS, P. P. (1967) 'What will the school counsellor do?', *Educational Research*, 9, 83–92.

EYSENCK, H. J., eds., (1960) *Behaviour Therapy and the Neuroses*, Pergamon Press.

EYSENCK, H. J. and RACHMAN, S. (1965) *The Causes and Cures of Neuroses*, San Diego, California, R. R. Knapp.

FULLER, J. A. (1967) 'School counselling: a first inquiry', *Educational Research*, 9, 135–6.

FULLER, J. A. and JUNIPER, D. F. (1967) 'Guidance, counselling and school social work', *Educational Research*, 9, 103–4.

KRUMBOLTZ, J. D. (1965) 'Behavioural counselling: rationale and research', *Personnel and Guidance Journal*, 44, 383–7.

KRUMBOLTZ, J. D. and SCHROEDER, W. W. (1965) 'Promoting career planning through reinforcement', *Personnel and Guidance Journal*, 44, 19–26.

KRUMBOLTZ, J. D. and THORESON, C. E. (1964) 'The effect of behavioural counselling in group and individual settings on information-seeking behaviour', *Journal of Counselling Psychology*, 11, 324–35.

LONDON, P. (1964) *The Modes and Morals of Psychotherapy*, New York, Holt.

MARKS, I. M. and GELDER, M. G. (1966) 'Common ground between behaviour therapy and psychodynamic methods', *British Journal of Medical Psychology*, 39, 11–23.

RAYNOR, J. M. and ATCHERLEY, R. A. (1967) 'Counselling in schools—some considerations', *Educational Research*, 9, 93–102.

RYAN, T. and KRUMBOLTZ, J. D. (1964) 'Effect of planned reinforcement counselling on client decision-making behaviour', *Journal of Counselling Psychology*, 11.

THORESON, C. E. (1966) 'Behavioural counselling: an introduction', *School Counsellor*, 14, 13–21.

TRUAX, C. B. (1966a) 'Reinforcement and non-reinforcement in Rogerian psychotherapy', *Journal of Abnormal Psychology*, 71, 1–9.

TRUAX, C. B. (1966b) 'Some implications of behaviour therapy for psychotherapy', *Journal of Counselling Psychology*, 13, 160–70.

WOODY, R. H. (1966) 'Behaviour therapy and school psychology', *Journal of School Psychology*, 4, 1–14.

WOODY, R. H. (1968) 'Integrating behaviour therapy and psychotherapy', *British Journal of Medical Psychology*, 41, 261–6.

WOODY, R. H. (1969) *Behavioural Problem Children in the Schools: Recognition, Diagnosis and Behavioural Modification*, Appleton-Century-Crofts.

WOODY, R. H. 'Reinforcement in school counselling', *School Counsellor* (in press, c).

WOODY, R. H. 'Training in behavioural counselling', *Counsellor Education and Supervision* (in press, d).

29

The school psychological service*

The School Psychological Service is mentioned in several Ministry of Education publications, for example the Report of the Committee on Maladjusted Children, 1955; *The Health of the School Child*, 1960, and Circulars 347 and 11/61. The Service has come into being during the past twenty-five to thirty years; it is, therefore, timely now to review its position and to anticipate probable further developments. The purpose of this document is to show the development of this Service and the way in which it works in relation to the School Health and Child Guidance Services.

The subject will be dealt with under the following headings:

   I. The Functions of the School Psychological Service.
  II. The Structure and Administration of the School Psychological Service.
 III. The Relationship between the School Psychological Service and the Child Guidance Clinic.
 IV. Future Developments in the School Psychological Service.
  V. The training of Educational Psychologists.
 VI. Summary.

The School Psychological Service is staffed by Educational Psychologists; since 1944 there has been a steady growth in the number of them employed by Local Education Authorities. Both as part of their work in child guidance clinics, and to a growing extent independently of it, psychologists act as advisers on psychological matters to Chief Education Officers, teachers, parents and others concerned with the

* Report by the *British Psychological Society*, 1962.

education and care of children. This clinical and advisory work together forms a psychological service to schools which aims at contributing to the healthy development of children through the application of psychological knowledge to education generally. Its concern is not only with the early detection of difficulties, but also with the introduction of preventive measures. Psychologists, therefore, have a part to play in the whole educational process both in and out of school, including the development and operation of facilities for normal, as well as for handicapped, children.

I. THE FUNCTION OF THE SCHOOL PSYCHOLOGICAL SERVICE

Educational Psychologists undertake, for the Authorities for which they work, both general advisory duties and also more specific functions relating to the problems of individual children. It is from extensive work with individual children that the principles have been developed on which the more general and advisory work of Educational Psychologists is based.

(a) General functions

Psychologists employed by an Education Authority are expected to advise and to cooperate with other officers of the Local Authority.

In framing policy Chief Education Officers may refer to psychologists. For example, many psychologists were consulted in connection with Ministry of Education Circulars 348 and 11/61 which invited Authorities to draw up development plans for maladjusted children and for educationally sub-normal children respectively. Psychologists also frequently take responsibility for the organisation of special educational provision for gifted or handicapped children, and some psychologists are consulted at a policy level about selection procedures in relation to 11 + examinations.

Secondly, psychologists advise Head Teachers on the choice of methods of assessment for the educational guidance of children in their progress through school. Some of the teachers' most pressing problems arise from the difficulties of individual children. These they discuss with psychologists who also help in this work by the individual assessment of particular children. Problems of educational guidance arise on admission to school and transfers. Advice may be sought, for example, on the admission of immature and delicate children at the age of five years and more frequently psychologists are consulted about transfers, especially at the secondary stage. A special aspect of educational guidance is the transfer of children at the secondary stage. This work may involve the administration of a comprehensive scheme for secondary selection and/or advising on problem or borderline cases.

Thirdly, collaboration with Medical Officers of Health and School Medical Officers is necessary with reference to learning difficulties and the educational needs of handicapped children, particularly the educationally sub-normal and the severely sub-normal.

Fourthly, organisers and Inspectors of Schools may seek the opinion of psychologists on results of recent psychological studies relevant, for example, to children's interests or to teaching methods. Collaboration at this level usually takes place on working parties, at conferences and in committee.

Psychologists also undertake the organisation of courses for teachers at which research findings relevant to school problems can be reported and widely discussed among colleagues. As a result psychologists have the opportunity to help formulate hypotheses needing investigation and, if the research involved is beyond local resources, they can channel the information to research institutes.

Extensive research projects can seldom be undertaken by psychologists working for Local Authorities, mainly because of the pressure of other demands; nevertheless awareness of need for research and some participation in it should constitute one of the psychologist's main contributions to the solution of children's difficulties. Whatever the day-to-day pressures psychologists must always be ready to undertake some fact finding to provide Chief Education Officers with information about local requirements on which development plans may be based.

(b) Specific functions

The functions outlined above refer to general matters: those that follow concern individual children. They mainly arise from the close contact between the psychologist and schools in the area, but also from his work with School Medical Officers, Health Visitors, Child Care Officers, Probation Officers, Education Welfare Officers and others who refer children to the School Psychological Service, for example, Children's Officers and Magistrates in the Juvenile Courts.

Among problems referred to the Educational Psychologist are those arising from

(i)   children's handicaps;
(ii) scholastic difficulties;
(iii) asocial or anti-social behaviour;

Although problems may be referred under one of these headings, further investigation often reveals the existence of additional or different difficulties. Responsibility for full appraisal of the individual child's condition rests with the Educational Psychologist.

The first stage consists of a thorough study of the child, including a psychological and educational assessment of his abilities and attainments based on an interview during which individual tests are given, and on knowledge about the environmental influences bearing on him. This assessment is always supplemented by discussion with the Head and class teacher of the school the child attends, and an interview with his parents. Many of the problems involve other agencies and, in particular, consultation with School Medical Officers.

This more detailed formulation of the problem leads to various courses of action. In some instances discussion with teachers and parents on the management of the problem may be enough to ease the difficulty. In other cases consultation and advice are not enough. The child may need individual re-education by the psychologist or referral to the Child Guidance Clinic for fuller investigation by the whole team or for treatment.

Some children also need to change their school. When this is the case, recommendations are made to the Education Department or Health Department regarding the special placement or facilities required. Over the years most Local Authorities have increased their special educational provisions and a wide range is now usually available, including remedial centres, units for the partially deaf, units for maladjusted children, schools for the educationally sub-normal and for severely subnormal children and training centres run by the Health Authority.

When a child is attending a Child Guidance Clinic for investigation the School Psychological Service can ensure that the Clinic staff is fully informed of the child's situation in school, his responsiveness, his backwardness, the demands on the group in which he works, his social behaviour and so on. Information from the Clinic that might be helpful to the teachers is also communicated by the psychologist; this is particularly important during the period in which children are under treatment in order that teachers may understand variations in their behaviour.

Through this channel of communication opportunities occur for informal discussion of other individual problems, and thereby further insight is gained into the educational and psychological needs of children.

The activities referred to in this section are representative of those undertaken by Educational Psychologists everywhere, but there may be local variations in emphasis. The School Psychological Service is still developing and we do not wish to suggest that present activities are, or will remain, the only duties of Educational Psychologists; it is expected that new functions will emerge and that present ones will be modified. Probable future developments are indicated in Section IV of this Memorandum.

II. THE STRUCTURE AND ADMINISTRATION OF THE
SCHOOL PSYCHOLOGICAL SERVICE

The direction of the School Psychological Service falls to the Senior Educational Psychologist who is responsible to the Chief Education Officer. This structure is favourable to the development of the Service and to effective liaison between it and other services for children. The Senior Educational Psychologist usually carries out much of the consultative work to which reference has already been made.

Although primarily responsible to the Chief Education Officer, in some areas the Educational Psychologist may be responsible to the Principal School Medical Officer for the administration of the Child Guidance Clinic. In either case close contact is maintained between psychologists, School Medical Officers and representatives of other local services; much information is exchanged in an endeavour to reach full understanding of children's problems and to secure effective treatment of them.

The staffing of Child Guidance Clinics was dealt with in the Report of the Committee on Maladjusted Children (1955). The ratios proposed were one psychiatrist, two psychologists and three psychiatric social workers to 45,000 children. So far as it applied to psychologists this estimate included only their work in the Child Guidance Clinic and school work on behalf of children attending the Clinic, but not the other work of the School Psychological Service as outlined in this document. The ratio of psychologist to population to cover both clinical work and a full psychological service to schools should be much higher than that just quoted. The following ratios would be in keeping with present-day needs, namely, one psychologist to 10,000 children in urban areas, and one psychologist to 6,000 in county areas. In Scotland the ratio is already one psychologist to 8,000 children for the country as a whole.

Each psychologist needs a separate quiet room suitable for interviewing in privacy; the nature of the work makes the sharing of a room undesirable. In addition, office space is necessary for administration and clerical work. Adequate secretarial help should be available to relieve psychologists of routine administrative work.

III. THE RELATIONSHIP BETWEEN THE SCHOOL PSYCHOLOGICAL
SERVICE AND THE CHILD GUIDANCE CLINIC

(a) *Functional relationship*

The main functions of the Child Guidance Clinic or Child Psychiatric
Unit are the diagnosis and the treatment of psychological disturbance
and developmental difficulties. This work is more clinically and psy-
chiatrically orientated than that of the School Psychological Service.
The psychologist working in the School Psychological Service has responsibilities not only to the child and his parents but also to the Chief
Education Officer, the school and other agencies. A different set of
values applies once a child is referred to a Child Guidance Clinic or
Child Psychiatric Unit; he then becomes a child patient. The effect of
this is to centre the treatment on him and to bring into effect more
confidential relationships with him and with his parents. At this point
also the case comes under medical supervision and becomes the responsibility of the psychiatrist, who has available all the resources of the
Local Authority and the National Health Service for the treatment of
the child.

In most areas the Educational Psychologist works in the Child
Guidance team as well as in the School Psychological Service. His role
in Child Guidance is threefold:

  (i) He contributes to the diagnosis of the child's problems by using
     psychological tests and techniques;

 (ii) He may undertake remedial work with individual children for
     whom the chosen treatment is re-education.

(iii) He is responsible for seeing that the facilities of the School
     Psychological Service are available for the suitable educational
     placement of the child, when a change is recommended, and
     for keeping the Clinic staff informed of the child's adjustment
     in school. At the same time, he confers with the school staff on
     the suggestions of the Clinic team regarding the child's treatment
     in school.

Research in Child Guidance is often neglected, yet it is essential in
evaluating the effectiveness of clinical work. The psychologist is normally well qualified in research methods.

(b) *Administrative relationship*

It is commonly held—and this we endorse—that the Educational
Psychologist makes his most effective contribution when he is a member of both the Child Guidance team and the School Psychological

Service. The psychologist often administers the Child Guidance Clinic and this has proved to be a satisfactory arrangement.

In the larger authorities, there may be a case for some specialisation on the part of psychologists. Some may specialise in aspects of educational work, e.g. provision for mentally and physically handicapped children, while others may concentrate on clinical work.

It is, therefore, recommended that the needs of the Child Guidance Clinic and the School Psychological Service be considered together when the employment of psychologists is under consideration.

IV. FUTURE DEVELOPMENTS IN THE SCHOOL PSYCHOLOGICAL SERVICE

Nowadays there is increasing stress on the need for research in education, therefore research in local authority areas may be expected to increase. The trained psychologist has experience of experimental psychology and the design of investigations. Moreover, he has a knowledge of local conditions, and there are many problems in education which can best be studied by those who have such knowledge. The combination of these two factors makes it likely that the Educational Psychologist will become more involved in research. He can make an effective contribution by providing objective evidence on questions which arise in forming policy. Two examples may be given of the ways in which Educational Psychologists, in cooperation with their colleagues, may further research:

First, provision of facilities for the education of all types of handicapped children is increasing. Consequently, there is a need to know more about the ways in which such children learn and about the difficulties of adjustment arising from their handicap.

Secondly, there is already available data from the field of social psychology on the formation of groups and their interaction. Although much of this work is relevant to the school situation it is, as yet, seldom applied. In the future more attention is likely to be paid to the social climate within which children learn and the bearing this has on their future development.

Recent developments in the Youth and Youth Employment Services may well result in requests to the Educational Psychologist for help in connection with, e.g. vocational guidance or handicapped school leavers or the implementation of the recommendations of the Albemarle Report regarding social misfits. Increasingly in the future it may be expected that the psychologist will help with the training of social workers employed by Local Authorities. It will always be an important part of their work to communicate to other workers in education and allied fields psychological findings that will be helpful in the day-to-day handling of children.

In the past the psychologist has been concerned with the problems of handicapped children and with abnormal rather than with normal behaviour. Although he will continue to be concerned with these problems and to work on them with psychiatrists, School Medical Officers and others, he can be expected, in the future, to contribute a great deal more to the educational guidance of normal children. Indeed it is likely that by increased activity in this particular field, he will be able to make an effective contribution to the prevention of maladjustment.

V. THE TRAINING OF EDUCATIONAL PSYCHOLOGISTS

Qualifications for Educational Psychologists are an honours degree in psychology or recognised equivalent, training and experience in teaching and post-graduate training in educational psychology. This training is essential to enable the psychologist to carry out the variety of work required in the Child Guidance Clinic and the School Psychological Service, work entailing, as it does, the application of psychological knowledge within the framework of education. To employ staff with an extensive or specialised knowledge of education, but limited psychological knowledge, is to fail to appreciate the full extent of the work. It is equally undesirable to appoint people who have inadequate experience in education and who may consequently fail to appreciate the nature of educational problems.

VI. SUMMARY

At present there is a trend in some regions to link Child Guidance more closely with the National Health Service by establishing Child Psychiatric Clinics in association with hospitals. This arrangement has advantages for those children who need the full range of medical services which only a hospital can provide. At the same time, it has disadvantages in the treatment of other children, of whom there are many, for whom the medical aspects of the problem are secondary to the educational and social aspects. In such cases an intimate knowledge of local conditions and facilities is invaluable. In Child Psychiatric Units there is usually less liaison with educational and social agencies. The Child Guidance Clinic, however, has traditionally been a place in which medical, social and educational considerations are reviewed with equal care.

The School Psychological Service has been developed, in part, to deal with the educational and learning difficulties of children. This service in most areas brings to the attention of Child Guidance Clinics cases which otherwise might not be referred. Moreover it pays considerable attention to preventive work.

In most areas all three types of service—Child Psychiatric Unit, Child Guidance Clinic and School Psychological Service—are required to meet the varying needs of children. Close consultation between them all is essential.

This document has been prepared to outline the functions of the School Psychological Service, to clarify the work of the Educational Psychologist and to comment on the relation between the work of the School Psychological Service, the Child Guidance Clinic and the School Health Service. While the objective, namely the healthy development of children, is common to all, there are differences in emphasis which, it is hoped, these notes have made clear.

Recommended reading

The following books are prescribed as required reading for students of the Open University course:

ARGYLE, M. (1967) *The Psychology of Inter-personal behaviour*, Penguin Books.

BOWLBY, J. and FRY, M. (1965) *Child Care and the Growth of Love*, Penguin Books.

EVANS, K. M. (1965) *Attitudes and Interests in Education*, Routledge & Kegan Paul.

HOLT, J. (1969) *How Children Fail*, Penguin Books.

HUDSON, L. (1966) *Contrary Imaginations: a psychological study of the English schoolboy*, Methuen, 1966; Penguin Books, 1968.

VERNON, M. D. (1969) *Human Motivation*, Cambridge University Press.

VERNON, P. E. (1963) *Personality Assessment*, Methuen.

CROCKER, A. C. (1969) *Statistics for the Teacher*, Penguin Books.

Another useful book on statistics is:

LEWIS, D. G. (1967) *Statistical Methods in Education*, University of London Press.

Index of Major Authors

Concept Index